media **ethics**

media ethics

an introduction to responsible journalism

JOHAN RETIEF

OXFORD
UNIVERSITY PRESS

OXFORD
UNIVERSITY PRESS

Great Clarendon Street, Oxford OX2 6DP

Oxford University Press is a department of the University of Oxford.
It furthers the University's objective of excellence in research, scholarship,
and education by publishing worldwide in

Oxford New York

Auckland Bangkok Buenos Aires Cape Town Chennai
Dar es Salaam Delhi Hong Kong Istanbul Karachi Kolkata
Kuala Lumpur Madrid Melbourne Mexico City Mumbai Nairobi
São Paulo Shanghai Singapore Taipei Tokyo Toronto

with an associated company in Berlin

Oxford is a registered trade mark of Oxford University Press
in the UK and certain other countries

Published in South Africa
by Oxford University Press Southern Africa, Cape Town

Media Ethics: An Introduction to Responsible Journalism
ISBN: 9780195781373

© Johan Retief 2002

Commissioning editor: Arthur Attwell
Editor: Alfred LeMaitre
Indexer: Mary Lennox
Cover designer: Christopher Davis
Designer: Christopher Davis

Published by Oxford University Press Southern Africa
PO Box 12119, N1 City, 7463, Cape Town, South Africa

Set in 10 pt on 13 pt Bodoni MT Book by RHT desktop publishing cc, Durbanville
Reproduction by RHT desktop publishing cc, Durbanville
Cover reproduction by The Image Bureau
Printed and bound by Mega Digital

Contents

Preface   viii

Part I Foundations

1   Ethics   3
2   The law: codes of ethics   25

Part II Ethical issues

3   Accuracy   49
     Case Study 1   Orders to kill?   57
     Case Study 2   Dead bodies necklaced   59
     Case Study 3   "The very opposite"   62
     Case Study 4   "Evidence" as truth   63
     Case Study 5   Background information omitted   65

4   Truth and deception   67
     Case Study 1   A bit too low   75
     Case Study 2   Paedophile's home filmed   76
     Case Study 3   Asked to lie   78
     Case Study 4   Dummy accidents   79
     Case Study 5   Teaming up   81

5   Fairness   83
     Case Study 1   A "possible suspect"   89
     Case Study 2   A bit more circumspection, please   91
     Case Study 3   A hostile climate?   93
     Case Study 4   Views not included   95
     Case Study 5   Focus on the conflict   95

6   Objectivity   99
     Case Study 1   How *could* you?   106
     Case Study 2   Criminal collusion?   108
     Case Study 3   A partial panel   110
     Case Study 4   His master's voice?   112
     Case Study 5   Participating in a smear campaign   114

7	Confidentiality		117
	Case Study 1	Not prepared to testify	125
	Case Study 2	Rumours, rumours, rumours	126
	Case Study 3	To be or not to be	128
	Case Study 4	Real sources?	129
	Case Study 5	Prepared to go to jail	130
8	Conflict of interest		133
	Case Study 1	From the same company	141
	Case Study 2	"Fertile ground for impropriety"	143
	Case Study 3	State money for a newspaper	143
	Case Study 4	Editorial (in)dependency	144
	Case Study 5	Agents of the state	146
9	Invasion of privacy		151
	Case Study 1	Elderly abuse	161
	Case Study 2	Bugged	162
	Case Study 3	A South African paparazzo	163
	Case Study 4	A widow's privacy invaded?	164
	Case Study 5	Pay up!	167
10	Trauma		171
	Case Study 1	On the (bloody) scene	181
	Case Study 2	Watershed at the Waterfront	182
	Case Study 3	Interviewing the dying	185
	Case Study 4	Blown to pieces	187
	Case Study 5	Hole in the head	190
11	Stereotyping		193
	Case Study 1	"A piece of fascist architecture"	205
	Case Study 2	"Love" or "hate" characters	206
	Case Study 3	Disgusting racist reporting	208
	Case Study 4	The mocking of stutterers	210
	Case Study 5	In lighter vein	211
12	Social responsibility		213
	Case Study 1	Obscenity, nudity, indecency	225
	Case Study 2	"Blasphemy"	228
	Case Study 3	Violence (not nudity)	230
	Case Study 4	Change of attitudes	231
	Case Study 5	Sliding down the precipice	233

13   Addendum: codes of ethics   237
      Institutional codes
      The Press Ombudsman of South Africa   237
      The South African Union of Journalists   240
      The South African National Editors' Forum   241
      The Freedom of Expression Institute   241
      The Broadcasting Complaints Commission
          of South Africa   242
      Professional codes
      Sowetan   244
      Sunday Times   245
      The Star   246
      Caxton *(Rustenburg Herald)*   247
      The SABC   252

Bibliography   253

Index   255

Preface

When a friend of mine heard I had been appointed to teach media ethics at the University of Stellenbosch, he burst out laughing. After he had had his fun, I asked him what was so hilarious. "Media ethics," he roared, wiping away tears of laughter. "Well, OK, maybe you will be able to talk for five minutes. But what are you going to say after that?"

This little anecdote serves as a vivid reminder that the public image of the media is not good, to put it mildly. In the US, study after study shows that public opinion of the media is extremely poor and appears to be worsening. For example, a Gallup poll conducted on 2–4 December 2000 (www.gallup.com) asked the following question: "[i]n general, do you think news organizations get the facts straight, or do you think that their stories and reports are often inaccurate?" Only 32% of the respondents said the media get the facts straight; an alarming 65% believed the media were often inaccurate; 3% had no opinion on this matter. When the same question was asked in July 1998, 50% of the respondents stated that they believed the media get their facts straight, with 45% disagreeing and 5% expressing no opinion. In only two years, the already alarming figure of 50% had sunk to 32%.

Andrew Belsey sums up this situation:

> They (the public) are suspicious of journalists and the way they practice their trade. Journalists are regarded in much the same way as politicians, as disreputable, untrustworthy and dishonest, pushing a personal or sectional interest rather than the facts of the case. If people are told that the essence of journalism is truth-telling, they will react with some scepticism or derision. If they are told that the practice of journalism is founded on ethical principles they will either laugh or, if they are prepared to take the matter seriously, point out that the typical tabloid story is trivial, scurrilous or invented. (Kieran et al. 1998, 1)

Moreover, the role of the media as the fourth estate has been eroded. Julianne Schultz is correct when she says:

> The ideal of the news media successfully fulfilling a political role that transcends its commercial obligations has been seriously battered. Its

power, commercial ambitions and ethical weakness have undermined its institutional standing. There is now a widespread, and reasonable, doubt that the contemporary news media can any longer adequately fulfil the historic role the press created for itself several hundred years ago. (Schultz 1998, 1)

In South Africa the situation is not much different. The local media are often accused of being biased, of a low standard, and irresponsible. It is often said that they are only interested in sensation and do not care how news is gathered or what harm they do. The popular perception seems to be that as long as the media make money they do not give a damn about anything else. The hundreds of complaints – many quite serious – received each year by the Press Ombudsman and the Broadcasting Complaints Commission of South Africa (BCCSA) show that the level of media ethics in South Africa leaves much to be desired. To be brutally honest, both the quantity and the seriousness of some of these complaints is appalling. The majority of the case studies in this book testify to this fact.

The inquiry by the South African Human Rights Commission into alleged racism in the media, held in 1998, supported the perception that the South African media cannot be trusted and should be monitored. Several reasons can be advanced for this state of affairs:

- a blatant indifference concerning the importance of practising journalism in a responsible way;
- sheer ignorance;
- the lack of codes of ethics in certain media circles;
- even where codes of ethics are in existence, they are not always used to good effect;
- a lack of literature focusing on journalism in South Africa;
- the accompanying problems that these situations create for the teaching of media ethics at tertiary institutions in this country.

Let us be clear about the following: there are no excuses for irresponsible journalism, and the concepts of "media" and "ethics" are not contradictory by nature.

One way of practising responsible journalism is to make use of codes of ethics. Fortunately, quite a number of such codes exist in South Africa (some of these will be discussed later), as well as bodies to mediate or arbitrate when complaints arise. Ethical codes are useful in that they help journalists to develop "ethical antennae", allowing them to recognize and analyze ethical situations and deal with them responsibly. If this book can make a modest contribution to practising journalism in a more responsible way, then the effort will have been worthwhile.

A South African Journalism Review

However, codes of ethics do not, in themselves, automatically lead to responsible journalism. At best, they serve as guidelines upon which journalists can base their ethical decisions. In ethical terms, the onus remains on the journalist to practise the profession in a responsible way.

One way of keeping journalists on their toes is to critique their work. This does happen from time to time in South Africa: for example, the *Rhodes Journalism Review*, published twice a year, fulfils a huge need. However, the lack of consistent critiques of journalists by fellow journalists or other knowledgeable people remains one of the most serious shortcomings in South African journalism today.

In the US, there are several professional reviews of the media of mass communication. The Nieman Reports, started in the 1940s, was the first publication to evaluate the press on a quarterly basis. In the early 1960s, the *Columbia Journalism Review* became the most influential of all subsequent critical reviews. An example of a more local review is the Chicago Journalism Review, which focuses only on that city.

These publications provide a valuable, and indeed essential, avenue "through which the often nebulous ethical codes of the profession are being interpreted and emphasized, given practical meaning and impact" (Hulteng 1976, 232, 233). Some prominent newspapers give regular publicity to the reviews, and some of these have been collected in book form. Granted, journalism reviews are unlikely to have a wide circulation. "But they do reach the people who count, the media circles in their communities and to some extent around the nation. And they are read at the schools of journalism, where future generations of journalists are forming their impression of the profession" (Hulteng 1976, 232).

Reviews of this kind are urgently needed in South Africa. A journalistically-minded philanthropist could make an important contribution by establishing a *South African Journalism Review*. A regular review magazine could be of the utmost importance to the future of this country's fledgling democracy.

JOHAN RETIEF

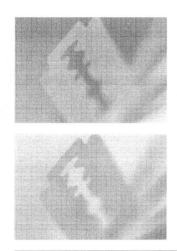

Part I | **Foundations**

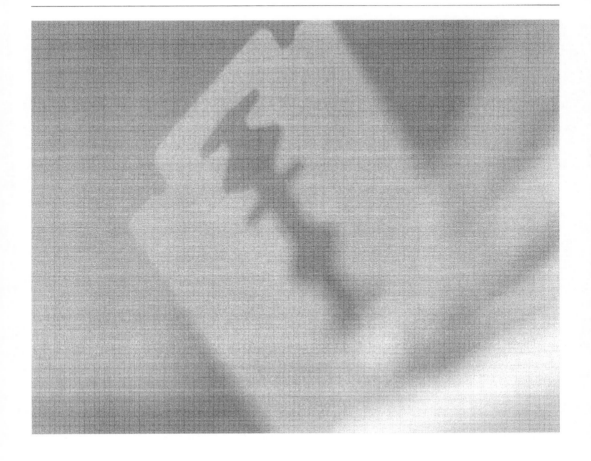

1 | Ethics

The subject of ethics – the word comes from the Greek *ethos*, meaning 'character' – has been debated by philosophers for thousands of years, and uncounted books and articles have been written on this subject. About 2 500 years ago the Greeks divided their philosophical world into three parts: aesthetics (the study of beauty and ways to analyze beauty objectively); epistemology (the doctrine of knowledge); and ethics (rational choices between what is good and bad for the individual and/or society).

A rational approach

In general, it can be said that the subject of ethics has now become a science. Like other human sciences, it uses a systematic, reasoned, or rational approach, based on a set of principles to determine what is "good", or ethical, and what is "bad", or unethical, in human conduct. These principles are sometimes also called values or norms (depending on the importance that is attached to them). In this wide sense, the subject of ethics deals with the philosophical foundations of decision-making (Black et al. 1995, 5). It can also be defined as the branch of philosophy that deals with questions of right and wrong, good and evil.

A distinction is usually made between metaethics, normative ethics, and applied ethics. This will be dealt with in the next section.

Morality

Although the concepts of ethics and morality are sometimes used interchangeably, there is a difference between the two. The Latin word *mores* refers to the customs and conventions that govern the ways people behave. More often than not, morality refers to prevailing customs.[1] For example, it is bad to pick your nose in public. The underlying ethical principle, though, is that it is bad to offend other people. However, the concern of this book is with (media) ethics rather than morality.

Media ethics

Media ethics is not an exercise for the elite. In fact, *everything* that a journalist does has ethical dimensions, to a lesser or greater degree. It is certainly not only editors who take those big ethical decisions to publish or not to publish. In fact, even minor journalistic exercises have ethical implications. Why? Because everything a journalist writes or says, or neglects to write or to say, in some or other way has an *influence* on people. And influences can be good or bad.

If, for example, you are too lazy to check your facts, you have neglected your responsibility (read: you have acted in an unethical way) to the public; if you did check your facts, the opposite is true. If you get the time of a tea party at the bishop's office wrong, you have inconvenienced some people. If you don't identify yourself to a source early and clearly enough as a reporter, you are misleading that person; if you do, you act in a responsible way. If you use a photo for sensationalist purposes while you have a better one, you have not told the whole truth; if you use the best picture regardless of its sensationalist impact, you have done well. If you don't report all the relevant facts, or you have your facts mixed up, you have failed on the ethical level; if you do, you have passed the ethical test.

These few examples can be multiplied a thousand times, and underline the fact that journalists must at all times be very careful *how* they do their job, and be mindful of their obligations (Christians et al. 1995, 20).[2] However, this is easier said than done.

Not so easy

"When we enter the area of journalistic ethics, we pass into a swampland of philosophical speculation where eerie mists of judgment hang low over a boggy terrain" (Merrill 1975, 8). Although pessimistic, this statement serves as a vivid reminder that media ethics is an extremely difficult subject. It is "…tantalizing, elusive, difficult to pin down in definite, concrete terms" (Hulteng 1976, 5), and, yes, it does rest upon philosophical thought. However, it really isn't *that* eerie, and it is much too important simply to give up all hope of finding a compass in the "swampland".

Here are some reasons why ethics is not an easy matter:

- *Ethics rarely (if ever) amounts to a mere choice between "right" and "wrong".* It is rather concerned with a wide variety of choices and actions – and the possible implications of those actions in the short and long term. One way to accomplish a high moral level of decision-making is therefore "to ask good questions of ourselves and of others, questions that force us to see shades of gray…" (Black et al. 1995, 47).
- *In the process of decision-making, ethical principles sometimes come into conflict.* A choice has then to be made between those principles (for example, a promise of confidentiality *versus* a compelling need to reveal a source).
- *Ethical decisions are by their nature contextual.* The intricate political, social and cultural dimensions of any given ethical situation can influence the decision that has to be taken. A knowledge of, and respect for, the context is essential.
- *Each and every ethical decision is by definition subjective.* No-one can really be objective, because each person has their own unique background that is influenced by millions of thoughts and actions, stemming from a myriad of sources. (This means that journalists would do well to consult their colleagues when confronted with difficult ethical decisions. Although fellow journalists are also subjective, the process of consultation encourages more balanced, responsible decisions.)

One thing is certain: the grey area between "right" and "wrong" is most of the time frighteningly large. Are journalists therefore going to run away from this issue? Fortunately, few real reporters are good at running away from anything.

Vital importance

Because the media have enormous influence, it is of vital importance that journalism be practised in an accountable and responsible way. When the media act irresponsibly, several things happen:

- Unnecessary harm is done to people.
- The media lose credibility.
- This weakens the media's vital role as watchdog.
- The wellbeing of democracy suffers.

Accountability

The question of accountability is of great importance, though this is also quite an elusive concept. Donald Gillmor defines accountability as the quality or state of giving an account, of answering, explaining, or of being liable and responsible (Dennis et al. 1989, 1). But that is where the questions begin. What are the ethical obligations of journalists? Who decides what those obligations should be? To whom should journalists be accountable? Who has the moral authority to call journalists to account? What is the nature of the relationship between personal responsibility and accountability? Should there be any penalties? What exactly should these penalties entail?

This book will provide some responses to these fundamental questions. For the moment, let us consider Gillmor, who asserts: "Ultimate accountability is with a public that decides which media die and which survive" (Dennis et al. 1989, 7). Although market forces may not work perfectly in ensuring accountability, John Merrill believes that "they do, indeed, bring the public into the ultimate process of accountability through a kind of economic (or 'public') determinism that goes a considerable distance in injecting audience values and preferences into the content decisions of our media elite" (Dennis et al. 1989, 11). And again: "Media that people accept and support will survive and thrive; media that people dislike or reject will suffer and die. This is *ultimate accountability*. And it is the kind of accountability in harmony with the spirit of individualism, democracy and freedom"(Dennis et al. 1989, 12).

Voluntary, self-regulatory systems of ethics are supplemental to market accountability in ensuring accountability. These systems can include press councils, ombudsmen, critical journalism reviews, codes of ethics, letters to the editor, and even litigation. Authoritarianism and state interference would, of course, not be acceptable forms of accountability within a free democratic society that rests on liberal values and that values the principle of the marketplace model, whose objective is to maximize individual and independent editorial responsibility in a pluralistic market system.

The goal

This is why the study of media ethics is of the utmost importance. According to Jan Larsen of the University of Wisconsin-Eau Claire:

> What journalism and journalists should be about is upholding the democracy. What we report, what we write about should be the stuff that helps people participate in and contribute to daily public life. Journalism is about society's connectedness, about justice and equal access and opportunity. This, and the traditional rudiments of solid report-

ing, including accuracy, thoroughness, fairness and balance, needs to be taught in the classroom. *Leadtime*, 4)

So what can the study of media ethics achieve? It is worthwhile to follow Louis Day's argument in this regard. Ethics instruction, he says, aims to "*promote* moral conduct by providing the means to make ethical judgements, defend them, and then criticize the results of one's choices" (Day 1991, 7). This process is known as moral reasoning. Day cites the following goals for the study of media ethics:

- *Stimulating the moral imagination.* Moral choices constitute an important part of the human existence and can lead either to much happiness or much suffering. "Stimulating the moral imagination develops an emotional empathy with others that is not elicited by discussing ethical issues in abstract terms" (Day 1991, 7).
- *Recognizing ethical issues.* It is not always easy to recognize or identify the moral dimensions of a situation. Yet this is of paramount importance, since nothing meaningful can be done to a problem if it is not identified as such. Furthermore, "Anticipation of possible dilemmas is an important objective of ethics training and the moral reasoning process" (Day 1991, 7).
- *Developing analytical skills.* The ability "to think critically about ethical issues is at the heart of the decision-making process" (Day 1991, 7). Fundamental abstract concepts such as justice, moral duty, and respect for others should be examined in order to apply them consistently and meaningfully to situations. It is also important to examine critically the arguments and justifications used to support one's moral decisions. The ability to *reason* is essential. That is why case studies are so important in developing analytical skills. What is needed is a rational decision, "based on a defensible moral foundation, ample deliberation, and consideration of the available options" (Day 1991, 8).
- *Eliciting a sense of moral obligation and personal responsibility.* As moral agents, journalists are accountable for their own actions. Journalism involves responsibility – and that responsibility cannot be delegated. "Media practitioners often emphasize freedom at the expense of responsibility. A course in ethics can redress that imbalance" (Day 1991, 8).
- *Tolerating disagreement.* "Before moral agents can make informed ethical judgments, they must take into account and respect other points of view" (Day 1991, 8). It is vital to tolerate differences and not to automatically label opposite points of view as immoral. The search for exact points of difference can help to solve disagreements by eliminating false distinctions.

This book deals with *media* ethics. The goal is to help journalists develop ethical antennae in order to identify ethical issues, so that informed, reasoned, and responsible decisions can be made that are "good", or, at least, take the best possible option between two or more conflicting values. What is needed, then, is an *ethical frame of reference* that can be used to make responsible decisions.

Sometimes it is necessary to identify the (conflicting) principles, values, or norms that underlie the ethical decisions the media make on a daily basis. This will allow journalists to use a systematic approach in their ethical decision-making and to defend their ethical decisions rationally. Both are extremely important, since journalists often find themselves in situations in which there is little or no time to reflect properly on the rights or wrongs of a given decision. If a journalist has learnt to identify the process of ethical decision-making, and understands the underlying values (and sometimes conflicts of values), then he or she should be able to make the best possible decision for the right reasons. Far too many decisions are taken on emotions alone, or on an ad hoc basis.

But firstly, journalists should dig deeper in order to understand properly the paradigms beneath the journalistic surface. Important ethical theories and different theories of the media should also be looked at more closely.

Metaethics

Metaethics is a purely theoretical field of study that focuses on the nature of ethics and searches for the meaning of abstract terms such as good, justice, and fairness. It also tries to identify moral values, and forms the theoretical foundation of codes of ethics and even of unwritten codes of conduct. Metaethics provides the broad foundation for making ethical decisions without being involved in the decision-making process itself.

The Latin word *meta* means "behind" or "underneath". In the journalistic sense, therefore, metaethics studies the paradigms that underlie the ethical choices – albeit sometimes unconscious – made by journalists.

At the risk of oversimplifying, it can be said that there are only two such paradigms. The first judges the ethical implications of the journalist's actions by the expected consequences that these actions can have (the so-called consequentialist approach); the other applies rules or principles of duty without necessarily taking the consequences of actions into consideration (the non-consequentialist, or duty-based, approach).

The consequentialist theory is called teleology; the non-consequentialist one is dubbed deontology. *Every single ethical decision that is made in journalism is based on one of these systems, or on a combination of aspects of both.*

Although these two systems are in opposition

to each other, they can (and should) be combined in certain circumstances. What is more, the same journalist who uses the one system in a certain case will use the other in another instance. "It is tempting to think of these alternatives as mutually exclusive, but in the real world, the lines between them get somewhat blurred" (Black et al. 1995, 41).

This means that journalists do not always (have to) choose between the two systems. Journalists should, however, know the various options and be able to make the best possible decision at any given time. Throughout this book, you will encounter many examples of consequentialist and non-consequentialist thinking, especially in the case studies. For this reason, it is worth exploring these concepts in some detail.

Theoretically, then, there are only the consequentialist and non-consequentialist paradigms. Yet there is a third option, the so-called golden mean, that must also be discussed.

Teleology

The Greek word *teleos* means "result" (or "consequence"). Teleology can be defined as an ethical system within which the moral worth of an action is judged by the relative goodness or badness of its consequences (Beauchamp 1983, 2). The act which produces the most good is right.

To the teleologist, Paul Husselbee and Amy Adams state, "nothing is inherently right or wrong about the act itself; only the result of the act can judged right or wrong" (*Newspaper Research Journal*, Vol 17, 1996, 43).

Most journalists take easily to teleology, for they quite naturally think in terms of consequences. But what is "good"? Teleologists differ on this point. Merrill (1975, 11) explains that egoists, for example, hold that an individual should always do what will promote his or her own greatest good, a view expounded by

Epicurus, Thomas Hobbes and Friedrich Nietzsche; utilitarians (or social ethicists) are convinced that something is right or good if it is, or probably is, conducive to the greatest possible balance of good over evil everywhere. Some utilitarians, like the nineteenth-century British philosophers Jeremy Bentham and John Stuart Mill, have been hedonists, connecting good with the greatest happiness or pleasure for the greatest number of people.

The most influential branch of teleology is utilitarianism. Bentham and Mill argued "...that we can assess the goodness or badness of actions and policies by reference to what produces the greatest possible balance of good consequences or the least possible balance of bad consequences" (Beauchamp 1983, 2). This, Beauchamp concludes, places morality (or ethics) in the social sphere because it is understood to include shared rules and principles. "The underlying purpose of ... morality, utilitarians insist, is to promote human welfare by minimizing harms and maximizing benefits" (Beauchamp 1983, 2).

Therefore, utilitarianism strives to achieve the greatest good for the greatest number of people. For Bentham and Mill, utility is what produces happiness. Utilitarianism boils down to this: if decisions have good results for the majority, then those decisions are good; if your actions harm the majority, then they are bad. Teleology strives for the greatest possible pleasure (against pain) and happiness (against sadness). It does not ask whether something is right or wrong per se, but whether actions will have positive results. If a news report makes the majority of the public happy or satisfies them, then it was a good decision to publish the report (even if certain people are unhappy with it).

However, Beauchamp quite correctly cautions against oversimplification. He argues that it is important to keep in mind what the utilitarian does *not* do:

- It is all too simplistic to state that utilitarianism teaches that the end always justifies the means. The *ends* of actions are different from their consequences. "The ends are what we aim at; the consequences are what happen as a result of what we do. A utilitarian consequentialist will always take both ends *and* means into account..." (Beauchamp 1983, 4).
- Promoting the greatest happiness is not the same as promoting the happiness of a simple majority. If, for example, it pleases 51 per cent of a society to enslave the rest, it seems plausible that the amount of pain suffered by the enslaved 49 per cent would offset the extra pleasure that the 51 per cent receive.

And yet, it must be said that, in general, in utilitarianism the end weighs heavier than the means.

Advantages

Utilitarianism has some important advantages. The mere fact that it looks at the results or consequences of reporting – both positive and negative – must be construed as positive. In this process, various alternatives are analyzed. This can only be beneficial to journalism.

In addition, utilitarianism is committed to the *maximization* of the good. The goal is "... to produce the *best* outcomes, not simply *good* outcomes" (Beauchamp 1983, 3). The conviction that something is good if the majority benefits by it implies that the public interest (and the public's right to know) is held to be of the utmost importance.

So-called Heintz dilemmas are easier to handle, but still present problems. A Heintz dilemma results from a situation in which two moral values clash. Heintz, a fictitious figure, is caught in a catch-22 situation. His wife is very ill and will die if she does not receive proper treatment. This treatment costs $2 000, but he can only come up with $1 000. Herein lies his dilemma: he can steal $1 000, which will save his wife's life, or he can refrain from breaking the law – and let his wife die. Is he allowed to steal in order to save a life? The consequentialist will find it easier to steal (or lie) than a non-consequentialist – on condition, of course, that this is the lesser of the evils and that the end result produces the greatest good for the most number of people.

There are countless examples of Heintz dilemmas in real media life. Should the media disclose sensitive material that could cause the state some harm? What about material the media have and the state wants? Can a journalist lie in order to get an important story? The list is endless. And the utilitarian will handle such difficult situations to the benefit of the majority of society.

Disadvantages

Journalists often find solace in the reasoning that the good that their story has done outweighs the bad. There can, however, be some serious disadvantages as well. For example, because of its focus on the majority, teleology can easily turn its back on (vulnerable) minority groups. Why is "good" necessarily what is "best" for the majority? This can easily result in a "give them what they want" ethical stance (Merrill 1975, 12). "This approach can place a disproportionate weight on justifying actions that serve the greatest good for the greatest number of people. Those individuals or issues that represent a minority perspective can easily lose out in a good-versus-bad-equation" (Black et al. 1995, 41). Achieving the greatest good for the greatest number of people may be unfair to vulnerable people and therefore unethical (Black et al. 1995, 41).

Another obvious problem is that it is extremely difficult to decide in advance what the consequences of your actions will be in the short term and, especially, what they will be in the long term. How do you determine what is really good for the majority of people? Or the consequences? Who makes those decisions? And what agendas do journalists have when making these decisions? How do we *really* know what the outcome of news reports will be (Hausman 1992, 21)? And what about the fact that reports can easily be slanted to get even better "results"? Public relations people are especially vulnerable in this regard.

Deontology

Teleology is not the only ethical system. In deontology, decisions are made according to the principles of duty. Deontology is derived from the Greek word *deon*, which means "duty". In this system, developed by the eighteenth-century German philosopher Immanuel Kant (1724–1804), your actions are based on principles and obligations. According to Kant, all people have a duty to behave morally correctly, even if it is contrary to their character or desires. Kant asks: what are your duties? What responsibilities do you carry? For Kant, the test for ethical behaviour is that it should be universally applicable.

What counts in this process is the intention, the motive behind the act, and not so much the consequences thereof. When applied to journalism, the duty – the ethical imperative – is the matter of distributing truthful information.

In the sense that deontology acts on the basis of principles (without taking the consequences of actions into consideration), it is the theoretical opposite of teleology. The determining factor is not the results of the ethical agent, but his or her intentions and motivations, the expectations of the community or religion or the intrinsic worth of the action. An action is justified if the intentions of the doer are good – regardless of the consequences of the act. In addition, a person acts ethically if that person would be willing to see his or her rule applied by everyone in a similar situation. This is Kant's categorical imperative.

What this means is that, in deontology, the end can never justify the means, precisely because the means (the way in which the journalist obtains information and publishes it) must be based on good intentions and ethical principles as well. For example, unlike in teleology, deception is taboo because the principle of truth would not allow it. Robin Hood is a thief – it does not matter that he steals in order to help the poor. Heintz dilemmas thus cause serious headaches. How do you choose between the desire to save a life and honesty?

Pros and cons

Like teleology, deontology has its pros and cons. On the positive side, a set of principles always makes it easier to make decisions (although this tends to take away some personal responsibility). And the journalist creates an image of trustworthiness and honesty by adhering to these principles. On the other hand, how do you divorce your duties from the consequences of your actions? Are those very same consequences really not important enough not to take into consideration?

Deontology tends to be absolutist (and therefore unrealistic), in the sense that your duty to obey the rules does not take into account that there may be compelling reasons to forsake your principles in certain situations. And Hausman asks whether blind adherence to a categorical imperative is an unrealistic ideal (Hausman 1992, 21). Teleology tends to be more flexible than deontology can ever hope to be.

The golden mean

Both teleology and deontology can (although not necessarily) lead to unacceptable extremes. On the one hand, media ethics should *never* consist of a list of musts, or shoulds, and must-nots, or should-nots – as if there are general or universal rules for each and every case. That would limit the choices that media practitioners should make

for themselves and ignore the unique nuances of situations to the detriment of all concerned. Strict rules that take away the moral agent's own responsibility rebel against true ethical behaviour.

The absolutist tendency of duty ethics can indeed easily lead to a form of legalism, and this has therefore taken away some of the appeal and force of deontology (Merrill 1975, 13). On the other hand, teleology can produce a form of antinomianism, a kind of "morality" that lacks rules, principles, codes, standards, or directives, and which tends toward relativism, anarchy, and nihilism. One of the big dangers in modern (or postmodern) society is that people tend to write ethics off as "relative" – as if there are no journalistic principles. Indeed there *are* such principles, as the remainder of this book would like to point out. Nothing is more detrimental to the cause of excellence in journalism than an "anything goes" attitude.

Both extremes should be avoided at all costs. Somewhere between legalism (absolutism) and antonomianism (anarchy), a golden mean must be found. This brings Aristotle to the fore. Teleology and deontology have one thing in common: they focus on the acts or decisions of the ethical agent, and not on the individual. In contrast to this, the ancient Greeks were rather interested in building character, which resulted in so-called virtue ethics. The idea was that the "good character" would also make "good" decisions.

The Greek philosopher Aristotle (384–322 BC), one of the main exponents of virtue ethics, held that a person with a good character shuns any form of extremity and always chooses a path in between. *Virtue lies somewhere between vices.* This is called the doctrine of the golden mean. It is important to note that the golden mean does not necessarily mean that the exact middle of the road, a "mathematical" compromise, a point of 50/50, must be found. "An editor who believes only in compromise for the sake of avoiding the hard choices on either end of the consequentialist–

non-consequentialist spectrum could produce what we might colloquially call a no-pain–no-gain statement" (Hausman 1992, 20). Sometimes the one extreme is closer to the truth than the other. The golden mean can therefore result in a 70/30 situation, or even a 90/10 one.

This doctrine can be applied fruitfully to most ethical situations that journalists handle. But then the character of the journalist comes into play. The golden mean is not a mere intellectual possibility between opposing values, it is indeed the considered option of a person of character. A journalist with a weak character will not look for the golden mean with the same passion as will a stronger counterpart. Hence the importance of the idea that journalists should build their character and work on it all the time, *to become the type of person who is likely to make sound ethical decisions for the right reasons.*

Normative ethics

Normative ethics builds on metaethics and develops general theories and principles for moral behaviour and for ethical decision-making. It reveals itself in theories of the media in general and in journalistic codes of ethics in particular. Normally, these principles and guidelines coincide with the fundamental values of society, which of course are closely bound up with a particular political and cultural ideology. Underlying any specific theory of the media are basic beliefs and assumptions (paradigms), which have philosophical and cultural bases and which give rise to a specific social system or a combination of political systems – which has everything to do with how the role of the media is seen.

> The press always takes on the form and coloration of the social and political structures within which it operates... It reflects the system of social control whereby the relations of individuals and institutions are adjusted. (Siebert et al. 1956, 1–2)

For this reason, different countries or political systems have different theories of the media. These theories have been identified by a number of authors.[3] There are, broadly speaking, *two* theories of the role of the media: the authoritarian and the libertarian. There are, however, important variations on each of these theories. In particular, the egalitarian (or social responsibility) model and the developmental concept are current in South Africa and will therefore be discussed.

Media theories

It is of the utmost importance that journalists are aware of and understand media theories.[4] This is especially true in South Africa, where different people work with different theories of the media, sometimes without even understanding the presuppositions that underlie these theories. This makes for all sorts of possible misunderstandings. In a country with more than one philosophical and cultural basis, such as South Africa, it is inevitable that there will be different (and even contrasting) theories of the role of the media. Identifying these different theories should help the media and society at large to understand these differences of opinions and the underlying thought processes, and encourage better communication between conflicting parties.

Authoritarianism

The authoritarian theory of the media is the oldest. It started with the invention of the printing press in the mid-fifteenth century, and came to be universally accepted in the sixteenth and seventeenth centuries. Within this system, the truth was conceived to be the product of a few wise men in powerful positions. Truth resided near the seat of power and functioned from the top down. The rulers used the press to inform the public of what they "should" know (read: the policies of the rulers that should be supported). The press belonged to the rulers and was in their service. Where private ownership was granted, this permission could be withdrawn at any time.

Of course, in this model the press cannot function as a watchdog of the government. It is rather the servant of the state. Criticism is "allowed", but only if it comes from within the circles of power, and if the loyalty of the press towards the government is not in question. The authoritarian model of the press still exists in many countries today.

Libertarianism

In direct reaction to the authoritarian concept, a new theory of the press developed around the turn of the seventeenth century and blossomed during the nineteenth century. This was the libertarian theory, and it undermined the authoritarian model at its core.

Libertarianism developed from "a synthesis of bits and pieces" of the philosophies of John Locke, Voltaire (François-Marie Arouet), Jean-Jacques Rousseau, John Milton, John Stuart Mill, Thomas Jefferson, Adam Smith, and Oliver Wendell Holmes (Merrill, in Dennis et al. 1989, 12). In this development the perception of the state–individual relationship underwent fundamental changes. Individuals were now conceived of as rational beings who could distinguish between truth and falsehood (and would do so, given the freedom to discern and choose), and not as dependent beings that had to be led and directed. Truth was no longer seen as the property of the powerful. Instead, the right to search for truth became an inalienable human right. In this search, the press became a vital partner.

Unlike in authoritarianism, the media now served as a watchdog of the government, acting as a check on the powers of the state. In order to fulfil its role as the "fourth estate" – the first three estates corresponding, respectively, to the executive, legislative and judicial arms of the state – the media had to become independent of government control and influence. A free "marketplace of ideas" had to become a reality. Censorship became taboo and criticism of the government was no longer punishable by governments. And all citizens had to be able to get access to the press.

Five ideas

Merrill (1989) identifies five historical ideas that have advanced and perpetuated the libertarian concept of the press:
- the philosophy of freedom and individualism coming out of the Age of Reason in Europe;
- the values of hard work and competition stressed by the Protestant ethic;
- the influence of social Darwinism, with its concepts of "natural selection" and "survival of the fittest" applied to business competition;
- Adam Smith's theory of capitalism, built on the free-market approach, whereby the laws of supply and demand determine the flow of goods and services;
- Justice Holmes and his "marketplace of ideas" (updating Milton's self-righting principle[5]), in which he spoke of the power of thought to get itself accepted in the open competition of the market. It is essential that the marketplace of ideas should be as free as possible, because this provides the best chance to obtain the truth and to disseminate information and opinions (Merrill 1989, 12).

Merrill (1989, 13) also formulates ten principal characteristics of the marketplace model:
- The media should be as free as possible from outside control.

- The media should strive to provide the greatest diversity of information and opinion as possible.
- The media should strive to gain and keep audience members (be competitive) and be economically sound.
- The media that deliver (provide desired services in the competitive market) will survive.
- The economic support of the various media reflects the basic satisfaction, or dissatisfaction, with them on the part of their audiences.
- Therefore, the media are dependent upon their audiences for existence and growth.
- If public support for a certain medium declines, policy should be altered and editorial content upgraded.
- If public support increases, the basic policy is considered sound and the editorial content at least adequate.
- This means that the media are directed (albeit indirectly) by the public. The media must satisfy and represent their constituencies.
- The media system, then, is an active–reactive mechanism that best reflects the wishes of the people and is, in the end, accountable to the people.

Towards the end of the nineteenth century the notion of rationalism came under attack, and with that also the classical form of libertarianism. For example, Freudian psychoanalysis "emphasizes the degree to which human behaviour is motivated not by rational but by irrational impulses" (Grossberg et al. 1998, 377). The two world wars seemed to validate this negative view of rationality. There seemed "no accounting for how a cultivated and civilized nation such as Germany could democratically vote into power an Adolf Hitler. And another 10 years later, the world was staggered by the horror of the Holocaust" (Grossberg 1998, 377). However, most non-communist countries adhered to the libertarian concept of the press during the twen-

tieth century. In the meantime, important new media concepts started to develop.

Egalitarianism

The egalitarian, or social responsibility, model is an important variant of, and counterpoint to, the libertarian concept of the media. Three main factors led to the development of egalitarianism: the communications revolution, the concentration of media ownership in the hands of large conglomerates, and evolving notions of the media's social responsibility.

The communications revolution

Advances in communications during the twentieth century revolutionized the media, making it possible to deliver news via television, and later via satellite, virtually as it happened. The influence of the media increased a thousandfold, and validated the maxim that all journalism is a form of social intervention. Whether they liked it or not, governments now had to take the presence of the media into account and make their decisions accordingly. More than ever, the media became part of the message. The outcome of a regional conflict could even be different just because the media covered – or did not cover – the event.

As a result of the communications revolution, the content of the message became all the more important. The issue of the quantity and "quality" of violence and sex, for example, forced itself into the sphere of social responsibility. One of the questions that arose was the extent to which the media should publish or broadcast explicit scenes of violence or sex that could do serious damage to younger viewers. Moreover, the newspaper networks that had enjoyed supremacy for decades through their control of the flow of news now found that they could no longer compete with their much faster competitors, such as television and the Internet. Consequently, newspapers the world over have resorted to the interpretation and analysis of the news. It makes increasingly less sense to report in tomorrow's newspaper what is already known via television and radio today. Although this change is vital for the survival of the newspaper industry, it is also dangerous. For the more you interpret and analyze, the more difficult it becomes to achieve the journalistic goal of impartiality and objectivity. These factors make it of vital importance that the media remain aware of the ever-increasing duty to be socially responsible.

Conglomerates

Since World War II there has been a major concentration of media ownership all over the world. This, of course, is due to capitalist market forces. Grossberg (1998, 389) quotes press critic Ben Bagdikian, who said in 1997 that if American newspapers, magazines, radio and television stations, and book publishers were owned by separate individuals, there would be 25 000 different owners. Yet there are only about ten owners. Since 1997, new conglomerates have been established, limiting media ownership and control even more.

The financial reasons for forming conglomerates are clear: it is more profitable to join forces, to synergize, and not to fight each other. But at what price? The formation of trusts, cartels, and conglomerates challenges the idea of a "free" marketplace of ideas in two ways. Firstly, how "free" is this marketplace really, if huge conglomerates mean that the media fall into the hands of a powerful few? When fewer and fewer people decide what is news and control the flow of news? When the hope of hearing independent viewpoints declines? When this happens, a shift in ideology takes place that mostly goes unnoticed. The point is this: *even in democracies where the libertarian (or even egalitarian) tradition is strong, the reduction of the marketplace of ideas inevitably leads to a new form of author-*

itarianism. This time it is not the state that is responsible for this state of affairs, but the media themselves – or, rather, the media as a business.

Secondly, many of the media conglomerates are part of larger multinational corporations, which of course have diverse interests. Grossberg poses this important question: "To what extent can the media perform other functions – information and entertainment – adequately if their major role is to make money?" (Grossberg 1998, 390). He adds an even more important question: to what extent is a media enterprise subject to the corporate goals and interests of a parent company (Grossberg 1998, 390)? Libertarianism emphasizes openness and variety; the political-economic counterpoint answers: "Only if there's a profit in it" (Grossberg 1998, 392). Some form of social responsibility on the part of the media is more important than ever.

The Hutchins Commission

Even before World War II, some media people in America began to realize that this new situation (due to the communications revolution and the growth of media conglomerates) demanded a special kind of social responsibility from media institutions. Their concern was that the media was too concerned with sensation, lacked depth, and was not concerned with journalistic excellence any more.

In 1942 the chancellor of the University of Chicago, Robert Maynard Hutchins, was commissioned to study the state of the American media. His specific task was to determine whether the freedom of the press was in danger. In 1946 Hutchins appointed a group of twelve academics to carry out this assignment. *Time* magazine publisher Henry Luce funded the initiative with $200 000, and later the *Encyclopedia Britannica* gave an additional $15 000. In 1947, the Hutchins Commission issued its report, entitled *A free and responsible press. A general report on mass communication: newspapers, radio, motion pictures, magazines, and books.* The commission concluded that the freedom of the press was indeed in danger, for three reasons (Altschull 1984, 180):

- The press had increased in importance and visibility.
- The few who ran the press had not provided a service adequate to the needs of society.
- This minority had sometimes engaged in society-condemned practices which, if continued, would lead inevitably to government regulation or control.

The commission also found that the press devoted too much effort to the trivial and sensational. Reports were meaningless, flat, and distorted, and perpetuated misunderstandings. They represented the exceptional rather than the representative, the sensational rather than the significant. In addition, the commission condemned the concentration of press ownership, and spoke about exaggerated drives for power and profit. In short, the press was not meeting its responsibility to provide a truthful, comprehensive, and intelligent account of the day's events in a meaningful context. Clearly, what was needed was greater responsibility. Freedom of the press was in danger unless it became an accountable (to conscience and the common good) freedom.

According to the Hutchins Commission, press accountability should be monitored and promoted by an independent press agency. The commission warned that the situation was so serious that, if this did not happen, the government could take upon itself that power and even regulate press performance. In effect, the watchdog should watch itself!

The commission's report identified five essential requirements against which the performance of media institutions might be measured (Day 1991, 35, 36):

- The press must provide a truthful, comprehensive, and intelligent account of the day's events in a context that gives them meaning. In this process, facts are insufficient; the truth about the facts (relevant background surrounding the facts) is also essential. Stories should be put into perspective and the credibility of conflicting sources evaluated.
- The press must serve as a forum for the exchange of comment and criticism.
- The press should project a representative picture of the constituent groups in society. Racial, social, and cultural groups should be depicted without resort to stereotypes.
- The goals and values of society should be presented and clarified.
- The press should provide full access to the day's intelligence.

This could be accomplished, the commission said, if the press were more responsible, journalists were better trained, and the press effectively regulated itself. It was understood that the media's duty now, more than ever, transcended the profit motive. Public service implied professional standards for journalists (read: reliable and responsible reporting).

Altschull has formulated the central theme of the Hutchins Commission's report as follows:

> The fundamental role demanded of the press by the Hutchins Commission was rooted in the democratic assumption, which holds that democracy is nurtured and furthered when an informed citizenry makes wise judgments in choosing those who will represent them in the government. To work towards this end is to be responsible. And in carrying out this role, the press must be accountable to the public, to the society that it serves. (Altschull 1984, 182)

The Hutchins Commission contained a well-reasoned and comprehensive analysis of the need for a socially responsible press (Day 1991,

35), and as such laid the foundation for the concept of social responsibility within the media. Within a decade, the American press community "had adopted the social responsibility thesis as if it, like freedom of the press and the public's right to know, had been handed down from some journalistic Mount Sinai" (Altschull 1984, 181). From the proposal that the media should regulate themselves developed the concept of a press council and later of ombudsmen – not only in America, but all over Western Europe and as far afield as India.

Similarities and differences

The egalitarian model can be classified as a variant of the classical libertarian tradition. Both models assume the existence of a discoverable truth and the rational ability of the public to discern between truth and falsehood. There are, however, important points where egalitarianism departs from libertarianism:

- While both are firmly steeped in the human rights tradition, libertarianism focuses on *individual human rights*, whereas the focus of egalitarianism is on *group rights*. Says Louis Day: "Whereas libertarianism emphasizes individual self-sufficiency, egalitarianism focuses on ensuring quality for all members of society. Egalitarians are more willing to sacrifice individual liberty in the name of justice than are libertarians" (Day 1991, 258).
- Unlike egalitarianism, libertarianism's emphasis on individual liberty makes it nearly impossible for libertarians to strive for social justice and to reach for the goal of being socially responsible.
- While libertarians would insist that government has no role whatsoever in the media world, egalitarians are convinced that "government should remain in the background, prodding media to be responsible through

self-regulation" (Grossberg 1998, 384). Egalitarians believe that if the media cannot regulate themselves, the government might have to establish its own media and more directly intervene to assure that the press is responsible. To effect this, government should be granted a limited role in intervening in media operations to ensure that public interests are adequately served – especially in the case of broadcasting, where government intervention is necessary to allocate frequencies and channels.

- In egalitarianism the media should be a "common carrier" of ideas because the press should be under an obligation to present all the voices and views in a particular community. To effect this, the media should effectively represent all sections of society and should reflect the diversities of that society. "This departed significantly from the libertarian idea that the media are wholly free – free, if they wish, to promote only those ideas of their own choosing" (Grossberg 1998, 383).

There are many forms of egalitarianism. In its most extreme form, egalitarianism demands equality regardless of merit (Day 1991, 258). However, as in most other systems of thought, egalitarian models are highly qualified. Louis Day explains: in the "distributive justice" form of egalitarianism, property, rights, and opportunities are allocated in equal shares according to merit (for example, equal pay for equal work). "Compensatory justice" holds that some form of moral compensation is required if an injustice causes harm. For example, programmes of affirmative action are meant to afford equal opportunity and to remedy injustices of the past (Day 1991, 258).

The question is whether the media can fulfil their role of social responsibility and still maintain their autonomy, which is of vital importance in a democracy. Day argues convincingly that "institutions, like individuals, must learn to be socially responsible. But there is no reason to believe that, in so doing, they must sacrifice their corporate autonomy. Institutional autonomy, like individual autonomy, consists of freedom of choice, but there is a price to be paid for making decisions that do not at least take into account the interest of others" (Day 1991, 37).

The developmental concept

Another form of authoritarianism developed in communist countries during the twentieth century. Under the communist system, the press belonged to the Communist Party and was owned by it. Communism suffered a fatal blow after the fall of the Berlin Wall in 1989, and the communist concept of the press perished with it.

However, authoritarianism did not disappear altogether; it merely found another avenue. One extremely important development has been the advent of a new authoritarian idea, namely, the developmental concept.

The developmental concept first emerged in the wake of political independence in impoverished nations throughout the Third World, especially in African countries since the 1960s. The developmental concept is "to some extent a critique of and reaction against the West and its transnational media. It also reflects the frustrations and anger of poor and media-deficient nations" (Hachten 1996, 30). Consequently, the developmental concept has many faces, based on different political and social conditions. There are, however, certain basic underlying convictions to this concept, namely the theme of *nation-building* and *patriotism*, whereby the media is seen to be central to the achievement of national integration and economic development.

Hachten (1996, 30, 31) identifies the following characteristics of the developmental concept:

- The media must be mobilized by the central government to aid in the great task of nation-building (fighting illiteracy and poverty, building a political consciousness, assisting in economic development). The government must provide adequate media services when the private sector is unable to do so, as is the case in many poor countries.
- Therefore, the media should support authority, not challenge it. There is no place for dissent or criticism, for the alternative would be chaos – or so it is perceived. Freedom of the press is of lesser importance than the developmental need of society.
- Information becomes the property of the state, as under authoritarianism. Information or news is a scarce national resource; it must be utilized to further the national goals.
- Individual rights of expression and other civil liberties are irrelevant in the face of the overwhelming problems of poverty, disease, illiteracy, and ethnicity that face the majority of these countries.
- Each country has a sovereign right to control both foreign journalists and the flow of news back and forth across its borders.

Theory and practice

In a 1984 study done in the US to determine the applicability of several normative theories of the media to television news, the research question was as follows: does the definition of what is news and the treatment and interpretation of news found in actual TV newscasts reflect what might be expected from its so-called philosophy? (Korzenny et al. 1992, 89). One week of TV news was monitored in eight countries, segmented among capitalist or Western (United States, West Germany, Italy, and Japan), socialist (the USSR), and developing (China, Colombia, and India) nations. The content was analyzed for its local and international reporting of economic, political, military, scientific, and other categories. The study also looked at the ways in which other nations were portrayed in the host countries.

A total of 735 news stories were coded. The level of reliability claimed by the researchers varied from 66 per cent to 90 per cent. The most important conclusions (Korzenny et al. 1992, 106–108) included:

- Developing countries were not as neglected in world news media as critics had suggested.
- The two socialist countries (USSR and China) almost never criticized or portrayed their governments, militaries, or economies as weak and often praised their government and individuals for social contributions.
- The USSR and China covered science and technology in a positive light, whereas other countries did not.
- Economic solutions (not problems) were most commonly portrayed in the socialist countries.
- The tendency to avoid "negative" news and criticism and to stress the positive characterized socialist news approaches more aptly than even the developing countries did.
- Third World countries showed less conflict and competition than their Western or socialist counterparts.
- Developing countries focused more on agriculture (and to a lesser extent industry) versus trade and commerce.
- Western countries are more "sensationalistic" (referring to the reporting of accidents, disasters, and crime).
- Human rights as a theme appears most in Western countries.
- Western newscasts were more frequently critical of their economies and governments (fulfilling the media's role of watchdog).

The general conclusion was that there was indeed some consistency between predictions made on the basis of political philosophy and the actual content of television broadcasts. This study was done a year after a comparative study between the nature and the role of the mass media in First, Second and Third World countries was published.[6] The results were remarkably similar.

Media theories in South Africa

At present, a curious blend of media theories prevails in South Africa. Underlying these theories are a number of political and cultural paradigms.

Libertarianism and authoritarianism

The first newspaper in South Africa, *The Cape Town Gazette and African Advertiser/Kaapsche Stads Courant en Afrikaanse Berigter*, was first published on 16 August 1800. According to De Beer et al. (1998, 87, 88), "this was the only newspaper that was allowed and it was printed on a government press" (De Beer et al. 1998, 87). This was an authoritarian start to the newspaper industry in South Africa if ever there was one. On 10 October 1800 the government announced that "it was improper and irregular ... to allow the editing of a public newspaper from a press in the hands of private individuals" (De Beer et al. 1998, 87, 88).

Other newspapers were soon established, and a period of media freedom followed. This freedom, however, was short-lived, and inevitably clashes occurred between the industry and the government, which resulted in Lord Charles Somerset confiscating the eighteenth issue of the *Commercial Advertiser* (Thomas Pringle and John Fairbairn, editors) and ordering that its publication be stopped (De Beer et al. 1998, 88). Says De Beer:

This was the start of a prolonged struggle between the press and the authorities, which culminated in Ordinance No. 60 of 8 May 1829. This stated that the government would act against publications only in the case of proven libel or when irresponsible statements were made. The press won the encounter and, ever since, the Ordinance has been described as the 'Magna Carta' of freedom of the press in South Africa... Since then, the names Pringle and Fairbairn have been closely linked to the struggle for press freedom against autocratic interference in South Africa... (De Beer et al. 1998, 88).

Since 1829, then, the (libertarian) principle of the freedom of the press has been firmly established in South Africa.

It should be noted that the authoritarian model was never the persuasion of the South African media – it was rather that of the government in power. However, a form of authoritarianism developed in the Afrikaans press when the National Party came to power in 1948 – even if it was steeped in the libertarian tradition itself.

The Cape Town daily *Die Burger*, in particular, saw itself as the official mouthpiece of the government. The criticism voiced in this period against the government was therefore circumspect, and when it was delivered, it came from a loyal "within". Here are a few examples (amongst hundreds) of this authoritarian approach, in which the extremely close relationship between the press and the party are evident:

- On 7 August 1948 *Die Burger*'s Dawie (the official political voice of the newspaper) stated he was overjoyed that Dr D. F. Malan had taken his place at the opening of Parliament as Prime Minister. "Your heart beat nice and warm because *your man* and *your government* is in power" (my emphasis), it was said (Louw 1965, 29).
- The National Party reinstated *Die Burger* as its official mouthpiece at its congress in September 1961. On 2 September of that year, Dawie commented: "This demonstrates our

mutual trust...". Mention was made of the idea that the Party and *Die Burger* were twin brothers, and even husband and wife. (Dawie also related a story about the woman who was asked at her golden wedding anniversary if she had ever thought of divorce. To which she replied: "Never – but I did contemplate murder!") Dawie added that an idea without organization is like a brain without muscle or sense (Louw 1965, 217, 218). The newspaper was obviously seen as (at least part of) the organizational tool of the ruling party.

- In 1964, British Prime Minister Harold Wilson visited South Africa. Before taking office, Wilson had undertaken not to export any weapons to South Africa. However, the previous British government was under contract to sell 16 Buccaneer fighter jets to South Africa. The opposition (English-language) press criticized the South African Prime Minister for warning the British government that it would violate the Simon's Town Agreement if Wilson did not comply. The English-language press feared that this attitude could endanger the whole deal. Wilson eventually decided to sell the planes to South Africa. Dawie's comment was significant: *"The South African press should make it a principle not to impede the country's position in such delicate matters by its arrogant criticism"* (Louw 1965, 277) (my emphasis).

When Piet Cillié, a former editor of *Die Burger*, was asked in a TV programme about the relationship between the press and the National Party, he responded that the press should not really be the bedfellow of the government, but that it could "sit at its bedside". Of course, the government exploited this situation. When President P. W. Botha, for example, did not like a certain news item on SABC TV, he just had to pick up the telephone and demand either a correction or an omission in the next news bulletin. It is also well known that Cabinet ministers served on the board of Die Nasionale Pers.

There are even more serious examples of this exploitation. In 1977 the government closed down the daily *World* without giving any reason and arrested the editor, Percy Qoboza. He was never brought before a court of law. Draconian media laws in the mid-1980s (during the states of emergency) prohibited the media from reporting on violent political scenes. Restrictions on both the local and international press were the strictest since World War II (De Beer et al. 1998, 104). Provision was made for the seizure of publications, and for fines of R20 000 or up to ten years' imprisonment. Several overseas magazines (such as *Time*, *Newsweek*, and *The Economist*) were censored with black ink. Fortunately, most of the restrictive measures were lifted after February 1990. The Constitution now guarantees the freedom of expression and access to information.

There is much debate as to when the "marriage" between the National Party and *Die Burger* (and the Afrikaans media in general) ended. To some, the divorce started in the early 1960s (De Beer et al. 1998, 88); others put it much later. However, even up to the early 1990s the Afrikaans media in general was so uncritical of the government that it could hardly function as the fourth estate.

In conclusion, the South African media have a firm libertarian tradition, even if different governments acted autocratically from time to time and even if a portion of the media briefly fell into the trap of authoritarianism.

Egalitarianism

The communications revolution and the influence of media conglomerates did not bypass South Africa. What implications do the phenomenon of media conglomerates have on the role and the message of the media in South Africa?

Before democratization in 1994, the South African media were almost exclusively owned by (a few) white people. Media ownership was largely in the hands of five media conglomerates: the Argus Company (now the Independent Group), Die Nasionale Pers (now Naspers), Times Media Ltd, Perskor, and Caxton. This concentration meant that the paradigms entertained by whites determined the process of news selection, and that the black majority was to a great extent bypassed.

After 1994, this had to change. It was of vital importance that the media's role in South Africa did not stay in the hands of a small group of editors and owners, but that it became a public matter in which the whole society could participate due to its interest in this issue. There have indeed been some changes to media ownership. The establishment of Nail (New Africa Investments Limited) was an important development. Times Media Ltd also became predominantly black-owned.

There is a growing (egalitarian) consensus throughout the broad spectrum of the South African media that the issue of media ownership should be addressed on a continuous basis, since the white media are not likely to cater adequately (both with regards to the market and ideology) for the black public.

In addition, the Hutchins Commission has had a remarkable influence on the media in South Africa. This, to a greater or a lesser extent, can be seen in the following:

- There is a growing emphasis on the social responsibility of the media.
- The media is expected to present all the voices and views in a particular community (for example, the "One City, Many Cultures" approach adopted by the *Cape Times*).
- The government should play some role in the media. (This is why the South African Human Rights Commission – a government body – investigated alleged racism in the media, and why the government controls the airwaves.)

- Justice for all (group rights) is often seen as more important than individual liberties.
- A programme of affirmative action should be implemented in media institutions (though some see this as a means to an end, and others as the end in itself).

The developmental model

The various theories current in South Africa have produced conflicting views on the role of the media. There are some telling examples in this process of why the developmental model should be taken seriously.

The *Mail & Guardian* published a very important leading article in this regard in its 22–28 August 1997 edition. The case in point was criticism that had been levelled by three journalists over the reporting of an arms deal between the South African arms manufacturing company, Denel, and Saudi Arabia. The first critic was Thami Mazwai, publisher of *Enterprise* magazine, who, in an article in *Business Day* the week before, had accused white South African journalists of working to a "secret agenda". He also implied that white journalists "do not care a hoot about those who face unemployment", and suggested they were intent on undermining the government in a generally treasonous manner.

Mazwai also pledged that the South African National Editors' Forum (SANEF) "will have to address the delicate balance between national interests and priorities and the public's right to know". Familiar words.

The *Mail & Guardian* pointed out that Mazwai's article was written in support of an earlier article by Jon Qwelane, a columnist and broadcaster, in which he described the disclosure that the Saudis were Denel's clients as an "abuse" of press freedom. The third critic, Njabulo Ndebele, followed suit in an article in *The Sunday Independent*.

The *Mail & Guardian* continued:

Common to all three attacks was the charge that the press was being unpatriotic in its reporting. As such it was of a piece with a recent complaint by the then Deputy President, Thabo Mbeki, that the media was undermining the interests of the country by giving prominence to reports on crime.

The article went on to say that if political leaders in countries like Zambia and even Nigeria (ruled by a military junta at the time) "were to urge their journalists to withhold information from the public on grounds of 'patriotism' they would be ridiculed for it". On Mazwai's pledge to SANEF, the *Mail & Guardian* had this to say: "The implication is that a bunch of jumped-up, self-appointed newspaper hacks – not the Constitution, not the law – will sit in judgment on what constitutes the national interest and what the public will be allowed to hear. We can conceive of no more dangerous a formula of the governance of South Africa." And for the media's role in keeping the public informed, it should be added.

This highlights one of the basic problems with the developmental model: who decides what constitutes the "national interest"? But criticism of the South African media does not only come from within certain circles in the media. Government officials, including members of the Cabinet, also sporadically accuse journalists of disloyalty – thus earning a mention in a 1999 US State Department human rights report (as reported by Johann Holzapfel in *Die Burger*, 1 March 1999). Concern was voiced in the US report that officials were oversensitive to criticism and wanted to tie the media down.

It must be said that recent reports have stressed that the government does not advocate "sunshine journalism" but rather "informed criticism" from the media. These reports are to be welcomed, for once government starts to believe it owns the news and tries to use the media to further "national goals", the slide is difficult to stop.

In general

The egalitarian concept is found, to a greater or lesser extent, in all the important media circles in South Africa. This means that there is some common ground. The situation, however, is not that simple, for not everyone arrives at the egalitarian model from the same starting position. Generally speaking, one section of the media departs from a libertarian model, resulting in a libertarian–egalitarian approach. Another section starts from the developmental (new authoritarian) concept, resulting in a developmental-egalitarian model. Of course, this is speaking in general terms. There can be thousands of permutations. Yet these different concepts (the libertarian–egalitarian and the developmental–egalitarian) should be kept in mind in order to understand the intricate media situation that exists in South Africa.

Applied ethics

Normative ethics leads to applied ethics, where insights derived from both metaethics and normative ethics are realized in practical terms. In applied ethics, contrasting values are often weighed against one another in order to find a responsible and practical way forward. This is a very important branch of ethics, since all the theoretical understanding in the world will not help much if properly reasoned ethical decisions are not taken. Part II of this book is devoted to applied ethics.

Guiding principles for journalists

The most basic maxims of normative ethics are to maximize truth, minimize harm, and act independently. These non-negotiable "commandments" are the most important ethical guidelines for journalists. According to Black (1995, 17, 18), this means:

1 **Seek the truth and report it as fully as possible (maximize truth).** The fact is that a journalist is in the business of telling the truth. Therefore:
   - Inform yourself continuously so that you can inform, engage, and educate the public in clear and compelling ways on significant issues.
   - Be honest, fair, and courageous in gathering, reporting, and interpreting accurate information.
   - Give voice to the voiceless.
   - Hold the powerful accountable.

2 **Minimize harm.** Your truth-telling can indeed cause a lot of harm. Therefore:
   - Be compassionate towards those affected by your actions.
   - Treat sources, subjects, and colleagues as human beings deserving of respect, not merely as the means to your journalistic ends.
   - Recognize that gathering and reporting information may cause harm or discomfort. Choose alternatives that maximize the goal of truth-telling and minimize harm.

3 **Act independently.** Your own integrity is always at stake. Therefore:
   - Guard vigorously the essential stewardship role that a free press plays in an open society.
   - Seek out and disseminate competing perspectives without being unduly influenced by those who would use their power or position counter to the public interest.
   - Remain free of associations and activities that may compromise your integrity or damage your credibility.
   - Recognize that good ethical decisions require individual responsibility as well as collaborative efforts.

Notes

[1] Black et al. 1995, p. 5: "Morality has come to mean socially approved customs, or the practice or application of ethics."

[2] Christians reminds us that journalists have an obligation towards themselves (integrity and conscience should play a major role in every journalist's work – be careful not to confuse this with your own egoistic self-interest); towards clients, subscribers and supporters; towards your organization (loyalty remains important, though one can follow company policy too blindly); towards professional colleagues; and towards society.

[3] For example, Hausman (1992, 16) refers in this regard to Siebert et al. (1956). See also Hachten (1996, 13–33).

[4] It has become popular to link modern journalistic dilemmas to classical thought. "While applying philosophical reasoning to journalism ethics is hardly a new idea, it is a fairly recent innovation in the classrooms of journalism and communications schools" (Hausman, 1992, 7).

[5] According to Milton's self-righting principle, the truth will be victorious against falsehood in a free marketplace of ideas. See Altschull 1990, pp. 36–42 for a discussion of this issue.

[6] See Martin et al. *Comparative Mass Media Systems*.

2 | The law: codes of ethics

A code which merely advocates ideal standards of behaviour for journalists, and makes no link between those standards and what people actually do, would be considered irrelevant by most practising journalists, and hence would be unlikely to influence their actions.[1]

The law and the media

An important distinction must be made between ethics and the law. These two concepts should not be equated. The legality of an action does not necessarily mean it is ethical; an illegal action is also not by definition unethical. A person can act lawfully, but unethically; or ethically, but illegally (De Beer et al. 1998, 299).

Ethics and the law

Louis Day is correct when he says that laws are not the cornerstone of a democracy – it is the moral respect for the law that provides the foundation for a democratic culture (Day 1991, 28). Two central concepts are introduced here, namely, "laws" and "morality" (read: ethics). The question therefore arises as to what the relationship is between the law and ethics. Here are some considerations:

- All laws should be morally just.
- If laws are morally unjust, a case can be made for acts of civil disobedience; for example, a journalist may ignore a ban on travel to a certain country or region if he or she feels compelled to document human rights abuses (Day 1991, 29). Of course, the journalist must then be prepared to face the consequences of his or her actions.

- All citizens, including journalists, have a moral responsibility to obey the law. Legal issues confronting journalists also have ethical dimensions (Day 1991, 30).
- Ethical questions cannot be resolved merely by resolving the legal ones. For example, even if the law does not prohibit the publication of the name of a rape victim, it still remains an ethical question whether the name should be published.
- A just law may only be violated in emergency situations or when a higher principle (or moral obligation) is involved.
- Not all ethical issues can (or should) be legally codified. How do you codify the breaking of a promise between friends?
- Violations of the law involve prescribed penalties; ethical misbehaviour does not.
- Media freedom "places a greater responsibility on media practitioners to consider the ethical ramifications of their actions than if they were prohibited from exercising that freedom in the first place" (Day 1991, 31).

There are many examples in South African history of where the media came into conflict with the law because of ethical considerations. Some of these cases are discussed in Part II.

The following discussion of the law and the media in South Africa is based on the unpublished report, *Legislation infringing freedom of expression: a call for amendment* by the Centre for Applied Legal Studies (Cals) of the University of the Witwatersrand.[2] The discussion is necessary not only in itself but also to illustrate the need for ethical behaviour as well as for ethical codes of conduct. The report analyzes the provisions of some important statutes presently in force which impact on freedom of expression and information in general and freedom of the press in particular. It was discussed in October 2000 by the South African National Editors' Forum (SANEF). What is presented here is a summary of the most important points in the report and is by no means exhaustive. Some of the laws that come under discussion may have been repealed or amended by the time this book is published.

The Bill of Rights and the media

There are two important aspects in the Bill of Rights pertaining to the media that have to be discussed first.

Freedom of expression

The Bill of Rights is contained in Chapter 2 of the Constitution of the Republic of South Africa,[3] Act 108 of 1996. Section 16(1) reads as follows:

> Everyone has the right to freedom of expression, which includes –
> (a) freedom of the press and other media;
> (b) freedom to receive and impart information and ideas;
> (c) freedom of artistic creativity; and
> (d) academic freedom and freedom of scientific research.

However, these rights are followed by some exceptions in Section 16(2):

> The right in subsection (1) does not extend to –
> (a) propaganda for war;
> (b) incitement of imminent violence; or
> (c) advocacy of hatred that is based on race, ethnicity, gender or religion, and that constitutes incitement to cause harm.

Access to Information

Section 32 of the Constitution, covering access to information, reads as follows:

(1) Everyone has the right of access to –
    (a) any information held by the state; and
    (b) any information that is held by another person and that is required for the exercise or protection of any rights.
(2) National legislation must be enacted to give effect to this right, and may provide for reasonable measures to alleviate the administrative and financial burden on the state.

Limitations

Freedom of expression and access to information are recognized by the Bill of Rights as basic human rights. However, neither are absolute. Not all legislation "which infringes the right to freedom of expression or access to information will be held to be unconstitutional and invalidated" (Cals 2000, 4). The right "to obtain and disseminate information and ideas is not absolute, it is constantly under pressure from other values such as privacy, national security, public order and public health amongst others" (Cals 2000, 4).

In particular, Section 36 places certain limitations on the rights set out in earlier sections. This section reads:

(1) The rights in the Bill of Rights may be limited only in terms of law of general application to the extent that the limitation is reasonable and justifiable in an open and democratic society based on human dignity, equality and freedom, taking into account all relevant factors, including:
    (a) The nature of the right.
    (b) The importance of the purpose of the limitation.
    (c) The nature and extent of the limitation.
    (d) The relation between the limitation and its purpose.
    (e) Less restrictive means to achieve the purpose.
(2) Except as provided in subsection (1) or in any other provision of the Constitution, no law may limit any right entrenched in the Bill of Rights.

This "may justify restricting freedom of the press and access to information for reasons including national security, law enforcement, privacy, confidentiality, commercial interests, international relations and government operations amongst others" (Cals 2000, 5).

Specific statutory provisions

There are several laws that have an important impact on the South African media. The following discussion will take a brief look at some of these laws.

Promotion of Equality and Prevention of Unfair Discrimination Act (Equality Act)

One of the aims of this Act, which "contains a number of legislative provisions that raise freedom of expression concerns", is to prohibit hate speech (Cals 2000, 5). Sections 10 and 12 are of particular concern.

Section 10(1) of the Act stipulates that:

no person may publish, propagate, advocate or communicate words based on one or more of the prohibited grounds, against any person, that could reasonably be construed to demonstrate a clear intention to –
(a) be hurtful;
(b) be harmful or to incite harm;
(c) promote or propagate hatred.

According to the Cals report, this does not distinguish between statements made in private conversation and public utterances. "It aims to regulate all (not only hate, but also hurtful and harmful) speech" (Cals 2000, 6).

Section 10(2) stipulates that cases dealing with the publication, advocacy, propagation, or communication of such hate speech may be referred by the courts to the Director of Public

Prosecutions. The report comments that Section 10 is "extremely constitutionally vulnerable in whole or in part" because the provisions "have the unintended consequence of unreasonably restricting freedom of expression in our society" (Cals 2000, 6). Moreover, "Section 10 is disturbingly wide as it effectively strives to protect citizens from speech which may offend them" (Cals 2000, 8).

Section 12 of the Act stipulates that:

No person may –
(a) disseminate or broadcast any information;
(b) publish or display any advertisement or notice,
that could reasonably be construed or reasonably be understood to demonstrate a clear intention to unfairly discriminate against any person: Provided that *bona fide* engagement in artistic creativity, academic and scientific enquiry, fair and accurate reporting in the public interest or publication of any information, advertisement or notice in accordance with Section 16 of the Constitution, is not precluded by this section.

This section "is also very wide as it also prohibits speech in instances where the communicator has no subjective intention to discriminate" (Cals 2000, 8). The provisos (art, academics, scientists, fair and accurate reporting) are also problematic. What if a journalist argues that his or her report does not contravene the Equality Act because he was engaged in "*bona fide* fair and accurate reporting"?

In the end, the main problem with sections 10 and 12 "is the powerful chilling effect that they are likely to have on the media. Editors who commit themselves to obeying this legislation will have to engage in self-censorship, undermining the public's right to know. Editors will also have to censor their advertisers" (Cals 2000, 9). For who is to know whether a part of society would find a particular report or advertisement hurtful or harmful?

Access to public trials and inquiries

The Cals report states that "access to courts may be an element of the right of access to information and intrinsic to freedom of speech and expression, including freedom of the press. Limitations on access to a trial may constitute an infringement upon these rights but the restriction may still protect an accused's right to a fair trial" (Cals 2000, 13). Section 153 of the Criminal Procedure Act and Section 10 of the Inquests Act permit the presiding officer in judicial proceedings to direct that a criminal trial be held *in camera* if it is in the interests of the security of the state or of good order, public morals, or the administration of justice.

The report concludes that limiting access to legal proceedings or banning publication of trial information should be an act of last resort.

If some limitation is required, it must be the minimum restriction possible to achieve the purpose. It is preferable to restrict what the media may print than to restrict public presence by holding hearings *in camera*. If an *in camera* hearing is reasonable and justifiable to achieve the ends of justice, a judge should bear the responsibility of updating the press on the proceedings. The onus should be upon the person seeking to exclude the public from the courtroom to justify the exclusion. (Cals 2000, 18)

Journalistic privilege

Everyone is aware of the fact that journalists frequently rely on relationships with sources who have "inside information". These sources are often willing to divulge information, but on condition that their anonymity is guaranteed. It is in the public interest that journalists should be able to protect their sources against disclosure. Therefore, a case can be made "for granting legal privilege to journalists in respect of their sources of information and the kind of information they acquire in confidence. Sources will be hesitant to give out information if they are aware that their identity may be extracted from journalists" (Cals 2000, 19).

There is indeed a public interest "in retaining and promoting particular confidential interactions for a greater access to information" (Cals 2000, 19). Yet, at the same time, it should be remembered that the administration of justice requires that all relevant facts should be available to a court. South African courts "have been reluctant to recognise privilege, other than the legal and marital privileges, which may result in the suppression of valuable evidence at trial, whether in relation to identity or communications" (Cals 2000, 20).

Section 205 of the Criminal Procedure Act is generally used to compel journalists to reveal relevant information – unless the journalist has a "just excuse" for failing to do so. When Section 205 was examined in the Constitutional Court,[4] the Court "found that Section 205 inquiries are not constitutionally objectionable in themselves" (Cals 2000, 21). This means, *inter alia*, that the decision about whether a journalist has a "just excuse" for refusing to reveal information must now be assessed in the light of the Bill of Rights. "An analysis of the right to freedom of expression should now figure prominently in any decision about whether a journalist has a 'just excuse' for failing to reveal his or her sources" (Cals 2000, 21).

The Cals report gives the following guidance about how journalistic privilege should be addressed:

- It has been suggested that information should be kept confidential only when it is in the public interest – and not if it is merely interesting to the public. A distinction between "need to know" (public interest) and "nice to know" (interesting to the public) should be made. Although this is an important distinc-

tion, "it may bog the courts down in defining and analysing the type and value of the confidential information seeking protection, instead of holding a presumption of privilege and allowing limitations in rare circumstances" (Cals 2000, 21).

- When the courts want a journalist to reveal his or her sources of information, the reporter "must assert and show that he or she received the relevant information in confidence, that the guarantee was necessary to assure that the relationship with the source was sustained and that the relationship would be substantially harmed by the disclosure" (Cals 2000, 21, 22). This amounts to a "just excuse". The onus should then be on the state to prove the overriding importance of disclosure. The state must then, *inter alia*, show that the identity of the informant is relevant evidence, that the evidence is highly probative to key issues, and that no alternative sources of information are available.

- On 19 February 1999 the Minister of Justice, the Minister of Safety and Security, and SANEF signed a Record of Understanding regarding the implementation of existing laws on the duty to testify and the protection of journalists' sources and information. The need to balance the interests of the maintenance of law and order and the administration of justice on the one hand with the right of freedom of expression on the other was accepted. It was also agreed to investigate the possibility of amending Section 205 of the Criminal Procedure Act. This is still to happen.

The Promotion of Access to Information Act

This Act regulates access to both publicly and privately held information. The Act cannot be used to gain access to the records of the Cabinet or its committees. It stipulates the following grounds upon which access to records *must* be refused:

- when information would involve the unreasonable disclosure of personal information about a third party;
- trade secrets or financial, commercial, scientific, or technical information that would be likely to cause harm (commercial or financial) to a third party;
- a third party's research;
- when information was supplied to the government in confidence;
- certain records of the South African Revenue Service;
- documents which would be privileged in legal proceedings;
- information that could reasonably be expected to endanger the life or physical safety of an individual.

Access to information *may* be refused on the following grounds:

- it affects the defence, security, and international relations of the state, or the economic interests and financial welfare of the country;
- it could compromise the security of certain property, computer, or communication systems;
- to enable criminal investigations and prosecutions to proceed effectively;
- some internal governmental communications;
- frivolous or vexatious requests for information.

Access to information must be *granted* when:

- it would reveal evidence of a substantial contravention of, or failure to comply with, the law; or an imminent and serious public safety or environmental risk;
- the public interest in the disclosure of the information clearly outweighs the harm contemplated in the provision in question.

When a request for information is made, the decision must be taken as soon as it is reasonably possible, but not more than thirty days after the request is received. This period could be extended for a further thirty days. If the request is denied and the requester appeals, another thirty days may elapse. A requester may only approach a court after the internal appeal procedure has been completed.

According to the Cals report, this Act has many good features, but there are a number of ways in which it can still be improved or augmented:

- The Act should provide a fast-track procedure for urgent requests for information.
- The Cabinet and its committees should not have received a blanket exemption from the terms of the Act.
- Legislation that provides for open meetings should be passed. (The 1996 draft of this Act contained a provision that emphasized the need for open meetings. In 1997 the open meetings section was dropped from the Act.)
- The Act implies that journalists could be requested to reveal their sources. Much more circumspection is needed.
- Limits on the dissemination or publication of information received in terms of this Act (as opposed to its reception) may still exist in terms of old legislation. This Act should therefore explicitly repeal or amend legislation that makes inappropriate incursions into the rights to freedom of expression or access to information.

National security

The following section considers the various pieces of legislation regulating national security and the need to balance the requirements of national security against the rights of free expression and information.

The National Security in the Promotion of Access to Information Act defines "subversive or hostile" activities as aggression against the

Republic; sabotage or terrorism aimed at the people of the Republic or a strategic asset of the Republic, whether inside or outside the country; an activity aimed at changing the constitutional order of the Republic by the use of force or violence; or a foreign or hostile intelligence operation. The main defence and security exemption in the Act is contained in Section 41(1), which provides that the information officer of a public body may refuse a request for access to a record of the body if its disclosure could reasonably be expected to cause prejudice to the defence or the security of the Republic.

Although the value accorded to national security is widely recognized as a vital and legitimate concept, this Act needs to be carefully defined and limited. "Vague definitions of the already nebulous concept of national security tend to skew the balance between freedom of information and national security in favour of the latter" (Cals 2000, 28). There is an urgent need to define the meaning of national security in a comprehensive and consistent way.

The following statutes, broadly speaking, restrict the disclosure of information for national security reasons, and require not only a clear definition but also analysis for potential infringement of sections 16 and 32 of the Constitution:

- **Defence Act 44 of 1957:** empowers the President to enforce censorship for the prevention or suppression of internal disorder, and to invade the privacy of anyone. However, "disorder" could entail legitimate dissent. Furthermore, Section 118(1)(a) states that no-one may publish any information relating to the composition, movements, or dispositions of the Defence Force, or any statement, comment or rumour calculated directly or indirectly to covey such information. Section 118(1)(b) adds the following absurd provision:

No person shall publish in any newspaper, magazine, book or pamphlet or by radio or any other

means any statement, comment or rumour relating to any member of the South African Defence Force or any activity of the South African Defence Force or any force of a foreign country, calculated to prejudice or embarrass the Government in its foreign relations or to alarm or depress members of the public, except where publication thereof has been authorized by the Minister or under his authority.

- **Armaments Development and Production Act 57 of 1968:** it is illegal to disclose any information relating to the acquisition, supply, marketing, import, development, manufacture, maintenance or repair of, or research in connection with armaments by or on behalf of Armscor or one of its subsidiaries (unless written authority from the Minister has first been obtained).

- **National Supplies Procurement Act 89 of 1970:** grants the state wide powers which may be exercised for the security of the Republic, with a view to ensuring that services and goods are available. It is illegal to disclose any information (without authorization) in relation to any person or business acquired in the performance of his or her duties. The Minister may, *inter alia*, prohibit the disclosure of any information in relation to any goods or services, or of any statement, comment, or rumour calculated directly or indirectly to convey such information.

- **National Key Points Act 102 of 1980:** the Minister of Defence may declare any place to be a National Key Point. Any person who furnishes information relating to the security measures applicable without authorization is guilty of an offence. This Act is impossible to adhere to as the only person whom the Minister must inform that a place has been declared a National Key Point is the owner of that place.

- **Protection of Information Act 84 of 1982:** intends to prevent certain government activities from being revealed by the media, by defining certain categories of information as "protected". The Act contains blanket restrictions on disclosure that take no account of the principles of openness and accountability.

Control of Access to Public Premises and Vehicles Act 53 of 1985

In general, the media should have the right to follow protest demonstrations onto public or quasi-public property without fear of prosecution, even if the demonstrators trespass. This Act aims to get control over access as a type of information control that restricts the media's freedom to gather news. Section 2(1)(a) of this Act grants the owner of any public premises or vehicles the power to do whatever is necessary for the safeguarding of those premises or vehicles and for the protection of the people therein or thereon. Section 2(1)(b) grants power to control access to the premises – which can result in barring journalists from entering certain premises.

Bogoshi, the media's best friend[5]

On 29 September 1998, the Supreme Court of Appeal liberated the media from the shackles of strict liability in media-related defamation cases. This landmark decision, known as the Bogoshi case, opened up new defences for the media when sued for defamation. These defences are in line with the constitutional avenues down which South Africa and its judiciary has marched since the introduction of the Constitution in 1996. In this landmark judgment, the Supreme Court of Appeal reaffirmed the constitutional value of freedom of expression and the pivotal role of the press in South Africa's young democratic society.

We must not forget that it is the right and indeed a vital function of the press to make available to the community vital information and criticism about every aspect of public, political, social and economic activity and thus to contribute to the formation of public opinion ... Conversely, the press often becomes the voice of the people – their means to convey their concerns to their fellow citizens, to officialdom and to government.[6]

This case is so important that it has to be covered in detail.

Before Bogoshi

Before Bogoshi, the media's defences were restricted by the so-called strict or absolute liability rule. Other defendants in defamation cases could escape liability by proving to the court that they had no intention of defaming the plaintiff or were not negligent. This defence, however, was not available to the media. This is the effect of the strict liability rule: the public media, faced with a defamation action, had to prove the article in dispute was true and in the public interest, or that it was the expression of an opinion based on facts which were substantially true (Carmel Riccard, *Sunday Times*, 4 October 1998). Qualified privilege and fair comment were the only other possible traditional defences in media-related defamation cases.

This was a very unfortunate situation, because sometimes the media, through no fault of their own, publish untrue allegations which could lead to a defamation lawsuit. Even if the media defendant took the most reasonable steps to verify the information before publishing it without knowledge of its false nature, it would be no excuse and the media defendant would be found guilty of defamation.

The facts of the case

National Media Ltd, the then owners of *City Press* newspaper, together with the paper's editor, printer, and distributor, were confronted with this dilemma when a Pretoria-based lawyer, Nthedi Morele Bogoshi, sued them for R1,8 million. Bogoshi claimed he had been defamed in a series of nine articles published in *City Press* between 17 November 1991 and 29 May 1994. In these articles the newspaper had alleged Bogoshi's involvement in fraudulent transactions with clients and the Motor Vehicle Accident Fund. The *City Press* articles also alleged that Bogoshi touted for business and was under investigation by the Auditor-General's office.

Bogoshi brought the claim in the Witwatersrand Local Division in 1996.[7] The presiding officer, Judge Frikkie Eloff, rejected an application by the media defendants to introduce an additional defence as an alternative to the defendants' traditional defence based on truth and the public interest. The essence of the additional defence was that the publication of the articles by *City Press* was indeed lawful, because of the freedom of speech and expression guarantee in the Constitution,[8] as well as the argument that the defendants did not publish the articles recklessly or negligently, that the publication was objectively reasonable and published without intent to defame.

The appeal

Eloff found that the 1993 Interim Constitution did not affect the common law of defamation, because the common law ensured an equitable balance between freedom of speech and the protection of a person's reputation. National Media Ltd took Eloff's decision to the Supreme Court of Appeal, who had to decide whether the proposed defence was good in law.

In his judgment, Judge Joos Hefer confirmed that the traditional defence of truth for the public benefit, fair comment, and privilege are not a closed list. He stated that the lawfulness of an act or omission is determined by the application of a general criterion of reasonableness based on considerations of fairness, morality, policy, and the court's perception of the legal convictions of the community. Hefer also considered the imposition of strict liability[9] on media defendants in defamation cases by looking at how the conflicting interests of a plaintiff's reputation and a defendant's freedom of expression are balanced. He said: "It would be wrong to regard either of the rival interests with which we are concerned as more important than the other". The court emphasized both these values as cornerstones of a democratic society. It concluded that the free flow of information and the task of the media in the process are severely handicapped by the strict liability rule. "Nothing can be more chilling than the prospect of being mulcted in damages for even the slightest error." Hefer overruled the strict liability rule, as it was "clearly wrong".

The effect of the ruling

This ruling allows media defendants to raise *absence of fault as a defence in defamation cases*. Absence of fault means that a defendant had no intention to defame or was not negligent in publishing the allegations. However, *media defendants would have to prove they were not negligent in order to escape liability*. A defence based on a lack of intention to defame would not be successful, because although you did not intend to defame, you might still be negligent. Hefer stated, "The approach adopted in this case is intended to cater for ignorance and mistake at the level of lawfulness, and in a given case negligence on the defendant's part may well be determinative of the (lack of) legality of the publication".

The court also looked at the grounds on which a media defendant could escape liability in a defamation case.

> The publication in the press of false defamatory allegations of fact will not be regarded as unlawful if, upon consideration of all the circumstances of the case, it is found to have been reasonable to publish the particular facts in a particular way and at the particular time.

The reasonableness of a publication depends on the nature, extent, and tone of the allegations. Factors that will certainly be taken into account in the determination of reasonableness are:

- the nature of the information on which the allegations were based;
- the reliability of the source;
- the steps taken to verify the information;
- the opportunity given to the person concerned to respond;
- the need to publish before establishing the truth in a positive manner.

However, this list is not intended to be exhaustive or definitive. Hefer emphasized the utmost responsibility of the media when it comes to the publication of defamatory matters:

> Ultimately there can be no justification for the publication of untruths, and members of the press should not be left with the impression that they have a licence to lower the standards of care which must be observed before a defamatory matter is published in a newspaper.

The Supreme Court of Appeal upheld the common law position on the onus/burden of proof,[10] in terms of which the media defendant has to prove that the publication was reasonable and that he or she was not negligent. Proof of reasonableness would usually be proof of lack of negligence. The common law rules should not be disturbed, because the facts upon which the defendant relies are peculiar within his knowledge.

Opinions on the judgement

The Bogoshi judgment was widely welcomed as a certain indication of the judiciary's intention to uphold and protect the constitutional value of freedom of expression and as an unequivocal recognition of the media's role in this regard.

> The Bogoshi judgement represents a substantial and long-overdue victory for freedom of expression and the media in South African society. It is submitted that the approach to justification and fault adopted in Bogoshi accords with the salutary imperative that the media have an indispensable role to play in our democracy, but that in fulfilling this role, the media should also act responsibly and with due regard to the importance attached to a person's reputation.[11]

Moegsien Williams, editor of the *Cape Argus* and chairman of the International Press Institute, commented: "People who had something to hide had used the courts to cover things up. This means we are freer in our reporting".[12] Carmel Riccard, reporter for the *Sunday Times*, said that "it was the first time South Africa's highest court properly affirmed the role of a free press in a democratic society and, flowing from this revised view of the media, made fundamental – and long overdue – changes to the laws regarding defamation" (*Sunday Times*, 4 October 1998).

Although the victory for press freedom can in no way be downplayed, some people felt that the ruling on the onus of proof was somewhat disappointing. SANEF described it as "an unfair onus on an accused" to prove innocence, one that should be imposed on the person who instituted the complaint (SAPA, 6 October 1998). Onus aside, however, 28 September 1998 marked the beginning of a new era for the South African media, an era in which any journalist who takes up a pen or speaks into a microphone will yell "Bogoshi" when a defamation suit rears its ugly head.

Codes of ethics

Whereas the law requires that certain rules and regulations must be adhered to, the field of (media) ethics relates to a self-imposed duty (De Beer et al. 1998, 297). It can be argued that, because the Constitution guarantees freedom of speech, the media have a special responsibility to regulate themselves without interference from government (De Beer et al. 1998, 298, 299). Hence the importance of codes of ethics, as one of the ways in which the media can regulate themselves.

A code is a code is a code

Media codes of ethics, as examples of normative ethics, are not a new phenomenon. The first journalistic code of ethics to be officially adopted was the Kansas Code, written by William E. Miller and endorsed by the Kansas Editorial Association in 1910 (Christians, in Dennis et al. 1989, 36). Other codes soon followed throughout the US. Codes of ethics have became commonplace since World War II. The most important goals of these codes were to safeguard media freedom and to prevent government regulation of the media.

Although South Africa has many such codes, there is also a marked absence thereof in certain (important) circles.

But what is a code of ethics, and what is it not? A code of ethics is a document that sets out guidelines aimed at proscribing certain types of conduct deemed unethical, and identifying other types of conduct as being ethical. Most professions have some sort of a code to give ethical direction to the profession and to serve as the conscience of the worker as an individual, and of the organization as a whole. The status of a code of ethics in journalism, however, cannot be compared with legal or medical codes, "…since in those fields ethical principles are enforced by licensing agencies and policing bodies" (Hulteng 1976, 229). That is why it is incorrect, and indeed dangerous, to link a code of ethics to the idea of journalism being a profession, as Hausman does (Hausman 1992, 125).

A code of conduct is not a legal document and can certainly not be enforced as such. "A code of ethics falls somewhere between societal and personal values on the one hand and law on the other. A code is not as subjective as personal beliefs and opinions, nor as rigid and enforceable as the law" (Black et al. 1995, 13).

This raises certain questions: should some enforcement mechanisms be formulated? If so, what kind of mechanisms? And, if not, how influential is a code of conduct for which there is no enforcement machinery? (Hulteng 1976, 229). For John Hulteng, "the hard fact is that codes without teeth, without an agency to enforce them, tend to be most influential with those who are *already* behaving responsibly and ethically; they often have little effect on the ones who need the guidance most…" (Hulteng 1976, 230).

So from where does a code of ethics derive its legitimacy? From the voluntary acceptance of the document by every worker, of course. This implies that journalists subject themselves to the code and be willing to be guided (and corrected, if necessary) by the code. It also means that a code is more binding than mere personal or societal values. This "in-between" status suggests that a code of ethics in the first and the last instance contains *guidelines* – nothing more and nothing less. It is a moral compass and contains broad ethical guidelines. It gives ethical direction; it points the way, like a road map, to the desired destination. The idea is not to cater for all possible situations – *nor should it ever intend to do so.*

The simple but profound reason for this is that a code of ethics should *never* function in such a way that it takes away even a small part of the responsibility that journalists should take upon themselves when making difficult decisions. Each journalist must paddle his or her own boat on the stormy river; a code of ethics only points to the dangerous rocks on either side of that river, helping the journalist to avoid a collision.

Personal responsibility

Yes, journalists can and indeed should allow themselves to be guided by the code to steer clear of the looming dangers; but it always remains *the journalist* who is ultimately responsible for his or her decisions. In a prophetic article, significantly titled "Media morality: more than codes of ethics" (*Open Media* 1987, 6–8), Alison Gillward[13] wrote:

> A vibrant and dynamic press run by ethical journalists will not simply rise out of the embers of apartheid, nor is it going to come about through media frameworks imposed from above, whoever is above. The media will only be able to perform its crucial role of ensuring that the will of the people is an informed one when individual journalists commit themselves to the free flow of information and the public's right to know. (*Open Media* 1987, 6)

Of course Gillward is correct: ethics are all about personal decisions and practices. All journalists should have that autonomy. And all journalists should be committed to freedom of, and access to, information. Her conclusion is also noteworthy:

> While ethics can be argued in terms of responsibilities at various levels ... it rightfully comes down to personal decisions and practices, and any journalist should have the autonomy to act on these. It is precisely for this reason that I suggest the major arena for developing humanist ethics – individual autonomy based on reason, humanity and spiritual principles – is at the training level. (*Open Media* 1987, 8)

Jan Larsen holds the view that "if we instill in our students a moral compulsion to concern themselves with justice and equality, if we teach them to value solid reporting techniques, we will have little cause for dismay about the future of journalism or its role in shaping democracy... In the future, I intend to be less timid about teaching these so-called absolutes. There's simply too much at stake" (*Leadtime*, 4).

What is needed is a deep sense of personal moral duty (commitment) and personal responsibility. Without this personal commitment, a million words aimed to "teach" media ethics will fall on deaf ears. Yet, while this is true, the tremendous value of a media code of ethics, if understood and used correctly, should not be underestimated – precisely because such a code can assist the individual journalist to make proper and informed choices for the right reasons.

Yes or no?

The debate over whether or not media institutions should operate under codes of ethics may never be settled. There are many arguments for and against the adoption of such codes. The arguments in support of the use of codes of ethics mainly go like this:

- It is better to have ethical guidelines than to have nothing at all. Younger journalists, especially, need to be told what is expected of them.
- A code helps to create an ethical consciousness, without which ethics easily become situation-based (where you act on an ad hoc basis, and base your moral decisions mainly on feelings or personal preferences).
- If ethical values are important enough to follow, why not codify them?
- A code of ethics is a meaningful way to ensure accountability.
- A code of ethics helps journalists not to take decisions independently of their colleagues. It is arrogant to think that you always know best; it is better to consult others.

- It keeps the profession on its toes and helps media institutions to fulfil their role as watch-dogs.
- It defines some potential problems.
- It creates public trust and therefore has an excellent public relations function. A code of ethics tends to convince the public that the media are sincere in their plight to act ethi-cally and responsibly at all times.

In an article published in *Rhodes Journalism Review* in 2000, Professor Francis Kasoma gives three reasons why he is in favour of the use of codes of ethics (Kasoma 2000, 20).[14] According to Kasoma, most African newspapers that criti-cize their governments are very unprofessional. Reports critical of the government are said to be highly biased, contain little truth, are one-sided and exaggerated, full of sweeping statements, based on hearsay, and not put into context. These reports, Kasoma claims, are characterized more by emotion than by understanding. In addition, Kasoma continues, newspapers are all too often guilty of advocacy journalism and sensational-ism. This always becomes worse during election times. Many so-called independent newspapers are nothing but mouthpieces for the opposition. Furthermore, journalists continually misuse an-onymous sources. Journalists say whatever they like, and then hide behind their so-called "sources". Kasoma concludes that the independ-ent press in Africa has apparently thrown all eth-ical norms overboard. Therefore, codes of ethics are necessary; they can help African journalists to come back onto the right track and to stay there, for if the media do not regulate themselves, the government will certainly do it for them.

It can be said that Kasoma is guilty of gener-alizing. After all, the press in Africa is so diverse that it can hardly be treated as a single entity, and his warnings do not hold water for the major-ity of the South African media. Nevertheless, media freedom is a scarce commodity in much of Africa, which means that Kasoma's warnings should be taken seriously. Although the South African media currently enjoy unprecedented freedom, that situation could change for the worse. The more responsibly the media behave, the shorter the stick with which the government can hit this particular dog. It is better to be pre-pared than to be caught unawares.

However, not everyone is convinced that codes of ethics are important or useful. The argu-ments against codes generally run as follows:
- Codes of ethics work against the independ-ence of a free press (because a "standard" is established).
- It leads easily to self-censorship.
- Being general and vague by definition, the finer nuances of different situations are easily ignored, making a code of ethics not a realistic, but an idealistic and therefore useless, tool.
- It can be used against journalists in a court of law.
- Values cannot be forced upon people.

Although there is a lot of truth in these argu-ments, none of them are compelling enough. The good that codes of conduct can lead to, if cor-rectly used, certainly outweighs the harm they can cause.

South African codes: common denominators

Some of the most important current ethical codes in South Africa are provided in the Addendum to this book. Some of these codes are institutional (used by institutions, serving a number of media organizations); others are professional (used by particular organizations). These include:
- *The press*: the Press Ombudsman of South Africa (used by many newspapers, as well as by the South African National Editors' Forum);

The Star (its code is used by Independent Newspapers); *Sowetan*; *Sunday Times* (representing Caxton); a code used by a local newspaper in Rustenburg (also part of Caxton); and the code of the South African Union of Journalists (SAUJ).

■ *The electronic media*: Broadcasting Complaints Commission of South Africa (BCCSA) and the SABC.

Institutional codes are usually much shorter, more general, and thus less specific, than professional ones. Institutional codes tend to underline the most basic ethical guidelines without which the media cannot, or should not, function. In contrast, a professional code serves the interests of a specific media organization, and typically uses these general guidelines to stipulate more detailed formulations. One example of this is the nature of the relationship between journalists and their sources.

Taking this difference into account, the current codes in South Africa are remarkably similar. In some instances, whole sections of the one code are often taken over in the other. An analysis of these codes will serve to highlight some common denominators.

The basis: the right to know

The preamble to the code of the Press Ombudsman of South Africa, the BCCSA, and the *Sunday Times* states:

> The basic principle to be upheld is that the freedom of the press (the electronic media) is indivisible from and subject to the same rights and duties as that of the individual and rests on the public's (i.e. the individual's) right to be informed and to receive and to disseminate opinions freely.

This means that *the freedom of the media rests on the individual's (or the public's) right to receive information*.

The Star states that the public's right to know about matters of importance is paramount. The newspaper should therefore fight vigorously any measure to conceal facts of public interest, any attempt to prevent public access to the news, and any effort to curtail the freedom of speech. The existence of the Freedom of Expression Institute (FXI) rests on this very conviction. Its principal objectives are to fight for and defend freedom of expression, to oppose all forms of censorship and to fight for the right of access to information. The SAUJ states that a journalist should at all times defend the principle of the freedom of the media in relation to the collection of information and the expression of comment and criticism. SANEF's first objective is to nurture and deepen media freedom as a democratic value in all the communities in South Africa and at all levels of society.

A word of warning is required at this point. The conviction that the public has a right to know is of the utmost importance to the freedom of the media and indeed also to the upholding of democracy. However, journalists often make the mistake of pointing out to their sources that they (read: the media) have a right to know. The media are far from being that special. Remember that the media are only vehicles through which the public can be informed. It is in the first instance not the media, but the public, who has the right to know. It is the individual's or the people's right to know that gives the media a reason for their existence. It is only on this basis that the media can function as watchdogs and that they need ethical guidelines to fulfil that function properly.

Guidelines

A careful analysis of the codes in question shows that ten common denominators can be identified. In the following section, we shall examine each of these in detail.

Accuracy

In its first sentence the Ombudsman's code states that the press shall be obliged to report news accurately. This means that news shall be presented in context, and without distortion, exaggeration, material omissions, or summarization. When there are reasons to doubt the accuracy of a report, it shall be verified (if practicable – otherwise this must be mentioned). Inaccurate reporting must be corrected promptly and with appropriate prominence. The BCCSA code has the same wording as the Ombudsman's.

SABC journalists shall report, contextualize, and present news honestly by striving to disclose all essential facts and by not suppressing relevant, available facts or by distorting the content by the use of a wrong, or an improper, context.

The *Rustenburg Herald* wants its journalists to be guided by the following principles: "report as fully as possible", and "be honest, fair and courageous in gathering, reporting and interpreting accurate information". The SAUJ agrees, adding that the right of reply should be afforded to persons criticized when the issue is of significant importance.

Although the media have the right to comment and criticize (the Ombudsman and the BCCSA), the expression of comment and conjecture as established fact and falsification by distortion, selection, or misrepresentation should be avoided. Both institutions say that comment shall be presented in such a manner that it appears clearly that it is comment, and shall be made on facts truly stated or fairly indicated and referred to. It shall be an honest expression of opinion, without malice or dishonest motives, and shall take a fair and balanced account of all available and facts. The Ombudsman adds: "where a report is not based on facts or is founded on opinions, allegation, rumour or supposition, it shall be presented in such a manner as to indicate this clearly". According to *The Star*, news and comment should be kept separate. Comment should be

clearly identifiable. Where there is reason to doubt the accuracy of a report, it should be verified. If this is not practicable, it shall be mentioned in such a report (the Ombudsman and the BCCSA).

The SABC states that its members shall do their utmost to correct timeously any information broadcast found to be prejudicially inaccurate. The Ombudsman and the BCCSA agree. A publication should make amends for publishing information or comment that is found to be harmfully inaccurate by printing, promptly and with appropriate prominence, a retraction, correction, or explanation. According to the SAUJ, "a journalist shall rectify promptly any harmful inaccuracies, ensure that corrections and apologies receive due prominence and afford the right of reply to persons criticised when the issue is of sufficient importance".

The Star mentions accuracy as its first responsibility, and also stresses the need to check facts carefully. Reports of a technical nature should always be read back to the source. Other reports should be read back for the checking of facts only (except when there is not enough time or there is a valid reason to believe the source will try to frustrate publication on grounds other than factual accuracy). The newspaper should not be afraid to admit error, and should publish corrections spontaneously, promptly, and with suitable prominence. Where an apology is appropriate, it should be rendered.

When quotations are used, the *Rustenburg Herald* says that these should be precise, used in the context of the conversation, and should be exactly what the speaker said.

Truthfulness

Although this goes almost without saying, the codes of the Ombudsman and the BCCSA state that news must be reported truthfully. To this they add one very reasonable yet somewhat strange condition: only what may reasonably be regarded as true may be presented as facts.

Deception to obtain news falls into the category of truthfulness. The media are in the business of truth-telling and must be careful not to be untruthful themselves in their mission to obtain the truth. The Ombudsman states that news obtained by dishonest or unfair means should not be published, unless there is an overriding public interest. The SAUJ agrees. All information should be obtained only by straightforward means, except when public interest demands otherwise. It adds that a journalist is entitled to exercise a personal conscientious objection to the use of such means.

According to the *Rustenburg Herald*, deceptive practices such as misrepresentation, impersonation, and the use of hidden tape recorders or cameras in news-gathering can seriously undermine a newspaper's credibility and trustworthiness. "These practices fall outside the bounds of general accepted journalistic behaviour." Where such measures are considered, the editor should give approval – and that only after thorough deliberation. In such a case, the deceptive practices and the reasons for them must be disclosed at the time of publishing the story. Journalists should not tape interviews without the knowledge of those being taped. Permission should be asked for taping. If this is not granted, the recording device should be turned off. Photographic manipulation should never mislead the reader. If it is necessary to manipulate a picture, the public should be informed as such.

The SABC states that its journalists shall identify themselves before obtaining any information for broadcast. Covert methods may be employed only with due regard to their legality and to considerations such as fairness and invasion of privacy, and the question whether the information obtained is of such significance as to warrant being made public although unavailable by other means.

According to the Ombudsman, headlines, captions, pictures, and posters shall give a reasonable reflection of the contents of the report or picture in question. They shall not misrepresent or mislead nor be manipulated to do so.

Finally, the SAUJ code states that journalists shall not engage in plagiarism and shall attribute information to the original source.

Fairness

The first sentence of the Ombudsman's code reads as follows: "the press shall be obliged to report news truthfully, accurately *and fairly*" (my emphasis). Fairness, according to the next sentence, boils down to *balance (and context)*. News shall be published fairly with due regard to context and importance. It adds that it is fair for newspapers to seek the views of the subject of serious critical reporting in advance of publication. News obtained by unfair means should not be published unless there is an overriding public interest.

The SABC says it always seeks balance as far as possible by presenting relevant viewpoints on matters of importance. This requirement may not always be feasible within a single programme or news bulletin, but should be achieved within a reasonable period. Fairness, however, does not require journalists to give all sides of an issue the same amount of coverage. In reaching editorial decisions, the SABC will rely on news merit and judgment.

The BCCSA mentions that, in presenting a programme in which controversial issues of public importance are discussed, a broadcasting licensee shall make reasonable efforts to present fairly significant points of view, either in the same programme or in a subsequent programme which forms part of the same series, within a reasonable period of time, and which are substantially in the same slot. A person whose views have been criticized on a controversial issue of public importance shall be given reasonable opportunity to reply "should that person so request".

The Star states that the newspaper should be fair in its reporting, aiming to give all sides of an issue the right to reply; it should present the facts without bias, undue emphasis, or omission. It should also endeavour to be fair when commenting on an issue. Every effort should be made to reflect all sides of a controversy – if not simultaneously, then in subsequent editions.

Impartiality

The notion of impartiality (objectivity or neutrality) is a thorny one. The main reasons for this are that impartiality is almost impossible to define and, due to the subjective nature of human beings, impossible to achieve. And yet impartiality – or rather the ideal of impartiality – is of the utmost importance if the media are going to be credible.

That is why the BCCSA does not shun this issue. The first sentence of the code mentions that the electronic media shall be obliged to report news with "due impartiality". This phrase was probably borrowed from the BBC's *Producers' Guidelines*. "Due impartiality" implies that only a "reasonable amount" of impartiality can be attained.

This is true as far as the reporting of the news is concerned, and even more so when commenting on it. Just about all the codes of ethics (for example, the Ombudsman) warn that any comment shall be presented in such manner that it appears clearly that it is comment. A definite distinction between news and comment is imperative. Comment shall only be made on facts truly stated; it shall be an honest expression of opinion, without malice or dishonest motives, and shall take fair account of all available and relevant facts.

The Star is a little less nuanced on this point. It states (apparently without envisaging any problem) that it should report issues in an impartial manner. It should report news without regard to its own interest or viewpoint, and without

favour to its advertisers. News and comment should be kept separate.

Confidentiality

On the matter of confidential sources, the Ombudsman, the SABC, the SAUJ, and *The Star* agree that a newspaper has an obligation to protect its sources, adding (supported by the BCCSA) that no payment shall be made to persons engaged in crime or to convicted persons or their associates, except where the information is in the public interest. Sources of news should be identified unless there is good reason not to, *The Star* states. Where a promise of confidentiality was made, the source of information should not be identified. The Ombudsman also states no breach of confidence is allowed, unless there is an overriding public interest. The FXI wants to work towards the establishment of a Freedom of Information Act that would include the right of journalists not to disclose confidential sources of information.

The *Rustenburg Herald* recognizes the critical importance of reliable sources. They should therefore be treated with courtesy and respect. A clear distinction should be made between personal and professional conversations. Whereas a politician can without hesitation be embarrassed by a journalist, this does not apply to ordinary citizens. They should be granted some leeway and courtesy. Attributions are very important because these tell the public "where our news comes from, that we have done our homework and that we are not inventing what we print", and gives the readers a chance to judge for themselves. However, confidential information should be kept as such. Be clear about when the conversation is on and when it is off the record. Confidential sources should be avoided as far as possible – using them places the newspaper's credibility at risk and robs stories of their vitality. Moreover, confidential sources make poor witnesses in cases of libel litigation. They should be used as a last resort if the information is of paramount importance, the source is believed to be reliable and truthful, and there are no other means of getting the information. Once confidentiality is promised, the whole newspaper is bound by that promise. However, if the source has misled the reporter, confidentiality can be withdrawn at the editor's discretion.

Conflicts of interest

It comes as no surprise that the professional codes of conduct give much more prominence to this point than do their institutional counterparts. The SABC starts off by affirming its commitment to the principle of editorial independence. The corporation shall be free from obligation to any interest group and shall be committed to the public's right to know the truth. Information should be evaluated solely on merit, and no advertising, commercial, political, or personal considerations should influence editorial decisions. Journalists shall not accept any gifts, favours, free travel, special treatment, or privileges which might compromise their integrity. Any such offer shall be disclosed.

This point is clearly very important to the *Sowetan*: staff should not accept any money (or gifts in kind) from anyone besides the official benefits, especially not from any person or organization that might benefit from enriching them. All suggestions of bribery and corruption shall be rejected. Any free offer must be referred for approval. Gifts of an insignificant amount of value may be accepted, as long as the credibility, independence, and integrity of the newspaper are not endangered. Nepotism is not allowed.

Sowetan recognizes the right of its journalists to associate freely with any lawful organization and to participate in its activities. Its members' preferences (sexual, religious, cultural, political, language, and the right to express any opinion as long as it does not infringe the personal rights of others) are respected. However, when these rights conflict

with the editorial stance of the newspaper, the *Sowetan*'s independence must take precedence over the rights of association of the individual.

The Star states, *inter alia*, that it should not pander to personal interests, but be solely concerned with the public interest. Members of *The Star* should be free of any obligation to news sources and special interests, including political parties. Even the appearance of any sort of obligation should be avoided, especially by political and financial journalists. No journalist may accept any gift, favour, or special treatment (including free or reduced-rate travel) if it puts her or him under any obligation to the donor. All such gifts should be referred to the editor.

The Star's journalists should avoid active involvement in public affairs where a conflict, potential or real, is likely to arise. News should be reported without regard to its own interest or viewpoint, and without favour to its advertisers. Matters concerning the newspaper or its staff should be reported in the same manner as it reports on other individuals or institutions. Staff at *The Star* may only accept outside commissions, part-time employment, or freelance work for other publications with the consent of the editor.

The SAUJ says journalists shall not accept bribes nor allow other inducements to influence the performance of their professional duties. Nor shall journalists lend themselves to the distortion or suppression of the truth because of advertising or other considerations. They shall not take private advantage of information gained in the course of their duties before that information is public knowledge.

Finally, the *Rustenburg Herald* believes that there is no such thing as a free meal.

Invasion of privacy

Although invasion of privacy is first and foremost a legal matter, it also has all sorts of ethical dimensions, and is therefore dealt with in the various codes.

The Ombudsman's code says the press shall exercise exceptional care and consideration in matters involving the private lives and concerns of individuals, bearing in mind that any right to privacy may be overridden by a legitimate public interest. The BCCSA and *The Star* concur. The SABC code states that it respects the legitimate rights to privacy of individuals.

Trauma

The Ombudsman as well as the BCCSA state that the identity of rape victims and other victims of sexual violence shall not be published without the consent of the victim. The SABC and the SAUJ say their journalists shall do nothing that entails intrusion into private grief and distress unless justified by overriding considerations of public interest.

While these institutions are all somewhat abrupt on this point, the *Rustenburg Herald* goes into some detail. It is understood that journalists will be called upon to make judgment "where private and public lives intersect". This judgment, it is said, should be based on relevance as well as on compassion. Information is the main objective – but not at the expense of victims and families "who have suffered enough without our intrusion". Victims of sex crimes are generally not identified, unless otherwise requested. Consultation should take place as far as sex crimes involving molestation of children are concerned. Collective judgment is needed for the identification of witnesses, mentioning background, the influence of headlines and posters, crime scene, photographs of carnage, etc. Suicides are generally not covered unless the identity of the victim or the circumstances have thrust the event into the public sphere. Traumatized people should be interviewed with due care and sensitivity.

Stereotyping

The matter of racism is very much an issue in South Africa, so it is understandable that the ethical codes devote a lot of attention to the issue. After the initial inquiry of the South African Human Rights Commission into alleged racism in the South African media, some effort has been made to clarify this issue further.

The Ombudsman's code states that the press should avoid discriminatory or denigratory references to people's race, colour, religion, sexual orientation or preference, physical or mental disability or illness, or age. The press should not refer to these matters in a prejudicial or pejorative context, except where it is relevant or adds significantly to people's understanding of the matter. The right of the press to report on matters of public interest must be balanced against the obligation not to promote racial hatred or discord in such a way as to create the likelihood of imminent violence.

The Star states that it should encourage racial co-operation and pursue a policy aimed at enhancing the welfare and progress of all sections of the population. It should not pander to sectional interests, but be solely concerned with the public interest.

The *Sunday Times* formulated a new code of conduct for dealing with issues of race, religion, and cultural difference. This newspaper also developed an extensive checklist of questions for use by reporters and editors when dealing with these matters. Both documents are included in the Addendum at the end of this book; they are too important to be summarized here and should be looked at in their entirety.

Like the *Sunday Times*, the *Rustenburg Herald* has several practical regulations. A person should be identified by race only when such identification is relevant or essential (for example, when there is reason to believe that a crime was racially motivated or as an important means of identification).

The SAUJ states that journalists shall not originate material that encourages discrimination on the grounds of race, colour, creed, gender, or sexual orientation.

The SABC says it shall be aware of the danger of discrimination being furthered by the media, and shall do its utmost to avoid promoting such discrimination based on gender, race, language, culture, political persuasion, class, sexual orientation, religious belief, marital status, or physical or mental disability.

SANEF wants to address and redress inappropriate racial and gender imbalances prevalent in journalism and news organizations and encourage the equitable spread of media ownership. Like the FXI, it wants to promote media diversity to foster maximum expression of opinion.

Sowetan respects the personal rights of colleagues as far as sexual, religious, cultural, political, and language preferences are concerned.

Social responsibility

The term "social responsibility" embraces matters pertaining to violence, obscenity, indecency, blasphemy, religion, and sex – with special reference to children. The Ombudsman warns that due care and responsibility shall be exercised with regard to the presentation of brutality, violence, and atrocities – and personal grief, adds the SABC.

As television is by nature such a graphic communication medium, it is understandable that the ethical codes of the electronic media must be absolutely clear about those aspects of their social responsibility. The BCCSA says that reports, photographs, or video material which relate to matters involving indecency or obscenity shall be presented with due sensitivity towards the prevailing moral climate. In particular, the electronic media shall avoid the broadcast of indecent or obscene material. It shall not, without due care and sensitivity, present material which contains brutality, violence, or atrocities, and shall exercise due care and responsibility in the presentation of programmes where a large number of children are likely to be part of the audience. The electronic media shall not present material which is harmful or offensive to public morals, or to the religious convictions or feelings of a section of the population, or which is likely to harm relations between sections of the population, or is likely to prejudice the safety of the state or the public order.

The SABC undertakes to exercise due care and be sensitive in the presentation of brutality, violence, and atrocities. The Ombudsman states that newspapers have a wide discretion in matters of taste, but this does not justify lapses of taste so repugnant as to bring the freedom of the press into disrepute. Reports, photographs, or sketches relative to matters involving indecency or obscenity shall be presented with due sensitivity towards the prevailing moral climate. The FXI is opposed to all forms of censorship and states its determination to fight for the freedom of expression and the right of access to information.

A paper intended for circulation to a general audience, says the *Rustenburg Herald*, should have no place for offensive language. This should be judged narrowly against what are reasonable taste and community standards and against the value and relevance of the potentially offensive language. The same goes for hate speech, particularly when it is directed towards minority, ethnic, or religious groups.

Ten "commandments"

Based on the common denominators described in the preceding section, the following brief code of ethics can be construed:

Preamble: The media shall be free because the public has a right to be informed.

You shall therefore:
1   Be *accurate* both in text and context (and correct mistakes promptly).
2   Be *truthful,* only using deceptive methods in matters of public importance if there is no other way of uncovering the facts.

3 Be *fair*, presenting all relevant facts in a balanced way.

4 Be *duly impartial* in reporting the news and when commenting on it.

5 Protect confidential sources, unless it is of overriding public interest to do otherwise.

6 Be *free from obligation* to any interest group.

7 *Respect the privacy of individuals*, unless it is overridden by a legitimate public interest.

8 *Not intrude into private grief and distress*, unless such intrusion is overridden by a legitimate public interest.

9 Refrain from any kind of *stereotyping*.

10 Be *socially responsible* in referring to matters of indecency, obscenity, violence, brutality, blasphemy, and sex.

In Part II we shall discuss each of these "commandments", starting with a more formal discussion and ending with some case studies. The purpose of each case study is to highlight certain aspects of the issue at hand.

Some of these "commandments" are not only ethical by nature, but also venture into the highly complicated field of media sociology. While the latter is an extremely important subject in its own right, the focus of this book is on media ethics.

Notes

[1] Belsey et al. 1992, p. 75.

[2] The report is unpublished but available from SANEF. See De Beer et al. 1998, pp. 267–285 for a discussion on media law in South Africa.

[3] Freedom of expression is also entrenched in various international human rights documents, such as Article 19 of the Universal Declaration of Human Rights, Article 19 of the International Covenant on Civil and Political Rights, Article 10 of the European Convention on Human Rights and Article 9 of the African Charter on Human and Peoples' Rights.

[4] Nel vs Le Roux 1996.

[5] This section was written by Handrie Basson while doing a BPhil in Journalism at the University of Stellenbosch. Basson is now a journalist at *Finansies & Tegniek*.

[6] Judge Joos Hefer wrote this unanimous decision. Judges Hoexter, Harms, Plewman, and Acting Judge Farlam concurred.

[7] Bogoshi vs National Media Ltd. and Others 1996 (3) SA 78 (W).

[8] Interim Constitution of the Republic of South Africa, Act 200 of 1993.

[9] As ruled in Pakendorf vs De Flamingh 1982 (3) SA 146 (A).

[10] As it was held in Neethling vs *The Weekly Mail* 1994 (1) SA 708 (A)

[11] Dario Milo, "The South African media: free at last!" www.ned.org/grantees/hurilaw/

[12] Jerri Eddings, 'South African court gives journalists more protection', www.freedomforum.org, 6 October 1998.

[13] *Open Media* No. 35 (1987). *Media in a new South Africa*. Cape Town: Idasa. At the time, Alison Gillward was a lecturer in the Department of Journalism and Public Relations at the Technikon Natal.

[14] *Rhodes Journalism Review* no. 1 (2000). Kasoma is Head of the Department of Mass Communication at the University of Zambia in Lusaka.

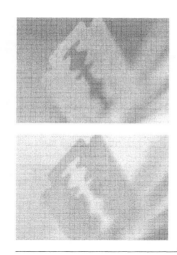

Part II | **Ethical issues**

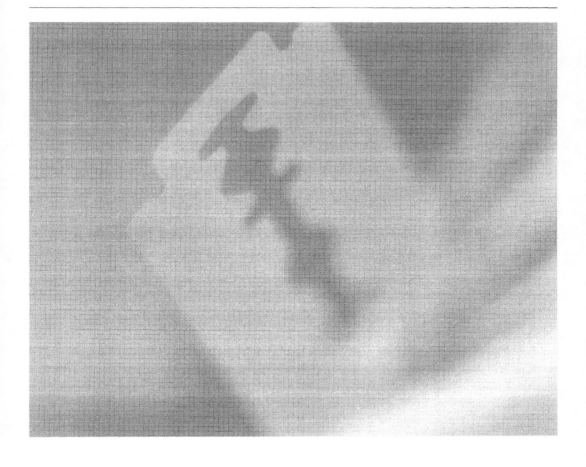

3 | Accuracy

Accuracy can be achieved only if the relevant facts are put into the proper context.

Introduction

A 1980 Gallup poll in the US found that 34 per cent of people who had personal knowledge about matters reported in the newspapers said the papers had reported inaccurately. Only 47 per cent believed the opposite. This compares extremely unfavourably with a similar poll conducted 23 years earlier, in which 70 per cent said that they believed newspapers reported accurately. This downward trend is worrying. There is no reason why the situation should be different in South Africa.

There are several important reasons why inaccurate reporting must be avoided at all cost:

- It can cause irreparable personal harm.
- It prevents the public from making informed decisions on important matters such as investments, voting, shopping, etc.
- It is very likely to affect the media's integrity as well as their credibility. Nothing erodes a journalist's credibility so quickly as inaccurate reporting. Remember: *integrity is what you think of yourself; credibility is what other people think of you.* You cannot maintain your integrity when you report inaccurately, and you will surely lose credibility if you do.
- The public rightly expects quality work from journalists, and has a right to be served by honest journalists. The public deserves, and indeed pays for, accurate reporting. On this point, the British Broadcasting Corporation (BBC) states: "The BBC must be accurate. Producers in all areas must be prepared to check, cross-check and seek advice, to ensure that the BBC's reputation is not diminished" *Producers' Guidelines* 1996, 22).

The 1980 Gallup poll found that people "who feel the press has been inaccurate in treating news items relating to their own lives are more likely to favor stricter curbs on the press than are those who feel the facts were dealt with accurately" (Goodwin 1987, 323). Consider what could happen if the government finds itself on this path...

Goodwin cites all sorts of excuses for inaccuracies in news reports (Goodwin 1987, 323), such as carelessness, ignorance, inadequate education, deadline pressures, the wrong information from sources, and oversimplifications. To these he adds the following rather interesting opinion: "Another cause of errors is the increasing tendency of journalists to isolate themselves physically and personally from their communities" (Goodwin 1987, 323).

However you look at it, there are no valid excuses for inaccurate reporting. No deadline, personal problems, or pressure of any kind will do as justification or serve as a valid excuse. There is simply too much at stake. One mistake is one too many. Of course, this requires hard work, most of which even your colleagues and immediate superiors will know nothing about, let alone the public. Reporting accurately is non-negotiable, whatever the cost. Accurate reporting is not the best way of doing journalism – it is the only way.

Not so easy

However, the concept of accuracy is a complex one. To report accurately is indeed much easier said than done. But before we delve deeper into the matter, consider the following statement: journalists can report "accurately" *and still be wrong*, causing immeasurable harm.

Consider this example: if it is reported that child pornography was found in the home of Person X, the public at large will forever believe that X is guilty. But what if the material belonged to a friend who visited him and X really did not

know anything about it? The report that the pornography was found in X's home will still be accurate, but not the insinuation that it belonged to him or that he even knew about it. The harm done to X's reputation will be immeasurable.

This is what happened to the well-known film critic, Leon van Nierop. On 1 August 2000, the three Naspers dailies, *Beeld, Die Burger*, and *Volksblad*, all reported on their front pages that Van Nierop and a friend, Tascoe Luc de Reuck, had been arrested in connection with the alleged possession and import of child pornography. A picture of Van Nierop was also used. It was alleged that the pornographic material had been ordered via the Internet. According to the reports, both Van Nierop and De Reuck were in custody and would appear the same day (as the publication) in court. Van Nierop did not have the chance to comment, and the reports certainly suggested some guilt on his part.

Eventually, on 23 September 2000, the newspapers had to report that the state was not going to prosecute Van Nierop as there was no evidence that he had known anything about the pornographic material in his home. The Director of Public Prosecutions in the Witwatersrand, André de Vries, said: "It is my opinion that the state cannot prove this case against him (Van Nierop) and that he is indeed not guilty". Van Nierop's reaction was noteworthy. He said, *inter alia*: "Those initial newspaper reports devastated me. Since then my whole career is on ice. I am also very sad about the way your newspapers treated me in that I was never given the chance to comment. I am also sorry about the harm those reports caused my listeners, friends and parents."

The point about the story is this: the newspapers were accurate in reporting that Van Nierop was taken into custody after child pornography was found in his home, but inaccurate in "suggesting" he was guilty.

Text and context

What is this "accuracy" that is so essential to any self-respecting journalist and media organization? Consider the following guidelines:

- Accuracy starts with the ability to gather *all* the *relevant* facts. This implies two things. Firstly, if a journalist leaves out one single detail that is important to a specific story, the report cannot be accurate. *All* the relevant facts must be included in the story. And secondly, the journalist must concentrate on all the *relevant* facts. There are always umpteen "facts" – too many to count and to include in any given story. Space (in newspapers) and time (radio, television) are always limited. So use them with care, or else irrelevant facts will creep into your story and distort the balance that is so essential for accurate reporting.

- After you have gathered all the relevant facts, you should *check and verify* your facts thoroughly, using more than one source. The reporting of facts before confirmation is a violation of one of the basic rules of journalism (Day 1991, 73). In 1981, the death of President Ronald Reagan's press secretary, James Brady, was reported as fact. The truth was that Brady had been badly injured during an assassination attempt on Reagan – but he was still very much alive.

  The BBC distinguishes between primary and secondary sources (*Producers' Guidelines* 1996, 22). *Never* rely on secondary sources. One of the worst things a journalist can do is to depend on hearsay or to perpetuate other people's mistakes. If you are in any doubt whatsoever about the facts, it should be revealed to the audience (Day 1991, 72, 73).

- Now you should *weigh all the relevant facts.* Not all the relevant facts are of equal importance. The really essential ones will go to the intro, and the facts of lesser importance will be used later in the story or not at all. The relative importance of each fact should be weighed against one another (*Producers' Guidelines* 1996, 22).

- Consider this example. You are covering a monthly meeting of a local council. An important decision to renovate the town hall has just been taken. Your story should include (not necessarily in this order) what the exact decision was, the reasons for it, the consequences (financial and otherwise) thereof, when the work will be completed, and some of the highlights of the debate. What you will definitely not do is to use up space or time to report what colour tie the mayor wore. That fact may be accurate, but it will certainly not be relevant.

- Here is another *scenario.* A prominent politician dies in a motor accident. You will start by saying who he was and what happened. You will inform the public about the other people who were involved. You will explain why the car left the road. Later you will report on who was on the scene and how fast the emergency services reacted (or whatever). The point is that you must sift through all the facts and arrange them in order of importance. If you don't do that, your opponent's report will be more accurate than yours, even if you have got all your facts straight.

- Put the relevant facts into the *proper context.* This is extremely important. Put the right facts in the wrong context and you are sure to get an incomplete and therefore an inaccurate report. For example: a ten-year-old boy was shot in a café and died on the scene. The incident occurred in Manenberg on the Cape Flats, so you include that in the story. But if you only stick to these facts, what you say will be accurate but what you omit will make it inaccurate. For this boy was the son of a leader of one of the gangs in the area. In addition, the twelve-year-old son of his father's worst enemy, the leader of a rival gang, was shot and killed a fortnight previously. This means that the incident suddenly becomes a revenge story. That is the context. Without this context, the facts that you portray in the story may be "accurate" but the report will not be sufficient.

- If a prominent organization takes an extremely important decision, the "facts" are what happened, and the context is that this happened (say) for the first time and that no other similar organization has done the same so far. Without this context the report will not be false, but it certainly will not be sufficient. Consider this real-life example. When the infamous Rodney King riots took place in Los Angeles in 1992, Richard Schickel wrote in *Time*: "television's mindless, endless (generally fruitless) search for the dramatic image – particularly on the worst night, Wednesday – created the impression that an entire city was about to fall into anarchy and go up in flames. What was needed instead was geography lessons showing that rioting was confined to a relatively small portion of a vast metropolis and that violent incidents outside that area were random, not the beginning of a march to the sea via Rodeo Drive" (*Time* 11 May 1992, 27). That particular perspective was absent. Remember that putting events into proper perspective is essential to the proper understanding of an event. Without that, the report will not be accurate.

Of course, when a journalist considers the context, he or she must be very careful. Putting your facts into the proper context involves not only the correct knowledge of the context, but also the ability to interpret soundly the background facts and historical perspective.

- Portray your facts (text and context) in a *fair and balanced way*. Give the different sides in your story the importance they deserve. Use fair language, without exaggerations or comment of any kind. The readers are not interested in your opinion. Keep it to yourself. According to the BBC, "it is not sufficient that we get our facts right. We must use language fairly. That means avoiding exaggeration. We must not use language inadvertently so as to suggest value judgements, commitment or lack of objectivity" (*Producers' Guidelines* 1996, 23).

- *Correct your mistakes immediately and properly*. Some journalists and news organizations are hesitant to tell the public when they have made mistakes. The BBC makes no bones about this: "When a serious factual error does occur it is important to admit it clearly and frankly. Saying what was wrong as well as putting it right can be an important element in making an effective correction" (*Producers' Guidelines* 1996, 23). The corporation also makes the valid point that inaccuracy can lead to complaints. If the error is acknowledged, "a timely correction may dissuade the aggrieved party from complaining" (*Producers' Guidelines* 1996, 23).

Selective media excuses

The media often make mistakes unintentionally, and these mistakes can cause a lot of unnecessary harm. Of course, one mistake is one too many, but what should the media do when it happens? Most people, and the media in particular, find it extremely difficult to say they are sorry. Is this because of arrogance (of which so many media people seem to have no shortage)? Although there are no hard and fast rules in this regard, it should be said in general that the greater the harm caused by the mistake, the more prominence the correction should receive. The truth is served in this way. It is absurd to expect a huge correction for small mistakes of no particular significance; it is unfair to make a small correction if the mistake was huge.

Quite a number of ethical codes stipulate that mistakes should be corrected promptly, without any need for pressure from outside, and in direct relation to the same prominence and space that was given to the faulty report.

Quotations

Are journalists allowed to alter direct quotations? This is a tricky question, but certainly a very important one. The general rule is *never* to alter a direct quote. If you are not happy with the precise wording, then don't use inverted commas. Rather use an indirect quote instead. If you are caught quoting somebody incorrectly, for whatever reason, it will take a very long time to regain your credibility. You could even get sued. So don't do it.

But why would a journalist in the first place *want* to alter a direct quote? Hopefully not because a quote does not suit his or her particular viewpoint! The only valid reason could be the desire to avoid embarrassment to the speaker. So what do you do:

- when a statement contains faulty grammar? Do you correct it to be fair to the speaker? It is better to put the correct grammar between brackets, or to add "sic". The faulty grammar really is your source's problem, but if you don't correct it the public will think your grammar is not up to standard.
- when a speaker has a slip of the tongue? Do you report his or her mistake as the truth, or are you allowed to report what the speaker clearly had *wanted* to say? Again, do not alter words when you use inverted commas. Rather put the intended words between brackets. If a politician says that R100 million is to be allocated to a project somewhere in Cape Town, but you know the politician really wanted to say Durban, it is your duty also to report what he had wanted to say. That is only fair. But

then you should not put "Durban" in inverted commas.

- with swear words? You can easily use the first letter of a swear word, followed by dashes or points. Most readers will understand if you report that your source said "f... you". That is not faulty reporting. Of course, it also depends on your type of media organization and therefore on your readers/listeners/viewers. A girlie magazine could quite easily spell out the f... word without thinking twice. It is unthinkable that a church magazine would do the same.
- with a statement that contains an assertion that you as a reporter believe may be untrue or inaccurate? In that case, a sound portrayal of the proper context becomes even more important. Associated Press (AP) states that "the newspaper should background, with the facts, public statements that it knows to be inaccurate or misleading" (Hausman 1992, 129). What is needed is background material (context), but be careful not to thrust your own opinion down the public's throat. In the end, it is the readers who must decide what they believe or disbelieve.

What if you don't know?

A news report can be inaccurate or misleading not only when false information is given, but also when vital information is lacking. A lie (inaccuracy) is not necessarily the telling of something that is untrue; silence or the lack of information can also constitute a lie. So what do you do when you know you lack some vital information? Should you acknowledge that fact publicly?

This is rather a tricky matter.[1] Some journalists have serious reservations about acknowledging or admitting a lack of knowledge. The arguments are that your readers will certainly ask why you don't know; an incomplete report will reflect badly on the journalist; it also weakens your story, it is often said. The strongest argument against acknowledging is that it can all too easily become a handy cover for bad (read: lazy) journalism. Sometimes journalists are too lazy to establish the necessary facts; the easy way out is merely to state you could not get that information. If you admit that this is the reason you don't know, it is, of course, inexcusable.

But there is another side to this coin – or, rather, three sides:

- The acknowledgment can assist the public to avoid coming to the wrong conclusions.
- Sometimes it is extremely difficult, if not nearly impossible, to get the desired information. State why this is the case, and the story may even benefit from that.
- Sometimes there simply is not enough time to establish all the facts. There is no harm in saying that, as long as you make sure to follow up the story.

All things considered, it is probably better to acknowledge your own lack of knowledge. Be careful, though; it is better to take your time and do some proper investigation than to make a habit of admitting to your own lack of information.

Plagiarism

Plagiarism occurs when a writer borrows another writer's work without attribution. Using phrases, clauses, or sentences directly without acknowledging that fact constitutes plagiarism (Black et al. 1995, 173). It is another form of inaccurate reporting, because the source of the material was lied about. It is, however, commonly accepted that borrowing ideas from someone else is in order. "The problem lies in determining the dividing line between borrowed ideas and verbatim theft" (Black et al. 1995, 173). The closer the two versions, the greater the need for source attribution (Black et al. 1995, 173).

In South Africa, a huge debate took place in 1999 about alleged plagiarism in the Afrikaans collection of short stories *Die mooiste liefde is verby*, compiled by the writer Etienne van Heerden and published by Tafelberg. This collection was subsequently withdrawn from shops (in December 1999). It was alleged that the story *Die redding van Vuyo Stofile* by Wilhelm du Plessis, then 25 years old, showed great similarities to *The Magic Barrel*, a short story written by the American, Bernard Malamud, in the 1950s.[2] Mr Hannes van Zyl of Tafelberg was quoted in *Die Burger* (13 December 1999) as saying that the similarities between the two stories are difficult to explain. "We would not have withdrawn the collection without reason", he said. Van Heerden said it was tragic that a young, talented writer could make such an error of judgment (*Beeld*, 13 December 1999).

It would be inappropriate to make any judgment about this matter in this book. However, the incident serves as a vivid reminder of what could happen if plagiarism is suspected. It also reopens the debate over where the dividing line is between plagiarism and mere re-creation of ideas. Whatever the facts, the whole drama could have been prevented if Du Plessis had acknowledged his debt (if any) to Malamud in the first place.

In another incident, the *Citizen* apologized formally to its readers early in August 2000 after a blatant act of plagiarism. This came after the newspaper reported the results of a "*Citizen* investigation" concerning the death of a man from Alexandra who had consumed toxic liquor. This story by Paul Letsoalo, a freelance journalist, was similar to a report that had appeared in the *Mail & Guardian* in September the previous year. The story was exactly the same; only the names and places had been changed. The editor, Tim du Plessis, explained that Letsoalo had been freelancing for the *Citizen* for a few weeks when the incident occurred. Letsoalo's services were terminated immediately.

Plagiarism is an extremely serious journalistic offence. Nothing destroys a journalist's credibility as fast and as certainly as when he or she is caught stealing another writer's work. It is considered such a serious offence "to be grounds for dismissal in many media companies" (Black et al. 1995, 173). *If text is borrowed, it must always be acknowledged as such.*

James Fallows, Washington editor of *The Atlantic Monthly*, has been quoted as saying: "This is something you never, never do. Every line of work needs clear rules. If you're a soldier, you don't desert. If you're a writer, you don't steal anyone's prose. It should be one automatic firing" (*Columbia Journalism Review* July/August 1995, 22).

Internet plagiarism[3]

Internet plagiarism is a burning issue, and one that gets hotter by the day. Frank Furedi (*The Times Higher* 14 July 2000, 16) states that even top universities are plagued by the problem. "Boston University in Massachusetts was forced to go to court to stop Internet sites selling essays online" (*The Times Higher* 14 July 2000, 16), he reports. There is even a site, cheathouse.com, which describes itself as "An Evil House of Cheating" and claims that it possesses the largest essay database on the Internet. According to Furedi, the business of providing course material is a lucrative one. "Anxious students with a bit of spare cash can request customized essays and receive them via e-mail within 24 hours" (*The Times Higher* 14 July 2000, 16).

Of course, Internet plagiarism is not confined to the United States. In July 1999 the examination results of 90 students at the University of Edinburgh were withheld pending an inquiry into alleged Internet plagiarism. A month later, students at Glasgow University also came under scrutiny. Furedi quotes Dr Fintan Cutwin of London's South Bank University as saying that universities are "overwhelmed" by plagiarism (*The Times Higher* 14 July 2000, 16). It seems as if universities are scared to tackle the issue. There are several reasons for this: the fear of the bad publicity that it would inevitably create; messy and time-consuming appeals and complaints procedures; and the ever-present possibility of litigation. (In the Edinburgh case, one student sued the university for defamation.)

Furedi says there are technical ways to counter Internet plagiarism, although these are time-consuming. An automatic detection system known as Moss (Measure of Software Similarity) provides an Internet service that compares letter frequency and length of sentences and also examines the structure of the text (*The Times Higher* 14 July 2000, 16). Other service providers such as plagiarism.org offer similar help. However, Furedi is correct in not wanting to get involved "in a technical game of cat and mouse" (*The Times Higher* 14 July 2000, 16). It is far better to explain to students why plagiarism is unacceptable, and to teach them to cite their sources carefully and to provide a proper bibliography. In addition, Furedi suggests that lecturers ask specific essay questions and demand that students engage with the literature provided by the lecturer. "Let us find an intellectual rather than a technical solution to the problem" (*The Times Higher* 14 July 2000, 16).

The Internet and character assassination

The Internet can easily be used in smear campaigns, spreading lies and half-truths at will. Yet this can also be countered. Joshua Quittner (*Time* 25 August 1997) explains: Internet muckraker Matt Drudge had sent e-mails to more than 60 000 people in which he claimed that a White House aide was a wife-beater. He later retracted this allegation and apologized. This apology was not enough for the aide's lawyer, William McDaniel, who sued Drudge for libel. "People who use the Internet feel they're not subject to the same constraints as everyone else", McDaniel was quoted as saying (*Time* 25 August 1997, 48). He felt a lawsuit would "deter Drudge and people like him from doing this in the future" (*Time* 25 August 1997, 48).

Quittner sums up the problem: everyone who has access to the Internet can compete "mouse to mouse" with the mainstream media. However, "many of the Net's would-be Woodwards and Bernsteins are journalistic novices and wouldn't think, say, to ask court or police sources to confirm a rumor" (*Time* 25 August 1997, 48). Character assassination can be devastating. Quittner cites the examples of fashion designer Tommy Hilfiger, who was falsely accused of racism; film star Brad Pitt, who was shown in the nude in unauthorized photos; and writer Kurt Vonnegut, who was falsely depicted as the author of a commencement speech he never made (*Time* 25 August 1997, 48).

A checklist for plagiarism

Black et al. suggest that the following checklist for plagiarism should be considered (Black et al. 1995, 174):

- Have you carefully attributed any material that is not your own?
- Are you working from your notes, or from your head? If from your head, are you certain that you are not taking out of your memory someone else's phrases or sentences?
- Will reasonable people recognize the difference between your writing and that of others?
- Are you well enough informed about the topic to be able to recognize potential problems with your work?
- Have you encouraged others to read your work to see if it triggers any memories that might indicate plagiarism?

Accuracy: a checklist

Consider the following checklist (Black et al. 1995, 54) for accuracy:

- Do you have a high level of confidence about the facts in your story and the sources that are providing them? If you have any doubts about your sources, can you delete them or replace them and achieve a higher likelihood of reliability?
- Have you attributed or documented all the facts?
- Have you double-checked the key facts?
- Can you provide the properly spelt name and accurate telephone number of every source cited?
- Are you highly confident that all the factual statements in your story reflect the truth?
- Are you prepared to defend publicly your fact-checking and whatever other measures that were taken to verify your story?
- Are the quotes presented fairly, and in context?
- Are you quoting anonymous sources? Why are you using those sources? Are you prepared to defend publicly the use of those sources?
- Are you using any material, documents or pictures provided by anonymous sources? Why? What is your level of confidence about the validity of this material? Are you prepared to defend publicly the use of that material?
- Have you described persons, minority groups, races, cultures, nations, or segments of society – for example, businesspeople, war veterans, cheerleaders – using stereotypical adjectives? Are such descriptions accurate and meaningful in the context presented?
- Have you used potentially objectionable language or pictures? Is there a compelling reason for using such information? Would the story be less accurate if that language or picture were eliminated?
- Do your headlines (or broadcast promos or teasers) accurately present the facts and context of the story to which they refer?

Orders to kill?

This case study illustrates how the simplistic equation of terms can lead to inaccurate conclusions.

Jessica Pitchford of the SABC reported on a meeting held by the Afrikaner Weerstandsbeweging (AWB) at Krugersdorp on 18 May 1999. The report, which led the AWB to lodge a complaint with the Broadcasting Complaints Commission of South Africa (BCCSA), was broadcast in English at 20:00 and in Afrikaans at 21:00. Pitchford's report went like this:

Presenter (Nadia Levin): Eugene Terre'Blanche returned to Krugersdorp last night, but not for another midnight tryst at Paardekraal. Instead, in an emotional address at the City Hall, he told the followers of the dangers that lay ahead after June the 2nd. But not everyone was impressed by the AWB leader's rhetoric.

Pitchford: The AWB orchestra was in fine form – as was the leader when he arrived with his so-called generals.

Eugene Terre'Blanche hadn't addressed a public meeting for almost a year and he certainly made up for lost time, blasting forth for an hour and forty minutes on everything associated with the new South Africa.

His return, he claimed, was because of the hundreds of calls and requests from followers, many of whom wanted him to contest the election to represent them in Parliament. But, he said, he could never enter what he called 'Dingaan se Kraal'.

The evening was also an opportunity to make some money. AWB memorabilia were on sale outside the hall, and pamphlets requested donations.

But not everyone was enthralled by Terre'-Blanche's animated address. AWB heavies had to silence the family of Deon Maartens, imprisoned for killing people at a roadblock in the run-up to the '94 election. Maartens and those serving life with him told the TRC [Truth and Reconciliation Commission] last year that the orders had come from Terre'Blanche. At the time, he denied it.

File (voice of Terre'Blanche, 23 April 1998): Ek beskou dit as 'n blatante leuen. Ek is nogtans jammer dat dié mense in die posisie geplaas is om te lieg. ('I regard it as a blatant lie. However, I am sorry that these people were put in a situation where they had to lie.')

Pitchford: Last night, to the anger of the Maartens family, he claimed he'd accepted responsibility.

Terre'Blanche: Sover ek weet, is dit nét ek wat onmiddellik sê: 'Ek het die opdrag aan die AWB's gegee!' ('As far as I know, it is only I who immediately say: "I have given the order to the AWBs!"')

Louise Maartens (wife): He's lying! He's lying! The night I phoned him, his words were: 'Ag Here, Mevrou!' ('Oh Lord, Madam!')

Cedric Maartens (father): Hoekom moet 'n mens eers tronk toe gaan voordat jou oë oopgaan om te sien wat die AWB werklik is? ('Why do first you have to go to jail before your eyes are opened to see what the AWB really is?')

Pitchford: Is u nog 'n lid? ('Are you still a member?')

Cedric Maartens: Ek? Guh! ('Me? That'll be the day!')

Pitchford: Despite his fiery address last night, Terre'Blanche doesn't think his followers will take him literally this time.

Terre'Blanche: Nee, ek dink nie daar gaan regse geweld wees nie. ('No, I don't think there will be right-wing violence.')

Pitchford: But that could well be because the only enthusiasm left in the AWB lies in its orchestra – Jessica Pitchford, Krugersdorp.

The AWB's complaint consisted of the following:

- The Paardekraal incident (referring to an alleged romantic rendezvous between Terre'-Blanche and Jani Allen, a journalist) was no longer news and took place years ago.
- What was meant by the phrase "so-called generals"?
- The AWB always sells memorabilia. It was

implied that the AWB was in financial trouble, and this aspect is in any case irrelevant.

- It was suggested that Terre'Blanche ordered Deon Maartens and his men to commit the murders for which they have been jailed.
- The essence of Terre'Blanche's speech was not covered.
- The coverage represented Pitchford's personal opinion.
- The enthusiasm that was "only" to be found in the orchestra amounted to an incorrect representation of what really took place at the meeting.

Clause 2 of the BCCSA's code applies to this case. The commission dismissed all the AWB's complaints, except the fourth one (concerning Deon Maartens). Here is a summary of the judgment:

- The inclusion of the Paardekraal incident does not invade Terre'Blanche's privacy, and it is entirely within the SABC's right to include such a matter.
- The reference to "so-called generals" is probably correct. Official generals are appointed by the state.
- Although the reference to sales was not countered by the fact that this has always taken place, this error is not relevant.
- Terre'Blanche spoke for approximately an hour and a half. References to "dangers that lay ahead" and "everything is associated to the new South Africa", as well as references to the amnesty matter, probably sufficiently covered his speech.
- The complaint about Pitchford's alleged slant against the AWB would probably have been upheld – if the AWB were registered as a political party for the (then) upcoming election. It is true that the report portrays a negative image of Terre'Blanche. However, this is not relevant in this specific instance.

- The reference to the band's enthusiasm is probably uncalled-for. Yet this is obviously a humorous note and would not have been taken seriously by viewers.

Now, back to the fourth part of the AWB's complaint. After a video copy of the full speech was studied on more than one occasion, it was clear "that the inclusion of Mr Terre'Blanche's statement that he had given 'orders' in the Deon Maartens case, was incorrect". Mr Terre'Blanche referred to these orders as part of evidence which he was prepared to give in the light of the Truth and Reconciliation Act, which requires that amnesty be granted only if certain requirements are satisfied. One of these requirements is that the person who applies for amnesty acted as a result of orders given. According to the BCCSA judgment:

He clearly stated in his speech that he was prepared to give evidence so as to fulfil this requirement. His speech also makes clear that he is prepared to believe that many of his organization's members could have been influenced by him in their actions.

Terre'Blanche also stated that he did accept "responsibility" for the actions of his followers. The judgment continued:

It was, however, clear that the word 'responsibility' has a wide connotation which is often used by leaders when applying for amnesty or explaining the misdeeds of their followers or employees. Although Mr Terre'Blanche did not spell out that he had accepted moral and political responsibility for the actions of his followers, it was clear that his reference to 'responsibility' was used in the wide sense. When dealing with the Maartens matter he referred to 'responsibility' and not to orders. The inclusion of the earlier part of his speech where he refers to 'orders' was accordingly not justified.

The commission did consider the possibility that, from a journalist's perspective, "orders" and "responsibility" were (within the context of the speech) in effect identical. "After due consideration… we have come to the conclusion that reference to 'orders' within a different general context differed substantially from 'responsibility' within the context of the Maartens' matter. We have accordingly come to the conclusion that the SABC contravened the BCCSA Code insofar as it quoted the 'orders' reference out of context." The BCCSA said that the mere fact of the finding against the SABC "is a sufficient sanction". The SABC was not directed to broadcast the BCCSA's decision.

Analysis

The BCCSA is indeed quite correct in saying that "orders" and "responsibility" do not necessarily mean the same thing. "Responsibility" has a very wide meaning, and is often used by politicians in this wide sense. "Orders", on the other hand, are direct, particular, specific – and damning. Pitchford's simplistic equation of these terms was irresponsible, and one that could have done a great deal of harm – especially to Terre'Blanche. Of course, Maartens would not have minded if Terre'Blanche admitted he had given orders to kill. That could have led to him getting amnesty for the murders. However, Terre'Blanche denied he had given Maartens the order to kill. The response of the Maartens family to this is there for all to see.

But more than the consequences (teleology) of that report are at stake here. Deontologically speaking, journalists have a duty to report truthfully. Not only was there no attempt to minimize harm (as far as the "orders to kill" is concerned), there was also little attempt to maximize truth. The media's duty to report truthfully includes that the journalist's interpretation (or at least the motivation for the interpretation) of words, phrases, or statements should at all times be above suspicion.

The fact that Pitchford was reporting on the leader of an extreme right-wing organization – certainly despised by millions of South Africans who abhor the apartheid regime in general and far right-wingers like Terre'Blanche in particular – should not have made any difference in this regard. As a professional journalist, she should have been above that kind of emotion. Pitchford's inaccurate reporting (for which she was found guilty by the BCCSA) combined with her overall attitude seem to suggest that she indeed could not rise to the occasion. Just as there is no excuse for the inaccurate reporting of facts, *there is also no room in responsible journalism for inaccurate conclusions.*

The BCCSA rightly dismissed the rest of the complaints. However, two questions remain:

- Is it in order to portray a negative image of any individual just because his or her party is not registered for an upcoming election?
- Would the viewers really have seen the reference to the enthusiasm of the orchestra as a humorous note that would not have been taken seriously by the viewers?

Dead bodies necklaced

This case is intended to illustrate that a lack of evidence (statements not adequately sourced) can easily lead to inaccurate reporting.

The Flame Lily Foundation, which has as its members ex-Rhodesians who have settled in South Africa, complained to the BCCSA about a statement made by journalist Max du Preez when reporting for the SABC during a report on the Truth and Reconciliation Commission (TRC). The BCCSA adjudged clauses 2.3 and 3.3 of its code, as well as Section 36 of the Constitution, were applicable in this case.

Du Preez's full statement in question reads:

Between September 1984 and August 1989, 771 people were necklaced or doused with fuel and burned to death. The myth perpetuated by the State then was that this was an example of African brutality. The truth, as we now know, is that this repulsive form of killing was first started by white Rhodesian security forces in the 1970s and then brought to South Africa by the Security Police. Policemen burned Siphiwo Mtimkulu and Topsy Madaka to ashes in 1982, the Pebco 3 in 1985 and Sizwe Kondile in 1989. May God forbid anything like this ever happening in our land.

In this report, on 9 February 1997, Du Preez described one of the scenes (the incineration of Maki Skosana, a young East Rand woman believed to be an informer) as the first TV broadcast of a necklacing. For a few seconds, a scene was shown of her being doused with petrol and set alight. However, the "balance of evidence" later showed that she had not been an informer. The then retired Col. A. H. G. Munro complained about the report, saying that it was not accurate (or was a misrepresentation of the truth). The complaint read, *inter alia*:

We (the Flame Lily Foundation) contend that the statement referring to 'white Rhodesian Security Forces' ...is both untrue and malicious. Necklacing ...was never practised (let alone started) by the Rhodesian Security Forces, black or white, and would have resulted in prosecution of the perpetrators of such a dastardly act if it were ever discovered. The allegation cast doubt on the integrity of all former members of the Rhodesian security forces, and causes distress for their families and friends.

Munro added that Du Preez gave no indication as to the source of this "truth" when he said "we now know". Munro asked the SABC to verify this statement. "Should the SABC be unable to satisfactorily substantiate the accuracy of the statement, please would you advise me as to what appropriate steps should be taken by the SABC to rectify this matter."

Du Preez claimed in his first defence that a primitive African belief is that a victim would die only if his or her soul was also destroyed. That, "the urban legend went", could only be done by fire. Du Preez wanted to debunk this myth. He therefore stated that the practice in South Africa "was actually not started by township people or the liberation movements, but by security policemen like Dirk Coetzee, Eugene de Kock and Gideon Nieuwoudt". Some of these people, Du Preez argued, repeatedly stated that they had similar experiences of "dirty war" in Rhodesia. According to Du Preez, there is "a substantial body of evidence" that necklacing was copied by South African policemen while they were fighting in the former Zimbabwe. If Zimbabwe had a Truth Commission, "they would not have been complaining about remarks like mine", Du Preez claimed.

In his second defence, Du Preez stated that the killings he referred to were not only instances of necklacing (hanging a tyre around a person's neck and setting it alight), but also of people who were (merely) burned to death. He repeated that "the account that South African security policemen copied the burning of the bodies of activists or guerrillas from the Rhodesian security forces, has been related several times by policemen who have themselves indulged in this method".

Du Preez also included the following, all of which allegedly testified to the above-mentioned statement:

- a handwritten statement by Dirk Coetzee;
- a transcript of a videotaped interview with Dumisa Ntsebeza, a TRC commissioner and head of the TRC's Investigations Unit;

- a faxed copy of the Zimbabwean monthly magazine *Parade* of August 1989;
- two documents, "The Man in the Middle: Torture, Resettlement and Eviction", and "Civil War in Rhodesia". Both reports were made after extensive investigations into the methods and practices of the Rhodesian security forces, Du Preez added.

He also sent a copy of the TV documentary, *The Hidden Hand*, which was shown on the BBC. "It contains ample proof of practices such as the large-scale poisoning of clothes and food supplied to opponents of the Smith regime which led to a large number of people dying an agonising death…"

Du Preez concluded, with reference to the Flame Lily complaint, that "there are individuals and organizations out there who could try and use your commission (the BCCSA) to make their own propaganda and harass journalists".

To all of this, the BCCSA concluded it had found no evidence (in the material presented by Du Preez) that live people were incinerated either by necklacing or being doused in petrol. Captain Dirk Coetzee recounted to the BCCSA that *corpses were sometimes incinerated to ensure that identification could not take place*. "But these acts do not amount to the incineration of *live* people, which lies at the core of necklacing and dousing."

The BCCSA then arrived at the following conclusions:

- There is no evidence that the SABC or Du Preez acted from malicious motives as alleged by the complainant.
- However, the BCCSA has not been provided with evidence that the alleged atrocities in Rhodesia of the 1970s included the incineration of live people by necklacing or by setting them alight after having doused them in petrol.
- Therefore, the statement that these forms of incineration of live people originated from the

Rhodesian security forces was not substantiated by the documentation placed before the commission.

The commission unanimously concluded that the Respondent had contravened the BCCSA code by having broadcast a statement that was not adequately sourced or shown to have been adequately sourced before the commission. The SABC was directed to broadcast this decision in an appropriate viewer- and time-slot.

Analysis

The BCCSA was correct in its decision. To Du Preez's credit, however, it must be said that he did try to assemble all the relevant facts, tried to check and verify them, and tried to put these facts into the proper context. Du Preez did everything right – except that his evidence seems to have pointed to the incineration of *already dead* people. The claim that people were killed by setting them alight could therefore not be validated. This means that, with the material at Du Preez's disposal, he should have been more careful with his conclusion (that necklacing/dousing originated in the Rhodesian army). Even if Du Preez's statement was accurate (the truth), the lack of hard evidence to this effect should have cautioned him to be much more modest. This meant that the truth was not maximized and that some unnecessary harm was done to the complainant and like-minded people because the complainant and the rest of the Rhodesian security forces were put in a bad light. This reporting probably also caused a lot of unnecessary distress to the families involved, as the complainant had claimed.

Harm in this case could very easily have been minimized, for example by saying that the practice of necklacing *could probably* have originated in the Rhodesian security forces, due to the fact that some enemies were indeed incinerated (albeit after their death). Or that necklacing could have been a practice *in some circles* in the Rhodesian army. This would have amounted to some kind of golden mean – although, of course, the real facts about the incineration of dead bodies should also have been mentioned. But

surely Du Preez cannot be accused of dishonesty (as the BCCSA quite correctly pointed out). The complaint of having been malicious was therefore correctly dismissed. Due to the seriousness of the matter, the BCCSA was correct in directing the SABC to broadcast its decision in an appropriate slot.

"The very opposite"

This case is intended to illustrate how the media can report the very opposite of the truth as truth.

In their respective broadcasts, SABC 3 (at 20:00) and SABC 2 (at 21:00) showed four Attorneys-General taking the oath at a hearing of the Truth and Reconciliation Commission (TRC). According to the reports, these Attorneys-General "admitted" they were at times influenced by the previous government to prosecute in cases relating to security legislation and the Group Areas Act.

At 22:00 on that same day (29 October 1997), Dr J. A. van S. d'Oliviera, an Attorney-General portrayed in the broadcast, lodged an urgent complaint with the Broadcasting Complaints Commission. The complaint was heard the very next day.

D'Oliviera said the news reports were substantially erroneous, completely wrong, and false. He had, *inter alia*, this to say:

No such admission was ever made. I am shocked and dismayed that anyone could have construed the evidence in that way. Such reckless reporting constitutes a grave disservice to our country and to the administration of justice. In fact what was said was the very opposite... I stated under oath that in my tenure as Attorney-General since 1 April 1986 I was *never* told or instructed in any specific case what to decide or to do... I submit that the error in reporting is of such a nature that it demands an immediate correction.

The BCCSA reported: "At the hearing D'Oliviera accentuated the importance of the office of the Attorney-General and how a reference to such influence impinged upon his and other Attorneys-General's standing in the community. The implication was that if this had occurred in the past, it could occur again."

The SABC said it understood the problem but that they could not, in the absence of the reporter, reply to the complaint. The SABC did, however, undertake to broadcast a correcting item (if found to be justified) as soon as possible. Mr Phil Molefe, TVN Head of News, added that the matter would get top priority. The BCCSA also saw this as a matter of top priority and "if the SABC's investigation confirmed the complaint, the complaint was also upheld". The BCCSA would convene again if the investigation led to a different conclusion.

The SABC then established that the complaint was justified. A correcting item was broadcast on both news bulletins on 31 October 1997.

Analysis

The central point in this case is that the *complete opposite* of what was reported was actually true. This does not happen very often. Mostly, in cases where news reports are not accurate, at least a part of the truth is told. Or the truth may be slightly twisted, or an important part of it omitted. It seldom happens that the opposite of the truth is presented as the (whole) truth. This reporter indeed succeeded in "reporting" the very opposite of the truth. What makes this case even worse is the fact that the report brought the whole administration of justice as well as the integrity of the Attorneys-General, into question. It could have had national and even international repercussions. And, as the BCCSA rightly pointed out, the implication was that if it could happen once, it could happen again.

None of the central requirements for accurate reporting was adhered to. The story was false, the context was distorted, and the report was definitely not verified. This is an extreme case of minimizing truth and maximizing harm. This is inexcusable. The credibility of the SABC took a dent, and with that, the South African media as a whole. The SABC earns credit in that it saw the matter as a top priority, and acted accordingly.

| "Evidence" as truth

This case shows how dangerous it is to portray unsubstantiated, untested "evidence" as the truth.

The SABC reported on 22 July 1997, in Afrikaans and English, that a few years ago the Supreme Court mistakenly found certain people (members of the ANC) guilty of the so-called Eikenhof murders. They received death sentences, but these were never carried out because the death penalty had been abolished in the meantime.

The reports on SABC news followed a confession by the Pan Africanist Congress (PAC) to the Truth and Reconciliation Commission the previous week that it (members of the PAC, and therefore not of the ANC) had been responsible for the murders in question.

Telephonic interviews with the prisoners were also broadcast. All the interviewees claimed that certain members of the police, including W. C. Landman, had tortured them. (In the BCCSA's documents, Landman is called "Major" as well as "Colonel".) At some stage in the report, Landman was said to be the chief investigating officer in this case.

Landman, who lodged a complaint with the BCCSA, made the following claims:

- There was no undisputed factual basis for the statement that the members of the ANC were mistakenly found guilty.
- He was not the chief investigating officer in this case, but merely responsible for arresting the suspects.
- The news reports referred to him as a controversial person because of his alleged links with the so-called death squads of Vlakplaas and the security police of the apartheid regime. He denied any such ties and called the allegations libellous.
- He had not been asked about these matters when interviewed by the SABC.
- He denied that the suspects were ever tortured.

Clause 2 of the BCCSA's code is relevant in this case. The BCCSA remarked that both the complainant and the respondent accepted that the SABC's reports were based on the PAC's testimony to the TRC. This evidence, however, was just evidence and did not amount to a verdict. It was therefore totally erroneous to conclude "factually", on the basis of this evidence only, that the Supreme Court had made a mistake. In so doing, the SABC had contravened Clause 2 of the BCCSA's code, it was decided.

On the matter of Landman's alleged links with Vlakplaas and the security police, the SABC did not put any evidence forward to substantiate these serious accusations, the BCCSA said. It therefore accepted Landman's word. This meant that the SABC mistake had caused him substantial embarrassment.

The BCCSA also decided that the SABC was free to report on the interviews with the convicted persons, including the allegations of torture (although, in the context of the report, this could have amounted to biased reporting). The fact that Landman's denial, as well as the Supreme Court's judgment on this issue, was also reported, "brought balance to the broadcast".

The mistake regarding Landman being the chief investigating officer was not deemed serious enough to make a judgment against the SABC.

The SABC was directed to broadcast a report, saying that it had erred when it stated that the so-called Eikenhof accused had been erroneously convicted of murder. The evidence before the TRC would first have to be tested in a court of law. The report also had to convey that the SABC had unjustifiably linked Landman with Vlakplaas and the security police.

Analysis

It is inexcusable to confuse "evidence" (before the TRC or anywhere else) with facts. Surely, the so-called evidence must first be tested in a court of law. To assume that the PAC's testimony (which was not even subjected to cross-examination) pointed to the fact that the Supreme Court had made a mistake is more than just bad journalism: it holds the status of the courts as well as the role of the judiciary in contempt.

The following quite serious question must be asked: why did the SABC accept untested, unsubstantiated testimony as "evidence" that the court had made a mistake? Why give credibility to "evidence" that had no undisputed factual basis? What makes matters even worse is that Landman was linked to Vlakplaas and the security police – *again, without any substantiating evidence*. Did the SABC make any attempt to check and verify these reports? It certainly does not seem so. This linkage could have caused an innocent person enormous harm – and since no substantiating evidence existed, we must assume that this is what happened to Landman. In this case, harm was maximized and the truth was minimized. In the end, neither the alleged "mistake" by the court, nor the linking of Landman to Vlakplaas, nor the allegation of torture, were proved to be accurate.

As far as the other complaints are concerned, the BCCSA concluded that the reports on the alleged torture were balanced because they included Landman's denial. But how ethical is it to make a statement (such as the one on torture) and then "balance" it with a denial? Can one say just about anything about anybody, as long as it is "balanced" with a denial? The mistake of calling Landman the chief investigating officer was not serious enough to justify a finding against the SABC, as the BCCSA had stated. The BCCSA was correct to direct the SABC to broadcast a report which had to say that the national broadcaster had erred in more than one way.

Background information omitted

This case illustrates what the withholding of information can do to the truth.

The Jewish Defence League (JDL) of South Africa lodged a complaint with the BCCSA about a radio talk show aired from 21:00 to 24:00 on 1 December 1998 on Radio 702, hosted by Jon Qwelane. The issue was the views expressed by a pupil, a certain Ms Cassim of Crawford College, to whose parents the JDL had previously sent a letter. Listeners phoned in and the host was outspoken in his criticism of the JDL.

Here are some of the comments that were made on the show:

- "The South African Jewish Board of Deputies has distanced itself from the criminal threats, the cowardly actions of the JDL."
- "The so-called JDL is nothing more than something with criminal intent – I have passed over the letters (sent to Ms Cassim's family) to the Human Rights Commission – I think that organisation also has to be looked at and if we are going to have that type of terrorist organisation in this country, we are going to have to use the might of the law to crush it."
- "If the people within the school are in concert with what I totally term a 'total criminal organisation with terrorist intentions' like the JDL… I have asked Dr (Barney) Pityana (chairperson of the HRC) to do something about this organisation. I will not live in a country with such sick terrorist minds."
- "This little pseudo-organisation… we are going to deal with it and we are going to deal with it just as we deal with any other that is hell-bent on terrorising its citizens."
- "I saw the letters and I handed them over to Dr Pityana and I have been given assurances that this criminal organisation is going to be investigated."

Mr Frank Startz, for the JDL, said in his complaint that there was absolutely no record of the JDL ever having acted illegally or having been involved in any act of terrorism. Radio 702 had seriously impaired their good standing by these "totally untrue, damaging, malicious and baseless" statements. Startz was also concerned about a "public broadcaster" providing a platform for airing uninformed and unaccountable opinions, which could recklessly induce, incite, and canvass other equally dangerous opinions.

Clause 3 of the BCCSA's code applies in this case. Radio 702 said the matter of the letter of the JDL sent to the parents of the Crawford College pupil had been covered extensively on several broadcasts. And yet, the BCCSA remarked, Qwelane failed to refer to the contents of the letter. In a second letter from the JDL, the latter apologized to the family, saying that the first letter had been based on a misconception. It was not clear whether Qwelane was also in possession of the second letter. "The fact that Mr Qwelane did not deal with the contents of the first letter (and, if he had it, the second letter) led to the likelihood that a substantial number of listeners… would not have been in a position to judge his comments on the organisation within the correct context", the BCCSA said.

According to the BCCSA, the first letter sent by the JDL to the family "could not have been interpreted by the family as an implied threat of violence". The JDL indeed had a clean record and they are totally against violence unless they act within the ambit of lawful self-defence, the BCCSA said. Nevertheless, the commission continued, "the content of the letter is problematic and open to misunderstanding…". The commission concluded: "… having commented on the organisation in a negative fashion, Mr Qwelane should, as background material at least, have quoted from the letter to the family (from the first one, as well as from the second one, if he was in possession of that)". This omission constituted a contravention of the code.

> It is accordingly unnecessary for us to decide whether the observations made in regard to the organisation were justified or not. ...The extremely derogatory comments of the host would normally be justified only under exceptional circumstances. It is, however, unnecessary for us to decide whether these exceptional circumstances were present in the light of our first decision that balance was absent.

Analysis

Qwelane's reporting was not exactly a shining example of responsible, ethical journalism. The JDL (correctly) complained, not because it merely did not like the content of the programme (surely, in a democracy different and opposing views should be aired) but because grave errors were made that placed the organization in an extremely bad light.

To be able to report accurately, journalists not only have to get their facts straight, but also to put the events into their proper context. Qwelane did not tell his listeners about the relevant background material, thereby omitting valuable information that could have made a material difference to the content of the story. Given the derogatory remarks made about the JDL on his talk show, the suspicion could easily arise that

Qwelane had been prejudicial towards the JDL.

For the reasons given, the BCCSA was correct in finding that Qwelane had contravened its code by omitting relevant material. But the BCCSA was far too lenient towards Qwelane, considering the derogatory remarks he allowed on his show. Why refrain from making a judgment on these remarks as such just because the Commission found that "balance was absent"? It is unfortunate that the above-mentioned statements, which could possibly have amounted to hate speech, were not adjudicated.

From a teleological as well as from a deontological perspective, this kind of journalism is unacceptable. We can only hope that some of the harm that was done to the JDL was undone by the BCCSA's decision.

Notes

[1] For example, see the article by Sinéad O'Brien, *American Journalism Review* December 1996, pp. 40–44 on this question.

[2] At the time Du Plessis was a lecturer at the University of Transkei and busy with his doctorate in linguistics. He was awarded the M-Net bursary in 1996 for exceptional writer's talent.

[3] For a comprehensive overview on Internet law in South Africa, see Buys et al. 2000. Topics discussed are, *inter alia*, copyright, contracts, taxation, gambling, freedom of expression (including defamation, pornography, and hate speech), privacy and the right to information, and regulation (such as censorship). The subject of media law (and ethics) and the Internet is a study on its own and cannot be dealt with meaningfully in this book. Buys' book is highly recommended.

4 | Truth and deception

"Telling the truth never needs any moral justification; lying and deception do." (Day 1991, 70)

Introduction

As the oldest, most highly regarded ethical principle of humankind, truth has been a fundamental journalistic value since Gütenberg developed the printing press. Truth is valued by philosophers, courts, religious people, and parents – and presumably will be of fundamental importance until doomsday. According to Day (1991, 68), "the commitment to truth is perhaps the most ancient and revered ethical principle of human civilization".[1]

The truth is the be-all and the end-all of journalism. The public rightly expects nothing less than the truth, the whole truth, and nothing but the truth. The reasons why truth is so vital to journalism are evident:

- Without the truth a journalist has neither integrity (what you think of yourself) nor credibility (what others think of you).
- The public needs accurate information to be able to make informed decisions.
- It demonstrates a respect for people as people (they are not objects to be manipulated).
- It builds a relationship of trust between the media and the public.

Day (1991, 72–75) identifies three concepts that underlie the notion of truth in reporting:

- Reporting must be *accurate*. The facts should be verified and based on solid evidence. If there is any doubt, it should be revealed to the audience.
- Reporting should *promote understanding*. A story should contain as much relevant information as is available and essential to afford the average reader at least an understanding of the facts and the context of the facts. All sorts of ethical issues arise when journalists intentionally withhold some facts relevant to the public interest.

- Reporting should be *fair and balanced*. Avoid reporter bias, accord recognition to those views that enhance the understanding of an issue, and present them fairly and in context. Certify the content and avoid any comment.

However, merely saying that truth should be sought is to oversimplify the matter. Yes, truth is a very simple concept, but it is simultaneously also a highly complex one. The point is that everything is relative and that all human beings are subjective. One person's truth is someone else's lie. Some people will call certain soldiers "terrorists", while for others they may be "freedom fighters". Truth often depends on our perspective. Hence the absence of the concept of *objectivity* in Day's three concepts underlying the notion of truth in journalism.[2]

J. Edward Gerald[3] argues that journalists like to see their role in terms of a model called the Tournament of Reason, after John Milton, or the Marketplace of Thought, after Justice Oliver Wendell Holmes (Merrill 1975, 136–142). "We all know the catchwords that identify the model: 'Let Truth and Error grapple. Who ever knew Truth to be put to flight in a free and open encounter?'" (Merrill 1975, 137). And so, "acting out our role, we sit in the press box and watch these two knights on horseback, Truth and Error, fly at each other with all the force at their command. Dipping into our knapsack of clichés, we label them the *White Knight* and the *Black Knight*. The playing field is rather large and we report only that part of the action which we can see" (Merrill 1975, 137).

But there is more here than meets the eye: "[t]he Black Knight, on the standard color scale, may be more purple than black and the White Knight may be, in several senses of the word, dirty. He may also be a mercenary soldier from hell, but because of his choice of colors and his self-depreciation we won't become suspicious of his motives" (Merrill 1975, 137).

These words must surely be of great concern to each and every journalist. For it is possible to think that you serve "the truth", but to find in the process you are actually undermining it. Don't be so naive as to think that "truth" or "untruth" (a lie) is a matter of 100 per cent right against 100 per cent wrong. This seldom happens: life (and journalism) is much too complicated for that. Mostly there are only varying shades of truth and untruth. For example, a person can lie "completely" (as in 100 per cent), or partially, or by keeping quiet, or by withholding some part of the truth, or by smiling, or by frowning, or whatever. There is more than one way of letting someone believe what you know to be untrue. However, the notion that the "whole truth" can never be reached in its entirety should not become "a stumbling block in the… inquiry into questions of truth-telling and falsehood" (Bok 1978, 13). The *search for the truth* remains a cornerstone of excellent journalism.

Deception

A vitally important moral question for journalists, who are in the business of truth-telling, is this: should the media indulge in untruthful, deceptive methods to gain information? Are journalists allowed to use deception – for example, by lying, doing undercover work, or using hidden cameras – as a way of getting information? Can they manipulate the news or photographs for their own purposes?

The issue of deception "is a significant ethical matter, for it deals with truth, and seeking truth is what journalism is all about" (Black et al. 1995, 119). Deception can take many forms: it can be outright lying, misleading, misrepresenting, or merely being less than forthright. "All of these actions are intended to cause someone to believe what is not true" (Black et al. 1995, 119) – or, rather, what you believe or know to be untrue.

Deception can take place in the process of news-writing as well as in news-gathering. The former happens most infrequently: "Only rarely, if ever, does a reporter or editor specifically and consciously give the wrong story" (Christians et al. 1995, 51). However, deception in *news-gathering* "...is a persistent temptation, because it often facilitates the process of securing information" (Christians et al. 1995, 51).

What is at stake here is not the unintentional misleading of the public or members of the public as such. It is rather the *intention to mislead* (Bok 1978, 18). Deception can be defined as the deliberate intention to mislead and constitutes therefore the opposite of truth-telling (Christians et al. 1995, 51). Intentional lying, Sissela Bok points out, has grave consequences. Like violence, deceit is a form of "deliberate assault on human beings" and it can coerce people into acting against their will (Bok 1978, 18). It also disempowers them: "To the extent that knowledge gives power, to that extent do lies affect the distribution of power; they add to that of the liar, and diminish that of the deceived, altering his choices at different levels" (Bok 1978, 19). And when the deceived learns of the deceit, they "...see that they were manipulated, that the deceit made them unable to make choices for themselves according to the most adequate information available, unable to act as they would have wanted to act had they known all along" (Bok 1978, 20).

Although truth is fundamental to human (and journalistic) ethics, dishonesty also seems to be part of human nature (Day 1991, 70). If and when an individual's own self-interest demands that he or she forsake the truth, it seems almost natural to resort to deceit. "In fact, it is safe to say that deceit, rather than truth, is featured more prominently in literature as a reflection of the human condition" (Day 1991, 70). People sometimes exchange the "White Knight" for the "Black Knight", even without knowing that they have

done it. Many people manipulate the truth to suit themselves (Bok 1978, xvi and following). Social scientists, lawyers, psychiatrists, advertisers, and journalists "...often have little compunction in using falsehoods to gain the knowledge they seek" (Bok 1978, xvii).

Maybe this is one of the reasons why codes of ethics the world over say so little about when deception is justified and when it not. "As a result, those who confront difficult moral choices between truthfulness and deception often make up their own rules. They think up their own excuses and evaluate their own arguments" (Bok 1978, 11). In addition, "contemporary philosophers, unlike their ancient predecessors, have virtually ignored the importance of truth in human intercourse" (Day 1991, 70). Day links this phenomenon with the present age of relativism:

> The problem is not that the relativists are entirely wrong: there are times when deception may be justified. But if we are to remain moral beings, both in our personal and professional lives, we should be prepared to defend our deviations from the path of truth based on some firm moral foundation. *Telling the truth never needs any moral justification; lying and deception do.* (Day 1991, 70)

Photojournalism and deception

Anybody who thinks that pictures cannot lie is simply uninformed – or very naive. People tend to believe implicitly what they see (or imagine that they see) and easily assume that a picture by definition represents "the truth". "We might exercise a little healthy scepticism about how representative the depicted scene was of what was actually going on..., but, as newspaper readers who have grown up with the conventions of photojournalism, we do not expect anything but a documentary photograph to accompany a news story" (Kieran et al. 1998, 126, 127). This makes deception in photojournalism potentially even more damaging to the newspaper's credibility than deception in written form.

This potential harm is not always completely overcome in "minor" or "well-intended" manipulation. Nigel Warburton asserts that "...what is wrong with lying is not that it tends to result in people acquiring false beliefs, but that it destroys the trust that is necessary for most co-operation and (the possibility of photographic) communication" (Kieran et al. 1998, 131). He goes on, offering this (understandably cynical) warning: "If trust were substantially undermined in this area, there would no longer be any point in sending photographers out to take news photographs. Provide them instead with access to a picture library and a computer and they will be able to come up with plausible-looking illustrations of whatever story print journalists care to write up" (Kieran et al. 1998, 132).

Three things can happen in photo manipulation: objects can be moved, they can be removed, and new details can be added. Even before the development of today's sophisticated imaging technology, pictures could be manipulated either to cut out or paste in some material. Nowadays this can be done without fear of detection. The electronic darkroom need not leave any trace of what the original picture should have looked like. Even a certain angle can misrepresent the truth: for example, two statesmen who are at odds with each other can be photographed whilst smiling at a photographer. The picture could then be manipulated in such a way so that they appear to be smiling at one another.

There are lots of examples of photographs that have been manipulated. In one instance, two Egyptian pyramids were moved closer to each other in order to fit the portrait format of the cover of *National Geographic* (Kieran et al. 1998, 123).[4] Warburton mentions that it is now common practice in fashion photography to enlarge the pupils of the eyes, or even to lengthen models'

legs. He concludes that "We can't trust what we see in photographs any more. Perhaps the only rational strategy in such circumstances is the Cartesian one of treating as false any belief acquired from looking at photographs, unless we can be absolutely certain that it is true" (Kieran et al. 1998, 123).

Different views

Many leading journalists maintain that the use of deception in the process of news-gathering is such a sensitive issue that it should be avoided altogether. The *Washington Post* does not allow any deception whatsoever. This is perfectly understandable in light of the Janet Cooke debacle of 1981. Cooke was a young reporter who tried to highlight the plight of heroin-addicted children on the streets of Washington, D. C. She produced gripping stuff on the life of an eight-year-old addict – and received a Pulitzer Prize for her efforts. The only problem was that the story, dubbed "Jimmy's World", was not true. She had made up this specific child. She lost both her job and her prize – and the newspaper lost a lot of credibility.

Karl Hausman quotes the following unequivocal statement by Benjamin Bradlee, executive editor of the *Washington Post*: "You can't break the law and you can't tell a lie... And you can't pass yourself off as someone you aren't" (Hausman 1992, 100). The *Seattle Times* agrees, saying its role is to find out the truth, not to obscure it. These, and other, journalists feel that no form of deception to obtain information is acceptable in a profession whose mission is truth-telling (Black et al. 1995, 119).

However, "others would argue that while deception is to be avoided, it may be acceptable in those rare instances in which the value of the information sought is of overwhelming importance, and the information can be obtained in no other way" (Black et al. 1995, 119). Some even feel it is the job of the press to do undercover work on public affairs of importance, and that deception is a journalistic tool to right serious social injustices. Is this position going too far? These journalists would stress that the distinction between forms of deception should always be kept in mind. For them, there is a difference "between outright lying and merely not revealing everything, between using hidden cameras in a public place and hiding cameras on the person of someone who is at the same time pretending to be somebody else" (Black et al. 1995, 119).

Ethical theories

Proponents of deontology and teleology will differ with each other on the question of deception. *Deontology* (duty-based ethics) is based upon certain principles, one of these being that the truth shall be spoken at all times. Under no circumstances is lying or deception allowed. This is despite the fact that truth-telling may cause serious harm. Truth is, as Kant argued, an absolute moral principle that should be applied to every situation and should be relevant in all circumstances (regardless of the consequences). In addition, the means are as important as the end. Just as the truth should be reported, the process of news-gathering should also be truthful.

Louis Day argues that, if rigidly applied, this duty-based approach to ethical decision-making is even more problematical when deception is not passive but active (Day 1991, 76). Whereas active deception involves overt misrepresentation, passive deception occurs whenever moral agents do not reveal their true identity or purpose. "Newspaper restaurant critics, for example, do not alert the manager of their presence for fear of influencing the quality of food and service accorded to them. This practice may be justified, because the critic is there to view the culinary

landscape from the perspective of the average consumer" (Day 1991, 76). Yet even this would be problematical for staunch deontologists.

Still, the deontological approach, whereby lying is taboo, does provide a good and necessary point of departure for the making of ethical decisions. The basic rule remains: the journalist is in the business of (reporting) the truth. But if this is taken as an absolute, we can easily ignore the uniqueness of events or situations. Situations can arise when "lying is taboo" cannot be your finishing point as well. What, for example, if serious corruption within the state can only be revealed if you, as a journalist, misrepresent yourself?

Utilitarians, on the other hand, who gauge the consequences of an act before making an ethical judgment, will argue that lying is acceptable as long as it is of some use to the public at large and in the public's interest. However, utilitarians would not easily assume that lies and deception are harmless: "The burden of proof is still on the moral agent to prove that a lie or deceptive act will promote the greatest good for the greatest number of people and that the benefits outweigh the harmful consequences" (Day 1991, 76). Unlike Kant, utilitarians stress the difference in degree between one lie and another, and weigh the consequences of each one: what good, and what harm, will it do to how many people? And, says Bok (1978, 49), that is exactly what journalists tend to do all the time. They tend to weigh up benefits against harm, and happiness against unhappiness.

The teleological approach is a more subtle and an equally important one. The consequences of the deception, both for the liar and the deceived, are indeed of great importance. So is the uniqueness of events and situations. But there are pitfalls in this approach as well: "The more complex the acts, the more difficult it becomes to produce convincing comparisons of their consequences" (Bok 1987, 49). It is difficult enough to gauge the consequences of a news report for one person, with all the different alternatives and their consequences, let alone to make estimates for several persons or long-term consequences. "The result is that, even apart from lying, those conflicts which are most difficult to resolve... cause as much disagreement among utilitarians as among everyone else" (Bok 1987, 49). The more complex a situation, then, the more difficult it is to "establish" the consequences for all involved.

Aristotle's *golden mean*, or virtue ethics, can provide a much-needed balance in this regard, especially "... in cases involving how much truth to reveal about a situation or the kind and scope of coverage to provide a news story" (Day 1991, 77). The golden mean can, for example, help journalists to exercise more restraint in covering sensational events like a terrorist hijacking (Day 1991, 77). According to Carl Hausman:

> The majority of opinion seems to rely on reasoning including both motivation and consequence, sort of a midpoint between consequentialist and non-consequentialist philosophies, and perhaps a good example of seeking a 'golden mean' between two extremes. In general, journalists condone deception when it is the only way to get a story and the story justifies special measures (the end justifies the means) but condemn deception when it is used indiscriminately or to gain privileges and access that could be dangerous or illegal, such as wearing a police uniform or impersonating a physician... (Hausman 1992, 102)

The Greek philosopher Plato argued that a person may lie in order to save a life, questioning whether the truth was always beneficial. "This advice, of course, blurs the distinction between fact and fiction and raises contemporary ethical questions concerning such issues as the use of composite characters in news stories and the use of the docudrama – the dramatic blending of fact and fiction – as a credible TV format for communicating historical events" (Day 1991, 52).

But not all lies have such a commendable motive. It is all too easy to manipulate the truth, to change the meaning of a word or a phrase ever so slightly to mix fact and fiction. Consider this example: Ulf Poschardt, a former editor of a weekly supplement of Germany's *Süddeutsche Zeitung*, was sacked in 2000 after it came to light that he had published fabricated "interviews" with Hollywood stars. A freelance worker based in Los Angeles, Tom Kummer, claimed to have interviewed, *inter alia*, Sharon Stone, Ivana Trump, and Courtney Love and submitted these "interviews" for publication. His fraud was uncovered when other Hollywood correspondents queried Kummer's "remarkable capacity" to make contact with the superstars. Kummer was apologetic and called his work "concept journalism".

The temptation to use deception in the news-gathering process, then, is alive and well in journalism. And that is perfectly understandable. "When newspapers or stations receive phone calls about violence in an orphanage, maggots in the bandages of patients at a nursing home, mechanics cheating on repairs, deception becomes one possible alternative for breaking the story. The important question, then, is whether deception can ever be ethically justified" (Christians et al. 1995, 52).

Jennifer Jackson puts it like this: "There remain two forms of justification for telling a lie: that your duty not to lie is overridden by another perfect duty more pressing in the circumstances, which makes telling the lie morally obligatory, or that your duty not to lie is overridden by another imperfect duty more pressing in the circumstances, which makes telling the lie morally permissible" (Belsey et al. 1992, 109). Doing it suggests that winning a prize, beating the competition, getting the story with less expense of time and resources, and doing it because "the others already did it" can never be used to justify deception (Black et al. 1995, 125).

Criteria for a "just lie"

In an effort to determine when the use of deception at whatever level might be justified, the participants in an ethical decision-making seminar at the Poynter Institute for Media Studies used the golden mean and formulated the following criteria (Black et al. 1995, 120) for a "just lie":

1 When the information sought is of profound importance. It must be of vital public interest, such as revealing great "system failure" at the top levels, or it must prevent profound harm to individuals.

2 When all other alternatives for obtaining the same information have been exhausted.

3 When the journalists involved are willing to disclose fully and openly the nature of the deception and the reason for it to those involved and to the public.

4 When the individuals involved and their news organization apply excellence, through outstanding craftsmanship as well as the commitment of time and funding needed, to pursue the story fully.

5 When the harm prevented by the information revealed through deception outweighs any harm caused by the act of deception.

6 When the journalists involved have conducted a meaningful, collaborative, and deliberative decisionmaking process in which they weigh:

- the consequences (short- and long-term) of the deception on those being deceived;
- the impact on journalistic credibility;
- the motivations for their actions;
- the deceptive act in relation to their editorial mission;
- the legal implications of the action;
- consistency of their reasoning and their action.

Only when *all* these criteria have been met may a journalist consider lying or the use of deception as a way of getting the relevant information.

It is essential for journalists to challenge themselves and each other to meet all of these criteria to justify lying. It is equally important for such soul-searching to take place at *the front end* of the reporting process, not after the fact (Black et al. 1995, 124).

No, but...

So, then, are journalists allowed to use deception? The answer to this simple but important question is: "no, but..."

> The simplest answer to the problems of lying, at least in principle, is to rule out all lies. (Bok 1978, 33)[5]

But it is also necessary here to use the golden mean and make some important distinctions. The *level* of deception obviously varies from case to case. It is one thing to operate a hidden camera in a public place, and quite another to go to a restaurant as a critic. In the latter case, you obviously cannot tell the manager what you are there for – it would defeat your purpose (which is not to mislead, but to tell readers about the food and the service). This is a much softer kind of misrepresentation and, although a form of deception, it is not in the same category as operating a hidden camera in a private place.

Karl Hausman argues that the need for deception has to do with "...the *amount* of artifice used by the reporter ... and the *necessity* of the artifice" (Hausman 1992, 98). If a reporter, he argues, anonymously takes a car to a repair shop to evaluate that dealer, then that misrepresentation is acceptable. Anybody could bring a car to that shop. "So when the amount of artifice is low, acceptance is high (in the public's eye). Too much artifice – pretending to be a police officer or doctor – brings almost universal condemnation" (Hausman 1992, 99). Remember that if a journalist goes overboard, the focus may fall on the practices and not on the story (Hausman 1992, 102). Deception can cause the profession serious harm, if used incorrectly. "Those who deceive can cause great harm to the credibility of journalism and may harm individuals who are deceived" (Black et al. 1995, 119).

It must be kept in mind that journalists do not have special privileges. They are members of the public, trying to serve the public, asking questions on behalf of the public, writing for the public. "Only if the average citizen, faithful to the ethical norms of society, would be willing to use deception to get a story could a journalist justify doing likewise" (Day 1991, 77). Day adds that "...regardless of what justifications are used for occasional deceptions, the line should always be drawn at violations of law, because illegal conduct by reporters undermines the respect for law" (Day 1991, 77).

Therefore, the most responsible position to take is probably to avoid deception, unless in the most extreme circumstances, in which the value of the information sought is of overriding public interest and can be obtained in no other way. In addition, no journalist should ever attempt any of these methods on their own. A process of consultation and deliberation is essential. The final decision must always be the responsibility of the editor.

The general rule for photojournalism is never manipulate a photograph. If, for whatever reason, a photograph *must* be manipulated, the newspaper *must* inform the public about it. If that is not a newspaper's policy, it can lose its credibility faster than lightning. This also goes for minor deceptions: "Toleration of minor deceptions for the sake of truth is the first step down a slippery slope towards general deception with total disregard for the truth. If you allow people to manipulate photographs without informing their viewers, then you will soon find yourself allowing photographers to invent reality" (Kieran et al. 1998, 132).

A bit too low

The following case shows how the "soft" manipulation of a photograph can damage a newspaper's credibility if the public is not informed about it.

In the most important case of photo manipulation in the history of South African journalism, and probably in the world as well, *Die Burger* in 1994 digitally altered a photo of the newly elected President, Nelson Mandela, to optimally utilize the available space on its front page. Mandela was standing on a balcony overlooking the Grand Parade in Cape Town. As he freed two white doves, symbolizing peace, the cameras were working overtime. However, the best picture was taken a split second too late. The distance between Mandela's outstretched hands and the doves in flight was a good 1,5 m – leaving a dead space in the centre of the picture.

Stefanie Hefer, the then chief sub who took the decision, said in an interview that the decision had previously been taken to "go big" with the event on the paper's front page. There was, however, only one suitable photograph available, which, if used as it was, would show only blue sky and the dove above the fold. The solution was to alter the "problem dove" electronically by bringing it closer to Mandela's hand. This was done *without* informing the public. Hefer's explanation is interesting:

I had (and still have) no problem in taking the decision to have the photograph manipulated. The point is that we did not recreate (alter) reality; we did not create a false image that never was there. The image *was* there, a split second before the flash went off. Only the photographer was not able to capture that very moment.

The then editor of *Die Burger*, Mr Ebbe Dommisse, later emphasized that, if there is no other way than to manipulate a photograph electronically, the public must under all circumstances be informed about it. His concern was obviously the potential loss of the credibility of the newspaper.

The manipulation of Mandela's photograph caused a worldwide sensation – so much so that the Poynter Institute uses this incident as a prime example of photo manipulation.

Hefer recalls a similar decision that she took in 1995. It was moments after the South African rugby team had won the World Cup at Ellis Park in Johannesburg. President Mandela was on the field with the South African captain, François Pienaar, who was holding the trophy above his head. Hefer had to choose between two pictures. There were, however, problems with both. On the one photograph the eyes of either Mandela or Pienaar (Hefer cannot remember clearly which one it was) were closed – but the smiles were excellent. The other photograph had open eyes – but no smiles. Hefer then decided to manipulate one of the pictures in order to have both open eyes and smiles. "The same principle applies in this case. The photographer was not able to capture the grand moment. But it was there. We did not alter reality", Hefer explained.

Analysis

Warburton's warnings concerning photo manipulation, as previously discussed, must at all times be taken seriously. Hefer rightly distinguishes between creating "reality that was there" (let us call it "soft manipulation", for the lack of a better term) and creating "reality that was not there" (we will call this "hard manipulation"). This distinction must be clear: hard manipulation, the alteration of reality, amounts to a downright lie,

to misrepresentation, and to nothing less than the deliberate misleading of the public – where the journalistic search for truth is forsaken. This can *never* be acceptable and *always* amounts to irresponsible journalism of the highest order.

The fundamental reason why there is indeed a distinction between "*soft*" and "*hard*" manipulation, is the respective motive of the ethical agents. In soft manipulation, the motive is not to mislead, but to inform. The motive is therefore not under suspicion, as is apparent in the Hefer examples. The opposite is true in hard manipulation.

Yet, a word of warning is appropriate here. Soft manipulation still amounts to deception, even if the motive is not to mislead the public. Once the public understands that photographs can be manipulated, and once a newspaper starts to do that without informing the public about it, the newspaper's credibility becomes fatally undermined. In the Mandela case, the public should have been informed about the manipulation. Dommisse's direction on this matter is heartening.

Paedophile's home filmed

The following case illustrates the principle that the home of a convicted criminal can be filmed secretly, as long as it is in the interests of the truth and of the public.

On 25 May 2000 the Cape Town Regional Court refused to extend bail for Benjamin Webber Emmerson, a 61-year-old retired accountant, after it was adjudicated that he had violated his bail conditions. He had been convicted in 1999 on six of seven counts of violating the Sexual Offences Act by abusing underage youths, paying them to have sex with him.

The main reason that Magistrate Vic Gibson refused bail was evidence from e.tv footage which showed street children loitering around Emmerson's home while he was on bail during his trial. E.tv journalists staked out Emmerson's home during the trial, and found that he had been in regular contact with street children, enticing them with offers of food and money. E.tv footage from 9 May showed three boys entering the alcove leading to Emmerson's house. It appeared that they spent 30 minutes in the alcove.

Prosecutor Bronwyn Hendry conceded that this did not prove that the boys had entered

Emmerson's house, but argued that it pointed to the fact that the boys loitered around his house at night. This was used as evidence that Emmerson had seriously violated his bail conditions. Emmerson denied any guilt on his part. Street children loiter in that area, but he never went out to speak to them, he said. He admitted that he greeted them when he met them on the streets and gave them money and food at his door. Emmerson added he felt sorry for them. He had not violated his bail conditions as the children had approached him, he claimed.

Peter Torrington, Emmerson's counsel, objected to his client being taken into custody on the strength of media information. According to Torrington, there was no evidence that his client would abscond, and said Emmerson already had been granted R2 000 bail after a formal application. Hendry argued that "bail was only valid pending judgment in a case, and did not automatically extend if an accused was found guilty", the *Cape Times* reported on 25 May. According to her, "the case was now more serious and it was in the interests of justice for Emmerson to be kept in custody until sentence was passed".

After viewing the TV footage, Gibson said that "due to the serious nature of the sexual offences, an extension of bail would lead to public shock and outrage at the criminal justice system" (*Cape Times* 26 May 2000). According to Gibson, media interest and protests by street children also militated against the extension of bail to Emmerson. Gibson commented that the children must have had some incentive to go to Emmerson's house regularly. He added he had been perturbed that various interest groups in this case (e.tv, NGOs, the Directorate of Public Prose-

cutions, and the police) "did not take some form of action earlier so that the rights of children would not be violated further".

Analysis

It would be highly inappropriate to attempt to make any sort of judgment on the merits of the court's decision. However, there are some ethical issues from the media's perspective that need to be addressed.

Of course, this was not a case of active deception. Nobody was actively deceived, misled, or lied to, although a hidden camera was used. How ethical was this action? Remember that the person in question was not an ordinary private person, but a convicted paedophile who had abused street children and was applying for his bail to be extended. It can therefore rightly be said that it was in the public's (and especially in the street children's) interest to know if he might possibly continue with his sexual predation. The street children were probably safer than they would have been had Emmerson received bail. The interest of the public at large was served, and the result was good for everybody concerned (except for Emmerson, of course) – a teleologist's dream.

Deontologists would presumably also be quite happy with e.tv's *modus operandi*. Nobody was actively deceived, and the truth (which is the media's duty to uncover in the first place) was served. In this process e.tv fulfilled its role as watchdog. An interesting question, however, is why e.tv picked Emmerson's house to film. Why not the house of any other of the thousands of people who are out on bail?

Asked to lie

The need not to comply when asked to lie, even if it is for a good cause, is the subject of the following case.

The media is often (rightly or wrongly) blamed for manipulating the news. But what happens if the shoe is on the other foot? What if someone tries to abuse you as a journalist? One example of the abuse of the media is the action of a police media liaison officer in Cape Town in July 1994. Captain Wicus Holtzhausen approached the *Cape Times* to write a fake report about a Bonteheuwel café owner, Abdullah Parker, 41, to say that Parker had been murdered, which was in fact not the case.

The scheme was an attempt to catch a business rival of Parker, who was thought to have hired somebody to kill Parker for R15 000. Only if this rival believed that Parker had been murdered would he pay the killer. Holtzhauzen wanted to provide this rival with some "proof" so that he could catch him handing over the money.

When Holtzhausen told them of his plan, the *Cape Times* refused to report that Parker had been murdered. The next day the captain approached *The Argus* with the same story. This time, however, he was more circumspect and did not disclose the fact that the information was false. *The Argus* reported the "death" of Parker in good faith. The rival was then arrested after he allegedly paid the R15 000 to the "hit man", who showed him the false report in *The Argus* as "proof" that the murder had been carried out.

Holtzhausen, who was severely reprimanded by police public relations commander Raymond Dowd, was quick to apologize. He said in a written statement that he regretted any harm to any institution or person and that he had misled *The Argus* because he had wanted to save a life. He "saw no other way out" because the life of a person was at stake (and had been saved) – the deception had been "vital in a crime prevention operation".

The media's reaction was fierce. The *Cape Times* wrote in its editorial on July 14 that this incident highlighted the necessity for scrapping the police media liaison structure, calling the incident "a creaky throwback to the total onslaught era when the police, faced with various states of emergency, followed the defence force in establishing a section to control and veto news about itself and its actions, backed up by a paralyzing web of laws".

Under the heading "Cynical manipulation" *The Argus* wrote, *inter alia*:

> The incident implies a belief within the police service that the media can be cynically manipulated by policemen for their own use. Although it might be claimed in some circles that the false information led to an arrest and the prevention of a murder, that end cannot justify the means.

Newspapers are watchdogs of the truth. They have a responsibility to the public to publish information which is accurate and dependable. With the planting of this incorrect report – published in good faith – the integrity of the reporter and the newspaper could have been called into question, *The Argus* protested in no uncertain terms: "In his letter of apology to *The Argus*, Colonel Raymond Dowd said: 'I can assure you this is not the normal procedure of operating and will not occur again'. We will make sure of that."

Analysis

By *intentionally* misleading the media (in order to catch offenders), the police undermine their own credibility just as badly as the media's own credibility is undermined when it intentionally misleads the public. However, this book is on media ethics and not on police ethics. The *Cape Times* must be commended for refusing to publish the story, for the simple reason that the story was not true. If that newspaper had published the story, knowing full well that it was not true, it would have rightly been seen as collaborating with the police. This would undoubtedly have resulted in a serious loss of credibility.

But that is not all. If the media are seen as collaborating with the police, all sorts of other problems will emerge, for, by definition, collaborating means sacrificing your own independence. And what if the media start collaborating with one group (setting itself up against another)? It has been stated that the basic ethical maxims for the media are: maximize truth, minimize harm, *and act independently*. The upholding of the media's independence is of vital importance in any democratic state.

This is not to say the fact that Parker's life could have been saved by a false report should not have been considered as a justification for publishing a false report. The true consequentialist would probably have published the story, believing the good of saving a life outweighs the bad of reporting a lie. Fortunately, however, the truth emerged as the winner between these two conflicting values.

The indignation of *The Argus* at being abused is perfectly understandable. In fact, the sharp reaction of both newspapers must be welcomed. However, one very important question remains: why did the media not demand that Holtzhausen be replaced? Surely that would have gone a long way towards restoring the lost faith in that specific department of the police service? How can the media ever trust this specific police spokesperson again? Or the department he works for?

The one lesson that emerges from this story is quite sinister: it is as difficult for the media to verify reports from spokespeople as it is for the public to verify media reports. True reporting is built on a relationship of trust. If that trust is broken, it is almost impossible to restore it.

| Dummy accidents

The following case illustrates how the use of deceptive methods by the media can sometimes be justified if these are in the interest of the truth and of the public.

The investigative journalists of *Carte Blanche*, M-Net's popular current-affairs programme, are certainly not shy to use deception – whether through hidden cameras or staged events – to obtain information. The two cases presented here are examples of how they do it.[6]

On 19 September 1999 *Carte Blanche* asked why ambulances sometimes take so long to arrive at the scene of an accident, and exposed the links between individuals on duty in the emergency control rooms and drivers of tow trucks "who will do anything to get there first".

It is well known that, in an accident, response time can mean the difference between life and death. So paramedics should be among the first emergency workers to arrive at an accident scene. "Ironically, the people who normally pull up to a scene minutes after an accident, are there for the cars – not the injured." Journalists from *Carte Blanche* spent several nights riding with Johannesburg's response units to see for themselves "whether tow-truckers were indeed so quick off the mark".

"It wasn't long before a pattern emerged. Time after time – no matter how quickly we responded – truckers beat us to every accident scene... So how did they manage to win the race when technically they shouldn't be able to?" It turned out that there was more to it than the scanning of the police, traffic, and emergency radio frequencies.

Eddie Duncan was one of the few truckers who were willing to speak to *Carte Blanche*. "We intercept the radio signals – it's been like that for years. But now there's a better step – the phone. The cellphone has taken over via the control centre. Before they can even dispatch emergency units they phone tow-truck drivers." Liz Stander, the owner of a breakdown company, said: "The guy gets phoned and he pulls out of the hangout... He gets calls from the control centres – fire, ambulance, and 10111".

Carte Blanche spoke to another trucker called Slurpy. One of the programme's undercover investigators filmed Slurpy. "Ashi's paying too much. R600 a car. I'm not mad enough to pay R600 a car", he said. When he was confronted by *Carte Blanche* about the payoffs, he said he could not remember anything, although he admitted that "the people in the control rooms" are involved.

Meanwhile, *Carte Blanche* received reports that officers at the Johannesburg Traffic Department were selling accident information to towing companies. Police investigators Charl Fourie and Richard Binder were already working on the case when *Carte Blanche* approached them about forming a team. They manufactured a "sting operation".

We set up a fake accident scene and Charl phoned the Traffic Control centre. Officer Dries van Wyk took the call, which went like this:
Fourie: 'I just drove past Kitchener, Milner, and Marathon. There's an accident. If you can just send some people to come and look please.'
Van Wyk: 'Now what street was that, sir? Kitchener and what?'

Fourie: 'Well, the intersection shows Kitchener, Milner, Marathon. It's three or four roads that cut together.'
Van Wyk: 'OK, sir, I'll send somebody there.'

Van Wyk should have taken down the caller's details and asked whether anyone at the scene was injured – but he didn't. Instead, he dialled a number on a cellphone. "Someone answered the call and promises to phone back. Less than a minute later, officer Van Wyk is on his cellphone. In this time, Van Wyk should have dispatched a traffic officer to the scene and alerted the ambulance control centre of injuries – which, in this case, was clearly impossible... since he never asked if anyone was hurt." Minutes later, a Super Towing truck pulled up at the scene of the supposed accident. Not seeing anything to tow, the driver moved on, but not without first making a quick cellphone call. Then Fourie phoned the radio room again. This time Van Wyk did ask for accident details. Minutes later, drivers raced to the scene. During all this time no call had been made on the emergency service radio. Why? Because Van Wyk never dispatched a traffic officer to the scene. That happened only 27 minutes after the accident was reported.

Two weeks later, *Carte Blanche* set up another dummy accident – and discovered that someone had stabbed a sharp rod through their hidden camera. When *Carte Blanche* later confronted Van Wyk, he denied having called any tow truck because it is against departmental policy. The towing companies denied any knowledge of this practice, but some did promise to investigate the matter.

Undercover footage of a conversation with a Super Towing employee suggests that management would have to investigate a few people for payoffs... Further investigations revealed that in one month there had been a substantial amount of illicit communication between the radio room and Super Towing drivers – 194 conversations to be exact...

Three people have allegedly died because of this practice.

The industry doesn't seem to have a fixed rate, but word on the street is that an accident tip-off can sell for anything from R200 to R600. All the call centre operator has to do to secure the deal is delay an emergency dispatch call unit until the tow trucker he tipped off gets to the scene.

Meanwhile victims can do little but wait for medical attention – and hope it doesn't come too late.

Analysis

Carte Blanche did not only make use of a hidden camera, it also explicitly lied by staging "accidents" that never took place, misleading the supposed perpetrators. How ethical is this action?

Several things should be kept in mind:

- *Carte Blanche* did not mislead the public at large, only the supposed perpetrators.
- The public's interest was served. The opening up of the scandal could have saved lives and was therefore of profound public importance.

- The possible harm prevented by this act of deception outweighs by far any possible negative consequences for the media.
- It is not likely that there was another way of getting the desired information.
- The journalists fully and openly disclosed the nature of the deception and the reason for it to the public.

The Poynter Institute's criteria for a just lie were fulfilled. However, this case is definitely not a deontologist's dream because deception was used as a method of gaining information. However, this deception helped to serve the interests of the truth (which is the prime duty of the media) and, in so doing, also served the interests of the public. The teleologist, on the other hand, will surely enjoy this one. The result is what counts.

| Teaming up

This case illustrates that teaming up with undercover agents can work for the media – but it can also be a dangerous practice.

Carte Blanche did a story on hospital theft on 30 August 1998. The presenter stated that over the last three years over R12 million worth of medical supplies and pharmaceutical products had been stolen from state hospitals. It was claimed that not much had been done about it, and certain government departments claimed the thefts had been exaggerated.

Carte Blanche teamed up with a private investigator who had been hired by a pharmaceutical company to find evidence of theft within their organization. This man used a secret

camera to show the M-Net team how easy it was to steal drugs from Hillbrow Hospital. A hospital employee received a "dummy shopping list" with drugs, syringes, and cotton wool balls on it for only R150 – much less than what the goods were worth. Some of the goods bought had already expired.

Other examples of corruption that were uncovered:

- The private investigator, using a secret camera and posing as a doctor, purchased three bottles of blood pressure tablets for R1 500 at a pharmaceutical company. The sale of those tablets would have amounted to R15 000.
- A pharmacist in Hillbrow accepted stolen drugs and paid very little for them.

- Linen bearing the Johannesburg General Hospital logo was illegally bought for a mere R50.
- An entrepreneur randomly decided on his own expiry date of drugs and reprinted the labels on the bottles of the expired drugs.

Carte Blanche said it took three years to put this story together. The relevant authorities were informed of how wide-ranging the theft of medicine and equipment from state hospitals really was. "However, there had been no obvious action taken to remedy the situation."

Analysis

Again, all the rules (see the Poynter Institute's criteria for a just lie) were followed. The harm prevented also outweighed the possible harm to *Carte Blanche*'s credibility. It was in the interest of the truth and of the public.

However, quite another ethical matter is at stake here, namely: how ethical is it for the media to team up with whoever in order to uncover corruption? In this case, *Carte Blanche* teamed up with a private investigator working for a pharmaceutical company. The latter had hired this private investigator not because it was concerned with corruption as such, but because the corruption affected its own bottom line.

It is a recipe for disaster if the media allow themselves to be used (misused) by people or companies for the latter's sake. The danger of the media losing their independence must not be underestimated. This could easily lead to a serious loss of credibility. Remember the basic ethical maxims: maximize truth, minimize harm, and *act independently*. *Carte Blanche* would argue, with some justification, that it did not sacrifice its independence. However, journalists should never lose sight of the looming danger.

Another question: why were the alleged perpetrators not named? Once some sort of corruption is uncovered, it is in the public interest that the media mention names. Not only does this make the story more credible, but it also adds to its effectiveness by enabling the public to make responsible and informed decisions. Let it be said, however, that it is not for the sake of the police that names should be mentioned. It is not the job of the media to apprehend perpetrators.

Notes

[1] Some of the earliest condemnations of lying are contained in judicial laws against false witnesses and perjury, such as the Code of Hammurabi and the Ten Commandments (Day 1991, 68, 69).

[2] See the chapter on neutrality and objectivity.

[3] Gerald is emeritus professor in the School of Journalism of the University of Minnesota.

[4] For details of this case and other similar cases, see Fred Ritchen, *In our own image*, New York: Aperture, 1990.

[5] The impact of St Augustine's thinking on this matter is immense. He claimed that God forbids all lies and that liars therefore endanger their immortal souls. He defined lying as having one thing in one's heart and uttering another with the intention to deceive (Bok 1978, 33).

[6] All the *Carte Blanche* information and quotes were obtained from the programme's website at www.carteblanche.co.za

5 | **Fairness**

Fairness first and foremost has to do with proper balance and context.

Introduction

Each and every journalist wants to be fair in his or her reporting – or, vice versa, does not want to be accused of being unfair. These statements sound reasonable, but this depends on your definition of fairness.

Forget fair?

It is not easy to define the word "fairness", as can be seen from the following example. Carl Hausman (1992, 54 and following) quotes John Parry, the editor of the *News-Tribune* (Rome, Georgia), who advises his fellow journalists to "forget fair". Parry uses this real-life example to explain: two men forced a night clerk at a con-

venience store in Rome to hand over the store's cash receipts. They then raped the clerk. The victim's name was not reported (which was, ethically speaking, the right thing to do), but the *News-Tribune* did mention the store's name and location.

A representative of the store claimed that this reporting was "unfair". If you identify the store, you also identify the victim, it was argued. The name of the store should therefore not have been mentioned, the representative said.

Parry wondered what a "fair" story would amount to, given the circumstances. "The only way the story could have been written to satisfy this complainant, Perry says, was 'A woman was raped last night someplace here'" (Hausman 1992, 55).

Thomas Griffiths, a news critic at *Time* (1986, 61), concluded: "People involved in the news do not really want fairness, he (Parry) insists, they want 'favor, exemption, protection from public notice'... They want only the 'good news published...' Parry believed that a newspaper's duty is to be 'accurate, timely, incisive and pertinent. Forget fair'" (*Time* 1986, 61).

Several questions arise from this: what does Parry understand fairness to be? Is it really true that people don't want fairness, as Parry would like us to believe? And *even* if the public does not demand fairness from the media, is that enough cause for journalists to "forget fair"?

No!

Says Hausman: "An essential difficulty with 'being fair' revolves around the reality that many factors contribute to our perception of fairness, word choice, the selection of elements which comprise a story, the perspective of the journalist and the occasional loss of perspective when a journalist bends over backward to hide his or her perspective, and the mechanics of news gathering and news routines" (1992, 54). But should that prevent journalists from striving towards fairness? Of course not! Fairness should be an important issue for all journalists because unfairness causes harm. Remember the most basic ethical principles for journalists: maximum truth, *minimum harm*. The more unfair you are, the greater harm you are likely to cause. This must be avoided at all costs. Not only is it completely unnecessary, but it can eventually also be detrimental to you as well as to your company.

Unlike Parry, the BBC makes no bones about the importance of fairness: "BBC programmes should be based on fairness..." (*Producers' Guidelines* 1996, 28). Simple words, without much qualification, or ifs or buts.

This is important to everyone involved. It reflects concern for the interests of the programme, the interests of the people who appear in it and the interests of the audience. All these interests are important, although none of them is automatically more important than others. (*Producers' Guidelines* 1996, 28)

Aspects of fairness

It certainly is essential to come to some sort of a definition of fairness. But let us first consider the following aspects of fairness:

- The *choice of words* in a news report is important. Words have semantic fields, and the same word can even have different meanings. In addition, the emphasis that is put on facts can distort their meaning. To be fair means to choose words to the best of your ability that justly reflect the reality you are reporting on.
- Without the quest for *perspective* (or context) no story can be properly communicated.
- The so-called *Rashomon effect*[1] – the phenomenon that people have their own (unique) interpretation of the same event – must always be kept in mind. The more complex the situation, the more important the journalist's awareness of the Rashomon effect becomes. It could even be that two witnesses fundamentally differ from each other about what they (think they) saw. To choose the account of one witness above the other means that you have not given your sources equal opportunity to portray the truth. That is unfair.
- Fairness means *balance*. A balanced report is one that looks at all the sides to an issue. If one concerned party is overlooked, the report cannot be fair.

However, fairness does not always imply that a journalist should *mechanically* balance every story by giving two opposing parties 50/50 coverage. Fairness does not always mean "equal opportunities"; it can also entail a *moderate amount*. One problem with fairness, Hausman argues, is that the common technique used to "balance" the news with mitigating quotes can easily compel reporters to give Judas equal space for his side of the story (Hausman 1992, 55). Consider this theoretical example: political party A has no representatives in Parliament, Party B has ten, Party C fifty, Party D sixty and Party E one hundred. The issue is whether Parliament must move from Cape Town to Pretoria. You are assigned to get reactions from the various political parties. Does fairness mean that you give 20% coverage to each of the five parties? Certainly not! In this case, fairness will imply that a moderate amount of space or time be given to Party A – but certainly more to Parties B, C, D, and E. It cannot be "a sort of eternal compromise – treading the middle ground so as not to offend or give any hint of sensationalism" (Hausman 1992, 58).

Yet it must be said that you are on thin ice when it comes to the above. As stated previously, Hausman says the technique to balance the news can easily result in compelling journalists to give Judas equal space for his side of the story. While it is true that fairness must not become a phobic search to give the same amount of coverage to both sides, it could easily happen that the "lesser" side of your story gets underplayed. Wouldn't many people, for example, just love to hear Judas' side of the story? Therefore, even if you are moderate in the presentation of your story, you could be unfair. There is certainly a fine line between equal opportunities and moderate coverage. Every important side of any given issue must be given due consideration.

We can be unfair not only in the end product of our work, but also in the way in which we gather and process the news (Hausman 1992, 64). *Element selection* is concerned with the difficult task of determining what goes into a news story. The content could even be altered after the event. For example, a TV news reporter can re-ask (and even rephrase) a question after a news source has made a statement, thereby giving the interview a totally different complexion (Hausman 1992, 64). That is definitely not fair.

Defining "fair"

According to the Oxford English Dictionary, fairness means, *inter alia*, ample, just, equitable, of moderate quality or amount, according to rules, above board, straightforward, and equal opportunities. Black et al. define fairness as "*pursuing the truth with both vigor and compassion, and reporting information without favoritism, self-interest, or prejudice*" (Black et al. 1995, 53). What is needed is "a basic sense of open-mindedness, avoiding biased reporting, stereotypical portrayals, and unsubstantiated allegations" (Black et al. 1995, 53).

There have been various other attempts to define this concept. When a group of reporters had an opportunity to react to questions from Media Studies Center Executive Director Bob Giles (*The Freedom Forum Online*, 16 December 1997) on a definition of fairness, they said: "weighing all sides", "presenting all sides in context", "looking at least at two sides to an issue", "being able to sleep at night", and "rarely if ever having to apologize for what you have written or broadcast". Chris Tollefson of the *Star–Tribune* (Casper, Wyoming) has said: "I know I've been fair when both sides complain".

Explaining what the BBC means by fairness, the *Producers' Guidelines* states that programme-makers should be "as clear as they can" about the nature of the programme and its purpose. The contributors have a right to know what the programme is about, what kind of contribution they are expected to make, and whether their contribution is to be live or recorded and whether it is likely to be edited.

The need for fairness applies equally to people asked for help or advice in the preparation of programmes. They should not have a wrong impression about why they were contacted. (*Producers' Guidelines* 1996, 28)

Any deviation from this stance "should happen only when there is a clear public interest, and when dealing with serious illegal or antisocial activity". And, again in the interest of fairness, all embargoes should be honoured (*Producers' Guidelines* 1996, 30).

"Fair"

So, then, here is an attempt to define this elusive term. Fairness is firstly an honest attempt to:

- balance your report in such a way that no party is misrepresented either by your choice of words or by the lack of the proper context (that would be unjust);
- ensure that all parties get their say (equality);
- give coverage to different parties in relation to their importance (moderation).

It seems that fairness, at least in the media-ethical sense of the word, boils down to *proper balance and the right context*. If those elements are absent, you have in some way not done justice to someone. Hausman's definition of fairness as "presenting the most accurate possible portrayal of events within their proper context" (Hausman 1992, 58) is therefore spot on.

Other issues

Quotes

Chapter 3 dealt with the question of what to do with quotations containing inaccurate or misleading information. Suffice to say here that journalists should be fair when dealing with such quotes. Hausman (1992, 129) advises not to print a statement out of context "when you know that simply printing the statement will mislead; use background material to paint a full picture".

It is also sometimes necessary (or fair) to protect people against themselves. Consider this scenario (discounting possible libel): a journalist interviews a worker – let us call him Claude – in connection with possible fraud by his immediate superior (James). Claude has never talked to the press before, and is very nervous. He also despises his boss. In a moment of emotion, Claude says: "Of course James is guilty! I am glad that this has come to light now; it has been going on for too long!" However, as the interview progresses, you get the feeling that Claude did not really mean what he said at the beginning of the interview. Later Claude confesses that he based his statements on hearsay and overstated in an emotional moment.

What do you do? Do you say: "Ah, you silly, now I have got these really juicy quotes! These are Claude's own words! Now this story will make the headlines!" Or do you say: "Well, Claude did stick his neck out. But in all fairness, if I include these quotes, will it really portray his intentions (and therefore the truth)?" An honourable journalist may just decide that the latter is the best option. This scenario changes dramatically, however, if Claude is a politician or a public official. They should not only know better, but the public has the right to know when officials are not able to comment in a reserved and balanced way.

The Fairness Doctrine

The histories of the print and broadcast media differ quite substantially. In 1949 the Federal Communications Commission (FCC), which regulates broadcasting and telecommunications in the US, formulated a policy which was later called the Fairness Doctrine.[2] The intention was "to guide radio and television station operators in dealing with issues of controversy" for, "if not everyone can have a radio or TV station of their own, then broadcasters have an affirmative obligation to see that all views are represented" (Grossberg 1998, 385).

In this process, the matter of fairness became a legal issue. The Fairness Doctrine basically required some degree of balance in the presentation of issues that are controversial. If the broadcaster supported one side of an issue, he or she was obliged to air contrasting viewpoints on the matter. This was later extended to include the requirement that if an individual was attacked, the broadcaster was required to inform that person and offer airtime for a reply.

Of course, the broadcast industry was heavily opposed to the Fairness Doctrine. Grossberg (1998, 385) cites the following as the main reasons for their criticism:

- The broadcasters, not the government, should decide what goes on air and what does not – using the libertarian argument of the free marketplace of ideas.
- Broadcasters would be discouraged from airing the views of a controversial side and would indeed steer clear of all controversies.
- New technology would ensure that more and more channels would become available to the public, which meant that less regulation would be needed.

In the 1980s the opposing forces triumphed over proponents of the Fairness Doctrine. In 1987 the FCC voted unanimously to suspend it (though not to repeal it). This meant that broadcasters were effectively relieved of direct legal requirements to be fair. The equal time rule (requiring broadcasters to provide equal time in comparable parts of the day to all candidates for political office) remained, however. The broadcasters argued, though, that they were still morally and ethically bound to fulfil their social responsibility role of being fair.

Public relations and advertisements

The public expects journalists to be unbiased (fair) and to report the truth as fully as possible. "On the other hand, consumers realize that public relations (PR) practitioners and advertisers are advocates and do not expect them to do anything that would be contrary to their self-interest or the interests of their clients" (Day 1991, 72). Hence the question: how much truth should be revealed by public relations practitioners and advertisers? Under what circumstances may these people withhold information that might be important to customers? Do the basic rules of fairness apply to the fields of public relations and advertisements as well?

Louis Day argues convincingly that journalistic standards cannot be entirely applicable to these other forms of media (Day 1991, 75). PR practitioners and advertisers are in the business of persuading. They are advocates of an idea or a product. "They come to the marketplace with a bias, and there is nothing wrong with that. Although we expect advertisers and PR personnel to adhere to the threshold requirement of truth – that is, that they not knowingly disseminate inaccurate information – they have no ethical mandate to provide balance in their public proclamations" (Day 1991, 75). But be careful here: there is a moral imperative to disclose fully all the relevant information, especially when the health or safety of the public is at risk (Day 1991, 75).

Aristotle's golden mean can be helpful in certain instances "…in an attempt to maintain that delicate balance between social responsibility and corporate self-interest" (Day 1991, 75). For instance, a beer commercial could contain an admonition to the audience not to drink and drive.

However, there are also some pitfalls in the business of persuading. The way that Castle Lager used, or rather misused, its gold medal (awarded by the Brewing Industry International Awards 2000) in advertising its product is a case in point (*Rapport* 2 July 2000). In a marketing campaign, Castle Lager claimed to be "the best lager in the world". Namibian Breweries then took South African Breweries (SAB) to task, saying that this advertisement was misleading – Castle Lager had received a gold medal in a certain class only.

The matter was taken to the Advertising Association of Namibia (AAN), who found that the advertisement broke the users' trust and exploited their lack of experience and knowledge. The AAN took the matter to the South African Advertising Standards Authority, and SAB subsequently undertook to withdraw the advertisement.

A checklist

Consider the following checklist for fairness by Black et al. (1995, 71):

- Is the meaning distorted by over- or under-emphasis?
- Are facts and quotes in proper context?
- Have you given the story the length and display appropriate to its importance, and have you presented it with dignity and professionalism?
- Are the headlines and teasers warranted by the text of the story?
- Have you done your best to report all sides of the story, or, just as problematical, have you portrayed two artificially polarized points of view?
- Have you been compassionate in your reporting?
- Have all relevant people, particularly those who may be affected or harmed, been given an opportunity to reply? If they have not been reached or have no comment, have you explained why?
- If sources are not fully identified, is there a justifiable reason?
- When substantive errors or distortions appear in your paper or on the air, do you admit and correct them voluntarily, promptly, and with a prominence comparable to that given the inaccurate statement?
- Are you fostering an open dialogue with your readers, viewers, and listeners? Do others, both in the newsroom and outside it, feel the story is fair to those involved?

A "possible suspect"

This case illustrates that it is blatantly unfair to label someone as a "possible suspect" without reference to well-sourced material.

Mr Saki Macozoma, the then Managing Director of Transnet, lodged a complaint with the Broadcasting Complaints Commission of South Africa (BCCSA) in his personal capacity with regard to reports by the SABC that implicated him in the theft of shipping containers. He was referred to as a "possible suspect".

The first report, on 3 September 1997, concerned money paid by Transnet to a security company to track syndicates involved in the theft of shipping containers. Further reports, on 4 and 21 September 1997, detailed the tapping of telephones and the impending disciplinary inquiry against an employee, a Mr Ndhela.

It was, however, the report on 23 December 1997 which was, according to Macozoma, the most damaging to him. Macozoma complained that this report:

- implied and insinuated that he was a "possible suspect" in investigations into fraud and container theft;
- stated that he had attempted to destroy evidence regarding the above-mentioned;
- said that he had travelled to Cape Town to meet representatives of Armstrong Security Services (the security company contracted to inquire into the theft), and that he had refused to pay them when they "refused to hand over the suspect files";
- insinuated that he was corrupt, involved in criminal activities such as fraud, theft, and extortion, and was trying to cover up his illegal activities – and was therefore undeserving of his position.

Macozoma also claimed that the SABC reporter, Mr Snuki Zikalala, made no attempt to contact him to give him the opportunity to respond to the allegations. In addition, Macozoma argued that Zikalala failed to report on some germane issues of which the latter was well aware. According to Macozoma, these were:

- the allegation that Armstrong Security Services were terminated by Transnet because their investigations came to nothing, and they had made use of illegal methods;
- a member of Armstrong Security Services was brought to court for theft of customs papers that were being sold by that member to syndicates at Transnet involved in fraud and container theft;
- Zikalala falsely claimed that investigations into fraud and container theft had ended. Furthermore, Transnet had invested in various other methods of combating theft, such as computer-based X-ray technology.

On 20 January 1998 Zikalala reported that Transnet had dismissed Ndhela – but Macozoma was again mentioned as a "possible suspect". And yet again Macozoma had not been approached for comment. The report was carried on various channels in several official languages. In its defence, the SABC argued that Zikalala had on several occasions attempted to contact Macozoma. With regard to the theft of containers, it was also indicated that supporting evidence could be given in regard to connected activities (this was denied by the Complainant).

The BCCSA came to the conclusion that the crux of the matter was two references to Macozoma as a "possible suspect". "Other aspects relating to the investigation of container theft would require an in-depth inquiry with witnesses, etc – an inquiry that would go outside the mandate of this Commission."

Clause 2 of the BCCSA code (clauses 2.1–2.4) applies to this case. The BCCSA had the following to say:

- Being the managing director of a huge concern that is managed in the public's interest, Macozoma can expect a variety of hard-hitting criticisms, some of which may not be well-founded. "A public figure simply has to live with such criticisms." A public figure is, however, also in a position to react publicly to criticism and the media channels would usually be open to such press statements.

- In order to label a person as a "possible suspect", the source of such a statement is of cardinal importance. "To base a statement that a person is 'a possible suspect' on the untested opinion of an investigation unit by a private … investigation firm, is highly risqué." It would have been a different matter if the statement had come from the office of the Attorney-General or from another official investigative agency. In that case, a newspaper or a broadcaster would be entitled to publish it. Furthermore, the word "possible" creates its own problem: "Even if a person is a definite 'suspect' publication of this fact would be highly risqué." It would require extraordinary circumstances to publish such a statement. Given the speed with which news items are dealt with, "a news broadcast would usually simply not be the correct channel to deal with such an assertion summarily". In this particular case the background material "falls substantially short of what would be necessary to base such a statement on".

The BCCSA found that the statement that Macozoma was a "possible suspect" fell short of Clause 2.3 of the code because the report was inadequately sourced. The SABC also did not even say that that statement was based on rumours – not that that would have justified the "possible suspect" statement. "The source of the news item was simply not shown to be good enough to even include the reference to the managing director as a 'possible suspect'."

Clause 2.4 of the code requires that where there is reason to doubt the correctness of a report and if it is practicable to verify the correctness thereof, it shall be verified – or else it shall be mentioned in the report. It was not possible to verify that Zikalala had attempted to contact Macozoma because the former was overseas during the hearing. Yet "… there should have at least have been a reference to the fact that attempts had been made to contact the Complainant".

In any case, the media "should not refer to a person as a possible suspect … without such a suspicion being based on well-sourced material mentioned in the item". An official source would usually be the most reliable. "If not, informal sources would have to be proved to be of special standard and experience." No such evidence was provided.

The BCCSA concluded therefore that the SABC had made a serious mistake in this case, and the corporation was directed to broadcast the following statement:

In reaction to a complaint by the Managing Director of Transnet, Mr Sakkie [sic] Macozoma, the Broadcasting Complaints Commission of South Africa ... held that news items which implicated Mr Macozoma in illegitimate activities were unacceptable in terms of the Code of the Broadcasting Complaints Commission of South Africa. The reports which implied Mr Macozoma had acted improperly in relation to investigations into fraud and container theft, were in clear conflict with the BCCSA Code. The BCCSA reprimanded the SABC for those items which improperly and unfairly prejudiced the good name of Mr Macozoma.

Analysis

The BCCSA was entirely correct in its adjudication of this case and must be commended for its direction to the SABC to correct its ("serious") mistake – or, rather, series of mistakes.

Zikalala had indeed made several grave ethical mistakes:

- If he did try to get in touch with Macozoma, he should at least have referred to the fact that he had made attempts to that effect.
- The fact that the statement of Macozoma being a "possible suspect" was based on rumour was never mentioned.
- The media should never of its own accord label someone as a possible (or a definite) suspect. Such an allegation must come from an official – and even then it is highly dangerous to report it.
- No apparent attempt was made to verify the allegations.
- If Macozoma is to be believed, Zikalala omitted some important background information (context).

- The references to Macozoma as a possible suspect probably caused him a lot of (unnecessary) harm. This amounts to unjust and unfair reporting of the highest order.
- It is more than scandalous to portray an innocent person as being corrupt, involved in criminal activities such as fraud, theft and extortion, etc, as this could be seen as libellous.
- These allegations were insufficiently sourced.

Given all of these considerations, it must be concluded that the SABC's report on Macozoma was blatantly unfair because it lacked balance on just about every count. However, one comment by the BCCSA should be questioned. Should Macozoma, as a public figure, really expect "a variety of hard-hitting criticisms, some of which may not be well-founded" – *and to live with that*? Why should anybody, public figure or not, live with unfounded allegations made against him or her? Surely there is a difference between hard-hitting criticism and unfounded allegations? And surely even public figures should not be asked to live with unfounded allegations?

A bit more circumspection, please

Great care should be taken to report in a balanced and fair way in situations of (political) conflict – otherwise the impression of bias can very easily be created.

In the 20:00 news broadcast on SABC 3 on 24 January 1999, a report stated that Sifiso Nkabinde, the assassinated National Secretary of the United Democratic Movement (UDM), had "lived by the sword and died by the sword", and that "he played God in sending many people to their graves".

The complaints made to the BCCSA were that these comments were neither truthful nor accurate, nor were they presented in the proper context or in a balanced manner. The news broadcast was intentionally biased and distorted and constituted a blatant misrepresentation of the facts. The complaints also pointed out that the SABC report omitted to say Nkabinde had been acquitted by a court of law of charges of murder and incitement to commit murder. This led the complainant to believe that the SABC and its reporter were acting as apologists and propagandists for the ANC, and were "intent on furthering the dominance of the ANC by not being impartial in its summarisation in reporting on the life and times of Sifiso Nkabinde".

The applicable clauses of the BCCSA's code are 2.1–2.5. In its adjudication, the BCCSA said that it was common cause that:

- Nkabinde was a controversial public figure and politician;
- he was born and lived in Magoda, Richmond, an area "plagued and engulfed in ... political violence which has resulted in many people being killed";
- there was a time when there were "no-go" areas in Richmond for persons depending on their political affiliation, and that "warlords" controlled certain areas for the exclusive patronage of certain political movements;
- political debate surrounding events in Richmond is highly charged and volatile, and that the central figures (for example, Harry Gwala) are perceived by some sections of the public to be controversial;
- political movements in Richmond have accused each other of inciting violence and of each murdering the other's supporters.

Therefore, the BCCSA said: "...any summarisation of the life and times of a major political person in Richmond, is bound to inflame passions and emotions, depending on which side of the political divide a person's sympathies repose".

Although the tone and style of the reporter came across as cynical and adversarial, the essence of the report was factually neither exaggerated, nor distorted, the BCCSA said. "Nkabinde was quoted extensively in the broadcast and he projected himself as not only a politician but as a militarist and as a skilful strategist and a brave soldier."

The words "warlord" and "who lived by the sword and died by the sword" are admittedly provocative, but these were "used in context having regard to the fact that Sifiso Nkabinde was often surrounded by automatic gun-bearing bodyguards, and was also seen wearing military fatigue uniform". According to the BCCSA the reporter did balance the report by stating that Nkabinde never admitted he was a warlord.

The BCCSA decided that its code had not been contravened and dismissed the complaint.

Analysis

The BCCSA could not have reached any other conclusion. Two essential issues dominate the context of the report: the political violence in the Richmond area, and local political leaders as controversial public figures. Both these issues were given proper attention. The fact is that Nkabinde projected himself as a militarist, as the BCCSA rightly pointed out. The exact wording of the SABC's report ("lived by the sword and died by the sword" and that Nkabinde "played God in sending many people to their graves") are indeed adversarial, as the BCCSA noted. Precisely because the context of Richmond was one of extreme tension and violence, this wording could have been chosen with more circumspection. Words like these can easily inflame an already volatile situation and make matters infinitely worse. The media must never underestimate their influence, especially in unstable situations like the one under discussion.

The report could have done better in minimizing harm – to the Nkabinde family in particular and to his followers in general. Because of this rather harsh wording, the complainant can be forgiven for thinking the SABC wanted to further the dominance of the ANC (although that was probably not the case). Statements like these can easily create the impression of bias. So the report was fair, but it could have been presented in a more sensitive, balanced, responsible, and circumspect way.

A hostile climate?

In the reporting of a court case, balance (fairness) should not only be judged by assessing individual reports, but also (and especially) by looking at the whole coverage of the event.

On 23 September 1998 Elna Boesak, the wife of Dr Allan Boesak, filed a complaint with the BCCSA. At the time Mrs Boesak was a co-accused in a trial in the Cape High Court. The complainant alleged that the SABC:

- in its reportage of the Boesak trial since February 1995 had, through comprehensive, repetitive, and one-sided coverage of untested allegations against Boesak, created and sustained a hostile and partially informed public climate in which a perception of Boesak's guilt – as yet unproven at the time – was encouraged;
- had not given adequate coverage to the cross-examination of state witnesses;
- made errors as to the amounts of money involved in so far as Boesak was concerned, and had erred in its translation into Afrikaans of the word "reconstructed".

The BCCSA directed that the complainant be more specific as to what broadcasts she was complaining about. Given the rule that complaints have to be lodged within 30 days of a broadcast, the BCCSA requested Mrs Boesak to limit her complaints to broadcasts during the preceding month. She complied. The SABC then, in its defence, added some other broadcasts to illustrate that it had not been biased in its reporting. Mrs Boesak was granted the opportunity to respond to these additional broadcasts.

The SABC conceded that it had made an error with regard to the translation of the word "reconstructed" to "*gereproduseerde*" ("reproduced") in an Afrikaans bulletin. It was also clear that there were confusing and differing reports as to the amounts of money involved.

It was true that the accent during the reporting of the state's case had been on the charges, and that less time had been given to the content of the cross-examination of witnesses. However, the SABC argued that TV news reporting concentrated on outstanding news events conveyed to viewers within sixty to seventy seconds, and that it was impossible to convey every aspect of a trial. *The emphasis would shift to Boesak's case when the defence commenced with its evidence,* the SABC added.

The BCCSA then pointed to the following guidelines that should be taken into consideration:

- Viewers are aware of the fact that charges and state evidence are not conclusive and that these only represent one side of the case.
- It would be very unwise for a broadcaster, given the short time at its disposal, to get involved in the details of cross-examination. The risk of reporting cross-examination out of context is high. Often it is sufficient only to report that cross-examination took place.
- Broadcasters should therefore limit their reporting to highlights of a case and not get involved in the details of cross-examination.
- The broadcaster should deal with the closing arguments and judgment in much more detail (when it happens), probably doing a news feature on the outcome.

In its conclusion, the BCCSA said:

- It could find "no evidence" to substantiate Mrs Boesak's first allegation (that the SABC created and sustained a hostile and partially informed climate).
- It is impossible to come to a conclusion on alleged bias before the case draws to a close.

"The matter has to be judged as a whole. Only in exceptional circumstances will it be possible to adjudicate alleged bias during the course of a trial."

- There was obviously considerable confusion in the media as to the exact amounts of money involved. The SABC was "requested" to ensure that further mistakes would not be made in this respect. All editors should be informed as to the exact amounts and the division thereof. "It would be prudent to obtain advice from the SABC legal department on this matter."
- The allegation that "reconstructed" was wrongly translated into Afrikaans as "*gereproduseer*" is well-founded. This error, however, amounted to a *bona fide* mistake, and the BCCSA could find no evidence of negligence in terms of its code.

The complaint was accordingly dismissed, but the SABC was referred to the BCCSA's third conclusion (the confusing reports as to the amounts of money involved).

Analysis

Of course, the accent of a news report will be one-sided if it was the state's day to put forward its charges. On another day, the emphasis will be on the accused's defence, and on that day the evidence will obviously be one-sided in favour of the accused. The matter should be judged as a whole, as the BCCSA rightly pointed out. That should provide the much-needed balance. In the meantime, with the very limited time at its dis-

posal, the broadcaster can only report the highlights of a certain event.

Even if some parts of the cross-examination proved to be important – and, of course, that would deserve attention – the focus of the news report should remain on the main events of the day. That does not make the broadcaster one-sided or biased against anybody. In this – the gist of the complaint against the SABC – the BCCSA was entirely correct in its finding.

However, the SABC did err on the amount of money concerned. The BCCSA was somewhat lenient in this regard. Was its "request" to the SABC to ensure no further mistakes were made really enough? Although there was some confusion in the media as to the exact amount involved, this did not justify sloppy reporting by the SABC. If there were any doubts, it would have taken only two seconds to make that clear. Should the BCCSA not instead have reprimanded the SABC in this regard?

It is understandable that an incorrect translation ("*gereproduseer*") could further the perception that the SABC was biased against Boesak as this implied that Boesak had lied. However, the BCCSA was probably correct in its finding that it was a *bona fide* mistake. Yet, let it be said that the media should make *no* mistakes in sensitive matters like the one under discussion – not even *bona fide* ones.

One last remark: the BCCSA stated that the matter must be judged as a whole, and that it could therefore not come to a conclusion on alleged bias before the case came to a close. That is perfectly correct – but why then limit Mrs Boesak's complaint to broadcasts of only one month prior to her complaint? How fair was that?

Views not included

Fairness means balance. The media should stick to this principle even where notorious individuals are concerned, and allow them also to voice their opinions.

On 19 January 1998 the SABC broadcast a programme entitled *Death of a Gangster*, which dealt with the death of a Mr Goosen. The programme contained interviews with Mr Ferdi Barnard, as well as several of the state witnesses in two trials against Barnard. At the time, Barnard was standing trial for the murder of Dr David Webster, and faced several charges of fraud relating to diamond and other transactions. Also pending was a robbery case in Klerksdorp, in which approximately R10 million worth of diamonds was said to be involved.

Barnard lodged a formal complaint with the BCCSA, saying that his views on the death of Webster had not been included in the report, which had aired the views of state witnesses who could have incriminated him.

Because the testimony of the programme's producer, Mr Jacques Pauw, could contravene the *sub judice* rule, his evidence was heard *in camera*.

The BCCSA asked itself this question: was it unfair to Barnard not to have included his views on the death of Webster, in order to counter the statements made by the state witnesses in that programme? With reference to Clause 7.2.2 of its code, the BCCSA concluded: yes, definitely. Although the BCCSA had no jurisdiction on the question of the *sub judice* rule, the commission said its code "would seem to have been contravened in this programme". Clause 7.2.1 was also contravened, the BCCSA adjudicated. Because Barnard could not take part in a subsequent programme (he was in jail at the time), "the only sanction this Commission could impose was to direct the SABC to broadcast this finding".

Analysis

Fairness demands balance. If a journalist portrays one side of a story, he or she is obliged to do the same to the other side – and let the public decide for itself what the truth is. Not only is it fundamentally unfair to do otherwise, but it also creates the impression of bias, and that is detrimental to the media's credibility. Perhaps the fact that Barnard was a notorious figure from the darkest side of the old apartheid regime caused the SABC to be less circumspect than it should have been. Nevertheless, this was not reason enough to throw the principle of fairness overboard. Great care should always be taken to give all sides to a story a chance to voice their opinion. The BCCSA's decision testifies to its own search for fairness. So does its direction to the SABC to broadcast its finding.

Focus on the conflict

It is not unfair to highlight a specific incident (although care should be taken to put matters in context).

On 5 August 1997 two prominent politicians, Mr Bantu Holomisa and Mr Roelf Meyer, jointly visited the campus of the University of Port

Elizabeth and were to speak at a venue called the Kraal. At the time they had started a new political initiative that eventually led to the establishment of the United Democratic Movement (UDM).

SABC 2 and 1 covered this event on its news bulletins at 21:30 and 22:00, respectively. A transcript of the full English report reads:

ANC-aligned student and worker groupings *prevented* [my emphasis] Roelf Meyer and Bantu Holomisa from addressing students at the University of Port Elizabeth today. The students said they were driven to protest against the two political leaders because of their association with expelled former Richmond leader Sifiso Nkabinde... Mkhokeli Thanda reports.

Students aligned to the South African Students Congress, the ANC Youth League and university workers from the NEHAWU union got to the university's Great Hall before the two political leaders. And they made it clear they weren't interested in listening to what Mr Meyer and General Holomisa had to say in launching their new political opposition. (Upsound: natural sound – toyi toyi)

There was no way the meeting was going to take place in the Hall...and later the two opposition politicians were moved to a nearby balcony on the university campus.

But their calls were in vain. (Upsound: Meyer – condemning the disruption)

The President of the Students Representative Council also thought the protesters were out of order. (Upsound: Evert Knoesen, President SRC)

But Sasco spokesperson Ngange Ngxiki says student bodies were not properly consulted before Meyer and Holomisa were invited to speak. They also objected because of Sifiso Nkabinde's involvement in the new political initiative. (Upsound: Ngxiki)

With questions still unanswered over Nkabinde's role in recent acts of violence in Richmond, both Meyer and Holomisa were careful not to associate themselves too closely with the former ANC strongman. (Upsound: Meyer and Holomisa)

Holomisa and Meyer are still only exploring the possibility of political alliances. But today's events demonstrates [sic] that it's not going to be easy for

them even to be heard in some places. Mkhokeli Thanda, SABC, Port Elizabeth.

A complaint was lodged with the BCCSA by the New Alliance Students Association (PE branch). It held that:

- camera shots were misleading because they created the false impression that the majority of students and people present were opposed to the appearance of the two speakers. In fact, only about 50 people out of 800 to 1 500 present protested. The rest insisted they had a right to hear the speakers.
- contrary to the SABC report, Holomisa and Meyer were not prevented from speaking. Both addressed the crowd – and they had a positive reception.

The complainant called the report biased and said it was to the detriment of the new movement (then called the National Consultative Forum).

Clause 2 of the BCCSA's code applies in this case. The second issue was dealt with first. The BCCSA asked itself this question: what exactly was meant by the word "prevented"? Did the statement by the reporter as well as the short visual of Meyer addressing students outside the Kraal from the balcony place a different perspective on the initial reference to them being "prevented" from speaking?

The fact is that the speakers were prevented from addressing the students in the Kraal, but not from speaking from the balcony. The word "prevented" was therefore "rather unfortunate", the BCCSA said. However, there was "sufficient correcting material" in the broadcast that shows that they did speak. As time is limited on a news bulletin, only the essence of an event can be conveyed to the viewers, the BCCSA added.

The first part of the complaint concerned the impression created that the majority of the students were not interested in what the speakers had to say. However, the BCCSA said video evidence showed how supporters of Meyer and Holomisa "attempted to shout down the protesters in the Kraal and that a substantial number of students were listening or attempting to listen to the address from the balcony in spite of the continued disrupting singing and shouting by the protesters, who had moved from the hall to the campus in front of the balcony".

The BCCSA was satisfied that a TV audience would realize that the protesters consisted of a small group only, although the news items did not accentuate the other students. The impression was not created that Meyer and Holomisa were treated unfairly. "They were all granted an opportunity to put forward points of view relevant to the whole matter."

On a production note, the BCCSA said that the SABC could be criticized for not highlighting the interest of the majority of students present. However, "once again on balance, (we) came to the conclusion that since the focus was on the disruptive aspect of the day, the interest of other students was not that important".

Analysis

On the use of the word "prevent": Meyer and Holomisa were (initially) "prevented" from speaking at the Kraal. The fact that they spoke elsewhere did not nullify that fact. A report to that effect would therefore be in order. As the BCCSA said, the main focus of the report was on the disruptive aspect of the day. To that extent, the SABC was well within its rights to report in the way it did.

The point is this: *the role of the media is not that of a secretary, whose job is to summarize a whole event. The broadcaster focuses on newsworthy events and tries to highlight them.* Yet it can be conceded that a more sensitive choice of words in the TV report would have been welcome. It would have been more accurate and fair if Thanda had said Meyer and Holomisa were *initially* prevented from speaking. It could also have given a bit more prominence to the majority of the students. Footage of Meyer and Holomisa speaking at another venue that same night on the very same campus did provide some perspective on the use of the word "prevent" and it gave the report more balance (fairness).

Notes

[1] The term "Rashomon effect" comes from an influential 1951 Japanese film of the same name. This film explores the different views, reactions, and perceptions of four people who are all involved in the same moment of violence. "The Rashomon effect is an informal term taken to mean a case where the viewpoints of the participants color their interpretations of events to such an extent that sifting out a 'fair' representation is all but impossible" (Hausman 1992, 62).

[2] For different viewpoints on the Fairness Doctrine, see Dennis et al., *Media freedom and accountability* (1989).

6 | Objectivity

A news report is a moment in a process of interpretation, and the specific interpretation chosen is "biased" by the horizon of the journalists and readers (Belsey et al. 1992, 120)

Introduction

Objectivity, neutrality, and impartiality all roughly mean not to take sides or to remain aloof. Some journalists say they are at all times neutral, objective, and impartial. They do not make the news, they just report on it – or so they say. They never get involved in any story nor do they allow their own convictions to influence a story – or so they claim. Their slogan is: "we just report the facts". These journalists say they never express or suggest a preference for one set of values over another or reflect their attitudes about the people and events involved. The only

response to this must be: how naive people can be.

Don't be naive

Louis Day warns that objectivity "is a controversial value and not one to which all journalists and media scholars ascribe" and says it is "probably impossible" to attain (Day 1991, 74). Make no mistake: objectivity is an indispensable journalistic ideal. The reality, however, is that all people are subjective, partial, and biased – and journalists are no exception. If you want to be a good journalist, you had better understand this. It is better to know the truth than to build on a false basis.

Always remember the Rashomon effect:[1] the reason why people perceive the same situation in a different way is precisely because of this subjectivity. What is important to one journalist may be of less importance to another; what stimulates one reporter may completely escape the attention of another. Take, for example, the situation in the old South Africa. Some journalists referred to members of the military wing of the ANC as "ter-rorists"; others called them "freedom fighters". The same people and events were involved – but, from a different perspective, contrasting types of reports were written.

This is admittedly an extreme example, yet it happens all the time. When cricketer Meyrick Pringle was selected to play for South Africa in the World Cup – the first time the country had participated – his recollection of how he received the news differed from that of his fiancée, who was also present at the time. *Die Burger* (20 January 1992) reported that Pringle said that he was so shocked when he first heard the news that he ran out of the house and jumped into the pool. He and his fiancée, Mrs Tania Moolman, hugged each other, drank champagne, and cried. Moolman, on the other hand, recollected that Pringle started to cry – and that *she* then jumped into the pool. The same event, but two accounts: in the excitement of the moment, the couple perceived (and remembered) the same event differently.

Journalists are no exception to this phenomenon. They often report the same event in different ways. This may be because they write for different markets, but it is also because no two people see things exactly the same way. Just think of that rugby report describing how and explaining why your favourite Currie Cup team lost an important match. Sometimes you wonder if the reporter really *saw* the match, or if the report is even about the same match.

Horizons

People mostly see what they want to see; they think in the way in which they have grown accustomed to think; they notice things because of their personal make-up and interests. Why? Because every person is an individual, born at a certain time in a certain place and raised in specific circumstances. Millions of factors are in play during your upbringing, influencing what you believe and think, as well as the ways in which you think and act.

These impressions influence each person in their own unique way, laying the foundations for paradigms – views of the world and of life that determine the ways in which we perceive things. A paradigm is like a pair of glasses through which you view the world. Paradigms are mostly unconscious presuppositions. People often do not even realize what their own presuppositions are – and therefore don't (consciously) understand the reasons *why* they behave the way they do or perceive events in a certain way.

Everyone views the world from his or her own perspective, through his or her own pair of glasses – and journalists are no exception. Every journalist has a specific journalistic horizon. Andrew Edgar states: "This horizon is constituted by the journalist's 'news values', which is to say, by the stock of knowledge and competences, typically taken for granted by the journalist, by which any event may be assessed as being newsworthy" (Belsey et al. 1992, 117). To which he adds: "The importance that the event has to the journalist is related to the...prejudices that take the form of frameworks for interpretation, within which events may be placed" (Belsey et al. 1992, 118). This horizon of interpretation is itself formed in a social tradition (Belsey et al. 1992, 118). He concludes by saying "Journalism is subjective... A news report is a moment in a process of interpretation, and the specific interpretation chosen is 'biased' by the horizon of the journalists and readers" (Belsey et al. 1992, 120).

Theodore Glasser goes so far as to state: "By objectivity I mean a particular view of journalism and the press, a frame of reference used by journalists to orient themselves in the newsroom and in the community. By objectivity I mean, to a degree, ideology; where ideology is defined as a set of beliefs that function as the journalist's 'claim to action'" (Hiebert et al. 1985, 51).

Glasser is adamant: "objective" reporting is biased in at least three ways (Hiebert et al. 1985, 52):

- in favour of the status quo (the prominent and the elite) – against the traditional role of the press as the fourth estate.
- against independent thinking. It emasculates the intellect by treating it as a disinterested spectator.
- against the idea of responsibility and morality. The day's news is viewed only as something journalists are compelled to report.

Yes, everything (in journalism) is subjective – from the importance attached to a certain event to the selection of facts and the interpretation of these facts. The journalistic ideal of "we just report the facts" appears to be more illusory than ever. It is important to realize this fact. It will help you recognize your own emotions, preferences, and dislikes, and your own paradigms and horizons. This is essential for the conscious process of attempting to avoid them as far as possible.

Reporting *is* interpretation

But more needs to be said. There are a number of (very important) questions to ask: *how* do you decide what is newsworthy and what is not? *Why* are certain events considered to be more newsworthy than others? Why will some journalists regard some events as "newsworthy" and others will disagree?

The first reason, as has already been stated, why the "just-the-facts" journalist is naive is because every individual is, inevitably, subjective. The second reason is that *the process of news reporting is by nature already interpretation (subjective)*. The media indeed never "just" report the news.

Reporting presupposes that a journalist decides which aspects of a given situation are more important than other aspects. This implies that the *process of selection* – of what is important and constitutes news and what is trivial – already is interpretation. We select the news on the basis of our interpretations thereof.

Consider what happens in the process of interpretation. Basically, there are three things at stake:

- The interpreter analyzes the factors that led to a certain situation. He or she focuses on the history of that case: how it came to be, what factors were involved, what decisions were taken, by whom, why, etc.
- Then the present situation is taken into consideration. Who are the players? What is at stake? What possibilities are open? What agendas can be pursued?
- Lastly the interpreter outlines possible scenarios, analyzing what will happen if choice A is made, or choice B, if more weight is placed on a specific aspect of a situation and less on another. Now the interpreter thinks about the future: what might happen? Why will it happen? When could it happen? And what will be the consequence if whatever does take place?

It is immediately clear that nobody can be objective in the above process. *Nobody can interpret objectively*. In fact, those words are contradictory to one another.

Due impartiality

The BBC has accepted that all journalists are subjective by nature, but also that the selection of what constitutes news amounts to interpretation – which is by definition a subjective act. That is why the BBC does not dogmatically ask its journalists to be "impartial". It rather talks about "due impartiality" – realizing that "absolute impartiality" does not exist (*Producers' Guidelines* 1996, 14). Due impartiality is at the heart of the BBC's beliefs. It is a core value, and no area of programming is exempt from it. It requires programme-makers to show open-mindedness, fairness and a respect for truth. While the whole spectrum of the diversity of interests, beliefs, and perspectives must be reflected, the BBC "is free to make programmes about any subject it chooses, and to make programmes which explore (or are presented from) a particular point of view." The term "due" is interpreted as meaning "adequate or appropriate to the nature of the subject and the type of programme" (*Producers' Guidelines* 1996, 14). The *Producers' Guidelines* continue: "There are generally more than two sides to any issue and impartiality in factual programmes may not be achieved simply by mathematical balance in which each view is complemented by an equal and opposing one" (1996, 14). And, very importantly: "…due impartiality does not require absolute neutrality on every issue or detachment from fundamental democratic principles" (1996, 14).

This is a very realistic approach. Again, it is better to realize your own subjectivity than foolishly to pretend otherwise. For example, *Sowetan*'s ethical code requires "impartiality". It is clear that its editorial staff has not really thought this matter through.

Strive to be objective

Once you have understood your own subjectivity as a journalist, the first hurdle has been overcome. The second hurdle is to take a deep breath and tell yourself: well, OK, so I'm only human. But now, more than ever, you must make a fundamental commitment to *strive to be objective*. By this is meant nothing more and nothing less than the commitment to report truthfully, comprehensively, and intelligently, putting an event into a context, and giving meaning to it as best you can. Various writers, such as Matthew Kieran (1998,

23–36) and Donald McDonald (Merrill 1975, 69–88) emphasize the need for objectivity. A journalist's subjectivity must never lead to adopting an attitude of "well, I can do nothing about my subjectivity. So, why worry?"

Journalists who have reached this stage have a lot to worry about. In a Gallup poll in February 1999 (www.gallup.com) the question was asked if the media were biased either for or against President Bill Clinton, or were not biased. A stunning 77 per cent of respondents believed the media were indeed biased (40 per cent for, and 37 per cent against). A mere 16 per cent thought the media was not biased in this matter, with 7 per cent of respondents having no opinion on this matter. Now *that* is cause for real concern.

Social intervention

The media are by nature subjective in their reporting of what is considered to constitute news, as well as in its interpreting of those items. As such, the media exerts an influence (in positive and negative ways) on society. This influence presupposes that the *effect* of the journalist's work is also not neutral. The question in this chapter is not *if* the media have some influence, but rather *how deliberate* this influence should be. (This question has a direct bearing on the discussion in Chapter 12.)

Jannie Botes[2] poses the following questions: "Should journalists become more directly involved in political or social issues as proponents of so-called civic journalism in the United States maintain they should? Or is it their responsibility only to 'report' as neutral and objective observers?" (*Crosslines Global Report* May/June 1997, 12). But he also goes a step further: "Aren't journalists playing an interventionist or mediating role in the resolution of wars whether they like it or not?" (*Crosslines Global Report* 1997, 12).

Botes argues convincingly that journalists often take on roles that are similar to those of conflict interveners. "They examine and analyse parties, investigate issues, often create options, pose possible outcomes, and in the process, sometimes establish (or destroy) relationships between disputants. The impact of journalism on conflicts and conflict resolution is therefore potentially much larger than merely being a channel of communication" (*Crosslines Global Report* 1997, 13). And, even more importantly, when journalists talk or write about the different sides in a conflict, "*they potentially change the dynamic of the conflict, and even its outcome*" (my emphasis) (*Crosslines Global Report* 1997, 13). All journalism, Botes concludes, is a form of social intervention. Moreover, this outside intervention "changes the dynamic of the conflict *irrespective of the journalist's intentions*" (my emphasis) (*Crosslines Global Report* 1997, 13). Although most journalists strive to be neutral, "the reporting process makes an intervener or third party out of journalists long before they have even considered covering the various participants' view on how to resolve the issues. This media involvement nearly always has an impact on the parties, the conflict and its resolution" (*Crosslines Global Report* 1997, 13).

The examples Botes uses are noteworthy, with the first being the role that the international media played in empowering the ANC during the apartheid era in South Africa. "By putting the ANC's cause on the international agenda journalists played a definite role in helping the ANC obtain freedom and justice for black South Africans" (*Crosslines Global Report* 1997, 13). More particularly, the American TV interviewer Ted Koppel took ABC's *Nightline* to South Africa in 1985 and Israel in 1988. Although Koppel's intention was to explain the complexity of these conflicts, Botes argues that Koppel assisted in transforming them. "In both cases, Koppel brought the parties to the table before they had begun speaking to each other through official negotiating channels" (*Crosslines Global Report* 1997, 13). By doing this, Koppel "not only empowered the weaker parties, but set an agenda for the type of public discussion, debate, and dialogue that had to be part of the resolution process" (*Crosslines Global Report* 1997, 13).

It is therefore essential that journalists understand the nature and the dynamics of conflict. This understanding will enable them to ask the right questions and to bring all relevant perspectives to the fore.

But be careful

Of course, this line of argument can be taken too far. It is one thing to understand that the media's reporting is an unintentional (but inevitable) form of social intervention, and quite another to believe (as some journalists do nowadays) that the search for solutions should be an integral part of journalism.

The task of the media can never be to facilitate solutions. *Beeld* carried a very important leading article on this issue in response to the view of the American expert on conflict, Dr Paul Wahrhaftig, that the media should play a role in the peaceful resolution of conflicts (*Beeld* 22 January 1999). According to *Beeld*, this viewpoint is only partially valid. The role of the media is to inform societies thoroughly about the full spectrum of issues in a conflict. The different parties are not capable of doing this on their own. As an example, *Beeld* outlined the relevant issues in the conflict between Pagad, the Cape Flats gangs, and the police. The media's role is to lay a foundation of valid information (via the reporting, as well as the authoritative interpretation, of facts) to enable leaders and communities to solve and avoid conflict, *Beeld* wrote. But no newspaper can stand between the warring parties and resolve their conflict. That is the role of an elected government and of the authorities over which the media is also a watchdog. An enlightened public opinion is the media's contribution to the solving of conflicts, the newspaper added.

What this shows is that it is dangerous to speak of the media's role in conflict *solution*; the media's task is more that of conflict *reporting* and conflict *analysis*. The media can definitely have a direct or indirect influence on events while doing their job of reporting and analysis. But if this distinction becomes blurred the journalist will deliberately become a player in events and thereby give up the goal of objectivity. It must be regarded as a bonus if a journalist makes a contribution towards actually solving a conflict. But the intentional solving of conflicts falls outside the scope of journalism.

More precisely

The issue of neutrality is always pertinent in situations of conflict where there are different points of view, and even contending paradigms, value systems, and beliefs. Journalists can easily take sides, even if this happens unconsciously. So a discussion about conflicts is necessary, together with the role the media can play in them.

First of all, make a list of the top twenty stories of the previous year. Most probably the majority are about conflict of some sort. It has been said that up to 90 per cent of all news reports are concerned with conflict in one way or another. This means that journalists should give serious attention to the nature of conflicts.

Robert Karl Manoff[3] calls attention to the fact that the twentieth century was characterized by organized group violence on an extraordinary scale (*Reporting Diversity Manual* 1996, 1): an estimated 110 million people were killed during the twentieth century, against an estimated 19 million people in the nineteenth and 7 million in the eighteenth century. Hence his question:

"What media-based initiatives would it be possible, and appropriate, to undertake in particular conflict solutions?"

Manoff's responses are worth noting – and fall more or less within the ambit of the above-mentioned position:

- Promote and help enforce national or international norms regarding human rights, the conduct of war, the treatment of minorities, or other issues.
- Relay negotiating signals between parties that have no formal communication or require another way to signal.
- Focus the attention of the international community on a developing conflict, and by doing so bring pressure on the parties to resolve it or on the international community to intervene.
- Establish the transparency of one conflict party to another.
- Engage in confidence-building measures.
- Support international peacekeeping operations in countries where they are active and in countries contributing military contingents.
- Educate parties and communities involved in conflict and thereby change the information environments of disputes, which is critical to the conflict-resolution process.
- Identify the underlying interests of each party to a conflict for the other.
- Prevent the circulation of incendiary rumours and counteract them when they surface.
- Identify the core values of disputants, which are often critical to helping them understand their own priorities and those of their opposite numbers.
- Identify and explain underlying material and psychological needs of parties to a conflict, clarifying the structural issues that are perceived to be at stake.
- Frame the issues involved in conflict in such a way that they become more susceptible to management.
- Identify resources that may be available to

help resolve conflicts or to mobilize outside assistance in doing so.

- Establish networks to circulate information concerning conflict prevention and management activities that have succeeded elsewhere.
- Publicize what should be public and privatize what is best left private in any negotiating process, although the definitions in each case are likely to be highly contested and should not be taken for granted.
- De-objectify and re-humanize conflicting parties towards one another, and avoid stereotyping.
- Provide an outlet for the emotions of the parties, the expression of which may be therapeutic in and of itself.
- Bring international pressure to bear on media organizations that promote xenophobia, racism, or other forms of social hatred.
- Encourage a balance of power among unequal parties where appropriate, or, where the claims of parties are not equally just, strengthen the hand of the party with the more compelling moral claim.
- Enable the parties to formulate and articulate proposed solutions by serving as a non-antagonistic interlocutor.
- Provide early warning of impending conflicts.
- Help leaders who are negotiating maintain credibility with their own constituents.
- Participate in the process of healing, reconciliation, and social reconstruction following conflicts.
- Signal the importance of accords that end conflicts by historicizing them as important public occasions in order to embed the resolution process in shared social memories.

One bridge too far

The well-known international journalist Ed Vulliamy, who covered the conflict in the former Yugoslavia during the 1990s, made a speech in Cape Town in 1999. Vulliamy talked about the Serb concentration camps that were "discovered" at Omarska and Trnopolje in Bosnia-Herzegovina in 1992 and which were run by the notorious Dr Radovan Karadzic.

According to Vulliamy, the most atrocious things happened in the camps. To cite but one example, prisoners were allegedly made to bite off the testicles of other prisoners – and as they died, live pigeons were stuffed into their mouths to stifle their screams.

What should a journalist do in such a case? Be neutral, because there are always two sides to a story? Just report both sides of the news? Give equal weight and credence to these sides? According to Vulliamy, "There are moments in history when crimes are being committed, and when neutrality is not neutral at all, but complicity in the crime. To be neutral is to be on the side of the criminal". He then distinguished between objectivity and neutrality. A journalist should never let go of objectivity, he said, but you can be objective without being neutral. "Why should we be neutral and not take sides between a camp inmate and the guard who beats, mutilates, and tortures him?"

Does Vulliamy go too far? Yes. For this amounts to consciously throwing overboard the journalistic goal of objectivity. Once a journalist does not even want to be neutral, he or she forfeits credibility. Why not just publish the facts as perceived – surely that in itself would be shocking enough, creating enough response? *A journalist does well to understand that he or she is by definition subjective; the journalist does even better by refusing to give up the journalistic ideal of neutrality, impartiality, and objectivity.* Moreover, Vulliamy's distinction between neutrality and objectivity is problematic. The point is that the journalist can *neither* be neutral *nor* objective, and that (again) a journalist's goal always must be to strive for neutrality, impartiality, and objectivity. Without that goal, a journalist becomes nothing more than a propagandist with an agenda, trying to force particular views down the public's throat.

Case Study | How *could* you?

The following case illustrates how emotion and subjectivity can cloud the media's judgment and reporting.

Hansie Cronjé, a former South African cricket captain, had enjoyed unprecedented success and was much loved and respected. In this case study, the focus is on press reaction to two events: the publication on Saturday 8 April 2000 of transcripts of an alleged conversation between Cronjé and a bookmaker; and a confession made by Cronjé a few days later. (This is not an attempt to describe or analyze all the aspects of the reporting involved.)

Under the heading "Hansie's a hero, not a crook", the *Cape Argus* wrote, *inter alia*, in a

leading article on 10 April: "The claim that Hansie Cronjé and three of his Protea teammates took money to throw a one-day international against India is patently nonsense. We have no doubt the accusations will prove as far-fetched in the end as they sounded in the beginning". The article described the evidence presented as "flimsy". "The scenario is so absurd it wouldn't have worked in a comedy."

A mere two days later, after new evidence came to light, the same newspaper led on its front page with one word: "Disgrace". There was no place for any other news on that page. Nor was there on pages 2, 3, and 4.

The leading article on 12 April makes interesting reading when compared to the one two

CAPE ARGUS

WEDNESDAY April 12, 2000 ★ CITY LATE

R2.30

Disgrace

JOHN YELD
Staff Writer

With Hansie Cronjé's life in ruins today along with the image of world cricket, one key question still eluded the unrelenting media spotlight: who had the disgraced former captain apparently not given all his confessors the same information?

Or if he had, why did only some of them choose to share it with the publicity?

At a news conference in Durban yesterday, United Cricket Board managing director Ali Bacher said that Cronjé had admitted taking between R50 000 and R5 000 (US$ 6 350-1150 in cash from a local South African on behalf of an Indian bookmaker based in London during the triangular home series with Zimbabwe and England in January.

One minute later Sports Minister Ngconde Balfour firmly denied Cronjé had made any admission that money had changed hands.

Dr Bacher, who said Cronjé had taken the money home but has not deposited it, said the South African cricketing authorities had been

Balfour fields the flak for a silent ex-captain

JOHN YELD
Staff Writer

For someone who must have spent the past five days agonising over whether to go public with his terrible confession and destroy his career, and who probably hadn't slept for at least 24 hours, Wessel Johannes Cronjé looked remarkably fresh at yesterday's press conference.

But the haunted, sad expression in his eyes, when he occasionally lifted them from their fixed gaze on the table in front of him, bore testimony to the unbearable emotional load he was carrying.

Wearing a neat white golf shirt and long khaki pants, and with his notoriously

City Park Hospital.

On Mr Balfour's right sat Pastor Ray McCauley, head of the Rhema Church and Hansie's spiritual leader.

While Mr Balfour read the two-page statement, Hansie sat with his arms folded across his chest, and kept his eyes mostly on the paper in the Sports Minister's hands.

At one point, as a barrage of cameras clicked in unison, he wiped an eye with his thumb, but whether from emotion or tiredness it was impossible to say.

Once or twice he glanced up anxiously at a question, but then looked down again.

Mr Balfour explained a reference to the statement to Hansie as "captain", although he had already been relieved of this position. "I called him, and I still do, until days earlier. It starts off by referring to its article on 10 April where the newspaper had reacted with "contempt and disbelief". Here are some excerpts from the 12 April article:

> In this (the leading article), the one patch of the newspaper in which we wear our hearts on our sleeves, we are driven by many motives.
>
> So, like many of you, we did not believe the charges emanating from India. We did not think for a moment that the massive investment of faith by South Africans into a national sporting team could be betrayed in such a fashion. We believed, instead, that the South African values we stand for had been embraced by Cronjé; that he represented an honest, decent present and the prospect of a brighter future. Finally, we believed we were reflecting a fundamental and positive truth about this country, about its leaders and about the path this country is going to pursue. We believed that in spite of the many problems we have endured over the years, we are at heart a good and decent people. We still believe in all that. If only we had been right.

In contrast to the emotional reaction of the *Cape Argus*, *Business Day* carried an extremely balanced leading article on 11 April. The first paragraph summed it up: "It seems almost beyond belief that SA cricket captain Hansie Cronjé, a devout Christian and a man seemingly obsessed with winning, should be at the centre of a match-fixing furore. But it is advisable to keep an open mind until the matter is resolved by hard evidence". The rest of the articles in *Business Day* were also well-written, critical, and rather unemotional.

The leading articles in *Beeld* and *Die Burger* handled the matter in much the same way as *Business Day*. They asked for more evidence, and displayed less emotion, than was the case with the *Cape Argus*. However, some of their coverage suggested a lack of objectivity. In one report in *Beeld* and *Die Burger* (not a leading article), Fanie Heyns wrote that if the allegations were true, then Cronjé's performance was worthy of an Oscar. Heyns analyzed some of the games that were allegedly fixed – and gave reasons for some poor performances, ranging from a stomach injury to dehydration. In other matches, it was explained, the performances of the players involved were very good indeed.

In a leading article on 10 April, *Die Burger* received the news with shock and dismay. It is extremely difficult for people who had come to know Cronjé as a true gentleman to believe these allegations, *Die Burger* said. The article asked that the matter be cleared up as soon as possible. The paper also published the report by Heyns. On 12 April *Die Burger* followed up with a well-balanced article that ended with the question: "How *could* you, Hansie?"

Analysis

When the scandal first erupted, the United Cricket Board, the government and the national cricket coach took Cronjé's side. That should have been no excuse for the media to do likewise. The media's serious lack of objectivity was nowhere more evident than in the *Cape Argus*. Hansie was a hero, not a crook, it was said on 10 April. There was not even an attempt to strive towards objectivity. The use of terms such as "patently nonsense", "far-fetched", "absurd", and "comedy" testify to this fact.

The subsequent "confession" by the *Cape Argus*, in the leading article, that it wears its heart on its sleeve, as well as that it is driven by many motives, serves to prove the point. One of these motives clearly is emotion – a hallmark of subjectivity.

In comparison, *Die Burger*'s article on the same day, as well as *Beeld*'s article the next day, came much closer to attaining the goal of objectivity. Note that *Die Burger* did not say that it was difficult for the newspaper as such to believe the allegations – the focus was on people who knew

Cronjé. There was a distance here between the newspaper and Cronjé that was totally absent in the *Cape Argus*.

However, the "report" by Heyns was not even an attempt at articulating the news. It was comment from start to finish. If that was the official view of the newspaper, it should have been included in its editorial page. It was not, and should therefore not have been published at all.

Otherwise, on the whole, these two newspapers covered the issue with as much balance as could be expected, while *Business Day* was exemplary in reporting the events. Thus, the initial coverage of the Cronjé debacle varied from no apparent attempt to be objective to a commendable attempt at objectivity. This is not to accuse, only to point out how difficult it really is even to strive towards objectivity.

Criminal collusion?

The media must be careful not to allow themselves to be misused for propaganda purposes, and not to become part of illegal acts.

SABC TV News reported at 20:00 on 27 April 1999 on a "kangaroo court" in Guguletu near Cape Town. The "court" was shown "meting out primitive justice by having alleged offenders flogged". In the case under consideration, a number of alleged rapists had been set free on bail. The rape victim complained to the taxi association, who took the law into their own hands. The alleged rapists, all of whom were sixteen years of age, were tied to lamp posts. They were told to undress – and the rape victim was given the opportunity to flog them. Members of the association followed suit. The floggings continued for two hours. Scenes of flogging were shown at medium range.

The news presenter, Alyce Chavunduka, began the report by saying: "As police struggle to control the country's escalating crime rate, there's evidence that local communities are taking the law into their own hands. In Guguletu outside Cape Town earlier this month, the local taxi association apprehended, tried, convicted, sentenced and punished five suspected teenage rapists. Our correspondent was given exclusive rights to film the event. Please note that the following visuals may be disturbing."

The Broadcasting Complaints Commission of South Africa (BCCSA) received a complaint about the report. Here is the gist of what was said in the complaint:

- The broadcasting "of such gratuitously violent material" is questionable – especially since it was stated in the introduction that this sort of "street justice" is inevitable when the court and the police (according to the SABC) have been remiss in their duties, not having investigated or prosecuted the case effectively.
- The "exclusive rights" claim revealed that the SABC knew about the flogging well in advance. The SABC was present when the accused were taken from their beds in the middle of the night. "They justified this by boasting of the 'exclusivity' of their coverage." This can amount to criminal collusion.
- This kind of "irresponsible behaviour from our national broadcaster" is quite extraordinary in the light of the tense run-up to the June election. Many may feel the alleged rapists got what they deserved, "but the precedent set by this kind of lynch-mob street justice is too ghastly for a society which aspires to the rule of law to contemplate".

The BCCSA said in its adjudication that the "primitive kangaroo court" is absolutely unacceptable. "The question is, however, whether

a broadcaster should ignore such an event."
The following argument is too important to
summarize:

> It is common cause that the Respondent's (SABC's)
> staff was invited to this flogging. To expect them to
> report the planned incident to the police conflicts
> clearly with a broadcaster's duty to report such a
> news event. It is highly unlikely that a court of law
> would find them to be associates in this crime. They
> did not, in any way, further the flogging or instigate
> it. There was also clearly no intention to associate
> themselves with what was happening. In any case,
> this is not a matter for the Commission to decide
> upon.

The commission said it had to decide upon two
things:
- whether the broadcast of the flogging
  amounted to the showing of violence for the
  sake of violence;
- whether the broadcast of this scene was
  offensive to public morals in the sense that it
  would further the aims of those who took part
  in the kangaroo court – or, alternatively,
  whether others would be likely to be
  influenced to do the same thing.

The BCCSA adjudicated as follows:
- It was satisfied that, given the newsworthiness
  of the event, it was necessary to show the
  footage of the flogging. This was shown at
  medium range. Although the cries of the persons being flogged could be heard quite dis-
  tinctly, there were no gratuitous film shots.
  The scenes were not too lengthy and the
  accent was on the event. "Our finding is
  accordingly that the scenes were not, as such,
  offensive to public morals. The newsworthiness of the event as well as the documentary
  nature of the material negated any conclusion
  of a transgression of the Code."
- Would the broadcaster of such a scene further
  the aims of this kind of extrajudicial intervention? Although the SABC had the "exclusive
  rights" to film the event, there is nothing in

the broadcast which shows any support or
sympathy for the "taxi association". The event
was filmed and produced as a news event and
falls into the category of a documentary. The
community's right to be informed, even of bar-
barous acts like this one, is of special significance in this matter. "In fact, we believe that
given the exclusive opportunity, the SABC
had a duty to photograph and broadcast this
event. We have come to the conclusion that
the footage could, in no way, further the aims
of kangaroo courts."

The complaint was therefore dismissed.

Analysis

The BCCSA's reasoning is basically sound, and
the public has a right to know. There are, however, some questions to be asked:
- Would the flogging have taken place if the
  SABC had not been there to film it? The
  BCCSA does not think so, but how can it be so
  certain? It is not enough to state that the
  SABC had no intention to associate itself with
  what was happening or that it did not stage the
  event. Would the attackers really have pro-
  ceeded with the (endless) flogging if the TV
  cameras were not rolling?
- Does being present at an illegal act like the
  one in question amount to criminal collusion?
- Why was the SABC *invited* to cover this
  event? To further what and whose aims? For
  propaganda purposes?
- The flogging continued for two hours. Of
  course the SABC could not be expected to
  report the matter to the police (or could it?).
  But what about the fact that journalists are
  ordinary citizens as well? There is a fine line
  between being a reporter and the duty of a
  normal citizen. Was that line crossed?

There certainly are no easy answers. It is, however, valuable to ask such questions.

A partial panel

The following case shows the dangers of choosing a panel that consists of like-minded people to discuss a controversial subject.

The SABC broadcast on 29 June 1997 at 22:30 a Christian-orientated programme called *Quest* on the topic of homosexuality. The question was whether being a homosexual and the practice of homosexuality constituted a sin.

After host Mark Manley had introduced the panel of three Christian congregational leaders, some background material (three interviews) was broadcast that called for more Christian understanding for homosexual relationships. In a further insert, texts were quoted from the Bible, all of which declared the practice of homosexuality to be a sin. The panel then did the same, in spite of several attempts by Manley to steer them in a different direction.

A psychiatrist and a psychologist, E. Allers and G. Grundling, lodged a complaint with the BCCSA about this programme. They said that they were consulted by many patients "who suffer severe trauma and psychological stress as a result of the ongoing espousal of societal opprobrium and exclusion on the grounds of their minority sexual orientation". It was argued that the programme was biased and one-sided. It failed to include the diversity of religious opinion on the issue and did not give homosexuals any opportunity to respond to the generalizations made. The panelists thereby "perpetuated arbitrary stigmatization and exclusion ... by creating the impression that the views expressed ... represent a universal and unanimous view of the church".

The arguments put forward by the SABC ran as follows:

- The focus of the programme was on what the Bible has to say on the subject. The panelists "simply represented the biblical view and that they had the right to do so as part of religious freedom". There are no verses that contradict these "clear statements".
- Where homosexuals were equated with criminals, alcoholics, adulterers, and idolaters, "this was a quotation from the Bible and not an opinion expressed by the presenters or any of the panelists". It is the Bible which condemns homosexuality, not the panelists, it was argued.
- The South African Constitution cannot be used to change what the Bible has to say on this subject.
- The background insert gave balance to the discussion and showed that there were different opinions on this matter.
- The panel debates were presented responsibly and with sensitivity.
- The programme did not advocate hatred and incitement to harm nor was there any offence to the religious convictions or feelings of a section of the population.
- No-one condemned homosexuals as persons.
- There was no intent to discriminate against or harm the homosexual community, "but rather to counsel those who might seek it via this programme".
- Several homosexuals were unable or unwilling to participate in the programme.

The SABC's defence could be summarized by the following statement:

> Given the focus of the programme, namely the biblical perspective on homosexuality, the discussion

was balanced, treated a sensitive issue with due care and responsibility, and neither attacked nor discriminated against gays. Being a Christian counselling programme, however, it conveyed a biblical point of view on homosexuality. It was never intended as a pros and cons debate.

The BCCSA acknowledged that, constitutionally, no restrictions could be placed on a panel discussion such as the one in question. Panelists have the religious freedom to express strong views against what they regard as sinful. The SABC also had the right to broadcast these views, *inter alia*, because it did not advocate hatred based on religion nor did it constitute incitement to cause harm. It also acknowledged that by its very nature a religious programme or channel need not be as fair (read: balanced, objective, neutral) as a public debate or an open channel.

Yet the BCCSA upheld the complaint, but not because of the views expressed by the three panelists: "It would be unrealistic to have expected from panelists to have changed their views just to accommodate the host. What was needed was an additional panelist ... who could have conveyed a more tolerant view ...".

The BCCSA did not direct the SABC to broadcast a correction; however, "... it would serve the interests of justice and fairness if the Respondent would consider dealing with the subject in a future related programme in a manner which would be in accordance with the guidelines given above".

Analysis

Like a number of other case studies, this one could also have been discussed in other chapters. It is used here to illustrate just how subjective the media can be, even in a programme that is not really supposed to be objective.

The BCCSA must be commended for acknowledging that religious programmes need not be as "fair" as other programmes. It is in the nature of religion to be biased and to take certain viewpoints and exclude others. Neutrality and objectivity certainly do not hold key positions here.

Although the SABC's defence was impressive (mainly because no hatred was advocated nor was there any incitement to do any harm), the BCCSA was correct in its finding that a fourth panelist should have been included who could have given a different perspective on the matter. The point is this: the subjectivity of the media is also revealed in the manner in which a panel is constructed. The result of this partial panel was that the programme amounted to a one-sided, subjective (although the claim is to be objective – based on biblical texts), and partial discussion. In addition, it is difficult to understand the SABC's argument that there was *no offence* to the religious convictions or feelings of a section of the population. Of course there was!

Two interrelated comments need to be made here. Firstly, the SABC defended itself by saying the panelists "simply represented the biblical view". But is there such a thing as *the* biblical view? And why would the three panelists have this particular wisdom at their disposal? Secondly, the SABC stated that the Bible – and not the panelists – condemned homosexuality (the panelists merely expressed what the Bible had to say on this matter). Any responsible theologian will admit that many issues in the Bible can be interpreted in more than one way. Throughout the ages the church has had to back down from previously held positions. It may just be possible that the issue of homosexuality will be one of those positions.

The complex issue of homosexuality should have been dealt with much more care, sensitivity, and openness. Is that too much to expect, even within the context of a religious (Christian) programme?

His master's voice?

Subjective (opinionated) journalism leads to the sacrifice of the media's independence, impartiality, and credibility.

On the evening of 18 December 1998 the SABC covered, on its three main channels, the opening speech at the annual conference of the Pan Africanist Congress of Azania (PAC) – a political party with representation in Parliament, and taking part in the elections that were due in May 1999.

The PAC complained to the Broadcasting Complaints Commission of South Africa, saying that *only one* sentence of the speech was reported – and even that was allegedly used out of context. According to the complaint, the President of the PAC, Dr Stanley Mokgoba, was quoted as saying that white people's commitment to this country and to Africa is their passport to become Africans. This report was preceded by *archive material* showing about eight Azanian People's Liberation Army (Apla) cadres chanting the slogan "one settler, one bullet" at a graveside. This material was first broadcast before the PAC suspended the armed struggle in 1992. The PAC's contention was that the SABC was "biased against it. This was irresponsible towards the People of South Africa by unfairly blotting the current reconciliatory stand of (the) PAC with its past militant stand." The PAC said it was public knowledge that:

- It had publicly denounced this particular slogan as a war cry by its armed wing two years before the 1994 general election.
- It had never officially endorsed this particular slogan.
- On the day in question this slogan was never chanted. Instead, a hand of friendship was extended to "all White tribes of South Africa"

and the listing of whites as PAC candidates of the 1999 election was approved.

- In reporting the previous annual conference of the ANC, the SABC did not use the particular slogan, "which was a war-cry for its armed wing and its youth league during the liberation struggle". When messages of the National Party were reported, past apartheid speeches were not similarly quoted.

The PAC concluded that the SABC had a hidden agenda and that it was "not in the interest of the SABC's political master (the ANC) to note such positive developments on the part of the PAC".

The SABC's defence was, firstly, that it had not been unfair to contrast the PAC's old and new approaches; instead, it was absolutely essential – in the interests of understanding – to do so. What was newsworthy was neither the conference as such nor its President's speech, but the fact that the PAC was changing its policy. Secondly, it was a valid question as to how the PAC, in the past, regarded whites. The answer was provided by the visuals of armed cadres chanting "one settler, one bullet". This sharp contrast "gave the necessary balance to the report". Finally, its reporters stated clearly that "this much feared PAC slogan is long forgotten".

The BCCSA agreed with the SABC that it is impossible to cover a lengthy conference fully and that the essence of Mokgoba's message was reported. However, the BCCSA had a problem with the introduction to the news item. Ronél van Zyl, who filed this report, stated in her introduction: "But, seriously hampering the PAC's performance, is a credibility problem...". By stating that, Van Zyl expressed an opinion. Then followed the visual of the cadres, chanting their slogan. Thereafter the dramatic change from the past (Mokgoba's speech) was shown. But nowhere in the report was the matter of "credibility" elaborated upon.

> This Commission is, accordingly, of the view that the visuals of the Apla cadres chanting the said slogan is, in effect, connected to the credibility problem... In this sense, the reference to 'credibility problem' amounts to unfair comment and to a contravention of Clause 3 of the Code of the BCCSA.

The BCCSA had a second problem with the report. Had the visuals of the Apla cadres been part of a historical overview of the PAC, the scenes would have been quite acceptable. "However, in a pre-election period the screening of such a scene which has a strong emotional effect tends to taint the image of the PAC." Together with the "credibility problem", this scene also contravenes the code, because it tends to question the sincerity of Mokgoba's call to all South Africans.

So, the news item amounted to unfair comment. However, the BCCSA found no evidence of any *male fides* (bad faith) on the part of the SABC.

> In the hurly-burly of news production, it would seem quite acceptable to add this historical text... We do not regard it as necessary to the SABC to publish a correction or even our decision. We believe that this judgment should serve as a guideline for pre-election broadcasts. If the specific news item were, in any case, to be discussed during a correction, the correction itself could be counter-productive by raising the spectre of the past once again.

Analysis

On the surface, the complaints boiled down to two matters: the concern that only one sentence of Mokgoba's speech had been reported; and that the context within which it was presented was unfair. The underlying issue, however, was the impression that there was no proper attempt at reporting as objectively as possible. Hence the PAC's conclusion that the SABC had a hidden agenda, because its "political master" was the ANC.

The matter of element selection is, as we have said, an extremely difficult one. A TV journalist sometimes sits the whole day in a conference, and eventually has only one minute to present the gist of events. This is no easy task, and only the best journalists succeed in doing it satisfactorily. The BCCSA was correct in saying that it is impossible to cover fully a conference of that magnitude. On the other hand, it is understandable that the PAC felt it was unfair to report only one sentence. However, one sentence could represent the heart of the matter – which is what happened to some extent in this case.

The BCCSA was also correct in its judgment on the context issue. Ronél van Zyl did express an opinion (on the PAC's alleged "credibility problem"). Van Zyl was free to think the PAC had a credibility problem (which she clearly linked to the much-feared slogan), but the public is not interested in her opinion. She was in the business of news reporting, not commenting on the news. Van Zyl's unprofessional conduct had the converse effect: it made her the one with the credibility problem. Journalists should keep their views to themselves if they are trying to report factually.

The reference to the PAC's past was, as the BCCSA adjudicated, not acceptable. The report was not a historical overview of the movement, but an attempt to portray what had expired. The sincerity of Mokgoba's call to all South Africans was indeed questioned by the context that was provided. This led to the PAC's accusation of the SABC being "his master's voice" (and therefore sacrificing its independence).

It is a sad day for the media if a perception is created that a news organization is so subjective that it takes editorial decisions that suit a particular political party. It does not really matter if that news organization is guilty or not – the perception is part of reality. The onus is on the media to do everything in their power not to create situations in which perceptions such as these can arise. The SABC could in this instance have minimized the harm it caused itself.

The only "mistake" the BCCSA probably made in this case is not to have instructed the SABC to publish a correction or its decision. The BCCSA's statement that it would seem quite acceptable to add that historical text in the hurly-burly of news production really lowers the standard of journalism. If it was an unfair and opinionated (subjective) report, as the BCCSA correctly decided, it was also not acceptable. Why live with it?

Participating in a smear campaign

The reporting of false allegations can lead to a perception that a media organization is hand in glove with forces orchestrating a smear campaign.

The *Mail & Guardian* reported in its edition of 30 April–7 May 1998 that the leader of the National Party (NP), Mr Marthinus van Schalkwyk, was being investigated by the police following allegations (and the laying of a charge) by a convicted thief that he (Van Schalkwyk) had paid the convict for sex (specifically, sodomy). At the time, sodomy between consenting adults was a criminal offence and carried a maximum ten-year prison sentence.

The main picture on the front page showed Van Schalkwyk standing next to the national flag, with the following words underneath the photograph: "Smear fears: A convict has laid sodomy charges against National Party leader Marthinus van Schalkwyk. But is it part of a dirty tricks campaign aimed at crippling the NP?" The story itself was run on page three. "The allegations bear all the hallmarks of a clumsy, very obvious attempt to smear or blackmail the NP chief", the second paragraph continued.

The story was that 25-year-old John David Hermanus had claimed that Van Schalkwyk paid him R20 for a brief sexual encounter in a Bloubergstrand house more than two years before. It was reported that Van Schalkwyk allegedly led Hermanus into a bedroom and

PHOTOGRAPH JAC DE VILLIERS

persuaded him to perform oral sex. Van Schalk-wyk then insisted on full sex, and did not use a condom, it was alleged. Hermanus also claimed that Van Schalkwyk had tried to buy his silence about the alleged incident, and that he had been liaising with the ANC about his story.

The following week, the first report in the *Mail & Guardian* mentioned the following:

- Van Schalkwyk's personal assistant, Mr Barnard Beukman, emphatically denied the allegations and said it was part of "some discrediting action".
- Hermanus was unable to identify the only witness (the owner of the house in Blouberg-strand). He spoke about a certain Mr Lloyd. However, none of the Lloyds in Blouberg-strand matched the description Hermanus provided.
- There was no record at the Voorberg prison, where Hermanus was serving seven years, of any visit in which NP representatives could have offered him money to keep quiet. (He had received three visits from journalists of the *Mail & Guardian*, and one from ANC branch executive Steve Carolus.)
- Hermanus produced a statement, dated 13 March 1998, in which he retracted his claims. The NP was to pay him R5 000 to release that statement should the allegations surface in the press, Hermanus claimed.
- The *Mail & Guardian* interviewed Hermanus on three occasions in the prison, and each time withheld the story "because of a lack of independent corroboration".

In its 8–14 May edition, the newspaper explained its decision to report on the matter: "The *Mail & Guardian* decided to report the probe last week following an approach by Senior Superintendent Attie Trollip – the province's top sex-crime sleuth who was quickly assigned to the case."

The NP then laid a complaint with the Ombudsman, a matter Van Schalkwyk described as "the first real test for the Ombudsman in the new South Africa" (*Die Burger*, 18 May 1998). This came after Western Cape Attorney-General Frank Kahn decided to ignore the charge because there was no truth in it. (He called the report a "*laagtepunt*" – a lowest point – in South African journalism.)

The Ombudsman, Mr Ed Linington, held a public hearing on 11 August 1998. Both the newspaper and the NP were given opportunities to state their case. The editor of the *Mail & Guardian*, Phillip van Niekerk, said that the crux of the matter was that his newspaper had decided to publish the story only after a formal complaint had been lodged that was being investigated by Trollip. He also said the statement in the second paragraph of the first report showed that the newspaper did not take the allegations seriously. However, if the most prominent policeman in the Western Cape investigates a sex charge against the Leader of the Opposition, it constitutes news, he added. The report was focused on the police investigation, and not on the allegations as such.

The NP countered by saying Van Schalkwyk had been slandered by the newspaper. It did not help to say first that the allegations were false, and then use the rest of the report to repeat these allegations in detail. The question was also asked if it was acceptable to publish allegations that were clearly false.

The Ombudsman decided on 20 August that the *Mail & Guardian* was within its rights to publish the story. The following comments were made, *inter alia*:

- The information in the report was accurate.
- The report was balanced because it stated the allegations could not be confirmed.
- The intention was not to give credibility to the allegations. The detail in the report was meant to show that the allegations could not be confirmed.
- The newspaper had known about the story for a long time, but only decided to publish when

it became clear the police regarded the matter in a serious light. Because of that fact, the newspaper was justified in publishing the report.

- South African newspapers do not hesitate to report on the private affairs of public figures.

However, the *Mail & Guardian* should have revealed the true reason why the police acted in the way they did. The newly elected premier of the Western Cape, Mr Gerald Morkel, had asked the police to investigate the case as a matter of urgency because he believed Van Schalkwyk was innocent. This would have put a whole new perspective on the matter, the Ombudsman said. (The *Mail & Guardian* reported on that matter in a follow-up article a week after the first one.) Linington also expressed his understanding for the fact that Van Schalkwyk felt victimized.

The NP appealed to the Appeal Board against this decision. The appeal was heard – and rejected (18 December 1998).

Analysis

There are many angles to this case. In essence, the Ombudsman was correct in his findings. The *Mail & Guardian* has to be congratulated for delaying its decision for so long. When the police started their investigation, the newspaper had every right to publish the story. It is news when a political leader is investigated on a sex charge. The public has a right to know. Likewise, Linington was correct in saying that reporting on Morkel's role would have put a whole new angle to the story. His understanding of Van Schalk-

wyk's frustration is also commendable.

However, there are other sides to this coin:

- Is it really ethically acceptable to publish allegations of this nature *if you seriously suspect there is no basis of truth to them*? Should newspapers publish untruths of all sorts and get away with it on the very flimsy basis that they admit these allegations may be false (or part of a scheme)?

- Should the *reason why* Hermanus laid this charge against Van Schalkwyk not have been taken into account? If it was part of a smear campaign against the NP leader, which the *Mail & Guardian* admitted it suspected, *why then participate in it*? The fact that an ANC representative visited Hermanus in jail *could* have pointed to a political plot. Of course this is not necessarily the case, but there had to be a reason for the visit. Why did Carolus visit Hermanus in jail?

- If there was a smear campaign and a certain political party was behind it, is it not understandable for the newspaper to be suspected of furthering the aims of that party? If that is the case, even the quest for objectivity and due impartiality may be said to have flown out the back door. For then the newspaper has sacrificed its independence.

Notes

[1] See Chapter 5

[2] At the time, Botes was a freelance correspondent for the SABC.

[3] Manoff was the Executive Director of the Center for War, Peace, and the News Media. This was extracted from a speech delivered at the colloquium on Science, Technology, and Government at New York University, 29 April 1996.

7 | Confidentiality

If you use an anonymous source, you must keep your promise – even if you have to go to jail for it.

Introduction

The relationship between a journalist and a source is by definition an ethical one, which can easily be abused by both the journalist and the source, for, to a great extent, this is a "used and be used" relationship.

Sources

Over the course of their careers, journalists develop various kinds of relationships with their sources. Not all these sources behave similarly. "Some of them facilitate the reporter's job, while some others compromise the central journalistic ethic of reporting the news honestly and fairly" (Hulteng 1976, 82). In this chapter it will

become clear just how careful journalists must be in their dealings with sources. To mention but one example: a source can use a journalist to further his or her own agenda and lie to further his or her own purposes. Indeed, "careful" is the word.

Journalists

Similarly, a journalist can also easily exploit a source, perhaps through the latter's lack of knowledge or experience, vanity or loneliness – and thereby shatter the relationship of trust. A journalist can also break a promise made to a source.

Just as there are two types of sources, when it comes to the relationship with sources there are two types of journalists: the "softies" and the "hardies". These extremes have everything to do with the personality of the journalist. The softies are usually scared of creating problems either with their bosses or their sources. That is their personality. They do everything in their power not to offend anybody. They therefore tend to get too cosy with their sources. In this process much of what could and should have been reported gets lost. On the other hand, the hardies tend to get cocky with their sources. They enjoy their power so much that it goes to their heads. Maybe they still have unfulfilled or childish dreams, or maybe they have just not had enough opportunity to push people around – and this is their chance. This type of journalist scares people away, but, like the softies, they find it very difficult to do their job properly.

For those who don't know, there does exist a golden mean.

"Confidential" is dangerous

Well-informed sources are the basis, the bread and butter, of any journalist's success. It goes without saying that the protection of these sources is a vital part of that success. And so is (the promise of) confidentiality. The amount of attention that most ethical codes give to this matter testifies to this fact.

There are, however, a number of important reasons why the use of confidential sources is potentially an extremely dangerous practice that should be avoided as far as possible. These reasons concern the public, journalists, and sources, as well as the people who may be attacked by these sources.

The following excerpt from an editorial in the *Washington Post* (12 February 1969) should serve as an eternal reminder of how easily journalists can misuse and abuse anonymous sources:

For the edification of those who may be unaware of the etymology, the family tree, so to speak, of the wellsprings of news, it goes something like this: Walter and Ann Source (nee Rumor) had four daughters (Highly Placed, Authoritative, Unimpeachable, and Well-Informed). The first married a diplomat named Reliable Informant. (The Informant brothers are widely known and quoted here; among the best known are White House, State Depart-

ment, and Congressional.) Walter Speculation's brother-in-law, Ian Rumor, married Alexander Conjecture, from which there were two sons, It Was Understood and It Was Learned. It Was Learned just went to work in the Justice Department, where he will be gainfully employed for four long years.

The reasons why the use of anonymous sources is dangerous include the following:

- An anonymous source can say *anything* to any journalist *without having to provide a single shred of evidence*. When a source is kept confidential, the reputation of the news organization "is being placed on the line, asking the audience to accept the information on faith" (Black et al. 1995, 197). All sorts of accusations can be made without any kind of hard evidence. Think about it. An aggrieved husband, a worried economist, a frustrated politician gives you "information" that could shake the universe. You publish it, whether you believe the source or not. This is a recipe for disaster.

- This means that *confidentiality can also easily be misused by the source (the latter's motives may be suspect)*. Always ask yourself: why doesn't your source want to be named? Of course there can be valid reasons for it. There could also be obscure ones. It is better to be cynical. Think about it. Check it out. Don't be a fool.

- The public has *no way of judging the validity of the information*. The public assesses the credibility of a certain statement or news report on the basis of who the source is. If, for example, an ordinary citizen says South Africa is in total anarchy, it carries little weight. If the President of the country makes the same statement, it would make news around the world. The public judges the validity of statements according to the importance (and knowledge) of a specific source. When an anonymous source is used, the public has no way of doing that, which tends to undermine the credibility of the media. The public (legitimately) expects sources to be fully identified.

- Anonymous sources can breed *distrust in the media*. If an anonymous source has been proven wrong and a certain newspaper (or TV/radio station) has consequently *once* broken trust, it is extremely difficult to build it up again. So make sure of your source's credibility and integrity. Very sure.
- *Confidentiality can also easily be misused by the media.* The following statement by Hugh Culbertson still rings true: "The unnamed news source has been called a safety valve for democracy and a refuge for conscience, but also a crutch for lazy, careless reporters" (*Journalism Quarterly* 57 Autumn 1980, 402–408[1]). In addition to often being an excuse for laziness, a journalist can use "evidence" from anonymous sources *because it suits his or her own agenda*. Unfortunately this happens all too easily. A journalist is very interested in a particular issue, and is looking for some substantiation for an all-too-flimsy story. There is no easier way to find that "substantiation" than by using an anonymous source. A journalist can even fabricate a source, and let "someone" say what he or she actually believes needs to be said.
- People who are accused by anonymous sources *do not know who is accusing them*. Remember that the anonymous source is saying something about someone. That "someone" doesn't know where the bullets are coming from. How fair is it to accuse someone if the person who is making the accusation hides behind anonymity?
- *It could bring the media in conflict with the law*. A complex question, as posed *inter alia* by Judge Arthur Chaskalson, is whether the press should be privileged by the law and, if so, in which respects (*Business Day* 17 October 1996, 13[2]). South African journalists frequently refuse to give information sought for the investigation of a serious crime and claim that seeking such information is an attack on its freedom. Yet "almost all countries have and enforce laws requiring such disclosures to be made" (*Business Day* 17 October 1996, 13). Chaskalson points out that the courts have in the past been fairly strict, "holding such material is not privileged and that the Press has no immunity against search warrants or subpoenas" (*Business Day* 1996, 13). This approach has been relaxed because the new Constitution guarantees freedom of expression and states specifically that this includes freedom of the press and other media. Still, "it is not clear what the implications of the Constitution will be on this issue, and whether it will result in greater protection being given to the Press against subpoenas and search warrants than in the past" (*Business Day* 17 October 1996, 13).

Chaskalson makes this very important point: information in the hands of a journalist is not necessarily confidential or privileged. Press freedom should not be seen in isolation. "It has an impact on other rights and interests and has to be balanced against them" (*Business Day* 1996, 13). Moreover, press freedom is not an absolute right. It "does not entitle a journalist to trample upon the dignity and privacy of others; a constraint that some journalists and newspapers are reluctant to acknowledge" (*Business Day* 17 October 1996, 13).

This means that it is still possible for a journalist who refuses to give information to be sentenced in a court of law. This can be done on the basis of Article 205 of the Criminal Procedure Act. Since the prosecution of *Beeld* journalist Andries Cornelissen (a case study in this chapter) this law has effectively been put "on hold". It is sincerely hoped in media circles that this law will be withdrawn, as requested by the Truth and Reconciliation Commission (TRC) in October 1998.

But sometimes also necessary

The preceding discussion does not mean that a journalist may under no circumstances use an anonymous source. Usually, the ground rule is that you fully identify your news sources, as this gives more credibility to your story. However, you may lose many important stories if anonymous sources are never used at all. There are indeed some stories that you cannot get otherwise.

The rationale runs thus: there are some kinds of news it is important for the public to know about (for example, the Watergate scandal) that cannot be obtained by conventional means. To get at such news, reporters must sometimes promise anonymity to the sources who constitute the only avenue to the news. When such a promise is made, it is in the public interest; the public's right to know is being served, and that right-to-know concept derives from the First Amendment. (Hulteng 1976, 97)

There are a few conditions that should be met before a journalist can contemplate the use of an anonymous source:

- The story must be of overwhelming importance and in the public interest.
- The story cannot be obtained by any other means.
- The trustworthiness of the source must be above suspicion.

So, you have a wonderful story and your anonymous source is willing to sing to the heavens. Go ahead, if there is no other way. But how do you proceed?

How to use anonymous sources

There are several things to keep in mind when using an anonymous source:

- Be very clear about your institution's stance on this matter. In some media institutions, a promise of anonymity may only be made if the editor, or at least someone on the editorial staff, gives permission. If you then make all sorts of promises without consulting your bosses, and you end up in court (being an individual of high integrity), you cannot expect your superiors to back you.
- Try (again) to convince your source to go public with his or her name. Your source could be worried about things of no real consequence. It might even turn out that anonymity is unnecessary. See what you can do!
- If the source won't comply, try to find the information from a different source. Perhaps you can find another source who will give you the same information. Who knows? It is worth your while to try. It goes without saying that it is always better to name a source than otherwise.
- Try to make a promise on condition that you are not bound to it if the matter goes to court. It could happen that you — and your source — end up in jail. This can be prevented by a simple arrangement. If you give a conditional promise of anonymity, you are not bound to your conscience when the law comes calling.
- If you promise anonymity unconditionally, you have got to stick to it, even if you have to go to jail for it. Sometimes a source will not be happy with a conditional promise. Then your integrity as a journalist is at stake. Once you have given your word, there is no way out. If you think there is, you should not be a journalist.
- Try to comply when somebody asks you to state that he or she is not the anonymous source. Sometimes the wrong people come under suspicion through the use of anonymous sources. A boss, for example, may wrongly suspect an employee of being a source and then discriminate against that person. If at all possible, try and find a

way. You do not have to publish this information; it could be enough to call the boss and say that he or she suspects the wrong person. Try to limit the amount of harm that your reporting can do. However, this can become very tricky.

- Make it clear to the public why you are using an anonymous source. It is not good enough to use anonymous sources to convince the public that you really know what you are talking about. The public not only has a right to know what concerns them, it also has a right to know why people who claim to have relevant information want to stay anonymous. Sometimes the reasons for anonymity are obvious, sometimes they are not.
- In political reporting, the political affiliation of the source must be mentioned. Don't underestimate the importance of this. Politicians are a species of their own. They use (and abuse) any opportunity that comes their way. Successful politicians do not even wait for opportunities – they create them. You will lose even more credibility than normal if an anonymous politician says all kinds of things about another party and you do not even mention his or her affiliation. So be careful, especially around deadline time. Some politicians understand deadlines; do not give them the opportunity of abusing you for the sake of their own propaganda.
- Reveal the name of your anonymous source to your editor if he or she insists that you do so. No responsible editor will easily demand that you provide the name of your source. But your editor will have solid reasons for asking – and you will have to comply. It is a good policy always to let your source understand in advance that your editor may demand to know his or her name. A good editor can be expected to keep that information confidential. However, would you deceive your editor if you suspect he or she would reveal your source?
- Always make sure that an anonymous source does not attack any person or institution. If a source who is willing to be named attacks someone else, the latter should have a fair chance to respond. But if your source is anonymous, the person who is attacked is at a disadvantage. Do not give your source that unfair advantage.

- If you find your source has lied to you, tell the public. All promises of anonymity are null and void if you discover at any time that your source has lied to you. Publish his or her name, and tell the public the source lied to you.
- Do not keep any records of confidential sources. If the police try to confiscate whatever they are after, they will find nothing of any substance if you have no confidential records. You are not an arm of the police, the security services, or whatever. Be smart.
- Never talk to anybody about anonymous sources or share any confidential information with them. This will not only protect you, but your sources as well. This goes especially for your family and your friends. Do not put them at risk.

Some other points

Consider the following general remarks on how to deal with sources:

- *Be clear when your conversation is on or off the record.* It is imperative that both you and your source are very clear when you talk on or off the record. If it is not clear to everybody, all sorts of problems can arise. Avoid this situation at all costs. Some journalists even refuse to accept any information off the record.
- *Never say "yes" to an off-the-record conversation after it has taken place.* All too often, a source divulges important information, only to have second thoughts afterwards. That is your source's problem, not yours. However, try to be fair.
- *Never tape any source without their knowledge.* Some journalists argue that a tape recording helps them to get their facts straight. It is a self-protection mechanism. Let's not argue against that. A tape recording is not ethical or unethical as such and can indeed save your bacon. But it is the ethical thing to let your source know that you are actually taping the conversation. That will make him or her more

careful of what is said, which is a good thing. A TV or radio journalist should be even more careful here: let your source know that you may possibly use his or her voice (or picture).

- *Never abuse sources nor be abused by them.* Do not, for example, put words into the mouth of a naive source. On the other hand, never let a source dictate to you what you should write.
- *Identify yourself as a reporter at the earliest possible moment.* A journalist has great power: you can cause a great deal of harm, or do a great deal of good. That power should be used with discretion. If a source does not know you are a journalist, or finds out too late, you put him or her at a serious disadvantage.
- *Try to verify all information.* This reduces the chances that you will be misled. The general rule is not to publish unless you have verified the information from another source.

Do you inform your source about your story?

Some journalists say, passionately, "no" to reading any story to a source (or faxing or e-mailing it) before publication. Other reporters are equally emphatic, but on the "yes" side.[3]

Some say "yes" because:

- you create goodwill and build a relationship of trust with your source;
- unnecessary mistakes can be corrected, especially if your source is inexperienced and may have misrepresented him- or herself;
- it gives journalists peace of mind;
- journalists should not be so arrogant as to think that they cannot make mistakes;
- sometimes you can improve your story (for example, by getting even better quotes or information);
- you do this mainly because you want the truth and not so much to avoid embarrassment.

Others say "no" because:

- you lose control over your own story and become a glorified secretary;
- it is your work as a journalist to write and you should take responsibility for that work;
- it is time-consuming;
- it can lead to all sorts of arguments, as sources may claim that they have been incorrectly quoted (and you are sure that is not the case);
- some sources think you are asking them to make a contribution to your story;
- your story can more easily be leaked to the opposition, especially if it is faxed or e-mailed;
- the source can contact your boss and put pressure on him or her to stop publication;
- sources can hold a media conference and deny your report, even before publication. (This happened in the US when some TV stations heard that the *Washington Post* was to publish a positive report on a person who was accused of a crime.)

A golden mean

If you are in any doubt about parts of the story, the gist of it, or some quotes, it is better for all parties concerned if you check. Rather correct possible mistakes before publication than afterwards. This especially goes for stories that are highly technical, such as medical matters, science issues, or economic affairs. In the first and last instance it is the end product that counts, not your ego.

If you do "consult", it must always be made quite clear that you maintain your journalistic integrity. And, of course, you must not change your style of writing – you are only checking some vital facts or quotes. However, this "checking" should be done as little as possible. Rather take responsibility for your work.

Examples

Let us look at two examples to learn more about the issue of sources.

Bob Woodward

American journalist Bob Woodward, of Watergate fame, regularly uses anonymous sources, and has regularly been taken to task for this. A public debate erupted in 1997 over an article by Woodward that appeared in the *Washington Post* on 2 March, in which he used nine unnamed sources (Robertson 1997, 11[4]). Woodward reported that Vice-President Al Gore had solicited millions of campaign dollars by way of a formidable fund-raising network, attributing his assertions to "records and interviews with more than 100 organizers, donors, and officials" (Robertson 1997, 11). Woodward referred to his sources, *inter alia*, as "Gore associates", "a donor", and a "senior Democratic official".

The *Post*'s ombudsman, Geneva Overholser, criticized Woodward, saying: "We should always assume that information provided by confidential informants is weaker than information attributable to real people" (Robertson 1997, 11). She added: "Besides, a reporter should always question the motives of sources who leak information" (Robertson 1997, 11). Managing Editor Robert Kaiser responded, defending Woodward: "When covering an important story, attribution is not always a realistic expectation" (Robertson 1997, 11).

The *Post*'s stylebook has the following to say on this matter:

> Before any information is accepted without full attribution, reporters must make every reasonable effort to get it on the record. If that is not possible, reporters should consider seeking the information elsewhere. If that in turn is not possible, reporters should request an on-the-record reason for concealing the source's identity and should include the reason in the story. (Robertson 1997, 11)

Woodward claimed that he followed these directions to the letter, claiming that the truthfulness of the story is the important thing, not the sourcing. Overholser reacted by saying there was a larger issue

at stake. She cited a 1985 American Society of Newspaper Editors survey in which 49 per cent of journalists polled approved of the use of unnamed sources while only 28 per cent of readers did. "Discomfort often seems a sufficient defense against being named, and pithiness reason enough to get a quote in" (Robertson 1997, 11). To which Woodward drily replied that the dispute created "a new awareness that the goal is to get things on the record if you can. It doesn't hurt to be reminded of that". However, Woodward's understatement is not enough; such awareness must do more than just "not hurt" – it should caution all journalists to use anonymous sources with great circumspection.

The Pentagon Papers

On 13 June 1971 the *New York Times* reported that it had received 7 000 pages of a secret – stolen – document that became known as the Pentagon Papers. This document had been commissioned by the then Secretary of Defense Robert McNamara, and detailed American involvement in Vietnam since 1945. By that time, thousands of Americans had already died in Vietnam, tens of billions of dollars had been spent on the war effort, and the nation was "acrimoniously divided", the Pentagon Papers revealed (Christians et al. 1995, 82).

After the second publication, on 14 June, Attorney-General John Mitchell asked the *Times* to stop publication. He argued that the papers contained "information relating to the national defense of the United States" (Christians et al. 1995, 81). Mitchell also claimed that publication was "directly prohibited" by the Espionage Law. In a statement made two hours after Mitchell's "request", the *Times* "respectfully" declined to withhold information, saying that it believed it was in the interest of Americans to be informed about this matter. On that same day the *Times* was enjoined from further publication, pending a hearing on the government's action. This time the newspaper obliged.

Three days later, on 17 June, the *Washington Post* obtained 4 000 pages of the same document. The question was obvious: to publish or not to publish. The *Post*'s lawyers advised against it, arguing that the *Times*'s case must first run its course. Publication could be interpreted as contempt of court. However, Ben Bagdikian, the then assistant managing editor for national news, saw the matter "strictly in terms of freedom of the press and journalistic responsibility to the public" (Christians *et al.* 1995, 81).

The next day, Friday 18 June, the Post published its first report – and was also immediately enjoined. The *Boston Globe* and the *St. Louis Post-Dispatch*, who had also started to publish parts of the document, albeit on a smaller scale, were also enjoined. The *Post* continued to publish, and on 30 June the Supreme Court ruled by six votes to three in favour of the press.

The questions arising from these cases that are relevant to the discussion in this chapter are:

- Was it ethically permissible to publish classi-fied (secret) material? The central issue for the press was whether it was in the interest of the state and state security to withhold publi-cation, or merely in the interest of a certain political party and certain politicians. Under normal circumstances it is ethically good to obey legally constituted authority. However, most codes of ethics make provision for civil disobedience in extreme cases. The Post was correct in defying the initial enjoinment. Although the government wanted the courts to rule that the information in the Pentagon Papers endangered state security, it was really a matter of convenience for a certain political party and certain politicians.

- Should newspapers use stolen documents as a source? From a deontological point of view, this question will always be answered in the negative. Stealing is wrong, and likewise for the publication of stolen documents. Utilita-rians will take the opposite stance. The mate-rial had enormous consequences for the US. The public had a right to know.

The golden mean would probably be to say that the information in stolen documents should be checked out before publication; should the infor-mation be of overriding importance, however, a case could be made for publication.

Not prepared to testify

It should be the media's prerogative to keep their sources and information confidential.

Rashaad Staggie, the leader of the Hard Livings gang, was murdered in Salt River, Cape Town, in the course of a march staged by People Against Gangsterism and Drugs (Pagad) on 6 August 1996. He was shot and his body was set alight.

On 22 August 1996 the police subpoenaed the editors of the Cape Town newspapers *Die Burger*, *The Argus*, and the *Cape Times*, as well as the SABC and two news agencies, the South African Press Association (SAPA) and Associated Press, to hand over information pertaining to Pagad. According to the subpoenas, all photographs, video material, and transcriptions of interviews with members of Pagad had to be handed over to the police. The names of journalists who were responsible for the coverage of that specific event also had to be made known to the police. The editors refused to comply. A suspect, Mr Ozeer Booley of Grassy Park, was later identified, without the help of the media, and the subpoenas were subsequently withdrawn.

In January 1998 a photographer from the *Cape Argus*, Andrew Ingram – who had arrived at the murder scene twenty minutes after the incident – was subpoenaed to give evidence against Booley. In the same month, another photographer, Christo Lötter of *Die Burger*, was also subpoenaed. Lötter, together with reporter Kobus Louwrens, had been injured at the scene of the crime.

In February 1998, the state suddenly withdrew its case against Booley. An inquest was then held, which started on 20 August 1998. This led to new subpoenas, dated 7 August 1998, which were served on the same media organizations mentioned previously. Seventeen people were subpoenaed. This time, Article 8.1 of the Law on Inquests was used. The editors again refused to comply and gave their reasons in court early in February 1999. The presiding official of the inquest, Mr Johan Venter, decided on 5 February that fifteen of the seventeen subpoenas were valid and that they could legally be enforced. If the media still refused to give the "evidence", they could be prosecuted under Article 189 of the Criminal Procedure Act. The media then took this matter to the Cape High Court.

The main reasons given by the media organizations for refusing to hand over any material to the authorities were:

- The independent task of the media of informing the public as accurately and as objectively as possible would be undermined if the perception is created that the media must do the job of the legislature.
- The situation will worsen if it looks as if the media is taking sides.
- Members of the media could become targets in the conflict. (Indeed, some received death threats.)
- It is an attack on the freedom of the media if their members are subpoenaed in their personal capacity to give evidence in a case that they covered in their professional capacity.

On 20 February 1999 the Minister of Justice, Mr Dullah Omar, and members of the media signed an accord on the controversial Article 205 of the Criminal Procedure Act. This accord stipulated that the media had a temporary right to protect their sources while further talks were held between the media and the government. Then another suspect, Mr Abdussalaam Ebrahim, was charged, and the subpoenas were again withdrawn. Advocate Koos Louw, for the Staggie family, said his client understood that the media must protect their sources. However: "We don't ask the media to act as agents of the police, but as responsible citizens and not to hide behind the privilege of press freedom".

On 20 October 2000 the case took a dramatic new turn when the police raided the offices of the SABC, Associated Press, and Reuters and confiscated video material that contained footage of the Staggie incident. The police raid, carried out in accordance with Section 21 of the Criminal Procedure Act, took place on 19 October – coinciding not only with World Press Freedom Day but also Media Freedom Day, set aside to mark the advent of media freedom in South Africa following the end of the apartheid era! The search warrant was granted by a magistrate and also authorized by the national Director of Public Prosecutions, Bulelani Ngcuka.

According to a newspaper report, the material, to be used in the trial of suspects in the Staggie attack, "was raw footage which had not been broadcast but which could not be obtained without a warrant" (*Cape Times* 20 October 2000). The South African National Editors' Forum (SANEF) and other media organizations, as well as several political parties, immediately condemned the raid. The footage was later used in court.

Analysis

Take another look at the reasons given by the media for refusing to hand over any form of possible evidence. *They are all valid.*

In the Staggie murder case, journalists were not the only witnesses to the crime. If they were, it would have been another matter (see also Case 5). It could then be argued that it is the civil duty of a journalist to testify – even if he or she becomes a witness to a crime in the course of professional duty.

However, where there are other witnesses, as is evidently the case in the Staggie murder case, the media should be left alone to do their job. It should be the media's prerogative to keep their sources and information confidential. This is essential in a democracy such as South Africa's, where freedom of the media is one of the cornerstones of society.

The police raids must be condemned in the clearest possible terms. Not only were relations between the media and government harmed, and the February 1999 accord broken, but the raids can also be seen as an attack on media freedom and a blatant example of the abuse of power. This is not the thing to do in a fledgling democracy.

Rumours, rumours, rumours

The use of anonymous sources to spread unfounded allegations and rumours can cause a great deal of harm – both to those who are victimized and to the media organization.

The murder of Mr Deon de Wet, a well-known businessman from Johannesdal (near Pniël, Stellenbosch) was in the news for several weeks. He had been shot fifteen times in the chest and head on 1 May 2000 in the main bedroom of his house, while his wife and two children were in the building.

A week later, a radio report on Kfm subtly linked the name of the 24-year-old rugby Springbok hero Breyton Paulse with De Wet's murder. It was reported that Paulse would not be questioned by the police in connection with his alleged relationship with De Wet's 30-year-old widow, Mrs Petronel de Wet.

The seed was sown that Paulse had a possible sexual relationship with Mrs De Wet. The police then emphatically denied that Paulse could in any way be linked to the murder. From what could have been established at the time, Paulse could have been a friend of the family, or merely an acquaintance. In the meantime, Mrs. De Wet was arrested on charges relating to her husband's death. She was suspected of having asked someone to kill her husband.

The next day, 12 May, the *Cape Times* published a story under the heading: "Breyton's friend on murder charge". Mrs De Wet "said to be a close friend of Springbok and Stormer rugby hero Breyton Paulse" was charged with murder after she had confessed to hiring two men to kill her husband, it was reported. It was also said that the police "confirmed" that Mrs De Wet was "close" to Paulse, but again denied that the latter was a suspect in the murder case.

At that time, Paulse was preparing for an important match in Durban and was not able to speak to the press. However, the paper reported: "Paulse went to ground yesterday as rumours surfaced of his relationship with the deceased's wife". The report continued: "'Everybody knew about Petro and Breyton', said a family member, who asked not to be named. 'He used to be at the house all the time, even when her husband was away. Deon even confronted her about it, but she denied it'."

The *Eikestad Nuus*, a local Stellenbosch newspaper, published a report on 19 May about the various rumours that were said to be floating around town. Ten rumours were mentioned. One of these was that Paulse and Mrs De Wet had "close ties". None of the rumours were attributed to a source. The media, for an undisclosed reason, stopped reporting these rumours soon after 19 May.

Analysis

This is a classic inversion of the journalist's guidelines, and involves maximum harm and minimum truth. The reporting on Kfm, as well as in the *Cape Times* and the *Eikestad Nuus*, testify to the danger that looms when the media make use of anonymous sources and spread unfounded

rumours. The mere fact that Paulse's name was mentioned in connection with the deceased's wife was bad enough. It was implied, albeit mostly as rumour, that Paulse could in some way be implicated in the murder. It was even insinuated that the murder took place because Paulse and Mrs De Wet were lovers.

The report that Paulse "went to ground...as rumours surfaced of his relationship with the deceased's wife" was scandalous, to say the least. Paulse did not duck the media – he was preparing with his team-mates for a match.

In this whole saga, the people who were responsible for the allegations against Paulse were never mentioned. The sources remained anonymous. They could say anything they wanted without having to prove anything – and the media, as mentioned before, were all too eager to spread these rumours. What makes the media's reporting even worse is that none of the allegations or rumours was verified. The reports were unfounded and untested.

The legal side of this tragic piece of journalism is one thing – Paulse could probably have sued the lot of them. The ethical side is another matter. This scandalous use of so-called anonymous "sources" to spread rumours can do members of the public, as well as the media, irreparable harm.

Case Study 3 | To be or not to be

The decision to protect a source, or to adhere to a promise made to a source, can be infinitely difficult – and dangerous.

The problem of gang-related crime and violence has plagued the Western Cape metropole for many years. But in the late 1990s, it suddenly seemed as if gangsterism was spreading to the rural areas as well. In one of these cases, the Terrible Josters gang became active in Bredasdorp towards the end of 1999.

Then, on 21 November of that year, about a thousand people from the local community decided they had had enough and took to the streets. When the incident was over, three alleged gangsters were dead (the crowd wanted to burn their bodies, but was stopped by the police), two shebeens (thought to be the headquarters of the gang) burnt down and six vehicles burnt out. The police, who used rubber bullets and tear gas, also shot and killed a community leader, Dennis Newman.

On 3 December 1999 the alleged leader of the Terrible Josters was shot twice (not fatally) in Hawston, a town some 100 km from Bredasdorp – just one day after another suspected leader and fifteen members of the gang had been arrested.

In mid-June 2000 the community of Bredasdorp again tried to drive out suspected gangsters. This was unsuccessful as the police were tipped off and prevented any further violence. Threats were made to the effect that this attack would be repeated shortly thereafter.

A month later *Die Burger* received a call from one of the leaders of the community. The caller spoke to Arnold Lombard (a pseudonym) and gave information as to where and when their next action was about to take place. It would be something similar to the events of 21 November 1999. The source, who identified him-/herself, specifi-

cally asked Lombard not to inform the police about the community's plan of action.

Lombard, who held a middle management position at the newspaper, took the matter to his immediate superior. A serious discussion was held: lives could be saved if the police were tipped off. Or should the media let things be and just report on what was to happen?

The decision not to inform the police was not taken lightly. "I had made a promise to my source, who depended on me. I would have lost the source if I broke the promise and told the police", Lombard said.

On 21 July 2000 *Die Burger* sent another journalist, Barnie Louw, to Bredasdorp to report on the possible violence. Louw reasoned along the same lines as his superiors. When he and photographer Johann van Tonder arrived at Bredasdorp they made contact with their source, who showed them the house that was going to be attacked. However, nothing came of the planned attack.

Analysis

It is commendable that the journalists debated this issue in depth. The situation in Bredasdorp was volatile and the conflict potential was huge. The fact that lives could be saved deserved serious consideration. People, with faces, names, and relatives, were involved. This was a matter of journalistic *versus* civic duty.

Yet their decision not to tip off the police was the right one. As has been said previously, the media's business is to report (and interpret) the news – and not to do the police's job for them. The media should disclose such information to the authorities only in extreme cases, as suggested earlier.

A few remarks need to be added:

- Had the journalists informed the police, they would have breached the promise of confidentiality between themselves and the source — and lost a great deal of credibility. If word got out that journalists from *Die Burger* could not be trusted, what source would even think of contacting that newspaper again?

- Even if the community was prohibited from action and lives were saved on that specific night, it would probably only have meant that the bloodshed had been postponed. Crime was a serious problem in that community and violence would probably have erupted anyway at a later stage.

- The motives of the Bredasdorp community leader should be questioned. The media must be extremely careful not to become involved in illegal acts or to be used by people for reasons of their own.

Real sources?

When confidentiality is used as an argument not to produce "evidence" that a journalist did not have in the first place, the rest of the media can justifiably feel stabbed in the back.

In a bizarre case, Hannes Smith, editor of the *Observer* in Windhoek, was found guilty in 1998 of contempt of court in a case pertaining to the death of advocate Anton Lubowski, a well-known member of the South West African People's Organisation (SWAPO). Smith claimed that he knew who Lubowski's murderer was and that he had documents to prove it. The editor said he paid a "certain source" in Johannesburg R4 800 for four documents that contained codes used by the murderer and his accomplices, a sketch of Lubowski's office, and pictures of his house. The source showed him how to decipher the codes, Smith claimed.

This case was followed closely in South Africa, because some members of the former Civil Cooperation Bureau (CCB) were said to be involved. Smith said there were eight codenames on the list, including Mr Martin Hennig of the Johannesburg City Council, Donald Acheson, an Irish mercenary, and Calla Botha, Chappies Maree, Donald Barnard, and Staal Burger, all former members of the CCB.

After being subpoenaed, Smith initially refused to disclose the "information". Later he said that, in mid-February 1996, he had put the documents in a drawer in his office and was unable to locate them. He testified that he and two colleagues had thoroughly searched the premises of the *Observer*, but without success. According to Smith, the newspaper had moved offices in December 1995 and the documents could have been lost at that time.

Judge Nic Hannah was frustrated by Smith's "hesitation" in handing over the alleged evidence. Hannah eventually found him guilty of misleading the court and sentenced him to four months in jail. The sentence was suspended until the next day at 9:00, on condition that Smith produced the documents. Smith failed to comply with the court's request and was then sent to jail. About one week later, he was released on bail of R1 000 and granted leave to appeal.

In an interview immediately after he received bail, Smith said he would hand over the documents to the Attorney-General of Namibia, advocate Hans Heyman, within two weeks. "I shall show South Africa and Namibia who Hannes Smith is. I shall solve this murder within three months. They will see. Everything that was not done the previous eight years by the police and the special investigative team, I shall do. I'll show them who the murderer is." This never happened.

Analysis

When examined at face value, Smith's initial refusal to hand over the alleged information to the relevant authorities seemed to be above board and to testify to his journalistic integrity. However, Smith later promised to produce the evidence. Why this change of mind? Eventually he failed to deliver on his promise that he would "solve" the case. This can only mean he never had the "information" in the first place.

So, hiding behind the sound journalistic principle of confidentiality, Smith not only misled the court, but his readers as well. On both counts, that is appalling. The loss of credibility in the Lubowski case must have had serious implications for the rest of the newspaper in particular and also for the media in general.

This is a disturbing example of how not to use the principle of confidentiality. When used as an argument not to produce nonexistent "evidence", it should be no surprise if fellow journalists feel betrayed.

| Prepared to go to jail

Normally, a journalist can only be forced to disclose information if the state cannot get it elsewhere.

In 1993 Andries Cornelissen, a journalist working for *Beeld*, was given a one-year jail sentence for refusing to answer questions in court under oath. (He was, however, prepared to hand in a sworn affidavit.) Magistrate R. G. le Roux found in the Johannesburg Magistrates Court in July of that year that Cornelissen did not have sufficient reason to refuse to testify in connection with a report on statements made by Mr Peter Mokaba, then leader of the ANC Youth League.

Cornelissen appealed, and won (on 10 March 1994). Faan Coetzer, one of Cornelissen's legal representatives, called the verdict an affirmation that the independence of the media is in the public's interest (*Beeld* 11 March 1994).

The court emphasised in its verdict the principle that a journalist must subject him to questioning only if it is necessary for the welfare of the community. When a journalist does not try to evade his responsibility towards society (but rather tries to fulfil his duty towards society) it gives him enough reason to refuse to testify. (*Beeld* 11 March 1994)

According to Coetzer, this case proves that it is a good defence against Article 205 of the Criminal Procedure Act when a journalist can say that he or she is not the only source of information. "For journalists it is a breakthrough to know that they will not be the only target in an investigation. Previously a journalist could only claim that his life or property will be endangered if he allows himself to be questioned. The court now defends the right of the media to report objectively" (*Beeld* 11 March 1994).

It is especially important to note what Judge P. J. Schabort said in his verdict (*Beeld* 11 March 1994):

- Cornelissen never claimed to be in a privileged position as a journalist or because he was involved in the press as an institution.
- *Beeld* has a continuous duty in the public's interest to gather newsworthy information and to publish it.

- The newspaper's ability to perform this task is, *inter alia*, dependent on the fact that its reporters have a relationship with the public which is built on trust.
- If the public believes a journalist acts as an informant for the police or identifies him-/herself with the police, his or her reputation can be badly damaged and access to important 'news sources seriously hampered.
- The police did not seriously try to get other witnesses, while such an investigation could easily have produced such witnesses.
- Cornelissen could have seriously damaged his public reputation as an independent and objective journalist if he had testified. He would also have seriously endangered his chances of getting political news in the future.
- Cornelissen would have damaged the image of *Beeld*.
- Cornelissen's willingness to hand in a sworn affidavit testifies to his good faith towards the police and the state.
- The sworn affidavit could not have been seen as choosing the side of a political figure because his report had already appeared in *Beeld*.
- The state negated the public's grave interest in the matter and Cornelissen's sensitive, dangerous, and important role as a reporter.

Judge M. J. Stegmann said that Cornelissen, by publishing his report, already did more than anybody to bring the matter to the attention of the public (and the police). "He did not want to be involved any further than that. His freedom under the law and his right of privacy of course allowed him to take that position" (*Beeld* 11 March 1994).

Hennie van Deventer, the then Chief Executive Officer: Newspapers for Nasionale Pers, described the verdict as a beacon for the press in general. "The result … is a much clearer picture of the role of newspapers in society and of the room that journalists can claim to report as uninvolved observers. Newspapers now know where they stand with Article 205" (*Beeld* 11 March 1994).

Analysis

Although this case is not strictly about the protection of sources (confidentiality), it touches on the related matter of whether or not to disclose information in a court of law.

Journalists are ordinary citizens and are, as such, not above the law. As Judge Chaskalson has rightly pointed out, press freedom is not an absolute right, and information in the hands of a journalist is not necessarily confidential or privileged. On the other hand, if journalists are forced to testify, the extremely important relationship of trust between the media and the public is destroyed. We must also take into account that press freedom remains one of the cornerstones of democracy.

That leaves us with the difficult but important question of where to draw the line between a journalist's duties as a citizen and as a reporter. The court's decision to uphold Cornelissen's appeal implies that the state can only force journalists to testify if they cannot get the necessary information elsewhere. This is a step in the right direction. However, what this will mean in future similar cases remains to be seen.

It stands to reason that the more important and exclusive the information, the heavier the journalist's duty to testify. If a journalist, for example, knows that some enemy is on the verge of dropping a nuclear bomb on Johannesburg, we would expect the reporter to disclose that information to the relevant powers as soon as possible. This is a difficult issue, but perhaps it can be said that in the most extreme cases, as when the security of the state is really at risk, journalists should consider telling the authorities about it. However, that is a slippery road, as can be seen in the Staggie case. In the meantime, Cornelissen's main concern apparently was his own credibility as a journalist as well as that of the newspaper he was working for. That is indeed commendable.

Notes

[1] As quoted by Christians et al. 1995, p. 75.

[2] The article in *Business Day* is an edited version of a speech Chaskalson delivered at the Commonwealth Press Union's Rainbow 1996 conference in Cape Town. Chaskalson is the president of the Constitutional Court of South Africa.

[3] Alicia Shephard looks at this question in more depth in the *American Journalism Review* March 1996, pp. 40–44

[4] *American Journalism Review* May 1997, p. 11 Lori Robertson is the administrative director of the Casey Journalism Center for children and Families at the University of Maryland College of Journalism. The Woodward issue is also discussed in the monthly *Brill's Content* (November 1999, p. 22 and following pages). In this article, Steven Brill raises some serious questions about Bob Woodward's book *Shadow: five presidents and the legacy of Watergate*, to which Woodward responds in the same article.

8 | Conflict of interest

Journalists must be free of obliga-
tion to any interest other than the
people's right to know (The Society
of Professional Journalists).

Introduction

In general it can be said that conflicts of interest[1] develop when the interests that a journalist may have outside his or her company clash or compete with the interests of the company itself. "Simply stated, a *conflict of interest* is a clash between professional loyalties and outside interests that undermines the credibility of the moral agent" (Day 1991, 156). It constitutes a situation in which the media are no longer free to act independently.

Conflict of interest "raises some basic questions concerning fairness and justice, two important and fundamental values" (Day 1991,

156). No news organization can allow a situation to develop in which doubt is cast on the organization's commitment to be duly impartial.

It has been stated several times that the basic ethical guidelines for journalists are to seek truth and report it as fully as possible, to minimize harm, and *to act independently*. The latter means journalists should not engage in any activity that could compromise their integrity or damage their credibility or that of their organization (Black et al. 1995, 94).

This is an extremely serious matter, because if there are conflicts of interest, the integrity and credibility of the reporter, as well as that of his or her news organization, is at stake. Journalists have a tremendous responsibility. "To abdicate that responsibility, to put awards or friendships or self-interest or economic gain ahead of public benefit, is unacceptable and unethical" (Black et al. 1995, 91).

Some of the most prominent international ethical codes make no bones about this:

- The American Society of Newspaper Editors: "Freedom from all obligations except that of fidelity to the public interest is vital."
- The Society of Professional Journalists, also in the US: "Journalists must be free of obligation to any interest other than the people's right to know."
- The BBC: "Our viewers and listeners should be confident that editorial decisions are made only for good editorial reasons. The outside activities of programme makers must not improperly influence, or be thought to influence, BBC programmes" (*Producers' Guidelines* 1996, 88).

It can happen easily

Journalists can be influenced by any number of factors – friends, family, personal beliefs, investments, outside interests, loyalties, and ambition. Consider this example: let's say you are a political reporter and are suddenly invited by a prominent politician for a game-hunting weekend somewhere in the Karoo. You see this as an excellent opportunity to build valuable contacts, and accept the offer thankfully. You have a wonderful time. Then Christmas comes, and you receive a box of biltong and a case of the best brandy available. You accept, albeit with reservations. In the meantime, this politician feeds you with great stories that are published under your name. But then, suddenly, it's election season. Payback time. *I've scratched your back, now it's your turn to scratch mine.*

If you think this is just a hypothetical example, think again. For this happens on a daily basis, and it comes in all shapes and sizes, in hundreds of disguises. Don't be naive. Never trust people who try to give you gifts and perks.

John Hulteng relates the following stories (Hulteng 1976, 29–30):

- Reporters discovered that about fifty Illinois

journalists had been on the state payroll for years – while they were supposed to provide impartial coverage of the state government. When this scandal was uncovered, these journalists had already received a total of $480 000.
- Half the sportswriters on New England newspapers were "consultants" to various racetracks in the area, earning up to $5 000 or more a year.
- Four members of the women's page staff of an Oregon daily received free service at a local hairdressing salon. Initially there were no strings attached – until the hairdressers began showing up in the newsroom and started giving suggestions for feature interviews on new techniques or products.
- Late in 1973 the story broke that 35 American journalists were on a secret payroll of the Central Intelligence Agency (CIA).

The list is endless. Under the apartheid regime in South Africa, some journalists were suspected of working for the security forces. Are there any such spooks working for the new regime? It is important that a journalist who wants to make a commitment to outside organizations first seeks the approval of superiors. Never do it on your own. If you get caught, you will even be more alone.

Some important issues

There are a number of other issues pertaining to conflict of interest.

Freebies

When journalists accept favours, gifts, or other special considerations from vested interests or news sources, it raises serious questions about their objectivity. "The mere acceptance of the thing of value raises questions about the moral agent's credibility and future independence of action, even if no favor is promised in return" (Day 1991, 158). Less spectacular freebies, such as meals, may not seem to be problematic. However, over a period of time the reporter's professional detachment could be undermined (Day 1991, 158). J. Russell Wiggens, former editor of the *Washington Post*, had this to say to his colleagues and to journalism educators: "It is as improper for a newspaperman to accept from any litigant...cash considerations, gratuities or favors as it would be improper for a judge to accept such inducements in his domain" (*Bulletin of the American Society of Newspaper Editors* no. 411, 1 August 1958, 3[2]).

The best thing to do when a potential news source sends you a gift is to return it promptly and politely. The bigger the gift, the more important this becomes. The fact is that gifts are regularly used to "buy" journalists, to make them soft, to try to ensure that the person or company who gave the gift gets the most favourable press possible. It boils down to bribery. As in all ethical matters, the question is where to draw the line.

The problem, of course, is that gifts and perks (such as meals, and other freebies) undermine the credibility of journalists. Yes, a meal may be in order if you feel you are building up a relationship with a news source or if the person who invites you may be able to provide you with genuine news. But it is always better to let your company pay for the meal. If not, be very careful. Never use your poor salary as an excuse for accepting free meals.

According to the BBC: "Individuals must not accept personal benefits, e.g. goods, discounts, services, cash, gratuities, or entertainment outside the normal scope of business hospitality, from organisations or people with whom they might have dealings with on the BBC's behalf" (*Producers' Guidelines* 1996, 95).

Free trips, with food and lodging thrown in,

present even bigger problems. Some organizations use this as a valuable public relations tool, and it is sometimes extremely difficult to refuse this kind of freebie – depending, of course, on the destination.

Peter Sullivan, the editor of *The Star*, asks: "Why do companies entertain editors? Or journalists, for that matter?" (*The Star International Weekly* 8–14 June 1995). Sullivan uses three examples: the launch of the airline of the United Arab Emirates at a "glittering occasion" in Sandton ("caviar, champagne, great dinner, the full bit"), after which "small discreet gifts" were handed out (for example, a solid brass clock the size of a matchbox). The next day, Sappi flew Sullivan to the bush in the Eastern Transvaal to tell him about how much water a tree consumes per day and about the involvement of the company in the bushveld within their tree farms, and gave him "a great Sappi jacket". Then SA Breweries flew him to Cape Town, Port Elizabeth, and Durban to watch rugby. He received a rugby jersey, a tie and SAB cuff links.

> It begs the question: what is the object of all this corporate entertainment? ...Is it because they think it will influence our editorial stance? It can't be in the hope of cheaper advertising, nor can it be to get their launch on page one (it was already there on news value)... It has a hint of bribery to it. (*The Star International Weekly* 8–14 June 1995)

The BBC has strict guidelines as far as this issue is concerned. "The BBC will not accept free places on a media facility trip unless it is the only way to report a significant event... If a media facility trip is open to a range of media and a programme wishes to accept a place upon it, the BBC should offer to make a realistic contribution towards the costs involved... If there is a clear editorial need to make a reference, it must be done in a way which avoids promoting or endorsing the (commercial) operator" (*Producers' Guidelines* 1996, 253).

Moonlighting

Some journalists do work outside of the company they are working for. This is called moonlighting. Permission must usually be obtained to do this. However, be careful that the interests of your moonlighting company do not clash with those of your own company. This also goes for the time and effort you are supposed to put into your company.

Affiliation to organizations

The problems that can emerge when journalists affiliate themselves to organizations are self-evident. These can seriously compromise your credibility and independence. On the other hand, some journalists argue that being affiliated to organizations gives them the opportunity to meet people, build contacts, and identify possible news sources.

Is there a golden mean here? Well, it depends on the type of organization. It is a highly problematic if the organization is a political one (see next section). This also goes for any other organization that is likely to become newsworthy. But if the organization is a chess or a bridge club, that obviously poses less of a problem. Similarly, there can be no problem at all if a journalist takes part in outside activities, be they cultural, religious, sporting, or whatever. The important point is that journalists remain sensitive and do not allow any situation to influence negatively their professional activities.

Political activities

The BBC outlines different stages of political involvement and deals with each separately (*Producers' Guidelines* 1996, 91–92). It is worth examining in some detail how the corporation does this; the issues raised will be discussed afterwards.

It goes without saying that anyone is entitled to belong to a political party, the BBC *Producers' Guidelines* states. That is the journalist's right. Office-holding may be acceptable for people in low-level editorial positions, but not for their more senior colleagues (with higher programme responsibilities). The name of a journalist can appear on a political party's "approved list" of potential parliamentary candidates. However, that person may not be able to undertake high-level programme responsibilities. The individual may be moved to a less sensitive position until the candidacy has been resolved. If a journalist is selected to fight a seat, and therefore becomes a prospective parliamentary candidate, his or her work for the BBC must be divorced from political issues.

The same goes for local government. However, an exception can be made for election to a parish council if the journalist stands as an independent candidate. But then he or she must not be involved at a senior editorial level or in programmes dealing with current political issues.

At all levels during election periods, candidates are allowed time off for the campaign. But then they should not appear in any programmes, except as candidates. No discrimination against politically active people, on the grounds that they gain publicity from their work for the BBC, is allowed.

Candidates who have been defeated in an election are to be judged afresh according to their future plans or aspirations. They are not to be excluded from topical editorial work just because they used to be politically active. Journalists who win an election cannot normally continue with their editorial work. Exceptions may be made for independent parish councillors.

So, how should we react to this stance? The BBC is strict – and so it should be – regarding journalists who want to appear in commercials or commercial videos (to name a few) on the basis that it will compromise their integrity. However, when it comes to an even more dangerous terrain, that of political involvement, the BBC is much more lenient. That is strange, to say the least.

Two things are likely to happen to a journalist if he or she is involved with a political party. Firstly, the journalist becomes friendly with politicians – and *certain* politicians (from a specific party) at that. That journalist will then rightly be seen by other political parties as partisan. Goodbye to credibility. But secondly, what happens if this political friend of yours is (for example) caught with his or her hand in the party's till? Would you be independent enough to write the truth? Or even worse: if this is a scoop for you, would you be able to write it at all?

Nothing compromises credibility more than involvement with a political party. Even if a journalist/candidate loses an election, he or she will always be associated with that party. He or she will have no credibility, whether writing against the opposition or about his or her own party.

Friends and relatives

This may be the most difficult aspect of the problem of the conflict of interest. Not all journalists belong to societies or organizations; not every one does some sort of moonlighting. But every journalist, it can be safely assumed, has some relatives and/or friends.

Picture this scenario. You are at a party with your friends or relatives. The fire burns high, the steaks are ready, the beer flows, the music is fine, and the company is excellent. One of your friends starts talking about his boss, a prominent public figure, who has been caught doing all sorts of strange things with his secretary. Just to make things more interesting, you don't happen to like that particular person very much, and you dislike his views even more. So what do you do with this scoop?

Of course, this scenario also touches on the relationship between journalists and their sources (see Chapter 7), especially when the "off the record" issue is discussed. But here we are talking about friends or relatives. Do you publish this information, knowing that your friend will feel that you have betrayed him?

If you do publish it without your friend's consent, you must know that you will lose friends as surely and quickly as South Africa lost the Rugby World Cup in 1999 – at the very first possible occasion. Your friend will not feel free to talk about confidential matters with you any more. If you don't publish the story, you will lose a scoop. A no-win situation?

Here is another scenario. Your best friend (or a close relative), a prominent public official, is disciplined by his or her company for fraud and corruption. It is in the public's interest to know about this, because this person had his or her fingers in the taxpayer's pockets. What do you do? If you don't report it, your conduct boils down to nepotism. A good journalist will always put his or her professional duties first. If you don't have credibility as a journalist, you may as well look for another job. It surely will pay better.

Paying for information

The hard-and-fast rule is never to pay for information that has been obtained by a person with a criminal record. However, the whole practice of "chequebook journalism" is deeply suspect. Louis Day says that this practice raises serious questions concerning the value of the information obtained.

Paid interviewees may feel financially obligated to perform or produce something of journalistic interest, which could lead to exaggerations, distortions, or even outright fabrications. Even if these outcomes don't materialize, the question is how much faith an audience should put in an interview that is conducted pursuant to a commercial arrangement between a news organization and a source. (Day 1991, 161)

Promotional activities

Journalists working on consumer programmes must be extremely careful. "They must have no commercial or other links which could appear to influence their attitude towards any product or service" (*Producers' Guidelines* 1996, 89). Promotional activities include, *inter alia*, appearances in advertisements, product endorsement, the making or appearing in corporate videos, attendance at commercial events, and public relations work (*Producers' Guidelines* 1996, 90). These activities associate the journalist with the product or service. "Any of these activities is unacceptable for BBC editorial people (including presenters and freelancers) when they might compromise public trust in the integrity of our programmes or of those who make them" (*Producers' Guidelines* 1996, 90). Engaging in promotional activities tarnishes the ideal of impartiality and neutrality, and will forever raise doubts about that journalist's impartiality.

Charitable activities

Generally, work for a charity is acceptable. But what if a particular cause or the way the money is handled becomes controversial? Talk to the head of your department. Each case should be dealt with individually.

Writing for other publications

It is accepted that a journalist may write articles for other publications without getting permission, provided that those publications form part of the company. Permission must however be sought if a journalist wants to write for rival organizations. Usually, permission will not be granted.

Who are the most vulnerable?

As the above discussion shows, all journalists are vulnerable to conflicts of interest. Everybody has friends and relatives, is offered gifts and preferential treatment, and lives in a community where all sorts of demands can be made. And yet certain types of journalists are more at risk than others. The following section looks at several of these types.

Journalists on local newspapers

Local newspapers are extremely vulnerable as far as conflict of interest is concerned – even more so than their provincial or national counterparts. The reasons for this are obvious: local newspapers are very close to their communities, and local journalists know each and every public official or businessperson. They play golf together, go to church together, party together, and watch the Big Match together. It can become very difficult to publish negative things about friends or about people whom you know very well. And the journalist must also face these people afterwards.

But the problem at local newspapers goes much deeper. These newspapers are much more dependent upon local advertisers than are the bigger newspapers. If a local newspaper alienates an important client by writing negative things about him or her, and that client decides to withdraw his or her advertisements from the newspaper, the newspaper could find itself in deep financial trouble. If it happens with more than one client, the financial health of the business could be threatened.

In a certain sense, it takes more journalistic skill for a local newspaper to survive than is required for its metropolitan counterpart. It is not impossible to maintain your journalistic integrity in a local paper, and there are some fine examples of local papers in South Africa that do just that. But the dangers and pitfalls are more prominent as far as conflicts of interest are concerned. Beware!

Travel journalists

Travel journalists give first-hand accounts of the places they write about. Their experiences add credibility to their stories. However, many of these articles are not investigative stories, but rather are written to promote travel destinations. "It is arguable whether reporters who depend on free trips from travel agencies can be objective in selecting information for their articles. A travel reporter is not likely to accept a stay at a luxury hotel and then write a scathing review of the accommodations" (Day 1991, 159). Smaller news organizations are especially at risk here. The bigger ones can pay their own way, whereas the smaller ones have to do everything in their power to stay competitive.

Financial journalists

In 2000, Jacques Dommisse reported from London that British newspapers were reforming their internal guidelines with regards to the giving of advice on shares (*Die Burger* 11 February 2000). There was a possibility that journalists would be prohibited from using information on shares (though not necessarily published) to buy shares for themselves.

This ballyhoo came after it was revealed that the editor of *The Daily Mirror*, Piers Morgan, had bought about R200 000 worth of shares in a firm called Viglen Technology. The next day *The Daily Mirror* carried a report urging the readers to buy these shares. Morgan explained that it was coincidence that his newspaper had reported on the shares a day after he had bought his. This led to other reports that journalists of *The Sun* (the biggest-selling tabloid in Britain) also publish tips on shares that they own.

The issue that is at stake is the role that journalists, guest writers, freelance journalists, and public relations officers play in "moving" share prices, as well as the role of groups that use journalists to move those prices. Financial journalists in particular must be very careful here. It can become very problematic if a financial journalist reports on shares in which he or she has a stake. This should rather be avoided. However, it is unrealistic to expect financial journalists not to own shares at all.

The BBC is clear on this matter: "Presenters, reporters and production staff should have no substantial connection with products or firms featured in the stories they are covering. Shareholdings are a right to be respected. They should be declared only if they are significant in size and connected with the programme content. On no account must early information acquired in the course of BBC programme work be used to trade ahead of the markets. It is illegal and unethical" (*Producers' Guidelines* 1996, 94).

Sports and political reporters

Sports reporters who travel with a team can easily fall into this trap. Fortunately, this does not happen very often – but beware, some South African politicians still try to cosy up to the media. For example, in 1999 a spectacular tour through Africa with one of the more prominent members of the Cabinet was on offer. Can a reporter remain impartial and balanced under circumstances such as these?

Freelancers

The BBC mentions that freelance programme people will by definition provide their services to a range of employers (*Producers' Guidelines* 1996, 89), *"But particular care needs to be exercised over the outside interests of regular freelance presenters in journalism programmes. Separate detailed examples of where to draw the line are reviewed from time to time and provided to freelancers by the programme areas involved"* (*Producers' Guidelines* 1996, 89).

Litmus tests

It is as impossible to catalogue all the problem areas as it is to "prescribe" certain reactions to them. The important thing is that the problem of conflict of interest should never be avoided. *Never look the other way*. Rather, take positive steps to deal with the problems. John Hulteng suggests two useful "internal tests of conscience" a journalist can apply (Hulteng 1976, 44):

- Can you honestly conclude that the favour or consideration involved – whether it is a cup of coffee, a cigar, a weekend in Miami, or a tour of the Middle East as a guest of the Arab League – is not likely to tinge your impartiality?
- Would the audience you serve be sure of your credibility, even if you have no doubts about it?

To which he adds: "Admittedly, these aren't simple tests to apply. They put to exacting trial the conscience of the individual journalist. But, if you choose to enter the media fields, you ought to bear in mind that no one has promised you a rose garden" (Hulteng 1976, 44).

Some checklists

Journalists must be aware of situations that create a real or perceived conflict of interest. Consider weighing your obligations against the impact of:
- involvement in particular activities;
- affiliation with causes or organizations;
- acceptance of favours or preferential treatment;
- financial investments;
- outside employment;
- friendships (Black et al. 1995, 92).

Journalists are ordinary citizens as well. They should take care that their primary obligation to the public is not eroded by other legitimate goals, such as:
- a quest for economic gain;
- the interest of being a good corporate citizen;
- the concern for their own employees;
- the desire to be competitive in the marketplace (Black et al. 1995, 92).

So ask yourself these questions:
- Am I being independent?
- Could my action harm my integrity or that of my organization?
- Is the mere appearance of a conflict enough to diminish my credibility?
- Am I willing to disclose publicly any potential conflicts (*Black et al.* 1995, 92)?

From the same company

The media should be very careful not to let a conflict of interest distort the truth when they report on matters in which they are involved – it could lead to a loss of editorial independence

The Freedom of Expression Institute (FXI) and others complained to the Broadcasting Complaints Commission of South Africa (BCCSA) that an item on the SABC's 20:00 and 21:00 news bulletins, informing viewers that the contract of the presenter of *Special Assignment*, Max du Preez, would not be renewed, was in conflict with the Broadcasting Code (19 April 1999).

The news item read as follows:

The SABC's Group Executive has endorsed the decision by TV news management not to renew Max du Preez's contract. The decision follows a two-hour-long meeting between the Group Chief Executive, Reverend Hawu Mbatha and Du Preez today. Last Thursday Du Preez was informed that his contract would not be renewed by the Editor-in-Chief Phil Molefe.

Molefe has again refused to discuss this matter with the media. It's however believed that Du Preez's contract was not renewed because of several incidents of gross insubordination towards management. This included the incident in which he swore at Head of News and Current Affairs, Themba Mthembu, in the newsroom.

Shocked members of staff saw an irate Du Preez in the middle of the newsroom pointing a middle finger at him and using an f-word. Du Preez later apologized and said he did not mean to insult Mthembu but SABC 3.

Lawyers acting for Du Preez tried to stop the statement from being broadcast.

It was alleged that the report lacked balance (failing to present the other side), accuracy, and editorial independence – amounting to managers using the airwaves to service their conflicts. The complainant, *inter alia*, further alleged:

- The statement that Molefe had again refused to discuss the matter with the media was "disingenuous and untruthful in the extreme". It was quite clear that Molefe and other officials had been consulted and were in fact the source of the report. Claims that Molefe refused to speak to the media created the impression that he was the aggrieved party.
- The sequence of events was presented in an inaccurate manner. The report linked an incident over two months old to Du Preez's dismissal and did not inform viewers accordingly.
- Although Du Preez was in the building at the time the news broadcast was prepared, he was not approached for comment. Certain individuals abused their positions to create a news item that would exonerate them and paint Du Preez as the villain.

The BCCSA did not deal with the matter of accuracy, since that dispute was being adjudicated elsewhere. The commission did adjudicate, however, on the alleged lack of balance in the news report and the corresponding alleged lack of editorial independence – which is the focus of this case study.

The latter complaint was dismissed. "Editorial independence can only be placed at risk when an *external force* [my emphasis] is active in demanding changes to a news item. The present matter deals with an internal dispute and there is no evidence that an external source was active in influencing the news editor." The BCCSA added: "… in not one of the more than 100 cases against the SABC which have come before this Commission had there been evidence that the SABC has compromised its independence."

On the matter of balance (fairness), the BCCSA contended that when a broadcaster is in dispute with an (ex-) employee, the demands for impartiality and balance are particularly strict. According to the commission's finding:

> ...the (news) item should have come to a close after the reference to Mr Phil Molefe's refusal to discuss the matter with the media. The moment when the newsroom added aspects concerning gross insubordination, swearing and the middle finger episode, it commenced to broadcast an opinion on what had happened. The references to insubordination, swearing and obscene signs, negated the balance which is required by Clause 2 of the BCCSA Code. These references created a duty on the SABC news room to at least obtain a comment of Mr Du Preez on it. It was not necessary to grant him an interview or even to place his photograph as part of the background material... But when the item ventures into these accusing background circumstances, there was no choice but to balance this material by stating Mr Du Preez's view as well.

Due to this lack of balance, the complaint (on this specific point) was upheld. The BCCSA directed the SABC to broadcast a summary of this judgment within three days. Molefe's refusal to comment on the matter was, according to the BCCSA, the correct one.

Analysis

Two issues need to be discussed here. Firstly, the BCCSA was quite correct in finding that the report lacked balance. Du Preez should definitely have been given an opportunity to state his views as well. The viewers were not given a realistic chance to make up their own minds as to whether the report was indeed true or false. That was blatantly unfair and amounted to inexcusable, irresponsible journalism. The rest of the BCCSA's finding on this issue is also to be wel-

comed (with regards to the f-word, the middle finger, swearing, etc.).

Secondly, and pertaining to the issue of conflict of interest, the complaint was that the SABC had compromised its editorial independence because Molefe was believed to have spoken to the SABC journalists. In rejecting this complaint, the BCCSA judgement contained the following very interesting remark: "Editorial independence can only be placed at risk when an external force is active in demanding changes to a news item. The present matter deals with an internal dispute...".

The matter of censorship provides a good analogy here. Usually, when the media are censored, it is due to some external force. There is, however, also such a thing as self-censorship. Likewise, there is always the possibility that a journalist will give up his or her editorial independence voluntarily – not as a result of external, but of internal, forces.

The same thing may have happened in this case as well. The report was not balanced – as the BCCSA rightly pointed out. The question, of course, is *why was the report not balanced? Because the SABC itself was involved and was always likely to give up its impartiality? Because it was a case of conflict of interest?* The mere fact that balance was lacking in the report suggests it was possible that the SABC did compromise its editorial independence in this case. Although it is difficult to state that as a fact, the BCCSA should at least have acknowledged that the SABC *could* have manipulated the news to suit its own needs. It is simplistic to state that no external forces were involved and that the SABC could *therefore* not have compromised its own independence.

The general (and irrelevant) statement by the BCCSA that there had not been evidence in more than one hundred cases against the SABC that the organization had compromised its editorial independence was also not helpful. So what if it had not happened before? Did all those cases relate to lack of editorial independence? The SABC's history was not the issue at hand. The media should be very careful when they report on matters in which they are involved.

"Fertile ground for impropriety"

Opportunities to take (financial) advantage of certain situations do arise and must be resisted.

The following case was reported in the *Mail & Guardian* in its 31 March–6 April 2000 edition. According to the report, the SABC television news camera section "was the focus of investigations that already have resulted in the suspension of the unit's manager, Mzi Mdude, and his deputy. At least six more suspensions are understood to be imminent". Mdude and his deputy were reported to have been suspended for paying "ghost" cameramen exorbitant rates for no apparent reason.

Within that context and amongst many other allegations concerning the misspending of money in the SABC, the article also focused on some alleged misappropriations during the (then recent) floods in Mozambique. The discussion will be limited to two incidents that allegedly took place.

The situation in Mozambique was reported by the *Mail & Guardian* to have provided "fertile ground for impropriety":

- A cameraman sold seats to foreign journalists on a rented helicopter for R1 000 each. The helicopter had been hired to enable journalists to cover the floods. "When discovered, the SABC cameraman said he had intended handing over the proceeds to the corporation."
- According to SABC sources, one crew member who captured dramatic, widely broadcast footage of a newborn baby being rescued from a tree, sold this footage to Reuters for $500 (then about R3 500) – although the footage was shot with an SABC camera. This deception only came to light when SABC executives saw their own footage on rival e.tv before it was aired by the public broadcaster.

Analysis

Again, it is not appropriate to make any statement on the truth or falseness of these allegations. However, if the alleged incidents did take place, they are classic examples of conflicts of interest, and would show how easy it is for a journalist to exploit circumstances (and people, even colleagues). As stated earlier, journalists in certain positions are even more vulnerable than others are. So beware! Such inexcusable behaviour (if it indeed happened) hardly requires comment or analysis. This incident is included as a case study in this chapter only to show how easily this sort of thing can happen.

State money for a newspaper

The media should guard unceasingly against being misused for political – or other – purposes.

Dr Connie Mulder was the crown prince of the National Party during the late 1970s. He was the

Minister of Information, and the leader of the NP in the Transvaal. There was a real possibility that he, and not Mr P. W. Botha, would take over as Prime Minister from Mr B. J. Vorster.

One of Mulder's problems, seen from his perspective, was the English press in general and the liberal *Rand Daily Mail* and the *Sunday Express* in particular. He had to make a plan to sink those newspapers. The need was simple: an effective (English-speaking) opposition that would scratch his and his party's back. The problem was serious: there was no such newspaper available. The solution was easy: create one.

Mulder established a new, conservative English-language newspaper – the only one of its kind in South Africa – which was called *The Citizen*. To do this, he illegitimately used about R32 million in secret, unaudited funds (money from taxpayers), which was given as a loan to Dr Louis Luyt, the former head of Triomf, to publish this newspaper. This happened in 1976.

In a sense, Mulder was vindicated in his belief that the *Rand Daily Mail* and the *Sunday Express* were his enemies, for it was those newspapers that broke the news of what was later to be called the Information Scandal. "In a major triumph they exposed the underhanded methods of his Information Department and its involvement in a great number of highly dubious operations, carried out covertly at public expense", the *Cape Times* wrote in a leading article on 14 January 1988, nearly ten years after Mulder resigned from Parliament, having lost to Botha by a few votes in the ballot to succeed Vorster.

The scandal involved some R85 million from secret funds that was used in a covert propaganda campaign that lasted for about five years. Some 180 projects were launched – all of them with the aim of improving the public image of the government of South Africa abroad. One of the projects of the Ministry of Information was an (abortive) attempt to gain control of the *Washington Star* newspaper. Vorster resigned in 1978 when the scandal was exposed.

The Citizen was later sold to Perskor and was amalgamated with the *Financial Gazette*. It is ironic, the *Cape Times* pointed out, that *The Citizen* was still around (and indeed still is). The newspapers that exposed the Information Scandal (the *Rand Daily Mail* and the *Sunday Express*) have since closed down.

Analysis

No newspaper created with state funds, whose express purpose is to further the ideology and goals of the government, can even think of attaining journalistic excellence. The conflicts of political versus journalistic interests are just too serious. It is clearly impossible to come even close to the goal of due impartiality and objectivity. There is no chance of acting independently.

This dark period in South African history may have passed, but who is to say what the future will bring? In the meantime, the story of the Information Scandal should serve as an eternal reminder of how the media should unceasingly guard against being misused for political (or whatever) purposes. If it serves this purpose, at least something good will have come out of the debacle.

Editorial (in)dependency

Great care should be taken by both the editor and the owner of a newspaper to maintain independence and to ensure that no conflict of interest arises.

The relationship between the editor of a newspaper and its owners is inevitably a sensitive one, especially when the owners are committed to some political party or movement (or, of course, to commercial interests outside the company). This also applies to the matter of editorial independence.

This issue came to the fore shortly before the general election of 2 June 1999, when Peter Bruce, the editor of the *Financial Mail* (or *FM*), in his editorial of 7 May, endorsed Bantu Holomisa's and Roelf Meyer's United Democratic Movement (UDM) and urged his readers to vote for that party – as well as to support it financially. This immediately provoked a response from, amongst others, Cyril Ramaphosa, the former General Secretary of the ANC. At the time, the *Financial Mail* was co-owned by the National Empowerment Consortium (NEC), through its shareholding in Johnnic – of which Ramaphosa was the chairperson. Ramaphosa also served on the ANC's national executive.

In an article in the *Financial Mail* (14 May 1999), Ramaphosa described Bruce's decision as "a travesty of the principles of unbiased reportage". Ramaphosa admitted that many media owners across the world prefer to remain at a distance from editorial affairs. However, Bruce's call to individuals and businesses to dig into their pockets to support the UDM forced him to react. "In this case editorial independence may well have been the sacrificial lamb at the UDM's altar." And again: "It is unacceptable for the editor to use the *FM* as a national and international fundraising platform for a political party". He summed up his criticisms by saying:

- The call to vote for a specific political party had seriously compromised the editorial independence and credibility of the *FM*. It had also tarnished the record of independence, fairness, and unbiased coverage of what the *FM* stands for.
- The action may have been seriously divisive within the *FM* community.
- Shareholders would be concerned about the commercial impact of the call to voters. Such

a bold endorsement ran the risk of alienating a section of its readership sufficiently for them to consider reviewing their loyalty to the magazine. Advertisers could be unnerved by the editorial in question.

In contrast, Ramaphosa said, the stance of *City Press* was "more responsible". *City Press* came out in support of the ANC, but was "careful and wise enough" not to urge its readers to vote for that party. *City Press* urged its readers to vote according to their consciences. There is a vital difference between endorsement and lobbying, Ramaphosa maintained. It is in order if an editor expresses personal views, but not if he or she joins a political campaign. Ramaphosa then took the opportunity, as spokesperson for the owners of the *Financial Mail*, to back the ANC.

Following Ramaphosa's criticism, the *Sunday Times* – 50 per cent owned by Times Media Ltd, of which Ramaphosa was also the chairperson – announced in its editorial of May 16 that it would no longer express its editorial preference for the forthcoming elections, as it had intended to do.

In his editorial on 14 May, Bruce said he was happy to print Ramaphosa's criticism. He defended his stance, however, and denied that editorial endorsement of a certain political party compromises a publication. Bruce said that Ramaphosa's response may appear to come close to interference in the editorial independence of the *FM*, but he can confidently say that it does not. Nothing was said about fundraising. Both Bruce and Ramaphosa denied that any pressure had been exerted on the editor to change his stance.

The editor of *Business Day*, Jim Jones, stated in an editorial that Ramaphosa's criticism had "compromised" the editorial independence and integrity of his own newspaper as well as that of the *Financial Mail*, although "not intentionally". (*Business Day* is in the same stable as the *Financial Mail*.) Meanwhile, the British media conglomerate Pearson, owner of the other 50 per cent of the *Financial Mail*, was "understood to have given its full backing to Bruce. Pearson...has a tradition of insisting on complete editorial independence for its editors" (*Mail & Guardian* 14–20 May 1999).

Analysis

The issue of editorial independence (conflict of interest) has two facets in this case: the actions of the editor (Bruce) and those of the owner (Ramaphosa). As far as Bruce is concerned, it is his right as an editor to have a certain political view and to express it in his magazine. After all, the media's task is not only to report on news events, but also to interpret the news. However, it is probably wiser not to support any party at all. For once you do that, all sorts of interests start to conflict with one another. Suddenly you are no longer so free to report as objectively as possible and with due impartiality. It is better to formulate your own principles, and analyze and evaluate news events according to those perspectives. *Then* the media can say: in so far as this specific party is very much in line with our views, we support it. This would allow the media to be fair to each and every party in so far as they are doing well (from your perspective); and to criticize the whole bunch if and when they fail. Still, it was certainly Bruce's right to endorse a political party.

But more needs to be said. Ramaphosa is correct: there is a (vital) difference between endorsement and lobbying (urging readers to support a party financially). It is the end of editorial independence when a media organization becomes a fundraising arm of a political party. This is conflict of interest *par excellence*.

Ramaphosa, on the other hand, also has a right to voice his opinion, even as an owner. The fact that Bruce's position as editor was not threatened certainly counts in Ramaphosa's favour.

However, keep in mind that Ramaphosa is also a politician. One of the key questions is whether Ramaphosa objected to Bruce's endorsement of the UDM as an owner of the *Financial Mail*, or as a politician. Would Ramaphosa have objected if Bruce had asked for financial support for the ANC? And why did Ramaphosa take the opportunity to back the ANC (in the same article)? Conflict of interests?

Both editor and owner can compromise editorial independence – which, to a certain extent, is probably what Bruce and Ramaphosa did in the end. The influence of an owner on the editorial process should start and finish with the appointment of an editor. If not, problems will arise. An editor, on the other hand, must jealously guard against interference from the owners. If he or she is not free to take a stance that differs from that of the owners, editorial independence is greatly devalued. The editor could also sacrifice editorial independence. It is a sad day when that happens.

Agents of the state

A poor salary is no excuse for falling into the trap of working as an agent for the state.

On 2 August 2000 the South African National Editors' Forum (SANEF) rocked the nation with a statement that journalists were being recruited as spies and agents for Defence Intelligence (DI).

The statement was made after *Cape Argus* political editor Adrian Hadland informed SANEF that the government's secret service had approached him "to establish a relationship in order for DI to acquire oral and written analyses of current events" (*Cape Times* 3 August 2000). DI offered to provide tip-offs for stories as well as better access to the official intelligence community, SANEF said, adding that DI claimed it had already recruited a network of journalists who had agreed to participate (*Cape Times* 3 August 2000).

The agent who had approached Hadland said the names of participating journalists would be kept so confidential that even cabinet ministers would not know which journalist had given what information. Journalists would be assigned numbers to help keep their names confidential.

On 4 August 2000, the day after the *Cape Times* published the report, *Die Burger* revealed that one of its senior journalists, Hendrik Coetzee, had also been approached by DI. Both Hadland and Coetzee refused to co-operate with DI. However, the agent who had approached Hadland claimed that "a network of journalists" had already accepted the offer. This claim was to some degree substantiated by Salim Vally, the chairperson of the Freedom of Expression Institute (FXI).

The Truth and Reconciliation Commission (TRC) had previously recommended that legislation be accepted that would prohibit journalists from acting as intelligence agents. Defence Minister Mosiuoa Lekota described this issue as "a complex one" that should perhaps be debated in Cabinet or in Parliament (*Cape Times* August 4, 2000).

A couple of months earlier, on 13 February 2000, *Rapport* had published a notorious document that indicated that the ANC had infiltrated South Africa's official spy service and used it to spy on local political partners. In particular, it was reported that well-known TV journalist Cliff Saunders operated as a spy for the National Intelligence Agency (NIA). *Rapport* said it had a document in its possession which "revealed" that Saunders had written a letter to the Minister of Intelligence Services, Mr Joe Nhlanhla, and to a certain Mr Zola Nglakani, in which they were asked to see to it that he (Saunders) be paid R50 000 in compensation for breach of contract.

In the letter, dated 7 February 2000, the writer warns the NIA that he would report the matter to President Thabo Mbeki and former President Nelson Mandela if he did not receive the money the following day. Mention was also made that legal action could be taken. Saunders was reported to have written in the document that he worked full-time for the NIA in 1995 and had received more than R1 million for his work. According to the document, the writer had turned down R10 000 a few days earlier as settlement for the ending of his services.

The names of Inkatha Freedom Party (IFP) leader Dr Mangosuthu Buthelezi and his chief adviser, Mario Ambrosini, were singled out as people on whom Saunders had to spy. According to *Rapport*, the document revealed that Saunders worked via an organization called Geofocus International, which spied on right-wingers and political parties worldwide, as well as in South Africa. Geofocus worked under the cloak of Newslink International – a news agency that belonged to another former SABC worker, David Bamber. Bamber had asked Saunders to work for Newslink and provided him with a press card that gave him access to certain places and people. Bamber told *Rapport* (27 February 2000) that he eventually found out about Saunders's spying activities, but that he could not expose him because he had no solid proof. However, Bamber reported the matter to the British Foreign Office.

To aid him in his work, Saunders allegedly made use of former SABC colleagues, without their knowledge. The journalist Jani Allan was involved; Allan reported to Saunders, but she allegedly became suspicious, especially when a bag full of British money was delivered. It was also reported that Allan was not allowed to see what commentary Saunders added to her reports before he sent them off "to some faceless employee".

Saunders denied that he was a spy for the NIA – neither during the apartheid era nor after 1994.

In a statement to *Rapport* (20 February 2000) Saunders said that whatever he did and for whom he worked, his intention was to further prosperity, stability, and security in South Africa. Nobody could prove otherwise, he said.

In an earlier article in *Rapport* (17 September 1997) a former chief of the covert Strategic Communication Unit (SCU) of the police, Superintendent Vic McPherson, told the TRC how the media was "used". Most of his "journalist contacts" did not know they were being used by the police, he said. According to McPherson, he had about forty such "contacts" at the Republican Press, BBC News, Reuters, SAPA, the *Sunday Times*, *Pretoria News*, *Rapport*, *Beeld*, *The Citizen*, *The Star*, *Insig*, *Huisgenoot*, and *Rooi Rose*. McPherson said four informants were paid from time to time, and twenty journalists unknowingly gave them information. McPherson said former President F. W. de Klerk approved "in principle" a "media project". In one instance, a report on thirty-seven communists in the ANC's National Executive Committee was "being placed" in *The Citizen*, while the police helped with the making of a documentary programme by Saunders on the ANC's offices in London. Another example of the SCU's work was when it provided photographs and detail to the media about the 1988 attack by the security forces in Gaborone, Botswana, in which 13 people died. "Everything was provided for the journalists. It wasn't necessary for them to think or to interview anybody", McPherson said.

Analysis

The outcry from various media institutions and other organizations against this practice is totally justified. SANEF rightly stated that the alleged DI activities smacked of the strategies adopted by the security community under the apartheid government. "This can only be interpreted as an attempt on a grand scale to turn all journalists and the publications into spies and agents for DI" (*Cape Times* 3 August 2000).

Hadland himself sums up the heart of the problem: "It is an extremely important issue in terms of the independence of the media. Governments should be strongly discouraged from, in effect, compromising the integrity and independence of the press" (*Cape Times* 3 August 2000).

Of course, the journalists who agreed to cooperate with DI compromised their independence in a fundamental way. This amounts to the most serious conflict of interest imaginable. Think also what could happen if that journalist swallowed the paradigms of the state and started to believe in all sorts of "causes". There is no question that this would seriously hamper his or her quest for objectivity and due impartiality.

In addition, if a reporter is rewarded for his or her work (even without believing in the "cause"), he or she can forget about being a serious journalist. Remember the maxims: maximize truth, minimize harm, *and act independently*. Journalists who sell their souls like this cannot even begin to act independently. For they are nothing more and nothing less than their master's voice.

The announcement that journalists were being recruited as agents for the state was an enormous slur on the media's reputation. A journalist's admittedly modest salary really should be no excuse for giving up one's integrity and credibility. It is in the best interest of South Africa's democracy to pass the appropriate legislation as soon as possible, in the hope that it will end this horrible practice once and for all. This may be a complex issue for Minister Lekota; for the media it surely is plain and simple.

It would be inappropriate to evaluate here the allegations concerning Saunders. His guilt has not been proven, and until such time (if ever) it is best to accept his word. However, McPherson's comments provide food for thought. It is an open secret that some journalists did work with and for the state during the apartheid era.

Notes

[1] Bruce Swain's book *Reporter's ethics* deals exclusively with the issue of conflicts of interest and can be highly recommended.
[2] As quoted in Hulteng 1976, p. 29.

9 | Invasion of privacy

The privacy puzzle, the game with no rules, is not an abstract academic problem. It affects private lives and public lives. In some cases it destroys lives. (Hausman 1992, 92)

Introduction

The concept of privacy is first and foremost a legal one. If the media invade someone's privacy, they can end up in court. Yet this issue is also an ethical one. In this chapter the focus will be on the latter.

To a great extent, it can be said that the media is in the business of invading people's privacy. The question is not *if*, but *when* and *why* the media are entitled to undertake this very serious exercise.

Background

The concept of privacy was absent in primitive communities, according to anthropologists. It took centuries for this concept to gain a foothold. The philosophical heritage of privacy, for all intents and purposes, hardly exists (Hausman 1992, 80). In fact, in classical antiquity a "very private person" was someone whose citizenship was questionable (Day 1991, 99).

In the seventeenth century landholders started to retreat to their estates to escape the concerns and pressures of public life (Day 1991, 99). Yet even in the eighteenth century privacy was not a media issue at all. Newspapers were in any case out of the reach of ordinary people. Privacy only started to become a real issue in the 1830s, when the "penny press" democratized the media for the public at large (Day 1991, 99).

An article called "The right to privacy", published in 1890 by the lawyers Samuel D. Warren and Louis Brandeis, was the first to articulate "the right to be left alone".[1] This was inspired by snooping reporters who had infuriated Warren by their coverage of a party held at his home. Warren and Brandeis argued that there are legal grounds for people to be left alone, and proposed that people who are exposed in the media be remunerated. This was arguably the first time that the matter of privacy was addressed as a legal issue (Hausman 1992, 80).

Fifteen years after the Warren-Brandeis article, the Georgia Supreme Court recognized the concept of privacy for the first time, in a case involving the use of an individual's photograph without his permission in a newspaper advertisement. Since then, the protection of personal privacy has received increasing legal attention and has grown in legal complexity (Christians et al. 1995, 115).

Privacy has now become a moral right for those who wish to maintain a sense of individuality. Today, almost every country in the free world recognizes some right of privacy, either in statutory or common law. Privacy is entrenched in various international codes and conventions.[2]

Moreover, the perception of what constitutes the invasion of privacy has changed dramatically since the Warren-Brandeis article. At the time, Warren was furious simply because he saw his name in print. In contrast, Hausman mentions a recent example in which a newspaper editor saw fit to order a journalist to call back the parents of a child who had choked to death on a Christmas decoration merely to find out the colour of the ornament (Hausman 1992, 81).

Some definitions

What is privacy? And what constitutes invasion of privacy? Privacy as "the right to be left alone"

is an oft-criticized concept. Judith Thomson (Beauchamp et al. 1983, 35) puts it this way: if somebody hits you on the head with a brick (and therefore has not left you alone), is that an invasion of your privacy? Is *every* violation of a right a violation of the right to privacy? Of course not.

Several definitions of privacy have been offered. Some say privacy has to do with *keeping personal information non-public or undisclosed*. According to David Archard, personal information is that set of facts about yourself that you do not wish to see disclosed or made public (Kieran et al. 1998, 83). Other definitions include control of access to your body and personal space, autonomy in personal matters, and solitude. Hyman Gross says that "Loss of privacy occurs when the limits one has set on acquaintance with his personal affairs are not respected" (Beauchamp et al. 1983, 26). These limits are twofold, Gross continues. There are restrictions on what is known, as well as on who may know it.

Belsey (1992, 83) distinguishes between three kinds of privacy:

- *Bodily or physical privacy* provides the space in which the body can exist, function, and move, free from physical intrusions (such as bodily contact and the intrusions of eyes and cameras).
- *Mental or communicational privacy* allows people to be alone with their feelings, thoughts, wishes, and desires.
- *Informational privacy*, which is more indirect, prevents the disclosure of personal information held in the files of public and private organizations.

It is difficult to pinpoint the essence of privacy. Carl Hausman states in this regard: "…the people who write the rules, the people who interpret the rules, and the people who break the rules all share a common problem – they don't know where they stand. As a result, we have what amounts to a high-stakes game with few, if any, rules" (Hausman 1992, 79). In the meantime, the concept of privacy is being redefined owing to the enormous explosion of electronic intelligence. "You have already zero privacy – get over it", commented Scott McNealy, chairperson of Sun Microsystems (*International Herald Tribune* 4 March 1999). Hausman explains: "First, we have increasingly sophisticated news-gathering technology. We can gather news quickly and transmit that news across ... the globe literally at the speed of light" (Hausman 1992, 85). Satellite transmissions and global communications have vastly extended the ability of a media organization to collect information damaging to another party (Hausman 1992, 85). The vexing question of how to contain the invasion of privacy on the Internet will probably not be answered in the foreseeable future.

It's important

The importance of the issue of privacy for the media cannot be underestimated because serious and unnecessary harm can easily be done. Hausman hammers the nail in: "The privacy puzzle, the game with no rules, is not an abstract academic problem. It affects private lives and public lives. In some cases it destroys lives" (Hausman 1992, 92).

Privacy is important, for people want to maintain an integrated personality in a social setting and wish to control how they appear to others (Gross et al. 1988, 28). Louis Day says that other people are not entitled to know everything about you (Day 1991, 98–99), and mentions four reasons why privacy is valuable:

- It is the hallmark of an autonomous individual. Others are not entitled to know everything about us.
- It protects people from ridicule and scorn.
- It helps people to control their reputations. The more others know about you, the less pow-

erful you become in controlling your destiny.
- It helps you to keep other people at a distance and regulates your social interaction.

When is privacy invaded?

Privacy can be violated by any means of communication, including the spoken word. This issue is usually divided into four categories (Day 1991, 99–100):

- *Intrusion.* This is the intentional invasion of a person's private affairs or solitude. Intrusion mostly focuses on some aspect of the news-gathering process. This can range from journalists who enter private property without the owner's consent (even if the police say it is in order to do so) to the use of telephoto lenses to document private moments. It may involve the wrongful use of tape recorders, cameras, or other intrusive equipment. Trespassing or the filming of something like an operation without the patient's consent can also be a form of intrusion.
- *The publicity of private facts.* Publication of truthful information concerning the private life of a person, which would be both highly offensive to a reasonable person and not of legitimate public concern, is an invasion of privacy. Liability is often determined by how the information was obtained and by its newsworthiness. Private facts about a person's economic status, health, or sexual activities can constitute an invasion of privacy.
- *False light.* This is when information is published that creates or supports a wrong public impression about a person.
- *Misappropriation.* This entails the use of a person's name, image, or photo without his or her consent, usually for commercial gain.

There are no hard-and-fast rules to establish exactly what constitutes invasion of privacy. It depends to a large extent, as we shall see, on *who* is involved and *where* people are at the time.

Public and private people

In the matter of invasion of privacy, it is important to make a distinction between public officials, public figures, and private citizens.

Public officials (including politicians)

Warren and Brandeis state that "... to publish of a modest and retiring individual that he suffers from an impediment of his speech or that he cannot spell correctly is an unwarranted, if not unexampled, infringement upon his privacy, while to state and comment on the same characteristic found in a would-be congressman would not be regarded as beyond the pale of propriety."[3] When somebody is or becomes a public person, "she, by that very fact, loses her privacy" (Kieran et al. 1998, 86). It is universally accepted that a person's privacy may be breached if the information disclosed serves *a proven public interest* (Kieran et al. 1998, 88). Detecting or exposing crime, matters of public health, preventing the public from being misled, corruption, gross inefficiency, criminal negligence, dishonesty – these matters are in the public interest, *provided* that these failings bear directly on the performance of public duties (Kieran et al. 1998, 88).

The reason for this is that citizens must know about the activities of public officials that have an impact on their work and therefore on society. Public officials are *accountable* to the public they are supposed to serve. They wield power in society – and all aspects of the exercise of power must therefore be open to public scrutiny (Belsey et al. 1992, 27). The media worldwide enjoy comprehensive protection when they report on public officials. To be successful in a case against a journalist, an official must usually prove *male fides* on the part of the journalist. For that to happen, it has to be proved that a journalist knew the information was false or blatantly ignored the truth.

The saying goes that a total loss of privacy is the fair price someone pays for fame. On the other hand, it is important to keep in mind that public officials do not lose all their privacy. They too have a right to a private life. The impact they have on society is what matters to the public; their private lives, in so far as they do not impact on society, are nobody's business.

David Archard warns: "The majority of cases where privacy is breached touch on matters of sexual morality and it is that much harder to see how the public interest is served by their disclosure" (Kieran et al. 1998, 88). Talking about public officials and public figures in the same vein,' the BBC's *Producers' Guidelines* puts it like this: "The public should be given the facts that bear upon the ability or the suitability of public figures to attain or hold office or to perform their duties, but there is no general entitlement to know about their private behaviour provided that it is legal and does not raise important wider issues" (*Producers' Guidelines* 1996, 34). Even if private behaviour is reported somewhere else in the media, the BBC says that this is not sufficient justification for reporting it too. When the personal affairs of public figures do become the object of inquiry, these officials or figures still "do not forfeit all rights to privacy" (*Producers' Guidelines* 1996, 34). BBC programmes, then, must stick to relevant facts and avoid gossip.

Of course, the relevant information must be important as well as true, and it is not enough to say that it is (merely) interesting (*Producers' Guidelines* 1996, 34). The BBC sums up:

It is essential that we operate within a framework which respects people's right to privacy, treats them fairly, yet allows us to investigate and establish matters which it is in the public interest to know about. (*Producers' Guidelines* 1996, 34)

Belsey argues that public officials are entitled to privacy – but not to abuse their right to privacy (Belsey et al. 1992, 78). What should be done is what is best, overall, for everyone whose interests are involved. Because we live in a society, there are limits to privacy. "The lives of those who exercise power should be above suspicion, which means that they must be open to scrutiny" (Belsey et al. 1992, 78).

Public figures

Public figures can be divided into two groups. Firstly, they are personalities who are created and sustained by publicity, such as people in show business, sport, arts, royalty – even people who join public debates on their own initiative or who put themselves in the limelight. These people would not be who or what they are without this exposure. "All such people live on the press and off the press; they require publicity and would shrivel without it" (Belsey et al. 1992, 84). To a certain extent, these people suspend their own privacy. The media then enjoy broad protection when reporting on them. Like public officials, they have decided to expose certain aspects of their private lives to scrutiny. They should therefore be willing to bear any possible embarrassment. Such people, Belsey argues quite convincingly, cannot claim the protection of privacy when they suddenly get bad publicity. "Claims to a right to a private life (then) shade quickly into hypocrisy" (Belsey et al. 1992, 84–85).

Secondly, it happens that people are thrust into the public eye involuntarily or unexpectedly. Two subgroups can be distinguished here. The first are people who are eminent or who have achieved much, such as scientists and writers. These people can be considered somewhat more public than ordinary citizens. The second subgroup is more "short term" and is typically made up of disaster survivors, the relatives of someone caught up in a tragedy, or the winner of the state lottery. If the events that both subgroups are involved in are public matters, the press can reasonably and legitimately report on them. However, the media should still exercise good taste in this regard. Resources are limited, "… and the press has more important tasks than to concern itself with senseless trivialities – among which, incidentally, I should include most of the activities of royalty" (Belsey et al. 1992, 85).

Private figures

A private figure is by definition somebody who is not a public figure. All (private) individuals have the right to be left alone and to lead their private lives without any publicity. Section 14 of South Africa's Constitution reads:

Everyone has the right to privacy, which includes the right not to have –
(a) their person or home searched;
(b) their property searched;
(c) the possessions seized; or
(d) the privacy of their communications infringed.

This entrenchment of privacy into the Constitution – as part of the Bill of Rights – makes the matter of (the invasion of) privacy a legal matter. But even before the Constitution was drafted, privacy was recognized in common law. The courts have always linked the right to privacy as part of the concept of *dignitas* (a person's dignity).

However, it is impossible to legislate privacy. Any such attempt will have disastrous consequences. "It is ethics, not law", Belsey concludes, "that should protect privacy" (Belsey et al. 1992, 90). A private individual has the right to keep personal information private. Other people do not have the right to know such information. The private citizen has the right to defend him-/herself against rejection and ridicule. Journalists do not have the right to suspend these rights. However, although private citizens can usually claim the right to be left alone, this right is not absolute. It has, *inter alia*, to be balanced against the right to freedom of expression (Section 16 of the Constitution) and the right of access to information (Section 32 of the Constitution). In addition, if a private individual is thrust into the spotlight because of his or her participation in a newsworthy event, any claims to privacy may be limited. Generally, corporations cannot claim privacy. Heirs can also not file suit on behalf of a deceased. The right to privacy perishes with the individual.

In public and in private

Another important distinction must be made, this time between people who are in public and those who are in private.

In public

The general rule is that anything that happens in public is by definition not private. Even private citizens who are in public places cannot expect the same degree of privacy as they enjoy at home (*Producers' Guidelines* 1996, 35). Arrests, for example, are considered newsworthy. The press is free to report these accurately. Courts usually find that individuals have no reasonable expectation of privacy when they are in public.

But beware: Some "public" places like railway stations, public transport, or shops may actually be private property. The BBC warns: "When considering secret recording in such places programme makers should be aware of the laws regarding trespass" (*Producers' Guidelines* 1996, 36).

Members of the media should keep in mind the distinction between legal and ethical. Two lovers in a park can legally be photographed because they are in a public place. No legal action can be taken against that – as long as a reasonable person would not consider the picture indecent. But is it ethical? What if the lovers are married, but not to each other? Imagine the harm that the publication of such a picture or video scene could cause them.

The BBC says that although it cannot guarantee that the broadcasting of recordings made in public will not cause individuals embarrassment, members of the corporation should not intend this unless the people are engaged in clearly antisocial activity (*Producers' Guidelines* 1996, 36).

The media can usually use public records, such as police reports, judicial proceedings, or birth certificates, without fear of being prosecuted. For example, a newspaper can publish a list of divorcees, based upon information from court records, even if it is embarrassing to certain individuals.

But be careful not to use privileged information, as this can lead to prosecution. A police detective's notes that are not part of the official police report, for example, are not part of the public record.

In private

On private property, especially in their homes, people (including public officials and public figures) may reasonably expect not to be watched or listened to (*Producers' Guidelines* 1996, 36). The BBC uses the following guidelines concerning the use of the surreptitious recording of people on private property (*Producers' Guidelines* 1996, 37–38):

- They will never place an *unattended* recording device on private property without permission of the owner, occupier, or their agent unless for the purpose of gaining evidence of serious crime.
- If permission has not been obtained, hidden cameras or microphones will generally be

used only where prima-facie evidence exists of crime or of significant antisocial behaviour. The journalist must then explain why an open approach would be unlikely to succeed, and why the information is necessary.

- There may be a narrow range of legitimate exceptions to the above-mentioned. For example, there may be prima-facie evidence against a group of people but not necessarily against known individuals in that group – for example, the exploitation of elderly people by some home repair workers. Where surreptitious recording is carried out in this way for the purposes of consumer research, the results should be presented fairly.
- The open recording in public when the subject is on private property is permissible, provided that it is not intended to intrude unreasonably on private behaviour. Prominent public figures must expect media attention – but the open use of cameras or other equipment on public property aimed at recording them on private property must be appropriate to the importance of the story.

These guidelines do not apply when programmes use secret recording for the purposes of comedy or light entertainment. In these instances, the BBC will ask people who feature prominently in the recordings to give their permission before the material is broadcast. The purpose should be not to expose people to hurtful ridicule or to exploit them. Assurances about the destruction of any material recorded should be given if asked (*Producers' Guidelines* 1996, 41).

Some problem areas

Anything can be a problem or become one. It can be a small matter, as when somebody complains about the publication of their age; or the reporting of a funeral (criminals can break into your unoccupied house). Or it can be bigger, such as the reporting of an illness (for example, AIDS), sexual orientation, or suicide. You may even break the law. Let us look at some specific problem issues and discuss possible actions that can be taken.

Surreptitious recordings

Journalists differ about the seriousness of surreptitious recordings. These include hidden cameras and microphones, as well as bugging. No other single incident has put this issue so much in the forefront than the death of Diana, Princess of Wales, who was killed in 1997 in a high-speed motor accident, together with her lover, Dodi al-Fayed, while being followed by paparazzi.

The use of long lenses to conceal the camera from individuals being photographed, or where people or equipment are used to give the impression of recording for purposes other than broadcasting, are surreptitious recordings (*Producers' Guidelines* 1996, 35). This is not ruled out as a legitimate way of getting information, but it should be applied with the greatest care. When it is necessary to operate secretly in public places, BBC personnel must get permission in advance from their relevant superiors (*Producers' Guidelines* 1996, 36).

In general, if there is prima-facie evidence that someone's behaviour is criminal, there is no other way of getting the information, and that person has repeatedly refused to give the required information without reasonable grounds, you may consider the possibility of using a surreptitious recording. However, the BBC never records telephone conversations for broadcasting purposes without the permission of at least one of the parties involved in the call (*Producers' Guidelines* 1996, 38). The same exceptions as in the above-mentioned issue are valid here. It is permissible without prior referral for journalists to record their own telephone conversations for note-taking purposes, or to gather evidence to defend the BBC against possible legal action (*Producers' Guidelines* 1996, 39).

In general, if you speak on the record on the telephone, you may tape the conversation. A tape recorder is not more or less ethical than the questions you are asking. This helps a journalist to get precise quotations and may come in very handy indeed when queries are made later on. Yet it is advisable and fair to inform the subject accordingly. For broadcasting purposes, however, you must get permission to tape the conversation.

Whenever surreptitious recordings are made for the purpose of exposing antisocial or criminal activity, whether in public or on private property, care must be taken to protect the reputations of innocent people who may be caught inadvertently in the recording (*Producers' Guidelines* 1996, 40). Their identities can be obscured or their innocence made clear if there is any likelihood of confusion.

Ambush interviews

An "ambush interview", also known as "doorstepping", occurs when someone is confronted for comment without prior arrangement. This happens often – and public figures are used to responding to questions when they enter or leave a building. That is part of journalism. Sometimes it is the only way of getting to a news source. However, ambush interviews should be seen as the last resort – especially in the case of serious crime or antisocial behaviour, and if a news source has repeatedly refused to react on reasonable requests (*Producers' Guidelines* 1996, 42). Do not use this method just to add drama to ordinary news reports. The element of surprise

means that some people may not give a considered response – and it is their basic right to have enough time to consider their response.

Trauma

Most people put a very high premium on privacy concerning their own physical health. A discussion here would therefore be in order. However, due to the seriousness of this issue, we shall look at trauma and the media in more detail in Chapter 10.

Sexual matters

There are people who are of the opinion that any kind of private immorality disqualifies a person from public office. Fitness for public office requires a morally untarnished character. The adulterer is seen as a hypocrite (who can be hypocritical in other spheres of his or her life as well) or a liar (someone who lies to a spouse can do the same to his or her country). To this, Archard responds: "The view has a charming Victorian resonance to it and is as utterly removed from reality as that period is from our own. We should set the standards of public office high but not so high as to require of our officers that they be angels" (Kieran et al. 1998, 89). Archard quite correctly states that in sexual matters it is important to be clear what kind of impropriety is at hand. If a politician's sexual misbehaviour is illegal (such as sex with minors or with animals), or it may compound other and perhaps more serious failings, it is clearly a matter of public interest (Kieran et al. 1998, 89). But a person who lies to a spouse is not necessarily a hypocrite in all matters. The politician who cheats on his or her spouse will not necessarily do the same to his or her country.

Most people can recognise the difference – in moral significance and motivation – between a personal betrayal and public treachery. (Kieran et al. 1998, 89–90)

The Hansie Cronjé saga is a perfect example of this. In 2000 this ex-captain of the South African cricket team was accused of giving information about matches, which many people believe boiled down to match-fixing. Then an ex-girlfriend of Cronjé, Debbie Coleman, from Chesterfield in England, sold her story to a tabloid newspaper. Her motivation was to say that if Cronjé could cheat on her, he could cheat on his own team and his own country as well. That is appalling. Cronjé's former relationship with Coleman clearly had nothing to do with the cricket scandal.

As a general rule, if a person's sexual orientation is mentioned, it must be relevant to the story. If, for example, someone is fired because he or she is gay, then it is relevant to mention that fact. But always ensure that you use sensitive language. The *Washington Post* decided in 1977 not to identify eight people who had died in a gay club – in order to protect their loved ones and families. The ombudsman took the opposite view, however: homosexuality is not so shameful that extraordinary steps had to be taken to protect the families of the victims.

As far as rape and sex crimes are concerned, it is a worldwide journalistic convention not to mention the name of a rape victim, except if the person died as a result or if permission was obtained from the victim before that person's name can be reported. There are, however, an increasing number of journalists who question this convention. Rape, they feel, has lost its stigma. I beg to differ.

Juvenile criminals

Juveniles are traditionally protected by law. However, there are (again) a growing number of journalists who feel that many juveniles can tell the difference between right and wrong and that they therefore do not need any protection – especially in serious cases. If a juvenile is old enough to commit murder, to rape, to use drugs, or to steal, he or she is also old enough to be punished for it, and certainly old enough to be named in a news report.

Accusations and gossip

Hausman correctly states that "The power of accusation can bring about a monstrous invasion of privacy" (Hausman 1992, 90). The question is how far can the media go in publishing unproven charges. "Do we … cloak ourselves in the First Amendment and say 'we accurately report real rumor?'" (Hausman 1992, 90).

Unfounded accusations are much like gossip. Sissela Bok defines gossip as informal personal communication about other people who are absent or treated as being absent (Bok 1982, 91). Gossip has no limitations of accuracy or reliability, and relies mainly on guesswork. Gossip, Bok continues, is not morally problematic in its own right.[4] There can be many harmless uses of gossip, such as talk about who might marry, have a baby, and so on. But gossip can also do a huge amount of harm, as when people lose their jobs or marriages are broken as a result of it.

The media must be very careful here. The right to know and the need to know are not always identical. There must be a *need to know* when someone's privacy is invaded; it is not enough to do it on a *nice to know* basis only.

Public interest (the right to know) vs privacy

The observant reader will have already picked up the tension between the right of the public to know[5] and the individual's right to privacy. Individual freedom will sooner or later encroach on the freedom of others. This means that individuals have to pay a price – a loss of privacy, to a certain extent – in order to be part of the society.

Sometimes the public has a legitimate need to know information that other people would like to keep private. The media's task is in essence *not* to leave people alone. No meaningful debate on issues of public interest can even start without some action that could be uncomfortable for someone. Public discussions "...that ultimately may bring some benefit often cannot begin without some invasive and harmful disclosure" (Black et al. 1995, 181).

The inevitable tension between public and private rights[6] ties in with two basic ethical principles in journalism: seek the truth and report it as fully as possible; and minimize harm (*inter alia*, by respecting the individual's privacy).

Neither the public's right to know nor the individual's right to privacy are absolute rights. Reporting on crime, corruption, and the misspending of public money are examples of the right to invade someone's privacy in order to serve the overwhelming public interest.

On the other hand, the right of the individual may from time to time outweigh the public interest. Deon du Plessis, former editor of the *Pretoria News*, makes a strong case to this effect: "As much as the nation, the public have rights, so too do its component parts – millions and thousands respectively – of individuals and institutions" (*Ecquid Novi* 1994, 15(1), 109). Each of these individuals and institutions, Du Plessis argues, must be protected as assiduously as the rights of the masses. If an individual, for example, has serious problems with his or her spouse and the matter has no wider implications, they should be left alone. The same goes for corporations. They have a right to plot their strategies and tactics in private – (again) provided that there are no wider implications that are of public interest.

Sometimes the line between the opposing interests (public and individual) is desperately fine. The media must always be careful not to use the argument of "the public's right to know" to cheapen the richness of the private–public relationship (Christians et al. 1995, 117). The trick is to find a balance between the two. Just where to draw the line, however, is a tricky question. The problem is that the media sail this sea of tension seemingly without any real moral compass.

A checklist

There is a high degree of responsibility on the media's shoulders when it comes to privacy. Consider the following checklist (Black et al. 1995, 182):

- How important is the information that I am looking for?
- Does the public have a right and a need to know, or do they merely want to know?
- What degree of protection do the individuals involved in the story deserve?
- How much harm might they suffer?
- What can I do to minimize harm?
- How would I feel if I were subjected to the same scrutiny?
- Can I clearly and fully justify my thinking and decision to those directly affected and to the public?

Clifford Christians cites the following three non-negotiable moral principles:

- Promote decency and basic fairness, even though the law does not explicitly rule out falsehood, innuendo, recklessness, and exaggeration.
- Use social values as the criteria for selecting which private information is worthy of disclosure. This guideline eliminates all appeals to prurient interests as devoid of newsworthiness.
- Do not malign the dignity of persons in the name of press privilege. Whatever serves ordinary people best must take priority over some cause or slogan (Christians et al. 1995, 117).

Elderly abuse

Invasion of people's privacy can be in the public interest – provided certain criteria are met.

On 23 January 2000 *Carte Blanche* revealed a horrible tale of elderly abuse at an old-age home. The presenter began the programme by saying "The nursing staff didn't know we were filming them and the frail aged people in their care could not defend themselves". These people in the old-age institution could no longer look after themselves and had to rely on others to care for them. "And only too often, when they can no longer stand up for themselves, the people who are supposed to care for them abuse them instead."

Carte Blanche's story began with the tale of an 81-year-old woman named Alice. She claimed to have been hit and showed a massive bruise on her right side. She was not allowed to use a telephone, her correspondence was confiscated, and her daughter, Karin, was prevented from visiting her. Alice eventually lost control of her world, including her financial affairs. She then signed an amended will in her "care-giver's" favour – to prevent him from hitting her again.

Karin contacted the police, women's organizations, and human rights bodies for help, all to no avail. Eventually Karin persuaded the welfare department to investigate the situation. After a number of visits, a social worker removed Alice from the care of the abuser, after the abuser got angry and pointed a gun at both of them.

Carte Blanche investigated and found that the problem was much bigger than was immediately apparent. The journalists contacted Marilyn Lilly, who ran an organization called Focus on Elder Abuse. She put them in touch with Gabriel, the administrator of an old-age home in KwaZulu-Natal, who gave the journalists permission to install hidden cameras.

He was one of the few managers who was willing to admit that he had a problem and needed to do something about it... He felt that the surveillance was his only option and so suggested to (us) that we install cameras in the wards and in the shower.

Gabriel admitted that the cameras were an invasion of privacy (being put up in the shower), but he also believed that the shower was one of the places where continuous abuse took place. According to the *Carte Blanche* report, "Our hidden camera showed that something is indeed very wrong – Gabriel was appalled at the extent of the taunting and physical abuse doled out by his staff". Gabriel said: "I never believed that the abuse would be as serious as what I have now witnessed. I also believe that if it's going on in my institution then it's bound to be going on everywhere". The abusers were caught and appropriately dealt with.

Analysis

Using the criteria established by the Poynter Institute to define a "just lie", it can safely be said that all of these criteria were met. The public's interest was served, and at least one of the perpetrators lost his job. Because of the seriousness of the case, and the fact that there was no other way to uncover the story, there was also little chance that the public's confidence in the media would be damaged. In addition, *Carte Blanche* did not act on its own; permission was obtained from the administrator of the old-age home.

The good that came from the intrusion into a public place, invading the privacy of the elderly, weighed heavier than any other consideration. A deontologist might not like *Carte Blanche's* actions, but a teleologist certainly would. Again, put yourself in the shoes of the abused elderly: would you have wanted the abuse to continue, or would you have preferred this action by *Carte Blanche*?

| Bugged

The media should avoid illegal ways of obtaining information when invading someone's privacy.

In one of South Africa's most famous cases of bugging, a newspaper and its co-editor, Mr Anton Harber, were found guilty on 1 April 1996 in the Johannesburg court on a charge of *crimen injuria*. This was the result of an incident in August 1992, when a bugging device was planted by the *Mail & Guardian* in the hotel room of Mr Staal Burger, an ex-policeman and ex-member of the Civil Cooperation Bureau (CCB) – a covert arm of the armed forces under the old apartheid regime.

The newspaper suspected that Burger was involved in so-called third-force activities. The "third force" is a phrase that was coined by Nelson Mandela in reference to a covert force bent on destabilizing the country to prevent political change. It was thought that some right-wing members of the armed forces were involved – and that Burger was a prominent figure in the whole matter. According to the charge sheet, Harber (later a runner-up for the International Editor of the Year award in 1995) gave the order to tap Burger's private conversations.

In his judgment, magistrate F. Roets accepted that the newspaper suspected that Burger was involved in meetings that were related to so-called third-force activities and violence. However, the court had to weigh up the public's right to know against the right to privacy of an individual. In this case, the latter weighed the heavier – and the newspaper was found to have acted illegally. However, due to the reputation of the CCB, extenuating circumstances were found. The newspaper was fined R3 000 and Harber had to pay R1 000.

Analysis

Mr Staal Burger was a public official and as such responsible for his actions to the public in general. His alleged involvement in third-force activities (very much in the news at the time) made his role in public life even more prominent. The question, however, is not whether the *Mail & Guardian* was correct in suspecting, or could be forgiven for thinking, that Burger was heavily involved in these covert activities. The issue is the bugging of a "suspect" in the privacy of his hotel room – irrespective of who the person is.

Some teleologists would say it was in the public's best interest to uncover third-force activities – no matter what means were used in the process. This may be so, but in this specific case the (illegal) means of obtaining the information should have been as big a consideration as the result of the investigation.

The media should be careful not to act like an espionage organization. Even with a burning issue such as this one, the media certainly have no right to infringe on someone's private life – not legally and certainly also not ethically. It would have been quite another case if the *Mail & Guardian* had filmed Burger in a public place, though.

| A South African paparazzo

Keep in mind the distinction between "need to know" and "nice to know" when invading someone's privacy.

"Diana knew how to manipulate the press for her own gain. People mustn't now point fingers at us so-called paparazzi." These words came from one of South Africa's paparazzi, Fanie Jason, just after Diana, Princess of Wales, died in a motor car accident in Paris in August 1997. Paparazzi were following Diana and her lover, Dodi al-Fayed, when the fatal crash occurred.

The previous year, on 14 August, Jason had been prohibited by an interim court interdict from harassing Earl Charles Spencer, brother of Diana, and his wife, Countess Victoria. The Guguletu freelance photographer was prohibited from taking pictures of Spencer, his wife, or their children without their approval, and from entering their property. He did not need their approval, however, if Spencer attended a public occasion as a public figure. At that time, Spencer lived in Hout Bay, near Cape Town, while the countess stayed in Constantia, a suburb of Cape Town.

Countess Spencer earlier said in a sworn affidavit that, ever since she came to Cape Town in January of that year, Jason had been following her when she did shopping or picked up her children at school. She also claimed that Jason threatened to publish pictures that he took of her in the swimming pool if she did not "co-operate". According to a report in *Die Burger* (5 June 1996), she said: "He (Jason) made an emotional wreck of me. It seems as if he knows all my movements and has targeted me. His conduct interfered with my right to privacy and this is traumatic for our children." She also claimed that Jason had set foot on her property without her consent and had taken pictures of her house.

The Earl said in his affidavit, *inter alia*, that he and his wife had come to Cape Town to get out of the limelight – especially for the sake of their children. "Nothing in our social or public life justifies the amount of publicity that we got as a result of our indirect ties with the royal family (in Britain)."

The central point on which the legal representatives of the opposing sides differed was the question of whether or not the Spencer family were public figures. Advocate Gerrit van Schalkwyk, for the Spencers, argued that Spencer was not necessarily a public figure, and his wife and children were definitely not. Advocate Colin Kahanowitz, for Jason, said they were public figures – Spencer because of his relationship with the royal family, and his wife because she was married to him.

Judge R. B. Cleaver granted the interim interdict on 14 August, saying he was especially worried about the children and the negative effect that photos and "sensational reports" might have on them. He said that on 25 November Jason could give reasons why a final interdict should not be granted.

Life went on – and so did Jason. After the interim court order, Jason took pictures of Spencer at an auction at the Mostertsdrif estate near Stellenbosch. Spencer claimed that he attended the auction in his private capacity and that Jason had followed him and taken several pictures. Spencer also claimed that Jason sent another photographer to take pictures of him and his "companion", Mrs Chantal Collopy, in front of the Cavendish Square shopping centre. (Jason denied both these allegations.) Spencer then asked that the court find Jason guilty of contempt of court.

Judge J. H. M. Traverso subsequently instructed Jason to file documents to explain why he should not be found guilty of contempt of court. "You must stop playing games with the court. Even the court can become fed up with you. If you end up in jail, you will only have yourself to blame", she said.

On 20 September 1996 Judge D. H. van Zyl gave Jason a suspended jail sentence of two months because he had ignored an interim court order and continued to harass Spencer. Jason was ordered to pay Spencer's legal fees – which, according to Jason, amounted to R20 000.

On 25 November 1996 the court confirmed an agreement (reached outside court) between the Earl, his wife, and Jason, abolishing the interim interdict. From now on, Jason could photograph only the couple and their children from a certain distance and with their permission. He was not allowed to communicate with them or threaten them. Jason had to be more than 30 metres from the Earl's wife and children, and more than 10 metres from the Earl. Jason could not photograph him without his consent in a place to which the public could get no access. He was also not allowed to be within 50 metres of the main entrance to their respective properties. The agreement meant that the court did not have to decide whether a person's right to privacy outweighed the freedom of the media.

Analysis

There is a difference between a private and a public figure. The Earl, being the brother of the Princess of Wales, could definitely be considered to be a public figure. To a lesser degree, the same could be said his wife and children. This meant that Jason to a certain extent fulfilled his role as a freelance journalist. The Earl and his family were fair game.

Yet, the difference between the people's *right* to know and their *need* to know is something that also has to be taken into consideration. Was it really *necessary* to know (a need to know) the whereabouts of these people, or was it merely *nice* to know? Many people would argue that it was not even nice to know!

In the process Jason certainly overstepped the boundaries and invaded their privacy. What the court decided on the legal aspects of the case can also be applied to the ethical issues at stake. Professor George Claassen of the Department of Journalism at the University of Stellenbosch once said: "It gives the media a bad name if a journalist peeps through holes or climbs a tree and takes advantage of a given situation". This is true, even if it is the paparazzi's bread and butter.

A widow's privacy invaded?

Normally, the media do not invade the privacy of the relatives of a person who dies in a public place when publishing a picture of the deceased.

On 29 January 1999 the weekly *Hermanus Times* published on its front page a full-colour photograph of Mr Peter van Zyl's body lying face down at the base of a cliff near the old harbour. He had apparently stopped in Hermanus to urinate while on his way from Gansbaai to his home in Rugby,

Cape Town. He presumably lost his balance and fell 20 metres from a cliff-top to his death. Patches of blood could be seen in the picture.

On 25 March 1999 his widow, Mrs Marcelle van Zyl, demanded – through her lawyer – an apology from the newspaper. She wanted this to be published in the *Hermanus Times*, and demanded the sum of R20 000 in "damages".

By way of motivation, her legal representative's letter to the newspaper stated that the publication of the photograph was not in the public interest. "On the contrary, the publication of the photograph constituted a violation of our client's privacy and, furthermore, at a time of profound sadness in both her life as well as the life (of) her son." The son was then six years of age. It was added that the publication of the photograph shocked both the widow and the son to such an extent that they had to receive medical treatment. The letter stated that this reaction was "reasonably foreseeable" at the date of publication, and concluded: "In the circumstances, the publication of the aforesaid photograph was not only distasteful but, in addition, negligent and unlawful".

Even before this complaint had been received, the next edition (5 February) of the *Hermanus Times* said in a leading article that the decision to publish the photograph had not been taken lightly. Consideration had to be given not only to the feelings of the relatives of the deceased but also to those of the newspaper's readers, who regard the *Hermanus Times* as a community, and not as a "hard news", newspaper. The reason given for publishing the picture was to achieve "an awareness of the possibility of this tragedy occurring again". Three people had lost their lives during the previous month, "in circumstances where the lack of facilities indirectly contributed to their deaths", the article stated. The *Hermanus Times* asked: how many more people must die before the authorities wake up? Thousands of people flock to Hermanus, particularly to that specific area, over many weekends of the year. "Is it too much to ask to make the place safe, or at least put up a sign to warn people of the danger?"

The newspaper reacted to the letter from Mrs Van Zyl's lawyer as follows: it disagreed with the idea that the publication of the photograph was distasteful, negligent, or unlawful. It was rather very much in the public interest because it could help to prevent a similar tragedy from taking place at that spot. "The cliff from where Mr Van Zyl plummeted to his death is right next to a sidewalk where there is no barrier at all. This fact could not be conveyed clearer to our readers, and the authorities, than by using the photograph." The photograph told the story of the danger of the cliff better "than a thousand words" could, it was reasoned.

The above-mentioned leading article was interpreted as an indirect apology to Mrs Van Zyl. The newspaper expressed its "fullest sympathy" with her in the same article, but refused to publish a formal apology or to pay the R20 000 in damages.

Mrs Van Zyl then sent an affidavit to Mr Ed Linington, the Press Ombudsman, dated 10 May 1999, in which she said, *inter alia*, that she had received "no warning whatsoever" that the newspaper was in possession of the photograph and intended to use it. She argued that her husband could hardly have been described as a public figure. His death, she argued, could not be regarded as a newsworthy item – "or at the very least was not in the public interest". Mrs Van Zyl added that the publication of the photograph constituted a substantial intrusion into the lives of her son and herself and further compounded their grief. She added that an apology from the *Hermanus Times* would have gone a long way towards pacifying her. In an accompanying letter, Mrs Van Zyl's lawyer said Mrs Van Zyl was not in a position to deal with this matter shortly after her husband's death.

In a letter dated 8 June 1999 the Ombudsman asked for a reply from the *Hermanus Times*. The complaint was summed up like this: the publication of the photograph invaded Mrs Van Zyl's privacy and was hurtful to her; and it was in poor taste and offensive to sensitive readers. The manager of the *Hermanus Times* at the time, Mr Danie van Niekerk, explained his side of the story in an undated letter to the Ombudsman, mainly repeating what he had told Mrs Van Zyl in a

was a lapse of taste so repugnant as to bring the freedom of the press into disrepute or to be extremely offensive to the public.

- The leading article on 5 February shows that there was serious intent behind the publication of the picture "which was entirely consonant with its contention that it was acting on considerations of public interest and not of sensationalism".

previous letter. In the meantime, the local council decided to erect a railing above the cliff from where Mr Van Zyl had tumbled to his death.

In a letter to Mrs. Van Zyl's lawyer, dated 11 June 1999, the Ombudsman gave his judgment. He said, *inter alia*:

- The crux of the matter is the fact that the publication of the picture was in the public interest. The publication resulted in a decision by the local council to erect a railing above the cliff. The press code recognizes the primacy of public over private interest, and in this case the former justified publication.
- Because Mr Van Zyl died in a public place and was seen by a number of people, the publication of the picture did not invade Mrs Van Zyl's privacy. "There would have been very special circumstances in which privacy required that newspapers may not publish what has happened in public."
- There is no doubt that the publication of the picture caused Mrs Van Zyl additional anguish. "One can only feel the deepest sympathy with her."
- The photograph was of such a nature that it could have offended sensitive readers as well as Mrs Van Zyl. However, it is doubtful that it

Mrs Van Zyl's lawyer reacted in a letter on 28 June. Mrs Van Zyl was not happy with the outcome and this time seemed to demand a direct – private – apology only. On 1 July the Ombudsman recommended that the *Hermanus Times* make such a private apology in writing, "on condition that this matter is thereby finalised". On 12 July 1999 Van Niekerk wrote to Mrs Van Zyl:

Council action calling for the erection of a safety barrier, subsequent to your husband's accident in Hermanus, confirmed this newspaper's position that coverage of the case was in the public interest. We are sorry that you and your family feel that this newspaper compounded your grief. Please understand that it was not our intention to cause you more anguish but rather to prevent a recurrence of the event. Please accept our apology on condition that this matter is now finalised.

Analysis

The Ombudsman's decision was altogether sound. The publication of the photograph was indeed in the public interest. The decision to erect a railing on the cliff testifies to that fact. Remember that a dead person's "privacy" cannot be invaded. Also, there is no way that this incident, which occurred in a public place, could have invaded Mrs Van Zyl's privacy. In addition, the publication of the photograph was not at all a matter of poor taste, negligence, or unlawfulness. Although Mr Van Zyl's blood could be seen, he was lying face down, 20 metres away.

However, two things must be said:

- It is definitely not clear *from the photograph*, as was stated by the newspaper, that the cliff was dangerous. The picture did not convey the danger of the cliff a thousand times better than words could have; it did not portray the uncovered sidewalk at all.

- Not enough attention was given to the fact that Mrs Van Zyl was not aware of the fact that the newspaper had this picture and was contemplating using it. To minimize some harm the *Hermanus Times* should at least have used a golden mean and informed (not asked) the widow in advance of its decision to publish this picture. This could have been done without minimizing the truth.

| **Pay up!**

Be careful not to give someone the right of veto before publication – publication of vetoed material could amount to an invasion of privacy

On 26 March 1996 *Huisgenoot* and *You* magazines were ordered by the Appeal Court in Bloemfontein to pay compensation of R5 000 to Ms Anna Jooste, a former friend of Naas Botha, former Springbok rugby captain, for invasion of her privacy. The case stemmed from the fact that *Huisgenoot* had published an article in which Jooste alleged that she was the mother of Botha's illegitimate son. She was also reported to have said that her son had begun asking questions and that she could not give him satisfactory answers any more.

During the first half of 1991, it became common knowledge that Botha was about to be married for a second time – to Ms Karen Kruger, a Springbok athlete. Jooste later claimed she did not know when the marriage ceremony was scheduled.

At the same time that Jooste instituted proceedings in the Maintenance Court against Botha, she contacted a journalist, Lucia Gomes, from *Huisgenoot*, and offered to sell her story for publication in *Huisgenoot* and *You*. Jooste said she wanted a "counter article" in *Huisgenoot* if she received negative publicity from the intended maintenance proceedings.

An agreement, part oral and part written, was reached on 8 June 1991. According to this arrangement, Jooste would receive R5 000 upon publication of this exclusive interview. However, Jooste first had to approve the contents of the article and the photographs to be used, and also had to agree to the date of publication.

Jooste's response to the article was that it was "very beautiful" ("*baie mooi*") but a bit too emotional ("*bietjies te emosioneel*"). She proposed nine amendments to the text and requested to see the final copy, as well as the English translation to appear in *You*. She tentatively suggested the first week in July as the publication date. A second draft was transmitted to Jooste. She was again not satisfied and proposed further amendments.

Before publication, the news editor of *Huisgenoot*, Tobie Wiese, requested Jooste to withdraw her maintenance application until the article had been published – for fear of the *sub judice* rule. Botha's attorney also telephoned her and, as she understood the call, threatened her with litigation. His corresponding letter was interpreted by Jooste as a summons.

On 19 June Jooste informed *Huisgenoot* and *You* that she was withdrawing her consent to publication. *Huisgenoot* placed the article, which was published on 27 June 1991, right next to Botha in his marriage clothes.

Jooste subpoenaed Nasionale Media and Mr Niel Hammann, editor of *Huisgenoot/You*, demanding damages of R20 000. Apart from the article being "a bit too emotional", it also appeared shortly before Botha's marriage, she said. According to Jooste, this looked like "sour grapes". The article created the impression that she had wanted publicity and wanted to launch a "total onslaught" on Botha, she added.

Huisgenoot countered that Jooste knew that her article was going to be published shortly before Botha's wedding. Jooste came to *Huisgenoot* for an interview, *not vice versa*. She had also accepted R5 000 as payment for the article.

According to Wiese, Botha's lawyer phoned Jooste when he heard that she had spoken to a magazine. Jooste got a fright and immediately wanted to withdraw the article, Wiese claimed.

Initially, the Cape Magistrates Court adjudicated against Jooste. Magistrate E. Putter found that Jooste could not claim that her privacy had been invaded because she had lost her right to protection when she went for an interview. She had wanted the facts to be published. These facts were admittedly private, but Jooste took a conscious decision to have them published.

Jooste appealed against this decision, and the matter went to the Cape High Court. This time she was successful. This court decided on 8 December 1993 that Nasionale Media and *Huisgenoot* had to pay R5 000 plus interest, as well as the legal fees.

Although it is true that the central facts around her relationship with Botha were known before the publication of the article, highly intimate details were revealed that were up to then not known, the court said. Unless it could be proved that Jooste consented that these intimate details could be published, the publication thereof was not justified. The public had no justified interest in knowing these facts. Jooste had the right to decide in what way facts about her and her son's private life were made known, the court said. She was not satisfied with the article. The court also said Jooste could not have withdrawn her consent for publication too late because she had never agreed to a date of publication in the first place.

This time *Huisgenoot/You* appealed to the Supreme Court of Appeal in Bloemfontein. On 26 March 1996 the Appeal Court upheld the Cape High Court's verdict. It stated that Jooste did not give her consent for the article to be published and that it was therefore published without her permission. Her privacy was invaded and she was pushed into the public's eye against her wishes. Because the final text had not been approved and Jooste had not agreed to 27 June as the date of publication, this amounted to a breach of the agreement. Jooste did not approve the final text, the court said, due to the fact that the article contained intimate details of her alleged relationship with Botha. "That, at the very least, was private and is worthy of protection", the court maintained.

Hamman described this decision as "unexpected". "Ms Jooste sold her story to us", he said. "She told us the whole story, posed for pictures, cashed the cheque, and then went to court. Her objection was not against the content of the story, but against the time of publication."

Analysis

Jooste took the initiative to go to *Huisgenoot*. Initially, she wanted to make known private "facts" about her and Botha's alleged relationship – if she received bad publicity from the maintenance case. *Huisgenoot* and *You*, therefore, believed (with some justification) that "This decision contradicted her right to privacy because she no longer had the wish to keep these facts secret. The publication of the article could therefore not impinge on her right to privacy."

Remember also that Jooste became a public figure by virtue of the fact that she claimed maintenance from Botha and because of the first *Huisgenoot* article. This provides even more justification for the magazine's decision to publish.

However, the Supreme Court[7] focused on the agreement, and therefore (rightly) responded: "This submission is unsound because it attaches no value to the agreement between the parties". According to the judge, a person was entitled to decide when and under what conditions private facts may be made public.

Huisgenoot should in the first place never have agreed that Jooste would have final approval of the article and when it should be published. This is a dangerous practice. It is one thing to give someone an unpublished article for perusal, and quite a different matter to give that person the right of veto. Had *Huisgenoot* not given these assurances, Jooste would probably have had no legal leg to stand on. But *Huisgenoot* did give those assurances – and eventually lost the case on that point. The magazines should have kept their word and withheld the article on Jooste's request. The placing of the article next to a photograph of Botha in his marriage suit was also unfortunate. Refer to the privacy checklist regarding the issues raised in this case study.

Notes

[1] The article originally appeared in the *Harvard Law Review* 4, 1890. Hausman (1992, 79) says that although the phrase "the right to privacy" is usually attributed to Warren and Brandeis, a former Associate Justice of the American Supreme Court, it actually originated with a judge named Cooley. The phrase was redefined by Brandeis, and later used by Justice William O. Douglas, who contended that "the right to be let alone is the beginning of all freedom".

[2] For example, Article 12 of the Universal Declaration of Human Rights (1948) states: "[n]o one shall be subjected to arbitrary interference with his privacy, family, home or correspondence, nor to attacks upon his honour and reputation. Everyone has the right to the protection of the law against such interference or attacks."

[3] As quoted in Kieran et al. 1998, p. 205.

[4] David Archard does not altogether discard the value of gossip either (Kieran et al. 1998, pp. 90–93).

[5] Carl Hausman (1992, 81–82) points out that the concept of the public's right to know was popularized by Kent Cooper, former general manager of the Associated Press, only after World War II. According to this view, the American Constitution guarantees the press the *right* to print the news freely; the people's right to know gives the press the *duty* to print it. "Thus developed the idea of a press serving as surrogate of the people and demanding access to news, as well as freedom to print it, on behalf of the people."

[6] Various journalists have recognised this inevitable tension. Hausman puts it like this: "[i]f a portion of our media is devoted to digging for dirt about celebrities or ordinary people consumed by extraordinary events, and a portion of the audience is increasingly devoted to consuming it, erosion of privacy seems a natural by-product" (Hausman 1992, p. 86). Belsey says: "[p]rivacy and alleged invasions of privacy by the media are central issues in the ethics of journalism. Clearly, we live in a society that values personal privacy, and are concerned about intrusions into privacy… Yet, perhaps paradoxically, we also live in a society that thrives on publicity, or at least one in which many individuals depend on publicity for their lives and activities" (Belsey et al. 1992, p. 77).

[7] Supreme Court Justice Louis Harms quoted the following from "The right to privacy" (Warren and Brandeis):

> The press is overstepping in every direction the obvious bounds of propriety and of decency. Gossip is no longer the resource of the idle and of the vicious, but has become a trade, which is pursued with industry as well as effrontery. To satisfy a prurient taste the details of sexual relations are spread broadcast in the columns of the daily papers. To occupy the indolent, column upon column is filled with idle gossip, which can only be procured by intrusion upon the domestic circle. The intensity and complexity of life, attending upon advancing civilization, have rendered necessary some retreat from the word, and man, under the refining influence of culture, has become more sensitive to publicity, so that solitude and privacy have become more essential to the individual; but modern enterprise and invention have, through invasions upon his privacy, subjected him to mental pain and distress, far greater that could be inflicted by mere bodily injury.
>
> Nor is the harm wrought by such invasions confined to the suffering of those who may be made the subjects

of journalistic or other enterprises. In this, as in other branches of commerce, the supply creates the demand. Each crop of unseemly gossip, thus harvested, becomes the seed of more, and, in direct proportion to its circulation, results in a lowering of social standards and of morality. Even gossip apparently harmless, when widely and persistently circulated, is potent for evil. It both belittles and perverts. It belittles by inverting the relative importance of things, thus dwarfing the thoughts and aspirations of a people. When personal gossip attains the dignity of print, and crowds the space avail-able for matters of real interest to the community, what wonder that the ignorant and thoughtless mistake its relative importance. Easy of comprehension, appealing to that weak side of human nature which is never wholly cast down by the misfortunes and frailties of our neighbours, no one can be surprised that it usurps the place of interest in brains capable of other things. Triviality destroys at once robustness of thought and delicacy of feeling. No enthusiasm can flourish, no generous impulse can survive under the blighting influence.

10 | Trauma

It is better to err on the side of caution than to compound distress through insensitivity (BBC Producer's Guidelines 1996, 53).

Introduction

More often than not, tragedies make newsworthy stories. People die in accidents, in crime-related incidents, in natural disasters; children disappear; women are raped – and journalists (usually crime reporters, but not always) must report what has happened.

In this process the media not only expose the victims or the next of kin to the public, but journalists themselves are all too often exposed to all sorts of traumatic events. Michelle Pieters believes journalists mostly dislike this as much as the victims or next of kin (Pieters 1999, 11–15[1]). In fact, most journalists hate to cover traumatic stories and are scared to speak to traumatized people (Pieters 1999, 15).

The reporting of traumatic events is certainly one of the most difficult tasks in journalism. Emotions run high – and naturally journalists focus on that, too. Journalists must also cope with intense emotions themselves. Yet this is the area where the media are most criticized for sensational and insensitive reporting.

It must be said that certain sections of the media deserve the blame for reporting sensitive matters in an insensitive and sensational way. All too often, it is the bleeding victims, crying relatives, dead bodies, and insensitive questions that dominate news reports. Events are often dramatized and presented so as to attract attention – in order to sell. The focus is on people's emotions, and often the traumatic events are recorded in unnecessary detail. Prominent headings and illustrations (or sound and dramatic music, in the case of the electronic media) often add unnecessarily to the drama.

When Pan Am Flight 103 exploded over the Scottish town of Lockerbie in 1988, killing 270 people, about a thousand journalists swarmed in to cover the story. The competition between media rivals was hectic. The more emotion that could be uncovered and the more personal the questions, the better a specific media organization was thought to have "performed". Afterwards, the media were heavily and deservedly criticized for unprofessional, unethical, and sensational reporting.[2] In the process the media *added* to the trauma.

South Africa's talk-show host Felicia Mabuza-Suttle provides us with another example. On 19 September 2000, broadcast of her talk show on e.tv was withdrawn at the last minute after a threat of litigation from the Western Cape Directorate of Public Prosecutions. According to a report in the *Cape Times* the next day, this came "after a five-year-old girl recognised the man she has accused of sexually assaulting her in a clip promoting the programme, *Wrongfully Accused* on e.tv earlier this week".

In *Wrongfully Accused*, Mabuza-Suttle interviews people who insist they did not commit the crimes for which they have been charged. During this specific show, the accused repeatedly asserted his innocence and threatened to sue the child's mother for reporting him to the police. Later, results of a polygraph test suggested he had been lying.

Fortunately this show was stopped in time. E.tv was to re-edit the programme to exclude any reference to the child's identity and would broadcast it at a later date after discussion with public prosecutors. Just think of the harm the broadcast of the programme could have caused the victim. In this case, e.tv certainly did not fulfil its responsibility to protect victims (especially children).

The potential to do serious damage to vulnerable people in situations like this is enormous – not only to the afflicted members of the public, but also to journalists (although this is not always immediately evident to the public, due to the actions of some reporters). Great care should therefore be taken not to aggravate already difficult situations, to handle matters such as these with great sensitivity, and to minimize traumatic effects to all parties concerned in the aftermath of the tragedy.

The word "trauma" is of Greek origin and means "wound". Journalists should try not to inflict more wounds, or make existing ones worse – whether for the victims, the next of kin, or themselves.

Handling the (traumatized) public[3]

It is important to understand that the way trauma is handled often is a normal reaction to an abnormal situation. People's view of reality easily becomes skewed in traumatic situations – they tend to see only the tops of the mountains, and not the valleys between them. (That is why a police report is generally more objective and reliable than the accounts given by traumatized people of the same events.)

There are no hard-and-fast rules on how to handle other people's stress (let alone your own). However, there are some guidelines that should at least help journalists not to aggravate the situation for other people. But first it is necessary to get a proper understanding of the profile of victims, as well as the reasons why traumatized people often react negatively towards the media.

A profile of victims

There are some typical reactions to tragic news, and it is important that journalists understand this. Of course not all people react in the same way, yet the following phases in traumatic situations can often be identified:

- *Denial.* "This is not happening" or "I don't believe it".
- *Blame.* A typical reaction is: "I should not have…" or "how could I have been so stupid?"

- *Despair or anger.* "How could this have happened?", or even "how could God have allowed this to happen?"
- *Psychic numbing* – to prevent further pain.
- *Gratitude.* A paradoxical feeling of deep gratitude for life.
- *Recollections.* Post-traumatic stress disorder. Recurring, intrusive recollections take place.

Victims' reactions towards the media

Traumatized victims often feel instantly overwhelmed and vulnerable. They do not instinctively and immediately know or understand why journalists want to talk to them in the first place. In addition, they often are completely unfamiliar with the news process. For many, this is the first time they have ever spoken with a journalist. This scares them even more. More often than not, journalists are seen as vultures, who want to make money out of other people's distress. Understandably, this can lead to quite vehement reactions.

In the longer term, victims often feel neglected. The courts, jails, and rehabilitation programmes spend millions of rands on perpetrators, but little, if any, on victims. At the same time, the media are not exactly known for their empathy.

Journalists and victims: empathy

It is important that journalists let people feel that they have empathy or compassion with them in their distressful situation. Some journalists fear that any form of empathy works directly against their ability to report as objectively as possible. They almost instinctively fear that they will become involved with the subjects of their stories, something that that would weaken their ability to inform the public, which is their primary task (Pieters 1999, 19). Compassion – getting involved – is seen as the opposite of detachment, in which the journalist remains an observer rather than a participant.

Pieters suggests competition as another reason why some members of the media feel they should suppress their feelings of empathy. Some journalists may feel bad about pushing a microphone in the face of a crying mother, but they know their professional rivals will do it (Pieters 1999, 19). So they oblige as quickly as they can and shove their press card in a victim's face. By doing this, journalists unfortunately lose their own humanity (Pieters 1999, 19).

The issue here is not one of objectivity. It is essential to have empathy with traumatized people. Not only does this enable journalists to handle those people effectively, it also helps them to write more than just mere clinical facts.[4] Gene Goodwin believes the lack of compassion in the way many journalists do their work (gathering news without regard for the people involved) to be one of the reasons that the news business is not more highly regarded by the public. "Even though compassion cannot be turned on and off like a faucet, encouraging more of it in news work and presentation might improve the public's perception of the journalistic enterprise. It also might improve the perception of news work by journalists themselves..." (Hiebert et al. 1985, 88).

On a practical level, saying something like "I know you are having a difficult time" may sound simple, but it can do wonders to put the subject at ease. Journalists can also say things like "I am sorry this happened", or "I am glad you are alive", or "it was not your fault".

On the other hand, there are two pitfalls that should be avoided:

- Your empathy must never get out of hand.
- Your behaviour must not be artificial.

Journalists with genuine empathy will testify to

the fact that members of the public generally respect them for their humane behaviour.

Journalists and victims: interaction

Journalists should first of all try to understand the phases victims are going through and why they react in the ways they do. Then, in dealing with traumatized people, it is important to create a "safe" environment – both psychologically and physically – within which the conversation between the journalist and the victim can take place. Without this safe environment no meaningful dialogue can take place.

A journalist should always identify him- or herself as such. This is even more important in cases of grief and distress. Journalists can easily make the disaster even worse by asking insensitive questions, or even by asking questions at all. Be very careful: people's feelings must always be taken into consideration.

It is extremely important to listen intently. You have two ears and one mouth – use them in the same proportion. Silence at the right time can be much more important than even the wisest choice of words.

It also helps to be calm and in complete control of yourself. The traumatized person must get the feeling that you are not afraid to listen to any information, no matter how gruesome it may be. The subject must feel it is acceptable to talk to you.

It does no harm whatsoever to apologize for intruding into a person's private grief – for that is exactly what you are doing when you cover the story. This helps to create a "safe" environment.

Victims feel (and often are) vulnerable. Journalists should therefore grant the victim a sense of power or control. It is best not to use a notebook or a tape recorder up front. Ask the victim if he or she minds if you take notes. Offer to take a break whenever he or she wants. Encourage the

victim to ask questions. Leave a visiting card, should the victim want to talk to you at a later stage.

Discuss the ground rules up front. Tell the victim that he or she does not have to talk to you. Explain what you want, and when and where your report will be published. It is always good to begin by asking people to "tell me your story". It helps them to feel more at ease and even in control. Small children, who by nature find it difficult to express their feelings and perceptions in words, could even be asked to act a scene out (if you *have* to talk to them). Consider asking them, "*show* me what happened".

It is wise to begin by asking a "when" question. This is not as emotionally laden as the "what" question. From there, you can cautiously proceed with other questions.

It is less painful to focus on the life of the deceased, and not on his or her death. Ask the next of kin what information they would want you to include in your report.

People feel secure if you promise to let them read the story before publication. Even if you are one of those journalists who do not like to do this, it may be wise to consider this option in highly traumatic situations.

Other important aspects include:
- Never ask a traumatized person how he or she feels. That is an absurd question, and it creates the impression that the journalist is out of touch with reality.
- Always be sensitive. Put yourself in the victim's shoes. Keep his or her expectations in mind.
- Do not talk while people are crying. Take your time, even if you have none. Although it is not your job as a journalist, it is not wrong to console traumatized people. A little word of encouragement or a gentle touch on the shoulder can transform the situation.
- Be honest with yourself and with the traumatized person. People will instinctively sense when you are putting on a show. There is no

harm in acknowledging that you are uncomfortable and a bit embarrassed. This makes you human in the victim's mind. But be careful not to draw too much attention to that fact. Your uneasiness is not the victim's problem, nor is it the issue at stake.

- Inform the relevant people immediately why you are at the scene.
- It may be a good idea to warn people not to say anything they do not want to see published.
- Prepare yourself thoroughly, if you have the opportunity to do so.
- It is even more difficult to talk to a traumatized person you know well. If at all possible, try to avoid such a situation by getting one of your colleagues to do the job.
- Always try to minimize the impression that you are competing for the story. Vultures do that kind of thing.
- Do not excuse yourself immediately after you have got what you came for. Tell people in advance that you will soon be leaving. And do not leave while somebody is crying. Rather ask if you could call someone or make the distraught person a cup of tea.
- Explain to the subject why it is important to cover the story. For example, it could be beneficial to the public to be informed about some reasons why people commit suicide.
- Never mislead a traumatized person.
- If you have to break tragic news to a person, do it in the most sensitive way possible.

Journalists and victims: reporting

The way you report the news should be as sensitive as the way in which you handle the victim or next of kin. Make sure all your information is accurate, and even monitor as far as possible what pictures, heading, captions, and lift-out quotes are used back in the newsroom. It is better to be safe than sorry.

The general rule is that journalists and photojournalists should be able to take the published report back to the victims or next of kin and show the traumatized people that it has been done with wisdom and sensitivity. Do not get so obsessed with a scoop that you become ashamed to show the end product to traumatized people (Pieters 1999, 20).

Again, great care should be taken to minimize harm. In particular, be very sensitive regarding the use of pictures. Think, for example, what impact it would have on a bereaved family if a picture of the deceased is put right next to one of a suspect, or if graphic photos of the dead body of a loved one are published. This can cause unnecessary pain and harm. Follow-up educational articles – on how to break the cycle of family violence, for example – can do a tremendous amount of good to traumatized people.

The BBC

In the chapter on "Privacy and the Gathering of Information", The BBC *Producers' Guidelines* devotes a whole section (*Producers' Guidelines* 1996, 43–46) to the reporting of suffering and distress, which can be helpful to all journalists. The chapter states, *inter alia*:

- In covering "accidents, disasters and disturbances", accurate reporting needs to be balanced "against the obligation to avoid causing unnecessary distress or anxiety". Journalists should provide, "swiftly and accurately", basic factual material (time, location, flight number, etc.).
- As first estimates of casualty figures often are inaccurate, information should be sourced in the early stages of reporting a disaster. If sources differ from each other, this should be reported. Alternatively, prominence should be given to the source that carries the greatest authority. Corrections should be prompt and prominent if earlier reports were not accurate.
- Long experience "...has emphasized the importance of compassionate coverage" of

traumatic events. "Coverage should not add needlessly to the distress of people who already know their loss..." Reporters on the scene as well as editors who make decisions "must take matters of taste and sensitivity very seriously".

- Traumatized people must not be pressurized to provide interviews against their wishes. It is often better to approach people in a state of distress through friends, relatives, or advisers. Do not interview such people just because they may be offered for interview by some authority. The use of material "which is voyeuristic or profoundly distressing" cannot be justified. An important purpose must be served by the reporting.
- Thoughtless questions cause distress and do damage. Try to edit the report without harming the sense of the interview.
- Sometimes victims co-operate willingly with the media or even ask for coverage. As this can upset audiences, background should be given to prevent misunderstanding.
- Needless or repeated use of traumatic library material should be avoided, "especially if it features identifiable people". Do not use it as "wallpaper" or to illustrate a general theme. Surviving victims or next of kin should be informed in advance as far as is reasonably practicable. "Failure to do this may be deemed a breach of privacy, even if the events or material to be used were once in the public domain." If there are objections from those concerned, the programme should proceed only if there is a clear public interest to do so.
- As far as is reasonably possible, next of kin should not learn bad news from a programme. "There may be exceptions for prominent public figures or because of some other special circumstances but otherwise names should be left out unless we are satisfied that next of kin have been told." While the withholding of

names may cause needless concern, the shock caused when names are received through the media is worse. Needless anxiety should be reduced as quickly as possible by narrowing the area of concern.

Tragically, the latter happened in the case of sixteen-year-old Liezl-Mari Goosen, a Grade 8 pupil from J. G. Meiring High in Goodwood, Cape Town. On 22 January 1997 Liezl-Mari was reported missing. When her dead body was found seven months later, Liezl-Mari's mother, Mrs Therena Goosen, heard the news on the radio while driving home.

The general rule is: "The more direct the impact of a tragedy, the greater the sensitivity needed in taking decisions...; it is better to err on the side of caution than to compound distress through insensitivity" (*Producers' Guidelines* 1996, 53).

HIV/AIDS

In recent years, HIV/AIDS has become a very contentious issue. In April 1992 a *USA Today* reporter asked the former tennis star Arthur Ashe[5] if it was true that he had AIDS. *USA Today* undertook not to publish the story without on-the-record sources. The paper, however, pursued the matter despite Ashe's objections.

Ashe felt he was forced to announce the fact of his illness – and held a media conference the next day. He was furious, and complained that his privacy had been invaded. He would have to lie if he wanted to protect his privacy, he claimed. Given the stigma that the community attach to HIV/AIDS, Ashe was especially worried about the effect of this public news on his daughter – even given the fact that he had contracted HIV/AIDS through a blood transfusion (and not through sexual intercourse or intravenous drug use). *USA Today* saw to it that Ashe did not have a choice of when (if ever) making it known.

A debate on the HIV/AIDS issue in South Africa was sparked off by the death of presidential spokesperson Parks Mankahlana on 26 October 2000. Although his widow denied it, there were rumours in the media that Mankahlana had died of AIDS. This led the Gauteng branch of the South African National Editors' Forum (SANEF) and the Freedom of Expression Institute (FXI) to convene a meeting on the media-ethical issues raised by Mankahlana's death. This meeting was held on 9 November 2000.

At a workshop on HIV/AIDS in Cape Town on 7 August 2001 Kerry Cullinan from Health-e News Service summarized a number of interesting points raised at that meeting. Here are some of them:

- Is the African approach to death different from that of other cultures? (Lizeka Mda of *The Star* appealed for journalists to respect the dead.) If so, do cultural concerns make it inappropriate to speculate in such cases?
- Does the fact that Mankahlana spoke out in the HIV/AIDS controversy mean that the cause of his death is relevant?
- If a prominent person dies, since when do journalists wait for his or her spouse or partner to inform them about the cause of death? How far should the media go with public figures?
- Why haven't the deaths of prominent whites been treated in the same probing way? Do the media polarize opinion along racial lines by writing too simplistically?
- Are the media taking a judgmental stance (by saying Mankahlana was promiscuous) to justify the rumours about the cause of his death?

These, and other, questions need to be debated fiercely by the South African media. *It is of paramount importance that all serious journalists enlighten themselves on this subject.* One way of doing this is to get hold of a copy of *HIV/AIDS –*

A resource for journalists, published by Soul City in partnership with SANEF, Health-e news service and the Department of Health. This invaluable booklet not only deals with facts about HIV/AIDS, statistics, socioeconomic issues, vaccines, and treatment, but also with ethical issues for journalists and legal matters.

To summarize the points raised in the above-mentioned booklet, the media-ethical issues around HIV/AIDS are as follows:

- Avoid *sensationalism*, which relies on emotion and usually offers a shallow view. For example, babies with HIV are often described as "innocent" – implying others are somehow "to blame". No one "deserves" to get HIV.
- *Subjects of reports and sources* should be approached as human beings who have the right to respect. Do not continue to devalue the lives and experiences of poor black people (as took place in the apartheid era).
- Do not publish the names of *people with HIV* without their permission (it could cause a tremendous amount of harm, such as rejection by family members and withdrawal of support). In the case of a person who has died as a result of AIDS, the family should be consulted.
- Use words *that do not carry value judgments* to describe HIV/AIDS. Words such as "infected person", "AIDS carrier", "sufferer", or "victim" should be avoided as these stigmatize people and imply they should be shunned. Rather say "people who live with AIDS".
- Inaccurate reporting fuels the epidemic. Do not repeat myths.
- Verify all "information" as far as possible.

Suicides

The reporting of suicides is another prickly issue. How does a journalist strike a balance between the benefits of the story and the consequences to the individuals involved? Normally the media do not report on suicides, unless a well-known person is involved, the method of killing is unusual, or it took place in public. For example, it is reasonable to expect the media to report the death of a man who jumped to his death from Table Mountain, or when a group of youngsters kill themselves in a death pact. The same goes for a public official or figure. The public has a legitimate right to know.

If a person takes his or her own life in the privacy of the home, the media should respect that privacy and keep a low profile. There can, however, be exceptions to this. If, for example, a private individual commits suicide in the privacy of his or her own home with poison purchased legally in a pharmacy, it is newsworthy.

Needless to say, all coverage of suicides must be done with the greatest possible degree of sensitivity. Again, the journalist must strive to minimize harm. To put it another way: do to others as you would like them do to you. Hausman asks whether the practice of withholding the cause of death in teenage suicides contributes to the mistaken idea that teenage suicides are not a problem – "an idea given spurious validity because we did not hear about teenage suicide because we never *reported* it. How did this silence affect situations where a teenager talked about suicide but no one took that talk seriously?" (Hausman 1992, 87).

People have the right to die with dignity. Take care not to report in a sensationalist way.

Funerals

Few journalists, if any, like to cover funerals – especially if the family did not want to speak to the media after the death of a loved one. It certainly is very unpleasant to feel unwelcome amongst mourners. One feels like a vulture and a scoundrel.

It must be in the public interest for a funeral to be reported on. For example, it is reasonable to expect the media to cover the funeral of a well-known public official or figure. But that is not the case with the funeral of a private individual.

Quite a few matters must be mentioned here:

- Journalists do not need permission from anybody to attend a funeral service. Such services are usually held in a church, which is by definition a public place. Yet do not be surprised if you feel like you are intruding into other people's privacy if you attend the ceremony without informing the next of kin in advance. It is good manners to inform the family of your presence at a funeral service.

- If a funeral service is held in the privacy of a home, permission must (of course) be obtained to attend.

- As church councils more often than not prohibit the taking of pictures in the church, permission must be obtained to take pictures. Even then, photographers must take great care not to intrude into people's private grief by pushing a camera into somebody's face. For that same reason, flashes should be avoided as far as possible. Long lenses are less invasive. Moreover, pictures should preferably not be taken while somebody is praying. Journalists should have the necessary respect for people's convictions and moments of devotion.

- A funeral ceremony, either in a cemetery or at a crematorium, is one of the most private moments imaginable. For this, permission to attend should usually be obtained. Journalists can cause a lot of unnecessary harm if they create the impression that they are sensationalizing the last rituals. Photojournalists in particular should show respect for the most private moment – when the coffin is lowered into the grave. It is unnecessary and insensitive to add to the trauma by going mad with clicks and flashes.

- Dress soberly out of respect for the deceased and the family. If you do not, you will be looked upon with even more suspicion.

Handling yourself

Potentially, journalists can become secondary victims of traumatic experiences. The symptoms include professional despair, anxiety, emotional and psychological numbing, flashbacks, post-traumatic stress disorder, substance abuse, marital problems, intrusive thoughts, and depression.

Some journalists, particularly photojournalists, are often exposed to traumatic situations. How do they handle it? Some say such journalists become "hardened". That is mostly not true (Pieters 1999, 55, 56),[6] but rather a matter of some journalists learning how to cope with their own stress and trauma.

And that is exactly what is necessary – to work out your own trauma, for it will surely catch up with you if you do not. Journalists (like other people) have a tendency to be affected by the traumatic experiences of other people. At best, this results in a degree of personal stress, but it could easily become worse and end up as acute or chronic trauma and depression.

Journalists often tend to deny their own stress symptoms. Some think it is an inherent weakness to acknowledge their personal stress and trauma. There is no place for sissies in the newsroom, it is often thought (and said), and therefore stress, trauma, and depression should be ignored. Such journalists are scared they will become known as "softies" and will only be given "soft" stories in future. However, the contrary is true: it is the weak ones who keep quiet about their stress, trauma, and depression. It really takes lots of guts and maturity to get over that kind of infantile attitude and to start doing something constructive about your own trauma. By the same token, media organizations must ensure that they provide adequate psychological counselling, and that such counselling is covered by the company medical scheme.

Again, there are no hard and fast rules to help you cope with your own trauma. However, here are some pointers:

- "Rate" the traumatic experience on a scale from 0 to 10. It helps you to see things in perspective, and to do something about them if and when necessary.
- Remember that trauma makes you tired.
- Remember that trauma tends to have a depressing influence.
- Realize that traumatized people do not see things in perspective, and that they can easily take out their anger on you. Do not blame yourself when this happens; it is bound to occur and it is not your fault.
- Confide in someone soon after a traumatic event – preferably someone you do not know. A few days after a traumatic experience, people (journalists) have the tendency to "forget" trauma as a way of "handling" it. In the meantime the memory is not gone at all – it is merely stored in the subconscious. If it stays there for too long, and other traumatic experiences are simply piled on top, the individual can slowly but surely start to withdraw from friends and family, and even from society and reality. It is of the utmost importance to have – and to use – support systems before it is too late.
- Do not be scared to identify your own trauma and to consult a professional person who can help you cope.
- Beware of assuming the status of a victim yourself. It is better to acquire a survival status. See the world in all its splendour and colour.
- Have a life outside of your work. Exercise, relaxation, and humour are important tools in handling your own stress, trauma, and depression.

Photojournalism

In many instances, pictures have bigger impact on the reader/viewer than words. This leads many people to say that "the photojournalist has the toughest job of all when it comes to journalism ethics" (Black et al. 1995, 155).

Photographs have an enormous potential for creating serious damage:

> Pictures engage the emotions of the viewer, draw him into the news situation being depicted, and let him share in a vicarious but vivid sense the excitement, the tragedy, or the exultation being experienced by the persons caught up in the news. (Hulteng 1976, 159)

By the same token, pictures can inflict lasting pain and suffering. Hence the ethical need "to consider the sensitivities of individuals as well as the larger need of society to be informed" (Hulteng 1976, 159). This especially concerns pictures of tragedy, suffering, and grief – the stuff that fills every newspaper – such as accidents, rape, murder, fires, natural disasters, violence, and war. "Readership surveys indicate again and again that readers linger over such pictures while ignoring many other aspects of the newspaper; these dramatic glimpses arrest the passing eye" (Hulteng 1976, 160).

Many times, the publication of tragic events can be justified by arguing that it will help to prevent further incidents of the same kind, or at least help to limit them. However, does the publication of explicit scenes of violence or death, such as car accidents, murders, or large-scale political uproar, really serve as a deterrent? Carl Hausman argues that "News media have, for years, run graphic photos of automobile accidents under the pretext that such photos would somehow let motorists know what awaits them should they become careless behind the wheel. But people continue to have auto accidents, and there is no evidence that conclusively demonstrates the deterrent effect of newspaper photos" (Hausman 1992, 87).

Photojournalism checklist

Black et al. (1995, 156) advise that the following questions be asked prior to taking a photo or recording on videotape:

- Am I invading someone's privacy? If so, is it for an appropriate reason?
- Is this a private moment of pain and suffering that needs to be seen by our readers or viewers?
- Does this photo tell the story I want? Would another photo be more appropriate?
- Am I shooting at a distance that is not obtrusive or potentially revictimizing individuals?
- Am I acting with compassion and sensitivity?

A further set of questions could be asked prior to publication or broadcast (Black et al. 1995, 156):

- What is the news value of the photo?
- What is the motivation for publishing the photo or using the video image?
- Who will be offended? Does such offence outweigh the value of presenting the image?
- How would I react if I were in the photo?
- Are there any alternative ways to present the information to minimize harm while still telling the story in a clear way?
- Are you able to justify your actions?

On the (bloody) scene

This case is intended to illustrate the stress some journalists work under and the trauma they experience.

On 21 March 1999 *Carte Blanche* broadcast a programme on the stress journalists work under and what helps them cope. What follows is a word-for-word account of that programme, as it appears on the *Carte Blanche* website:

Alistair Lyne has been a cameraman for the past six years. His film archive contains some of the most harrowing scenes ever shot. What helps him cope? 'When it's all happening around you it's the technical stuff that helps. Picture focus, checking your exposure. Thinking about your family and especially your kids make you more sensible about the job.'

In 1996 he shot footage of a man being stoned to death in Kinshasa, Zaire. 'I haven't looked at it since. I wouldn't look at it ... not in colour.' Alistair's world is a black and white one through the viewfinder of his camera. 'When it gets really hectic you tend to hide behind it a bit', he admits. 'The scariest moments I've ever had is when my camera went down on me in Liberia. It's then that you start thinking, 'What am I doing here?' You find the fear is that much greater because you have nothing to think about.'

Rob Cilliers, originally from Zimbabwe, managed to dodge the bullets for ten years. Until 1992, that is, when he was in Sarajevo. A WTN cameraman filmed the entire incident as Rob was hit by shrapnel while he was filming. 'There was no pain, it was just shock ... like, I've been shot... Gee', he says. His wife Jill feels it was just a matter of time before something happened. 'You have to expect bad news, thank God it was just an arm injury. I think that sometimes they think they are invincible behind that camera, like somehow they are detached from all of it. I don't think they realise quite how bad it can get,' says Jill.

Clinical psychologist Brian Dyke speaks of the trauma the profession can cause to a family, 'seeing images and knowing that your family member is filming it, not knowing if they're alive, not being able to make contact. I don't know if there is a word to describe the anguish these people must feel.'

Alistair's wife Sorena remembers the day she stopped watching her husband's work. 'I was watching CNN, I knew Ali was close to the front line. I saw this really hard-core violence and thought, "thank God, he's not crazy enough to go in there". The next moment this voice asks the soldier he is filming, "where are you heading next?" It was Alistair's voice.'

Victor Dlamini also bears the emotional and physical scars of the job. He was ambushed by a group of guerrillas in Burundi in 1995. He narrowly escaped with his life after dragging himself three kilometres to find help. His colleagues however were not as fortunate. 'Just a minute before we were all talking and it was nice. All of a sudden they were no more, they can't say anything. My friend was screaming, he had been torn in two.'

It's a fine line to walk. A journalist is the messenger and not the missionary, they are ethically bound not to act. 'I'm a human being... When you see someone suffering you tend to sympathise with them', says Victor.

Brian Dyke feels it's this professional ambivalence which can create psychological problems. 'It's the most awful catch-22 situation. They have such a huge responsibility, perhaps it's this that makes them think "I can't back off, I can't leave the field".' Alistair echoes these sentiments. 'No dead person has ever been just another dead body. I find that I shoot stuff even though it is not going to be used. It's like you are justifying that person's death by documenting it. For a person to die the least you can do is document their going.'

Analysis

This is an extreme, yet not uncommon, example of what journalists endure from time to time in the course of their careers. Clearly there are different reactions to this kind of trauma reporting. Some journalists seem to thrive on the adrenaline; others have more difficulty in coping; still others never return. It really takes a special breed of journalist to cope with this kind of pressure. Consider the following:

- Alistair Lyne copes by focusing on the job at hand, thinking about the loved ones far away, and not looking back at the pictures taken. At

least he is documenting the last moments of a person's life.

- Victor Dlamini has opted out (and could anyone really blame him?). It is impossible not to sympathize with a victim, even when you are a journalist.

Hopefully both "types" of journalists receive the necessary counselling on an on-going basis. They need it more than most journalists do.

Watershed at the Waterfront

DIE BURGER

Terreur ruk Waterfront

Journalists must work through their own trauma – and not ignore it.

On 25 August 1998 a powerful pipe bomb exploded just after 19:00 in the Planet Hollywood restaurant at the V&A Waterfront in Cape Town. Two people died and 26 were injured.

Karin Cronjé, a night and crime reporter at *Die Burger*, happened to be about 100 metres from the scene when the bomb went off. She rushed to the restaurant, as did Roger Sedres, a photographer on the same newspaper. The two of them were the first people on the scene, together with a security guard. This case study examines the trauma of a journalist. For practical reasons the discussion is limited to a single individual.

Karin's immediate dilemma was whether she should first act as a journalist or help the injured. She decided first to help carry the injured out before informing her newspaper. She recalled the scene:

> I think I saw a foot. And pieces of human flesh. It was dark, with just a few dim lights burning. The statue of Arnold Schwarzenegger in the entrance was shot to pieces. There was blood all over it. Broken glass was strewn all over the place.
>
> A shocked woman covered in blood came stumbling out of the restaurant with her hands above her head, shouting: 'Where are my legs?' People were screaming and shouting all over the place.

When Karin had carried out three or four victims, a chef from a hotel next door arrived with buckets of ice. They shoved people's bruised bodies in the icy water to try and stop the bleeding. In the meantime, she was aware that another bomb could explode at any time. But she was not scared. "Maybe it was the adrenaline rush", Karin explained. "What did freak me out, however, was all the people who asked me if I had seen their loved ones, whom they then described to me. And the horror on their faces."

Karin phoned her newspaper about ten minutes after the blast. She stayed at the scene and filed reports throughout the night, only leaving at 5:00 the next morning. Her family and friends kept on calling her to find out if she was safe. "When I got home at about 6 am, it was the first time that I came to a halt. I was tired to the bone. I sank down to the floor, sat with my back to a wall and started crying. I felt better afterwards."

That same afternoon she was back at work, working on the same story and talking to several victims.

The next day, when she arrived at the office, she saw the front pages of *Die Burger*, the *Cape Times*, and the *Cape Argus*. "One read something like 'Bloodbath turns into hell'. I realised I could not work on the Planet Hollywood story any more. I went to the news editor, Pierre Steyn, and told him how I felt." He asked her what she was doing at work at all. All the journalists who were involved had been booked off for a week, and they all had to go for counselling, he informed her. Pierre also said that he was considering taking her off the crime beat. According to Steyn, she had been a crime reporter for too long and that was against newspaper policy anyway. Karin replied that she would resign from the newspaper if he took her off her beat.

Karin recalled that she did not want to go for counselling. All she had wanted to do was to stop working on the Waterfront bomb story. Pierre then persuaded her, and she went (reluctantly) to a friend who was a psychologist. "The one thing I could not understand was my tiredness. I was also nauseous. I had not eaten, just drank coffee and smoked lots of cigarettes. I felt as if I was on the go all the time, even when I tried to sleep. I could not come to rest."

Karin had to tell the psychologist everything that had happened. "She explained to me I had symptoms of what she called post-traumatic stress disorder. That also explained why I felt guilty all the time. Apparently people in extreme situations sometimes feel guilty because they were not victims themselves, or because they did not sufficiently help the victims. The latter was true in my case. Of course, rationally, this feeling did not make sense at all, yet that was the way I felt. I did not feel guilty because I was not a victim. I understood that it was fate."

Karin realized the bomb incident at the Waterfront was her watershed. She was a very experienced crime reporter and had witnessed many people who had been murdered or maimed. This time, however, it was different. "My friend explained my tiredness was because of toxins that were released due to the adrenaline rush. I had to go for a massage, or take a long, hot bath. She also prescribed some homeopathic medicine."

That night Karin slept well. The following morning she had to write down everything she had experienced. She had to go back to her friend for another session. "I had to decide if I wanted to continue to be a crime reporter, or maybe to change my whole life and do something totally different. I had become morbid, cynical, 'dark'. But I knew that was what I wanted to do, so I decided to continue."

Two or three days after the incident Karin started to get heavy nightmares. She dreamt about blood, accidents, and that she was dying. "I dreamt five times in a row I am in an aeroplane that was on the point of crashing. In the dream I was also outside the plane, watching it happen."

She also dreamt of real events, like a pipe bomb explosion some months before in which a young boy had died and his sister had lost both legs. The psychologist instructed Karin to speak to her family and friends, even to the police, about the event and her feelings as much as possible. This she did not want to do. "I closed up completely."

Every time she went past Planet Hollywood, her stomach turned. For a whole year she never returned to that restaurant, until she was asked to relate the events to a group of school journalists. "I could not eat with them in that restaurant. I was nauseous the whole time. I told my story, reacted to questions, and left as soon as possible."

Two years later, Karin had to do a story commemorating the issue. Although this was very taxing for her, she felt she had to do it. "It was a baby that I had adopted."

Then Planet Hollywood went bankrupt, and again it was Karin who had to do the story. This time something strange happened. When the restaurant closed down, she felt as if she also closed that specific chapter of her life. "That day will forever remain a date of extreme emotional disturbance. I'll never forget the images of muti-

lated bodies – lying in what seemed like a true movie scene. But I have now learnt to cope with the stress."

According to Karin, the Planet Hollywood bomb never affected her in any way in the course of her career as a crime reporter – with one exception. It was not blood, but a tear in a child's eye that suddenly took the carpet from underneath her feet. "This little girl was sitting in a cot in a hospital. She had to undergo a kidney transplant (the kidney coming from her twin sister). The tears in her eyes stopped me in my tracks. I left without doing the story."

Analysis

Karin Cronjé had no time to prepare for this traumatic event. She had to act immediately.

Karin cannot be faulted for her split-second decision to help the victims first (she could have saved lives) and then to inform the newspaper. She did her duty as a citizen, which can be expected from any journalist in an extreme situation like the one in question. It was only ten minutes later that she did phone her newspaper – still very much in time for the first deadline.

Anyone who believes a journalist should never become involved in events is welcome to talk to the victims that Karin helped. They will surely be of a different opinion.

Pierre Steyn's sensitive but firm handling of the situation provides a textbook example of how to deal with traumatized journalists. Not only did he book Karin (and the rest of the staff who were involved) off for a week, but, much more importantly, he insisted that they go for counselling. If trauma is not handled and it is kept bottled up, it is stored away – from where it sooner or later will do damage. It will not go away on its own.

Young as she is, Karin is one of the most competent and experienced crime reporters in South Africa. The reason she found it difficult to cope is because she is, after all, only human. That showed when the tears of a dying child stopped her in her tracks.

Karin's reluctance to talk to a psychologist, as well as to her family and friends, is understandable, but not wise. Fortunately she herself experienced that it is much easier to work through your trauma by talking to people than it is to lock it all up inside. If you deny your own stress symptoms, you will never work through your trauma. That can only end in chronic trauma and depression.

Interviewing the dying

The media's "weapons" are notebooks and cameras, not first-aid equipment or guns.

In March 1994 three members of the right-wing Afrikaner Weerstandsbeweging (AWB) were shot to death by a member of the Bophuthatswana police. The men were part of a (poorly) organized right-wing resistance force which invaded the former Bophuthatswana to ensure that President Lucas Mangope, who was facing a military coup at that time, stayed in power. Members of the Bophuthatswana police and AWB members were exchanging gunfire in Mmabatho and Mafikeng at the time. It was like war.

Andriette Stofberg from *Beeld* and two photojournalists, Phyllis Green and Christiaan Kotze, arrived at the police headquarters in Mafikeng just after the three AWB members had been shot. One of them, Sarel Fourie, was already dead. According to Stofberg's account of the events, which appeared in an article in *Die Burger* on 16 March 1994, it seemed as if AWB members Fanie Uys and Alwyn Wolfaardt had sustained only light wounds. They did not complain that they were in any sort of pain, but did ask Stofberg for medical aid. Stofberg recounted (Pieters 1999, 28) that Wolfaardt lifted his head when she knelt in front of him and spoke to him in Afrikaans. Wolfaardt said the Bophuthatswana security people did not want to help him and he pleaded with Stofberg to do so. Stofberg then asked one of the policemen who was at the scene for help. The policeman referred her to a white officer who was close by. This officer said he could not do anything. An ambulance had already been summoned from the military base eight kilometres away.

At that point, the policemen shouted at Stofberg and her colleagues that the AWB was coming and that they had to leave the scene immediately. Shots were fired higher up in the main street, and Stofberg and her colleagues went to investigate. Vehicles full of armed AWB members raced past them. They pointed their guns at pedestrians and motorists. While this was happening, shots were fired a few blocks away. A Bophuthatswana policeman had killed the two wounded AWB members next to their blue Mercedes.[7]

The last moments of the lives of Uys and Wolfaardt were shown on television, and seen by millions of people – including the families of the dying men. Fourie was at that stage already dead. Pictures of the two dying men were also published in full colour on the front pages of most South African newspapers. Naturally, the next of kin were highly upset by this media coverage.

Amelia Uys, the wife of Fanie Uys, told the Tebbutt Commission in February 1997 that she and her children had received the news of her husband's death on television. Both her children had to get medical and psychiatric help afterwards. Her ten-year-old daughter later tried to commit suicide by jumping from a moving train.

Analysis

The media were severely criticized for acting unethically by conducting interviews with two wounded AWB members and taking pictures of them before and after they died, whilst not attempting to give them medical aid.

Journalists are also ordinary citizens, and situations can arise where they feel compelled to act as such. However, there were two valid reasons why the journalists acted the way they did. Firstly, the situation was extremely volatile. A full-scale gun battle could have erupted at any time. If the journalists could have rescued the men, it might have been another matter. Perhaps a case could then have been made that they should have saved the men first and worried about their work as journalists later. But the journalists were completely powerless. They were not armed, and, even if they were, they could not reasonably have been expected to enter into a gun battle with trained armed forces.

Stofberg was quoted as saying: "We (members of the media) carry notebooks and cameras, not first-aid equipment. It is the media's only weapon in a dangerous situation not to become involved" (Pieters 1999, 27). That does not mean to say the media are insensitive and would leave wounded people alone without trying to help. Any kind of interference in that specific situation would have caused even more confrontation and could have led to greater loss of life.

Secondly, Stofberg did ask a policeman for help. That was her civic (and human) duty and she fulfilled that duty as well as the situation allowed her.

So the journalists could not have saved the men's lives. The reporters were neither soldiers nor doctors. But was it ethical to interview the wounded and to take pictures of the dead? Of course it was! The journalists were sent by their newspaper to cover a war-like story. It was their duty to inform the public about what was happening. If Stofberg had refused to talk to the wounded, and if the photographers had refused to take pictures, they would have refused to do their duty.

It is indeed extremely regrettable that some of the deceased's next of kin saw the murders on television. However, due to the enormous public interest in the tragic events, the public interest in this specific case has to weigh heavier than the concerns of the individuals. It was not reasonable to expect the media to withhold that kind of information just because the next of kin had not officially been informed (as the Press Ombudsman also later stated). Normally, the bodies of dead people are not shown explicitly because of the traumatic effect, especially on the families of the deceased.

Blown to pieces

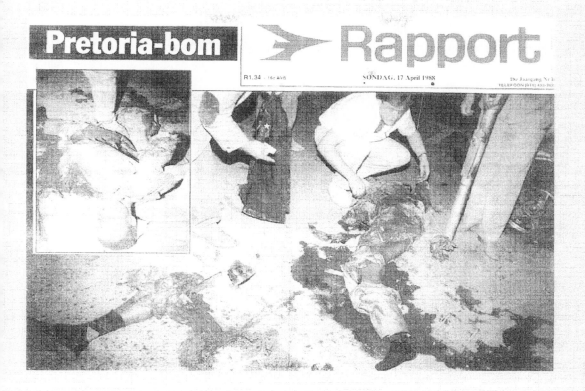

Be careful not to use traumatic pictures to advance your own ideological convictions.

On Sunday 17 April 1988 *Rapport* published two extremely gruesome photographs – a big picture and a smaller insert – on its front page. The photographs showed a person who had literally been blown to pieces in a bomb attack in Pretoria. The newspaper reported that a limpet mine had apparently exploded while a terrorist was trying to attach it to a motor vehicle in a parking lot near Sterland.

A similar picture had been published in *Beeld* the previous day. The picture had been used smaller and was not as colourful as the one in *Rapport*. *Beeld* also did not use an insert picture. The former Media Council received several complaints against *Rapport*. The only complaint against *Beeld* was withdrawn.

In its leading article on 24 April 1988, the editor of *Rapport* defended his decision to publish the pictures. It was stated that *Rapport's* circulation was approximately 400 000 and that the number of complaints, seen against this background, was extremely low. Of course, the editor wrote, the pictures were published with the knowledge that readers would be shocked. However, it would amount to a misconception and a serious simplification to assume that such a picture would have been published with the intent to shock. He argued that these are the kinds of pictures a newspaper always publishes with some hesitation, and hopes not to publish again. But how can the public fully understand what happened if they do not see the full extent of the event, he asked.

One of the complainants, Mr D. J. Sheasby, told the Media Council that he was irrevocably opposed to terrorism. However, he wanted civil standards to be upheld and was of the opinion that *Rapport* had acted irresponsibly. Sheasby's nine-year-old daughter had been with him when he bought the paper and she had been deeply shocked. He argued that if members of the public were going to be exposed to pictures like that, they would later see it as normal. Sheasby said he would probably not have lodged a complaint if the pictures had not been used on the front page and if an appropriate warning had been published on the front page.

Another complainant, Mr L. J. Vosloo, argued for ten other complainants that the use of such large pictures amounted to sensationalism. This was unacceptable and in very poor taste. Vosloo said *Rapport* actually furthered the aims of the terrorists, whose goal was to instil fear. Vosloo admitted the pictures were newsworthy, but argued that *Rapport* had published them to boost its circulation.

Advocate A. W. Mostert, in *Rapport's* defence, referred to a report by Professor J. van der Westhuizen, the Director of Unisa's Criminology Institute. Some 1 200 average readers were asked their opinion on the matter, and 91,2 per cent approved in principle of the publication of the pictures. Mostert also pointed out how difficult it was to establish criteria in this regard.

The respondent told the Media Council that he had consulted an expert, Paul Johnson, a well-known historian and former editor of the *New Statesman*. Johnson wrote a weekly column in the British magazine *The Spectator* on ethics in the media. According to Johnson, to justify

publication the pictures must be in the public interest and for the benefit of the community – like warning the public against the atrocities and dangers of terrorism. Johnson also said it is one thing to publish a picture of an innocent victim, whose next of kin have moral rights in the matter, and quite another to publish the body of a terrorist ripped to pieces by his own bomb. By coincidence, Johnson wrote in his column on 23 April 1988:

> Newspaper editors are not normally people who command much sympathy from me. But there is one topic on which I feel for them. How and where do they draw the line on publishing material, especially photographs, which in one way or another shocks readers? In this as in other respects the Permissive Society has introduced not so much freedom as confusion.

If the Media Council interfered, it would add to that confusion, Mostert continued. It is in the discretion of the editor, and the editor alone, to decide what appears on the front page of his newspaper, he added.

Prior to this, the editor had explained to the council that it was in the public interest to be openly confronted with the consequences of terror and to be informed about what had happened. The Media Council argued that the question was not how many people were shocked by the pictures, but whether its code had been breached. Both pictures contained violence and atrocities, but could it be proved that the editor did not exercise the necessary care when making his decision?

Other questions on which the council deliberated included:

- Was it necessary to use the pictures that large?
- Would black-and-white pictures have been less shocking?
- Did these pictures have to be on the front page?
- Was the public interest high on the editor's agenda?

- Did the editor understand the sensitivities of members of the family, friends, and children?

The Media Council said that *Rapport*'s editor had more than enough time to come to a decision, as the incident had taken place on the Friday evening (*Rapport* is a Sunday newspaper). In addition, in light of the editor's written explanation the council concluded that the editor did consider the matter carefully. The motivation for his decision was logical, and although many people would not agree with his argument, it cannot be said that the editor made this decision without circumspection and care.

Then, with regard to the bigger picture, the Council asked: was care and responsibility exercised with regard to the presentation of the violence and atrocities? The answer was that although the picture carried a shocking message, it was in itself no breach of the code. It was all a matter of degree, the Council said. *Beeld* had run the same picture, but had used it smaller, and the colour of the blood was less realistic. If *Beeld*'s was fine, then *Rapport*'s should also be. None of the factors (size, colour, front page) constituted a breach of the code, the council found.

However, the council said that it was not necessary to use the smaller insert picture to convey the message – to warn against the threat of terror – that the editor had already portrayed in the bigger picture. In addition, the smaller picture was unnatural, having clearly been staged for dramatic effect. *Rapport* gave no explanation as to why this picture was used in this way. The Council decided that this unnatural picture had been used for the sake of sensation. In this instance, *Rapport* was found guilty because the editor did not exercise proper circumspection and care. One member of the council was convinced that both pictures constituted a breach of the code. *Rapport* was then told to publish its finding as soon as possible on its front page.

Analysis

The Media Council's decision on the small insert picture was undoubtedly correct. It was obviously staged and used for sensational purposes only. The decision on the use of the bigger photograph, however, was different. Yes, the incident occurred in public. And yes, the picture was of the terrorist and not of some innocent bystander. And yes, again, publication could serve to warn the public about the dangers of terrorism.

However, if the article that accompanied those horrible pictures is taken into account, it could be concluded that the decision to use them was ideologically tainted. It will suffice to quote only the intro of the article: "Panicking suicide terrorists are now being sent across our borders by the ANC. They are ill trained and desperate". In any self-respecting newspaper, the use of the first person (I, we, us, our) is reserved for the newspaper itself. "We" or "our" should refer to *Rapport*; in this instance, it clearly refers to South Africans. Would it be wrong to suppose the "our" refers especially to white South Africans? Or more specifically, to white South Africans who supported the Nationalist government?

The point is this: at the time the ANC was seen by the average *Rapport* reader as a terrorist organization. This is not to deny that the ANC did not commit terrorist crimes. However, the government of the day came to that same party with a passion (as later revealed to, *inter alia*, the Truth and Reconciliation Commission). It is therefore legitimate to ask whether *Rapport* would have published these pictures in the same way if the person in question had not been a member of the ANC? And what if the dead terrorist had been white?

To use or not to use those pictures? Apart from ideological considerations, the decision also boils down to a matter of taste. It is safe to say the pictures in question were probably the most tasteless ever published in a South African news-paper. If that does not transgress the code of any press monitoring body, perhaps it is time to rethink such codes.

It certainly was not good enough for the Media Council to say merely that the editor had enough time to deliberate on this matter and that he *therefore* used his discretion with care. The ample use of time does not guarantee that it is used in a responsible way (as the use of the insert photograph proves).

Lastly, the council stated that the use of the same picture by *Beeld* was only a matter of degree and that the council could therefore not fault *Rapport*. To be honest, that is an extremely dangerous position. Are there no borders?

Hole in the head

A gruesome picture can be published even if it offends members of the family or sensitive readers – if it is in the overriding public interest.

On 29 January 1999 the *Vaal Weekly* published on its front page a full-colour picture of a man who had first killed his girlfriend and then shot himself in the head. The hole in his head could clearly be seen, along with the pistol and the pool of blood oozing from the gaping wound. He died in hospital. A picture of the dead woman, whose name was mentioned, was inserted. She was partly covered by a blanket and her face could not be seen. The police requested that the man's identity not be revealed.

Underneath the pictures the story was told. Here is the gist of it:

> Gauteng MEC for Safety and Security Paul Mashatile tasted the wrath of the ever-escalating crime in the Vaal when police who were awaiting him had to leave in a hurry to attend to an incident in Zone 6, extension 5 where a man had shot dead his girlfriend and then turned the gun on himself.
>
> Mr Mashatile was to visit the families of the vic-tims of a massacre in Evaton West where seven people were shot in cold blood while watching tele-vision... A 26-year-old man from Evaton had allegely [sic] shot his girlfriend, Elizabeth Majoe (22) in a fit of jealousy before turning the gun on him-self.

> Police who were waiting for the MEC to arrive were called on the car radios and hastily left for the scene of the crime.
>
> According to the neighbours the man apparently ran amok after he had quarreled with the girlfriend over one of their children whom he claimed was not his own.
>
> He then pulled out a 9mm pistol and shot his girlfriend, killing her instantly.
>
> In a state of panic, after realising he had killed his girlfriend, he put the 9mm pistol to his chin and shot himself.
>
> When our team arrived at the scene together with the police, the assailant was lying in a pool of blood still breathing. He was rushed to the Sebokeng hospital in a critical condition...

Analysis

The insert of the (smaller) picture of the woman is not in question. She is partly covered and her face cannot be seen at all, which is in line with normal newspaper practice. The picture merely tells the tragic story how this woman's life came to an end. However, the main picture is very explicit, showing the gaping wound in the head as well as lots of blood. The publication of this picture presents some ethical questions. The conflicting issue at stake is whether the harm that would be caused to the man's family and friends justifies the publication of the picture. What should weigh the heavier: the truth about what had happened or the minimizing of harm (to the family in the first instance and, secondly, also to sensitive readers)?

Normally, a picture like this one would be too offensive for publication. The amount of blood, as well as the gaping wound in the head would be too much for most editors to stomach. This picture was also bound to cause serious harm to the man's family and friends. Moreover, the use of the picture could not have been justified as an attempt to prevent any further murders and incidents of suicide. The opposite argument can even be advanced, namely, that the reporting of such events can lead to "copy-catting".

However, the particular circumstances of this incident do make a fundamental difference in assessing the issue. Several important points must be taken into consideration here:

- The incident was part of the "ever-escalating crime" in the area. The MEC was to visit the next of kin of the seven victims of a massacre in Evaton – the same township as the two deceased. The publication of the picture (more than mere words) accentuated the spiral of violence in the area, which the public should know about.
- Although extremely gruesome, the man was not dead at the time the picture was taken.
- At that stage, the attempted suicide was not an isolated incident. It happened just after a murder had been committed.
- The incident happened in public.
- The injured man was not an innocent victim.

It is doubtful whether the story could have been told as effectively by not using the picture. Although this is a borderline issue, a case can be made – based on the above-mentioned considerations – that the maximizing of truth in this instance weighed heavier than the minimizing of harm. The newspaper should therefore be given the benefit of the doubt for publishing this explicit picture in colour on its front page as it did. Yet perhaps a golden mean could have been found by blotting out the gaping wound. The picture could also have been used in black and white to minimize the dramatic effect of the blood, or not on the front page.

Notes

[1] Mini-thesis for the MPhil degree (Journalism) at the University of Stellenbosch. Pieters came to this conclusion after interviewing several journalists.

[2] For a discussion in greater depth, see Pieters 1999, pp. 9–10.

[3] Much of what follows in this section was borrowed from lectures given by Dr Mariëtte van der Merwe in 2000 in the Department of Journalism at the University of Stellenbosch. Van der Merwe is a social worker who specializes in treating traumatized children. She wrote her doctorate on the effect of media trauma on children. Mr Bun Booyens, a former lecturer at the same department, also made a huge contribution to this section.

[4] Pieters 1999, pp. 21, 22 cites some interesting examples.

[5] Ashe was the most prominent black male tennis player in history. He won the US Open tennis championship in 1968 and Wimbledon in 1975.

[6] Pieters cites Professor Michael Blumenfield, a psychiatrist at the New York Medical College in Valhalla, who had studied post-traumatic stress in journalists in 1990, from Deppa, J. et al. *The media and disasters: Pan Am 103*. London: David Fulton Publishers Ltd.

[7] Four years later, Sergeant Bernstein Menyatsoe of Thaba Nchu in the Free State, admitted at an amnesty hearing of the Truth and Reconciliation Commission that he had killed the two wounded men.

11 | Stereotyping

Introduction

The issue of stereotyping is a particularly relevant and important one for South Africa. Stereotyping is a process that mainly targets ethnic, racial, religious, sexual, and physical groups. In certain respects – mainly, of course, the racial one – this country's troubled past makes the issue of stereotyping even more sensitive than it is in other countries.

But first things first. The word "stereotype" comes from the Greek word *stereo*, meaning "solid", and denotes a "fixed mental image of a group that is frequently applied to all its members" (Day 1991, 279).[1] The result is an uncritical and oversimplified view of the world and society, based on a set of preconceived ideas, distortions, and prejudices.

The most "common", and perhaps most controversial, areas of stereotyping are racism and sexism. However, the use of unfair labelling extends to virtually all areas of social interaction.

This goes for fat people (they are "lazy"), politicians (thought to lack moral principles), the elderly ("slow, forgetful, childlike, stubborn"), the handicapped ("helpless, vulnerable"), and for teenagers, teachers, construction workers, farmers, clergymen, lawyers, doctors, homosexuals, and bankers. The list is seemingly endless.

Why it happens

Stereotyping provides an "easy", though highly problematic, way to handle social relationships. Once you have identified certain types of people, it gives you a sense of security. Now you (psychologically and emotionally) can "handle" the Jews, blacks, whites, fat people, women, the elderly, the handicapped, whoever. People seem to have an inbuilt tendency to categorize other people. The use of these ideological spectacles helps people cope with the intricacies of life. And it makes them feel safe.

Why is stereotyping so dangerous?

The celebrated American journalist Walter Lippmann (as cited in Rabe[2] 2001, 4) once said:

> The subtlest and most pervasive of influences are those which create and maintain the repertory of stereotypes. We are told about the world before we see it. We imagine most things before we experience them. And those preoccupations, unless education has made us acutely aware, govern deeply the whole process of perception.

Charles Zastrow suggests that the categories we create for other people may contain some useful information about a member in any category. "Yet, each member of any category will have many characteristics that are not suggested by the stereotypes and may even have some characteristics that run counter to some of the stereotypes" (Day 1991, 280).[3] The big problem, therefore, is that stereotyping leaves no space for individual differences and merit. And that is fundamentally unfair, for not all fat people are lazy; not all whites are racist; not all blacks are poor; not all women are bad drivers; not all elderly people complain; not all Americans are loud; not all Russians are corrupt.

This contempt for a person's individuality means that people are dehumanized. Their right to determine who they are or want to be is fundamentally violated. Lippman once said: "The attempt to see all things freshly and in detail, rather than as types and generalities, is exhausting, and ... practically out of the question... We notice a trait which marks a well known type, and fill in the rest of the picture by means of the stereotypes we carry about in our heads" (Day 1991, 280).[4]

The media and stereotyping

The attempt to move away from stereotyping people may be exhausting and "practically out of the question", yet the media have, for various reasons, no other option.

Not supported by metaethics

Louis Day points out (Day 1991, 285, 286) that journalism which perpetuates stereotypes cannot be justified by either deontology or teleology:

- Deontologists would argue that racism and prejudice should never become universally recognized standards of conduct. Stereotypes undermine the fundamental idea of respect for people (which is crucial in ethical decision-making).
- Teleologists would believe that, because stereotyping is unfair and offensive to certain segments of society, stereotypes must be rejected as harmful to the self-image of those groups. Stereotypes also breed prejudice and discrimination within society at large.
- The golden mean suggests that characters who are representative of some individuals within a group (such as the flamboyant gay or the traditional housewife), but are seen as prejudicial to the group as a whole, should be treated with sensitivity while not portraying them as typical of the whole group. It also calls for balance in trying to portray the range of lifestyles within a certain group.

Moral responsibility

Journalists are very much in danger of falling into the trap of stereotyping, precisely because most of the time they write about people. And because journalists have their own subconscious beliefs and are highly subjective in their thinking, they easily fall into the trap of generalizing, of creating "boxes" into which people can be fitted.

If journalists fall into this trap, the media perpetuate these images – and influence people to judge others on the basis of preconceived ideas. That could be detrimental not only to the media's future, but also (and especially) to the future of a country like South Africa.

Granted, stereotypes do reflect qualities or characteristics of members of groups. The point, however, is that these reflections "reinforce the notion of a culture anchored in superficial values" (Day 1991, 284). Louis Day asks this important question: what is the media's moral responsibility in promoting such values? Should the media merely reflect societal norms, or do they have an affirmative obligation to promote positive images (Day 1991, 284)? The influence of the media, perhaps not so much in creating as in sustaining already existing stereotypes in society, should never be underestimated. It is the moral responsibility of the media consciously to break those stereotypes in order to lay a foundation for a better society.

The worst scenario

Stereotyping in the media occurs often, despite conscious efforts to avoid it. It inevitably occurs in what is popularly called "parachute journalism". This term denotes journalists who come from "high heaven", "parachute" in to report on particular situations, and then fly away to do more damage somewhere else. Parachute journalism does not take seriously the complicated nature of a given situation; it has little or no room for nuances; it ignores the intricate social, economic, political, and religious aspects of life. As such, it almost inevitably reverts to stereotyping and one-dimensional reporting. Once a journalist starts to use clichés and think in stereotypes, he or she tends to ignore whatever does not fit in with his or her preconceived ideas. What is

reported may still be accurate to a certain extent, but it represents only part of the truth.

> There is a danger of coming to broad conclusions from two hours walking around in a neighborhood... It's a good idea not to rush in and come to some stereotypical conclusions so you can fill 15 inches on the jump page. (*American Journalism Review* July/August 1997)[5]

Journalists who work in another country are especially at risk here. Yet, for two reasons – time and the lack of knowledge – no journalist is free of this risk. All journalists know what it is like to be pressed for time. Deadlines are deadlines. The temptation often is to "parachute" a story, knowing full well that the proper context could be lost on you. The other danger (the lack of knowledge) is as real. Journalists often have to report on matters they know little or nothing about. That is indeed a recipe for disaster.

But don't retreat entirely

Even though the use of stereotypes is dangerous, Louis Day believes that their elimination would infringe on artistic freedom (Day 1991, 286). He uses Mark Twain's *The Adventures of Huckleberry Finn* as an example to show that no society can retreat entirely from its cultural heritage, and that many classic works of art and literature contain stereotyped characters. Some people have criticized this book because it contains racist material, and there have even been efforts to ban it. "Such drastic actions would be an affront to a democratic society. Under such circumstances the contemporary artistic marketplace should be the proper mechanism for remedying whatever prejudicial lessons might be reflected in American cultural history" (Day 1991, 286). Even then, however, efforts should be made to change those stereotypes that are particularly degrading and prejudicial. "Increases in minority employment and minority media ownership should help make media institutions more sensitive to this moral dilemma" (Day 1991, 286).

In the following section, we will look at three issues deemed of sufficient importance to be the subject of legislation, namely women, racism, and the handicapped.

Women

In the 1950s the American media generally portrayed women as homemakers preoccupied with better ways to do the laundry and discovering other ways to please their husbands. "Television programmes featured the perfect wife, who maintained a spotless home for the family patriarch and the children and displayed none of the signs of stress that one associates with contemporary living" (Day 1991, 283). In the 1970s the TV roles of women began to change. Programmes such as *M*A*S*H*, *The Mary Tyler Moore Show*, *One Day at a Time*, *Murphy Brown*, and *The Golden Girls* began to feature female characters who were assertive and self-sufficient (Day 1991, 283). Today, the submissive housewife has virtually disappeared from TV commercials and has been replaced by a new stereotype – the "super mom" (Day 1991, 284). This new mother can skillfully balance the demands of her professional career with her family responsibilities.

In general, women are now portrayed as being preoccupied with beauty, fitness, slimness, and sex appeal. However, the 1970s also saw the rise of the soap opera – for example, *Dallas*, *Knots Landing*, and *Dynasty*. Contemporary "soapies" such as *Days of our Lives*, *The Bold and the Beautiful*, *Loving*, and *Egoli* depict beautiful women as conniving and manipulative and interested primarily in power (Day 1991, 284).

Although television arrived in South Africa only in the mid-1970s, these American stereotyping patterns, which did not display reality,

held true for the rest of the local media until the 1980s and even later. To a large extent, the media have for decades perpetuated society's stereotypical ideas about women.

Professor Lizette Rabe is convinced that the status of women in the media is far from being equal to that of men. The life experiences and ideals of women, she believes, are grossly neglected by the media. Citing the Global Media Monitoring Project (GMMP) from time to time, Rabe makes, *inter alia*, the following remarks about how women are portrayed in the media:

- They are by far in the minority. For example, the GMMP found in 1995 that the ratio was 17 per cent women to 83 per cent men. In a similar study in 2000 the figures were 18 per cent to 82 per cent – which represents no significant change.
- They are portrayed in stereotypical situations, such as victims – people who are not in control of their own lives.
- The reason for this is that the definition of what constitutes news is still mainly determined by men.
- The media identify women with regard to their marital or family status (wife, mother, daughter); conversely, men are identified with regard to their occupation or profession, as well as their status in the community.
- The only place where women are in the majority is in pictures. For example, in photographs of uproar and demonstrations women represent 70 per cent of participants. However, statistics show that only 23 per cent of demonstrators are female. The conclusion: women are being used for decorative purposes.
- The perspectives and opinions of women are often missing, even in stories that affect them more than men (for example, wages for nurses and abortion).
- The Dutch media researcher Liesbet van Zoonen argues that a fundamental element of Western culture is the exhibition of women as

objects, to be viewed by the (male) audience. The use of women to "decorate" advertisements is common.

The (relative) absence of women in the history of the South African media is part of a wider social picture, Rabe believes. On the portrayal of black women in particular, Rabe cites Phumla Mthala, who makes the following rather disturbing statement:

> With black women it goes further: there is a 'near invisibility' of black women in the news. When they appear, it is mostly in the following stories: underdevelopment, oppressive traditions, high illiteracy, rural and urban poverty, religious fanaticism, overpopulation, disasters (burning of shacks) and violence against women. (cited in Rabe 2001, 7)[6]

Rabe also has the following to say with regards to women in the media workplace:

- Women are by far outnumbered by their male counterparts.
- Although the number of female journalists is increasing, not enough women find themselves in decision-making positions.
- According to a GMMP study, female TV presenters are younger (between twenty and thirty-four years of age) and male presenters older (fifty plus). The conclusion: looks are of greater importance in female appointments than in those of males.
- A GMMP study found that women report mainly on local news (entertainment and health); men report on politics and crime, sport, and national and international news.

Female journalists have to cope with several serious problems that their male colleagues don't have to deal with. Rabe quotes Wilma Randle who sums up the problem: "Among them (the problems): access to jobs and training, equitable wages, discrimination and sexual harassment, and balancing work and family" (cited in Rabe 2001, 10).[7]

Quo vadis?

One of Rabe's conclusions is that the challenge is not to better the situation with a few percentage points. Journalists must be sensitized on how they write, both as far as content and presentation are concerned. The time when news was determined by a predominantly Western patriarchal society should be long gone. *At stake are the structures, the values and the practices that determine how news is selected and presented.* What is especially necessary, she believes, is a *fundamental transformation* that will ensure that the rights of women (to communicate) are better understood, respected, and implemented by the community and the media. This will not happen spontaneously – ongoing study, media monitoring, and advocacy are necessary to ensure these issues are taken seriously.

The SAHRC and racism in the media

On 11 November 1998 an inquiry was launched by the South African Human Rights Commission (SAHRC) into racism in the local media. This came after the Black Lawyers Association and the Association of Black Accountants of South Africa requested that the *Sunday Times* and the *Mail & Guardian* be investigated.

The SAHRC was commissioned to:

- investigate the handling of race and possible incidents of racism in the media and whether such as may be manifested in these products of the media constitutes a violation of fundamental rights as set out in the Constitution;
- establish the underlying causes and to examine the impact on society of racism in the media if such racism is found to be manifested in the products of the media;

- make findings and recommendations as appropriate.

This investigation, which culminated in August 2000, highlighted the issue of stereotyping in general, and racism in particular, in several dramatic ways. Several leading newspapers such as *The Star*, *Business Day*, *Cape Times*, *Beeld*, *Die Burger*, and *Rapport* were implicated.

It is worthwhile to note at this stage what the ANC had to say in its submission to the SAHRC on the matter of stereotyping in South Africa. The ANC cited novelist J. M. Coetzee (author of *Disgrace* and two-time winner of the Booker Prize) who believes that white South Africans, including journalists and even foreign correspondents, still hold a particular stereotype of Africans (*Rhodes Journalism Review* August 2000, 21). According to this view, Africans are defined as immoral and amoral, savage, violent, disrespectful of private property, incapable of refinement through education, and driven by hereditary dark, satanistic impulses.

This stereotyping, the ANC continued, influences the definition of what is news, how news should be prioritized and interpreted, the presentation of the activities and the views of blacks in positions of authority, and the portrayal of blacks in positions of authority. According to the ANC, this means that the white stereotype of the African causes stories to be prejudiced right from the start:

> The stereotype directs that the news that must be found and reported is precisely of the events and occurrences that the stereotype prescribes as being typical of the behaviour of the African barbarians 'once the whites have departed' from their positions of power. The news must therefore be about crime, corruption, government ineptitude, moral decay and economic collapse. It must show that when the African barbarians took over from the civilised whites, the rot started and is escalating beyond control. (*Rhodes Journalism Review* 2000, 21)

These extremely serious allegations against the South African media cannot pass without comment. Firstly, it is stereotypical in itself, in that it talks about the white stereotype – as if all whites fall into that trap. Secondly, it ignores the fact that blacks also stereotype whites. And thirdly, the ANC makes it sound as if there is some subversive conspiracy in the mainstream media against the new South Africa – which is pure nonsense, of course. And yet the media must ask if these allegations are completely without foundation. If not, what can be done about it?

It is noteworthy that *while* the debate concerning the SAHRC's report raged on, several examples of racism in the South African media surfaced. For example, in March 1999 a blatantly racist article in *Ilanga*, an Inkatha Freedom Party publication, led to the suspension of its editor, Amos Maphumulo (*Die Burger* 27 March 1999). In the leading article, whites and especially Indians were severely attacked because they were said to have enslaved blacks in their own lands. Indians were accused of inciting violence in KwaZulu-Natal. As if that was not enough, the editor expressed the wish that a South African Idi Amin (the bloodthirsty Ugandan dictator of the 1970s) would rise up to get rid of the Indians.

The far-right newspaper *Die Afrikaner* is another example of blatant racism in the media (see Case 3 in this chapter).

A history of stereotyping

Before we discuss the SAHRC report, and the criticisms of it, several observations should be made about racist stereotyping in this country:

- The mere fact that a public inquiry into alleged racism in the media took place points to the fact that South Africa in particular has a history of political and social stereotyping.

- A serious rift developed between white and black editors over the way the SAHRC's efforts were perceived. The white editors were mainly of the opinion that the inquiry was an assault on freedom of expression (largely due to the fact that most of them were subpoenaed to appear before the commission, and threatened with a jail sentence if they did not). Over and against this, a significant number of black editors supported the probe. Several black editors told the SAHRC that they were worried about the slow pace of transformation in the media. In a joint submission, five black editors[8] "indicated that media owners were paying lip service to affirmative action while a coterie of white editors who wield enormous power continued to dictate public opinion and influence government policy" (*FXI Update* May 2000, 10).

  These editors added that SANEF's response to the subpoenas was an example of an assumption that white editors can and do necessarily speak for black editors. "We witnessed with concern the attempts to give the public the impression first that the subpoenas were an assault on the freedom of expression of all editors, and secondly that the inquiry was part of a secret agenda by the commission to intimidate white editors", the five added (*FXI Update* May 2000, 10). Mike Robertson, editor of the *Sunday Times*, sided with Johan de Wet, his counterpart at *Rapport*, by criticizing the black editors for their stance (*Die Burger* 11 March 2000).

- This rift between white and black editors is characteristic of the one that so deeply characterized the old South Africa.

- It also shows that these two experiences still exist, which shows that some things have not changed in the new South Africa.

- The responsibility that these realities place on the South African media (in the sense that stereotyping should be avoided at all costs) is awesome.

Criticisms of the report

Both the interim report by Claudia Braude and the SAHRC's report, entitled *Faultlines: Inquiry into racism in the media*, came under heavy criticism in the South African media.

According to the critics, the impression was created that Braude had to please her masters (the SAHRC). It had already been decided that racism in the media does exist; the only thing left to do was to find some examples. One such "example" was a photo of a crow and marabou, which was supposed to signify white anxieties about decaying urban infrastructure... This, more than anything else, testified to Braude's one-sided and unscientific approach. In addition, Braude was a sociologist rather than a media expert. The limited time she had spent on her research, as well as the fact that she worked alone on the interim report, were also causes for serious concern. It would have made much more sense if an experienced and representative team had investigated the matter.

Criticism of the final report was directed both at its content and the process embarked upon by the SAHRC. The Freedom of Expression Institute (FXI) probably summed up the gist of the criticism: "Many media and human rights organisations, both in and outside the country, saw the Human Rights Commission's investigation into racism in the media as a threat to the right of freedom of expression, a right which the Commission is expected to protect" (*FXI Update* May 2000, 10, 11). To be fair, the FXI also said that, despite this criticism, the investigation has also been seen as a breakthrough in trying to eradicate racism in the South African society.

Other criticisms from various circles included (not in order of importance):

- Dr Barney Pityana, the chairperson of the SAHRC, prejudged the issue of racism in the media by declaring that it existed (even before the investigation began).

- The report is unscientific, incomplete, and unreliable.
- While it is true that the media in South Africa is still largely white-owned, business factors should be kept in mind. The media are, like any other business, target-driven. Target markets based on economic demographics are of the utmost importance if a media organization is to succeed.
- Not a single instance of racist reporting could be found in the mainstream media. The SAHRC therefore had to revert to the highly subjective term "subliminal" racism. Is evidence not important to the SAHRC?
- How does one regulate something that is not being consciously done?
- The report's observation that the "South African media can be characterized as racist institutions" is a broad generalization and totally unsubstantiated by factual evidence. It is unfair to label all South African media institutions as racist.
- If a white person denies he or she is a racist, that person is said to be "in denial" and evades the issue – thus "confirming" the accuser's charge. This is counter-productive as it is discouraging for white journalists striving to be part of the new South Africa.
- The experience of an act as racist by a reader is seen as more important than the intention of the person who is accused of racism. The SAHRC are in fact saying: "you are racist because I say so."
- Bad or incompetent journalism is not necessarily an act of racism.
- The focus of the study should have included class and gender as well.
- While it can be said that racism is everywhere in South Africa, and therefore in the media as well, racism is probably less prominent in the media than outside.
- The subjective nature of the whole process and the final report may well have inhibited a

healthy debate on this crucial issue, instead of stimulating it (which was the purpose of the inquiry in the first place).
- The SAHRC announced the forthcoming inquiry prior to a general election. The timing of the announcement was therefore suspicious. Was it a plan to discredit journalists who were critical of the government?

In the article in *Rhodes Journalism Review* entitled "Where the HRC went wrong", Sean Jacobs[9] voices an interesting opinion. The inquiry took place at a time when the media felt under siege from the government, Jacobs suggests. This was not only a legacy of the apartheid experience, but "visions of a government and ruling party-led crusade against them" (*Rhodes Journalism Review* August 2000, 5) were also conjured up after criticism from both President Thabo Mbeki and former President Nelson Mandela. In late 1994 Mandela questioned the media's *bona fides* in properly relaying the complex nature of the South African transformation process. At the ANC's national conference in 1997, Mandela referred to the media as part of a broader "counter-revolutionary" conspiracy against this process. Mbeki followed suit, and seemed to remind the press at every opportunity of their racial character. This was to point out the inability of the overwhelmingly white press to write about the process of transformation from the experience of being a minority. This, of course, further exacerbated the media's fear of being targeted by the government. "As a result, the HRC could hardly rely on any cooperation from the media" (*Rhodes Journalism Review* August 2000, 5), Jacobs concludes. But that is not all. The basis of this "assault" on "press freedoms" was "a poorly formulated complaint by a group more interested in their advancement as a racial class", he adds.

Jacobs also highlights three issues that stood out from the debate on the process held by the

SAHRC. Firstly, an individual complaint from two organizations against two specific newspapers became conflated with a broader social inquiry: in other words, a micro-level complaint led to a macro-level inquiry. Secondly, the SAHRC could have adopted a less confrontational approach. The furore that ensued after its decision to exercise its legal powers and subpoena editors "compromised and severely damaged the prospects for a substantive inquiry into racism in the media" (*Rhodes Journalism Review* August 2000, 5). And lastly, not only was the research sloppy, it also lacked definition. The debate over what constitutes racism should have been settled before the public hearings started, Jacobs contends.

As a result of the media's perception of being under siege, as well as the SAHRC's mistakes, Jacobs suggests, "What was lost as the HRC became the subject of the investigation, was the real subject: racism" (*Rhodes Journalism Review* August 2000, 5). He points to two "useful lessons" that can be drawn from the inquiry: a wide-ranging public debate should have preceded the inquiry; and a fresh approach and new perspectives into the problem of racism in the media is required.

Perhaps the most serious criticism of the SAHRC report stems from its fifth recommendation, which calls for one legalized regulatory framework for all South African media. The idea is that the Independent Communications Authority of South Africa (ICASA) and the Press Ombudsman should be merged. At present, the former watches over the electronic media in South Africa, while the latter takes care of the print media.

This calls for some comment. Firstly, the electromagnetic frequencies available to broadcasting stations are limited. This determines how many TV and radio stations can be on air. This means that broadcasting requires some degree of control – which is not the case for the print

media. In addition, if the envisaged new regulatory body is to be set up by legislation, it is folly to say that the new body would be under the control of the media alone. Of course the government would have a say as well.

The WAN

Another contribution to the debate came from the World Association of Newspapers (WAN), whose membership includes 57 national newspaper publishing associations, 17 news agencies, and 7 regional media groups. The WAN expressed its concern about the SAHRC's inquiry in no uncertain terms. The organization's chairperson, Mr Bengt Braun, described the inquiry as an unacceptable violation of press freedom (*Die Burger* 26 January 1999, 14). In a letter to President Nelson Mandela, the WAN was especially concerned about the SAHRC's powers of search, confiscation, and arrest.

Of course, racism is intolerable and the media should do nothing to further it, the WAN argued. Yet it is totally unacceptable for a government commission to act as a judge in media matters and to interfere in any way in the editorial content of newspapers, the WAN stated.[10] Racism should be tackled within the framework of existing legislation that is applicable to all citizens. Any specific regulation that is only applicable to the media is an unacceptable violation of press freedom, the letter continued.

On the positive side

Having referred to the criticisms, there are also several positive things to be said about the SAHRC's inquiry and subsequent report. These include:

- It advocates the retraining of journalists.
- It should make journalists sensitive to racial issues in South Africa.
- The investigation has a symbolic value, particularly for black people.
- Various media organizations acknowledged the need for ongoing transformation in newsrooms and boardrooms of media organizations.

- Journalists should indeed be exposed (as much as possible) to the cultural diversity of the country. This diversity should be reflected both in the personnel of a media institution (reflecting its readership) and in the content of the reporting.
- Codes of conduct should indeed be reviewed to include matters of diversity and sensitivity with regard to racial issues (as happened in the case of the Press Ombudsman).

A policy

In a leading article published on 19 January 2000, *Beeld* set out its policy on when a person's race should be mentioned and when not. It is safe to say that, in general, these guidelines are usually followed by the mainstream media in South Africa. In general, a person's race is never mentioned. There are, however, some exceptions:

- when a person's race is relevant, for example to identify a suspect (surely, that is in the public interest);
- when people who were asked for comment or who were involved in the news event, mention the race of other people concerned (in order to explain the event);
- when it is mentioned in a court of law and is relevant to the case at hand.

The handicapped

In February 2000, a furore was created over an advertisement for Nando's chicken restaurants. In the advertisement, an elderly blind woman carrying a packet of Nando's chicken is walking with a guide dog. The dog purposely leads the woman into a pole so that she falls and he can snatch the meat. The dog runs away with the chicken while the woman lies helpless on the pavement.

Protest marches were held in Johannesburg, Cape Town, and Durban against this advertisement. Many visually handicapped people saw it as the misuse (and mocking) of blind people by

Nando's to sell its product. The SA Guide Dog Association for the Blind also objected. Guide dogs love their owners and would never endanger their lives, it was said.

Nando's maintained that the advertisement was meant to be funny and that the company had not intended to offend anybody. However, Nando's withdrew this advertisement soon after these events.

This is just one example of the media being insensitive towards the handicapped. Unfortunately, this is not an isolated case (as can be seen in Case 4). Handicapped people are often portrayed as "helpless and incapable of fending for themselves and meeting the challenges of our complex society" (Day 1991, 284, 285). The media have a special responsibility not to perpetuate stereotypes about handicapped people. It certainly cannot be funny to be handicapped. To make fun of, or to exploit, handicapped people for financial gain is simply not acceptable.

Giving voice to the voiceless

The most important way for the media to avoid stereotypes is to give voice to the voiceless. The media should ensure that attention is given to minorities and that these minorities are given the opportunity to voice their own opinions. Although journalism should be a mirror of reality, news coverage is often not balanced, putting minorities at a disadvantage. Even the majority can suffer the same fate (mainly due to media ownership and market-related forces).

And how fateful stereotyping can be! The American media scholars James and Sharon Murphy tell the chilling story of how the media for two centuries either neglected or stereotyped the American Indians (Hiebert et al. 1985, 372–383). Much reporting was done in such a way that it condoned, and even encouraged, the ill-treatment and killing of Indians. The media was at least partly responsible for the savage murder of many innocent Indians, including women and children. The Murphys' conclusion will sound all too familiar for South Africans:

> How many Americans know of the conditions on reservations or among urbanized Indians? How many are aware of the true story of how Indians came to be dispossessed of their land? How many have any more than a naïve, misleading vision of eighteenth- and nineteenth-century naked savages running through forests whooping and hollering and making off with the innocent children of equally innocent, brave, and honest white settlers? The story of America's birth and its early nationhood is laced with accounts of how white men tamed the wild land, educated the savages, and gradually assumed benign dictatorship over nomadic peoples unable to control their own destiny and unwilling to rear their children as God-fearing, civilized citizens. (Hiebert et al. 1985, 382)

During the apartheid era, how many South Africans knew the ways in which blacks had been stereotyped for decades, and even centuries, or what was happening in the townships, or the atrocities the minority government was guilty of, or the inadequacy of black education? Of course, whites (another minority) in South Africa are also stereotyped. The most common stereotype is that they are all racist. The problem with stereotyping minorities is that it misleads the public and desensitizes people. And that can have catastrophic consequences if the voiceless are not given a voice.

But stereotyping – and its inevitable dangers – can be avoided. Black et al. cite an excellent example of how the tendency to stereotype can be reversed. A group of journalists at KRON-TV in San Francisco decided "to develop a formal policy governing (KRON's) coverage of a multicultural population" (Black et al. 1995, 136). A process of consultation was followed for a number of months. Eventually, a policy was adopted to seek a balance in the station's portrayal of the (Bay Area) community by:

- actively pursuing stories that accurately reflect the diverse make-up, needs, and concerns of that population;
- covering and presenting the stories in a way that does not reinforce stereotypes;
- seeking to better integrate members of the minority population into the mainstream of daily news coverage.

The policy applied not only to race, but also to groups such as the disabled, gays and lesbians, and the elderly.

The KRON-TV policy also emphasized:

- *Coverage.* A monitoring system was put in place to assess newsroom performance on multicultural coverage. Minorities had to be included in nonracial stories. An expanded network of minority sources and experts was established.
- *Education and outreach.* In-house seminars were set up to lay the foundation for an overall multicultural policy, and a calendar was created of outside multicultural events for staff members to attend to increase awareness.
- *Terminology.* A glossary of terms and rules was provided as a reference guide to suggest certain appropriate uses and to identify certain abuses that had to be avoided.

We should not be naive in this regard. Not everyone in the newsroom thought this was a good idea. The policy also had to be implemented, which was much harder than formulating it. *The point is, though, that an approach like this provides a solid basis for reflecting a balanced picture of a multicultural society. Perhaps the South African media could learn from this San Franciscan experience.*

A checklist for diversity

To ensure diversity in reporting and eliminate stereotyping, consider the following guidelines (Black et al. 1995, 134):

- Cover the story with sensitivity, accuracy, and fairness to all the people involved.
- Consider the likely consequences of your story. Who will be hurt and who will be helped?
- Seek a diversity of sources. The use of one minority person can amount to tokenism.
- Do not allow preconceived ideas to limit your efforts to include diversity.
- Be flexible about the possibility that the focus of your story may change when different sources are included.
- Develop a meaningful list of minority sources that can bring perspective and expertise into the mainstream of daily news coverage.
- Spend time in minority communities.
- Avoid letting place names become code words for crime or other negative news.

"A piece of fascist architecture"

Even when the feelings of sections of the population are not protected by ethical codes, the media should be careful not to stereotype and thereby offend people unnecessarily.

Barry Ronge, the well-known broadcaster, critic, and journalist, caused an uproar in certain sections of the Afrikaner community during a programme on Radio 702 on 10 April 1999. With him on the programme were host Graham Scott and Claire Johnston of pop group Mango Groove. Under discussion was a plan to hold a pop concert on 1 May 1999 at the Voortrekker Monument in Pretoria. Here are excerpts of parts of the dialogue in question:

> *Ronge*: I have always looked at that old stupid monument to the past, called Voortrekker Monument, and have decided that the only sensible thing to be done with it is to paint it pink and turn it into an enormous gay disco at which they can have drug-crazed raves. Now that would be exactly what it deserves. (laughter)
>
> They are not going to do that, BUT they're going to make it rock. Now how the rocks (rocks = rock spiders, rock heads = derogatory term for Afrikaners, Boere) that built it will feel about it. (laughter)
>
> (The Voortrekker Monument is) a huge piece of fascist architecture...

One individual and twenty-six Afrikaner organizations complained to the Broadcasting Complaints Commission of South Africa (BCCSA). They argued that the monument symbolized the Afrikaner heritage and that it was built to honour the efforts of the Afrikaner Trekkers. "Since the Trekkers also believed that God had helped them in their efforts and the Monument also symbolizes this for many Afrikaners, the broadcast was not only offensive to the feelings of the Afrikaner

but also to the religious feelings of a section of the South African nation…" Complainant 2, Mr A. G. Visser, asked what would happen if a similar broadcast were to be directed at a monument in honour of a Jewish or black hero?

Section 7.1 of the code applies in this case. The findings of the commission were as follows:

- The "feelings" of a section were not protected as such by the code. Even if that were the case, the broadcast was not so scathing as to amount to being "offensive" in law. "Offensive" has a narrow meaning in law and does not include material that is merely displeasing or annoying. The broadcast was annoying, but not to such an extent that it became repugnant and "offensive".
- There had been no encroachment upon religious convictions or feelings, but only on what for some people would amount to religious sentiment.
- The fundamental rights laid down in Chapter 2 of the Constitution must also be taken into consideration, especially Section 16(2) as an exception to the guarantee of freedom for the media and the arts. This section, *inter alia*, prohibits speech which advocates hatred based on race, ethnicity, religion, or gender, and which constitutes incitement to harm. The broadcast, "judged as a whole", was not calculated to further hostility between sections of the community. The words spoken were meant to provoke debate and were in line with the kind of material often found on Radio 702: provocative, satirical, ironical, light-hearted.

The commission went on:

> Conversely, it is also clear that the words were regarded as particularly disrespectful and stinging

by a substantial number of Afrikaners. Yet, it is the opinion of the Commission that so as to ensure that the inestimable benefits of free speech remain intact as far as possible, the present broadcast, despite its questionable nature for so many, did not go so far as to place relations at risk.

Visser's remark was also dismissed: "Each case must be judged on its own merits and much depends on the context and the history and characteristics of a particular section". The complaints were accordingly dismissed.

The BCCSA, however, warned that broadcasters must take into consideration the fact that the cultural heritage of any given section of South African society is a sensitive subject and should be treated as such. "Even if it is judicially speaking not a transgression, it remains a question if it is suitable to broadcast such statements in the present sensitive transitional climate in South Africa."

Analysis

This is a difficult case, and the BCCSA must in general be praised for a job well done – especially on the matter of religious sentiments and the Voortrekker Monument. The warning at the end also puts their considerations into perspective. There is, however, one aspect of the BCCSA's adjudication that has to be criticized. The use of the word "rock", a derogatory reference to Afrikaners, does cross the line. Would a reference to blacks as "kaffirs", coloureds as "hotnots", and Indians as "coolies" not justifiably have caused a similar uproar? Offensive references such as these can only lead to polarization – and therefore to hatred.

And yes, it is one thing to be insensitive towards people's *convictions*; it is altogether another thing to be snooty towards *people themselves*. Ronge can count himself very fortunate that he was not found guilty of hate speech.

"Love" or "hate" characters

People whom some love and others hate can easily be stereotyped by the media – all too often leading to inaccurate, untruthful, and unfair reporting.

In his capacity as the President of the Golden Lions Rugby Union, Dr Louis Luyt, a former President of the South African Rugby Football Union (SARFU), lodged a complaint with the BCCSA against the SABC. Luyt's complaint concerned a broadcast of Dr Wilf Rosenberg on the programme *On the Edge* on 28 May 1998 between 22:00 and 22:30 on SABC 3. Rosenberg had stated that Luyt and his family controlled 84 per cent of the funds of Ellis Park Stadium (Pty) Ltd and/or the Golden Lions Rugby Sports Trust.

According to Luyt, this assertion was totally incorrect, completely false, and had never been the case. It was contended that the Golden Lions

Rugby Union holds the entire issued share capital and debentures of Ellis Park Stadium (Pty) Ltd, and that this has been the position since 1989. Luyt demanded that an apology and verification (the "true facts") be broadcast in the same programme the following week. Luyt undertook to sign a waiver if the SABC agreed to broadcast the following correcting statement:

During last week's edition of *On the Edge* Dr Wilf Rosenberg stated that Dr Louis Luyt, his family and friends control 84 per cent of funds of Ellis Park Stadium and/or the Golden Lions Rugby Sports Trust. This statement is false and devoid of all truth and the SABC, Dr Rosenberg and the producers of the programme tender their unconditional apology to Dr Luyt. The true state of affairs can be gleaned from all the Union's annual reports published since 1989 when Ellis Park Stadium Ltd was delisted on the Johannesburg Stock Exchange to become a 100 per cent owned affiliate of the Union. Similarly, the Trust is 100 per cent owned by the Golden Lions Rugby Union.

Luyt was not prepared to accept the following proposed statement from the SABC:

> During last week's edition of *On the Edge*, Dr Wilf Rosenberg stated that Dr Louis Luyt and his family control 84 per cent of the funds of Ellis Park Stadium and/or the Gauteng Lions Rugby Sports Trust. Dr Luyt has responded by saying this is not the case, and *On the Edge* is happy to withdraw the statement. The latest Annual Report of the Gauteng Rugby Union indicates that the Gauteng Lions Rugby Union holds the entire issued share capital and debentures of Ellis Park Stadium (Pty) Ltd. We apologise for any inconvenience caused.

Luyt rejected this proposed statement because this "left the ordinary reasonable viewer with the impression and perception that there could be some truth in the contents of the broadcast complained of". The SABC then conceded that the report was factually incorrect and that a correction as suggested by Luyt be broadcast by *On the Edge* on 11 June 1998 between 22:00 and 22:30. The SABC explained that *On the Edge* was an out-of-house production and that the SABC had no control over the production, content, or Rosenberg.

The BCCSA found that:

- the SABC had contravened Section 3 of the code – the programme was factually incorrect and not fair and balanced;
- this finding had to be broadcast, together with Luyt's correcting statement;
- the SABC was guilty of gross negligence by not previewing any productions which are to be broadcast to ascertain whether they comply with the Code of Conduct;
- irrespective of the nature and origin of the production, there is a duty on the SABC to monitor that every broadcast substantially complies with the dictates of the Code of Conduct.

The BCCSA reprimanded the SABC and stated that "it did contemplate imposing a fine in view of the gravity of this contravention".

Analysis

This case could have been discussed in the chapters on accuracy, truth, or fairness. Sometimes the reason for such irresponsible journalism is stereotyping. When this happens, the "spectacles" through which a journalist views the world somehow distort the subject so that all nuances disappear. Then a matter becomes either 100 per cent right or 100 per cent wrong – without the option of a golden mean. This could have happened in this case.

Stereotyping occurs frequently with public figures that some people love with a passion and others hate with an equal passion. If you love the person, you tend to accentuate all his or her good points and do not want to hear anything bad; if you hate the person, then you will believe just about anything you are told about him or her. Luyt is, through his own fault or not, one of these figures – which makes a serious and conscientious attempt at accurate reporting all the more important (which apparently did not happen in this case).

The BCCSA's finding was undoubtedly the correct one – harsh as it was. Not only were the facts not straight, but the report also lacked balance and fairness. The false information was certainly not fair to Luyt, and it probably caused him some (unnecessary) harm. There was also no clear attempt to verify the "facts" properly, and there is no evidence that more than one "source" was used. As if this was not enough, the "facts" were not presented fairly in that Luyt was not asked for his opinion.

Why all these journalistic errors? It would be unfair to Rosenberg to claim that his motives were consciously malicious. But it is difficult to understand how he could have made such a grave error if he had not at least partly been influenced by his own presuppositions, likes, and dislikes. Journalists must be very careful when reporting on "love-or-hate" characters. Dangers loom around every corner. The truth, whether in teleology or in deontology, is always at the heart of good journalism. In this case, the truth was minimized (and harm maximized).

Two more comments need to be made:

- The SABC's first attempt to correct its mistake was pathetic. Mistakes should be corrected *immediately and properly*. This was not done. Luyt correctly refused to accept the first "apology", for this would indeed have given the impression that there could be some truth in the report.
- The SABC's excuse that it was an out-of-house production (and that the broadcaster therefore had no control over the content, production, or Rosenberg) was even worse. Of course the SABC should take responsibility for its programmes!

These gross journalistic mistakes – the biggest one being falling into the trap of stereotyping a public figure – caused the report to be factually inaccurate.

Disgusting racist reporting

This case illustrates how racist stereotyping can influence reporting.

In November 2000 the SABC broadcast video footage, shot by an amateur, of six policemen inciting their dogs to bite three black people. The three victims of the dog attacks were illegal immigrants from Mozambique. *Die Afrikaner*, mouthpiece of the Herstigte Nasionale Party, a far-right political party, reported on this matter in its 10–16 November edition, and led with a story under the heading: "Hysterics over police dogs totally misplaced".

The report alleged that the incident was yet another example of the fact that the ANC could not be trusted with objective reporting. Although the action of the policemen was reprehensible, the crime situation in South Africa as sketched by the "ANCBC" (referring to the SABC) was totally distorted. The Mozambican immigrants were criminals (because they were illegally in South Africa). Not one of them died – unlike so many farmers, the report continued. White women were raped before they were killed, often in front of children. The murdered farmers were often elderly people who could not have defended themselves as young people could do. These murderers got bail, unlike the policemen in question. Not only the "ANCBC", but also newspapers ignore the murders that are committed during car hijackings, it was alleged. And yet they all reported the dog incident on their front pages. After using another "example", the report concludes that the "ANCBC" purposefully distorts the news to stir up blacks against whites. "They purposefully create feelings of hatred in blacks that lead to further atrocities against whites."

In its edition of 17–23 November *Die Afrikaner* led with "Disgusting racism over police dogs continues", placing above that story two photos of white farmers who had been murdered. This report stated that the "hysterics" about the dog attacks continued unabated. Newspapers even tried to outdo each other with "hatefulness" and "sheer racist reporting". The most disgusting exploitation of the incident was said to be a picture in *City Press* (12 November). Firstly, this report alleged, the dog in the picture was not a police dog. It was not even an Alsatian. Secondly, the blood on its mouth was fabricated: "This is evident from the 'blood' on the upper jaw of the dog, but especially the strip of blood that was drawn in on the lower teeth. All the blood is on top of the teeth, and it does not run down. This is so unnatural that a layman can identify this as a fabrication to rouse emotions…"

According to the report, these immigrants had still not been repatriated to Mozambique. And if they were, "it was so enjoyable in South Africa with its dogs and all, that they came back". The report also alleged that the "propaganda campaign" of the media and the ANC had failed dismally in that they had not succeeded in rousing the emotions as intended.

The following week, *Die Afrikaner* led with the following headline: "Photos of murdered farmers cause a sensation". This story was accompanied by another story on the dog-biting incident. The lead story stated that *Die Afrikaner* had been inundated with queries and requests for more copies of its last edition (which published the pictures of the murdered farmers). Both stories mainly repeated what had already been reported in the previous two editions.

In November 2001, one policeman was sentenced to an effective five years' imprisonment, and the other five to four years in jail, respectively.

Analysis

Die Afrikaner accused the SABC and the printed media of purposely distorting the news, and of racist reporting in order to try to rouse racist emotion (which would lead to further atrocities against whites). In the meantime, *Die Afrikaner* did exactly what it accused the other media of doing.

Of course, the dog-biting incident was news, but many factors have an influence on what constitutes news. One of them is the uniqueness of an event – such as the one in question. By linking this incident with the murder of farmers *Die Afrikaner* only succeeded in distorting the news. Although it admitted that the actions of the policemen were reprehensible, the whole focus of *Die Afrikaner's* reporting was not on this incident at all but rather on the murders of farmers. There was no real sympathy for the immigrants. They were criminals, they were enjoying life in South Africa with its dogs and all – and remember, none of them had died…

What is more, *Die Afrikaner* quite unashamedly mixes news and comment. To be sure, the reporting in question does not even pretend to strive towards objectivity. It is extremely doubtful whether *Die Afrikaner* would have adopted the same approach if the police dogs had been incited to attack white people, which makes its reporting racist. Moreover, it is simply not true that the media underplay farm murders.[11]

These extremely serious accusations can be explained only in terms of stereotypic thinking. Perhaps the ANC's submission to the SAHRC inquiry on how whites still hold to a particular stereotype of the African holds true for *Die Afrikaner*.

The mocking of stutterers

Spiteful humour has no place in the media.

On 8 July 1998, Jeremy Mansfield, the presenter of the Highveld Stereo's early-morning radio programme, *Rude Awakening*, pretended to stutter badly when referring to a stutterer's convention. He also, *inter alia*, said: "The convention would take three days to do what could be done in one".

The Broadcasting Complaints Commission received a complaint and adjudicated it with reference to Clause 7.1.1 of its code.

The general manager of Highveld Stereo, Malcolm Fried, explained that Mansfield's co-host, Sam Cowen, always attempted to moderate his sometimes provocative views. "When Mansfield does, infrequently, venture into territory (sic) such as stuttering, Cowen indicates firmly that this is not the kind of thing he should be doing." Fried also justified this type of material on the grounds that it had attracted more listeners.

The BCCSA commented that Cowen therefore plays the part of the "straight man" – an established comedy technique "where the comedian is offered serious lines against which to butt his humour". However, the "interpolations" came across as utterly synthetic and contrived. They "served to exacerbate the offensiveness of what was taking place rather than the opposite" – in the sense that they "set up" each new "joke".

The commission held that the item was grossly insensitive. The "three days" comment was of "bar-room level". "This essentially spiteful form of humour should have no place on public radio, any more than jokes about paraplegics, cerebral palsy victims, or any other dysfunctionalities. This cannot seriously be termed 'poking fun at taboos' nor as humour or satire."

Fried's mention of the specific material that attracts more listeners is "specious". "There is little doubt that if his station broadcast forthright pornographic material, its listenership figures would increase even more. To imply that a radio programme's popularity is some sort of yardstick against which offensive material may be offset is without reasonable basis."

The complaint was accordingly upheld. Highveld Stereo was directed to broadcast a formal apology at the corresponding time when the offending insert was broadcast.

Analysis

This was a case of maximum (and not minimum) harm. Insensitive comments like these have no place at all in the media – not even as part of a so-called "humorous" insert of a programme. It does not take the feelings of this particular (stuttering) minority group seriously.

What did Mansfield hope to achieve? A bigger audience? The BCCSA's comment in this regard is correct. If such insensitive "humour" is aimed at creating a bigger audience, then the lowest form of communication (pornography) should do the trick even better.

The South African media can do without this shameful type of nonsense. If a journalist cannot *be* funny, he or she should not *try* to be funny. Only the lowest common denominator would enjoy such humour. And perhaps not even them.

In lighter vein

Humour should not be used as an excuse to stereotype people.

In the following case of stereotyping, the BCCSA found that the complaint in question was made in lighter vein and was not meant to hurt anybody — and dismissed the complaint on that basis.

On 4 August 1999 Radio Jacaranda broadcast a clip about an accident suffered by rock star Robert Plant in Greece on the same day 24 years ago. One anchor then said: "What do you expect from Greeks, Greek drivers are bad drivers".

Part of the transcript reads as follows:

Karl: 1975 on this day Robert Plant is seriously injured in a car accident whilst in Greece... and I'm not surprised, the way they drive...

Mairhi: You're not talking about the way Zeppelin drives... you're talking about the way Greeks drive!

Karl: That's a debatable point... We don't have time for that! (laughter)

A commissioner dismissed the complaint lodged by Mr Ai Papadelis. He appealed, and the matter was referred to a full panel of the BCCSA. The panel found:

It would be insensitive for this Commission to ignore the sensitivities of the Complainant. On the other hand the observation was made in lighter vein and was not intended in any way to advocate hatred against a person on the grounds of his or her race. Section 16 of the Constitution of the Republic provides that the freedom of speech guarantee is limited in cases where a person advocates hatred based on race, religion, gender or ethnicity. Once it has been found that words have advocated such hate, it must also be clear that those words incited to harm. To our minds neither of these requisites has been satisfied... Some may say that the observation was in questionable taste, but that is not sufficient to base a finding against a broadcaster on."

Analysis

It is difficult to understand why the BCCSA adjudicated this case against the complainant, but found in favour of the complainant in Case 4. The BCCSA may be correct in its interpretation of the Constitution, and therefore find that there are not sufficient *legal* grounds to uphold the complaint. It is, however, a different matter with regards to the *ethical* issue at stake. The use of the "lighter vein" argument, in supposing that no harm was intended, is really skating on thin ice. Would a light-hearted remark about white people being racist or black people being uneducated be treated in the same way? And why would that not be the case? Is it permissible to stereotype people as long as you laugh while doing it?

The finding of the BCCSA points to the fact that it is difficult to find against a media organization on the grounds of poor taste. This means that it is the responsibility of the individual media organization to make sure that (ethical) boundaries are not crossed.

Notes

[1] In this regard, Day (1991, 279) cites Charles Zastrow and Karen Kirst-Ashman, *Understanding human behaviour and the social environment* (Chicago: Nelson-Hall,1987), p. 556.

[2] Address by Professor Lizette Rabe, Department of Journalism, University of Stellenbosch, 26 September 2001. Published as *Eva-lusie: Die vrouestem in Suid-Afrikaanse media.* '*n Besinning oor die status van vroue in die media* (2001). She cites this from M. E. Gist, 'Through the looking glass: Diversity and reflected appraisals of the self in mass media', in P. J. Creedon (ed.) 1993. *Women in mass communication* (Newbury Park, California: Sage Publications), pp. 104–117.

[3] Cited in Zastrow and Kirst-Ashman, p. 556

[4] Day (1991, 280) quotes *Public Opinion* 1922, pp. 88–89 in this regard.

[5] Sharyn Wizda (*American Journalism Review* July/August 1997) quotes Stephen Seplow of the *Philadelphia Inquirer* in this regard.

[6] Rabe cites Phumla Mthala, "Gender: The next step", *Rhodes Journalism Review* (August 2000), p. 7.

[7] Rabe cites Wilma Randle, "Women and gender in the African media", *Rhodes Journalism Review* (December 1999), p. 27.

[8] They were Kaiser Nyatsumba of the *Daily News* in Durban, Phil Molefe of the SABC, Mike Siluma of the *Sowetan*, Cyril Madlala of the *Independent on Saturday* and Charles Mogale of the *Sowetan Sunday World*.

[9] Sean Jacobs works for Idasa, where he researches the relationship between media, power, and democracy.

[10] The late Parks Mankahlana, spokesperson for the President's office, denied that the SAHRC had anything to do with that office and maintained that the SAHRC was an independent body.

[11] See Chapter 12.

12 | Social responsibility

A typical American child will witness 40 000 murders and 200 000 other violent acts by the age of 18 (Stossel 1997, 90).

Introduction

The media have a significant influence on both perceptions and behaviour. But what is the nature of that influence? And what, if anything, should the media do about it?

In a 1997 article in *The Atlantic Monthly*,[1] Scott Stossel argued that a huge body of evidence, including 3 000 studies in America alone prior to 1971, suggests a strong connection between watching television and aggressive behaviour (Stossel 1997, 87). Reed Hundt, chairperson of the Federal Communications Commission (FCC) in the US, said in a speech in 1995: "There is no longer any serious debate about whether violence in the media is a legitimate problem".[2]

The public agrees. In a Gallup poll done in September 1999, 44 per cent of all respondents indicated that violence in the media bothered them more than sexual situations (22 per cent) or lewd and profane language (23 per cent). In that same poll, an alarming 52 per cent of respondents said that they had been shocked by something they saw in the media (www.gallup.com).

An important contribution to understanding the influence of television on behaviour was made by George Gerbner, who was appointed in 1968 by the US government to analyze the content of television entertainment shows. This was the start of the Cultural Indicators Project (CIP) – the longest-running, continuous media-research undertaking in history.[3]

Both the quantity and quality of TV violence were monitored, and the CIP produced stunning results. In 1997, there were on average more than five violent scenes in an hour of prime time and five murders a night. There were 25 violent acts an hour in Saturday-morning cartoons. The CIP reckons that "the average American child will have witnessed more than 8 000 murders and 100 000 other violent acts on television by the time he or she leaves elementary school" (Stossel 1997, 90). Another study (published in the *Journal of the American Medical Association* in 1992) found that a typical American child will witness 40 000 murders and 200 000 other violent acts by the age of 18 (Stossel 1997, 90).

"The sheer quantity of violence on television encourages the idea that aggressive behavior is normal", Gerbner concludes (Stossel 1997, 91). Viewers become desensitized – or militarized, to use Gerbner's term – by the avalanche of television violence. However, Gerbner is careful not to imply that television violence directly "causes" anything. Of course there are other factors that have a decisive influence on aggressive behaviour. However, he firmly believes that television *contributes* to aggressive behaviour (Stossel 1997, 92). For the direct cause, we need to look at overall patterns rather than at the effects of specific shows. "It is the long-range exposure to television, rather than a specific violent act on a specific episode of a specific show, that cultivates fixed conceptions about life in viewers" (Stossel 1997, 92).

Of course, television shapes not only behaviour, but also perceptions underlying behaviour. For example, a study sponsored by the American Jewish Committee's Institute for American Pluralism found "that ethnic and racial images on television powerfully shape the way adolescents perceive ethnicity and race in the real world. In dealing with socially relevant topics like racial and ethnic relations", the study said, "TV not only entertains, it conveys values and messages that people may absorb unwittingly – particularly young people" (Stossel 1997, 95).

South African examples

In South Africa several claims have been made that the media have an antisocial influence. Here are a few examples:

- During the late 1990s, attacks on farmers reached frightening levels, with 560 murders committed during farm attacks from 1994 to September 1998. In an article in *Beeld*, Professor Neels Moolman quoted from a report entitled *Bloodstains on our food*, which said: "The prominence of farm attacks in the media will lead to an increase in these attacks because it over-emphasizes the vulnerability of a specific group of the South African community" (*Beeld* 10 November 1998).[4]

  According to this report, there was on average more than one newspaper report per day on the issue of farm attacks. "Many of these reports repeated the same things over and over again", Moolman said (*Beeld* 10 November 1998). The report asked that the media give less attention to the attacks on farmers and that the Truth and Reconciliation Commission (TRC) "under no circumstances" continue with its activities pertaining to that matter. According to Moolman, the public hearings of the TRC and accompanying racial tension also contributed to attacks on farmers. "Statistics show that these attacks escalated since 1995, when the TRC started its activities, to the (then) present highest level ever" (*Beeld* 10 November 1998).

  It is a terrifying thought that Moolman just could be correct – that at least some of these atrocious acts were committed because of the influence of the media on certain people. But true or false, the fact remains that the *perception* exists that the media have an antisocial influence. And perceptions are as real as "facts".

- "… people living in a violent township are more affected by the news than they would be by a violent scene in *The A-Team*. The opposite is true for people living in more stable areas who find violence in an episode of *MacGyver* more upsetting than real-life incidents on the news", recounted Dr Daan van Vuuren (*Sunday Times* 24 July 1994).[5] He added that "This scenario sums up the disparate situation":

Little Thabo watches a train massacre on the news.
Little Tommy watches it too.
Thabo's daddy rides that train.
Later, Tommy tells his mommy he wants to grow
    up to drive a choo-choo.
(*Sunday Times* 24 July 1994)

According to research by the SABC's Broadcasting Research Unit (headed by Van Vuuren), "violence, such as that broadcast in news programmes, has a greater emotional effect on viewers who are exposed to similar violence" (*Sunday Times* 24 July 1994).

- On 30 August 1994 five people were murdered in three separate incidents in KwaZulu-Natal. The possibility that these murders could be linked to the broadcast of the controversial television miniseries, *The Line*, was investigated. According to Mary de Haas, an independent human rights monitor at the University of Natal, there were rumours that people who had watched this broadcast were chosen as targets and shot.

Negative enough?

According to Professor George Claassen, head of the Department of Journalism at the University of Stellenbosch, "There is no doubt that violence and sex depicted in the media do have some sort of influence on consumers. The difficult question is whether this influence is negative enough to affect consumers – and especially children – in such a way that their behavior becomes deviant" (*Ecquid Novi* 1994 15 (1), 88).

The rest of Claassen's article is important enough to follow its reasoning. Claassen states that in South Africa there are "numerous examples of young boys being injured when they tried to take off from roofs after the screening of the first *Superman* film in the country's theatres" (*Ecquid Novi* 1994, 89). We cannot deny, Claassen continues, that the South African media "have played a vital role in changing perception of sexuality, violence and, for that matter, the way apartheid is seen" (*Ecquid Novi* 1994, 90). He cites J. Q. Wilson and R. J. Herrnstein,[6] who make the valid point that it would be absurd for advertisers to invest so much money in advertising if the media had no effect on people's behaviour. "And if the media changed only the noncriminal aspects of our behavior, that would be only slightly less remarkable" (*Ecquid Novi* 1994, 90). And furthermore, "One of the dangerous behavioral effects the media can have on society is man's inherent trait to copy others, the so-called 'monkey-see, monkey-do' principle" (*Ecquid Novi* 1994, 90). Claassen also quotes *Newsweek* (23 March 1987, 28) in connection with a spate of suicides among teenagers in the United States: "There is no question that news of a youthful suicide often triggers others, and it may be dangerous even to discuss the problem" (*Ecquid Novi* 1994, 91).

In contrast, Dr Ruth Teer-Tomaselli, a member of the SABC board, is of the opinion that threat of copycat killings is not to be taken seriously. "There is no evidence to indicate that the majority of offenders imitate what they see on the screen. In fact, the number of copycats is so small as to be discounted" (*Sunday Times* 24 July 1994). The number of copycats may be small, but that does not take away the fact that the media do have an influence on the public. The question concerns the nature of this influence.

Reinforcing concepts

Carl Hausman quotes some rather interesting studies (Hausman 1992, 44) to suggest that the media is a powerful tool for *reinforcing* ideas and concepts, but not so much for *creating* ideas.[7] "When people are exposed to contradictory messages, they tend to reinterpret them in such a way as to agree with their prejudices" (Hausman 1992, 44).

But not all studies support this position. Louis Day is quite sceptical. The *number* of injuries, deaths, and other violent acts flowing from any given programme, movie, or article is very small, he says. "Thus, the evidence would appear to suggest a cautionary approach in fashioning a moral framework within which to evaluate the impact of the media on antisocial behaviour" (Day 1991, 203).

It would take years of study to determine exactly the extent of the media's influence on human behaviour – if it could be done. Such a study is certainly beyond the scope of this book. Suffice to say that the media has a marked influence on (some) people, whether it serves to create, reinforce, or change their views. And precisely *because* of this influence, the media have a huge ethical – and social – responsibility.

Sufficient to change?

Scott Stossel asks this very important and pertinent question: "Shouldn't the weight of thousands of ... studies (that depict the connection between TV and aggressive behaviour) be sufficient to persuade broadcasters, required by law since the 1930s to serve the public interest, to change the content of television programming?" (Stossel 1997, 88).

Few issues command as much attention from media reformers as violence on television and in film (Christians et al. 1995, 263). The current crime wave in South Africa makes this issue even more urgent. Call one violent incident on the Cape Flats a step towards a gang war, and the media might just trigger that war...

On the other hand, Louis Day argues quite correctly that it would be unreasonable and unrealistic to avoid all controversial content, even when the effects on the audience are unpredictable. "The goal should be to devise strategies to promote the responsible treatment in the media of antisocial behavior and to avoid approaches that encourage moral degeneration" (Day 1991, 204).

J. K. Hvistendahl asks this central question: "Are the news media responsible for the *effects* of what they publish, or just for getting the information from the source or the event to readers or listeners fairly and accurately?" (Merrill et al. 1975, 186). Does the assumption of power carry a concomitant responsibility to the people affected by that power? Or is the only responsibility of the media to show a profit (Hausman 1992, 45)?

We would hope that the latter is not the case. But how do we, for example, explain the use of pornography? Surely, the *sole purpose* of pornography can only be to "entertain" in order to make a profit? And what about sensationalism? Or the publication of a picture of a gruesome killing or a terrible accident? Surely the freedom of the press can never mean the absence of responsibility, the leeway to do what you please, an "anything goes" philosophy. Real freedom should always be accompanied by responsibility. In fact, the bigger your influence, the greater your responsibility.

Blasphemy, obscenity, pornography

Matters such as blasphemy, indecency, and pornography are, like the issue of violence, part of the media's social responsibility. Most people are offended by speech containing blasphemy, obscenity, and indecency. But is that enough reason to censor such speech? Anthony Ellis remarks: "There is nowadays little support for restrictions on speech that does not adversely affect others…" (Kieran et al. 1998, 172). The way in which the Broadcasting Complaints Commission of South Africa (BCCSA) has handled these matters testifies to this fact. The mere fact that even a majority of people would probably think that blasphemy is immoral is not sufficient grounds for making it illegal. "The mere intrinsic immorality of speech will not generate a legitimate reason for censorship" (Kieran et al. 1998, 177).

In the United States it is unconstitutional to prohibit blasphemy, as this would violate two provisions of the First Amendment: the clauses prohibiting the state from establishing a religion, and from abridging the clause that guarantees freedom of speech. In England and Wales blasphemy is still a criminal offence – but the last prosecution for blasphemy took place in 1976 (Kieran et al. 1998, 176).

The classical argument against pornography (Kieran et al. 1998, 153) goes like this:

- The depiction of certain sorts of act causes occurrences of those acts.
- Pornographic acts are of a socially harmful kind.
- Society has the right to constrain the activities of individuals in order to prevent harm.
- Thus, society has the right to constrain the activities of those who would produce and distribute pornography.
- Society consequently has a right to confine the activities of those who want to view it.

So the people who believe that publishing pornography is harmful to society will also be in favour of all kinds of restrictions. But are South Africans *really* ready for more censorship? And is it *really* true that the publication of pornography is harmful?

According to Graham, there is a lack of convincing evidence to that effect. Citing Howitt and Cumberbatch,[8] Graham argues: "No study has

revealed any clear statistical connection, and even the seemingly plainest and most telling instances do not clinch the matter. This is partly because the theories of psychological motivation with which they must ultimately be supported allow interpretation in different directions" (Kieran et al. 1998, 155).

Is pornography harmful or not? In a certain sense, all these questions have become purely academic. The explosion of the mass media (movies, videos, magazines, the Internet, and satellite television) is such that official (governmental) censorship is out of the question. Pornography is now a *fait accompli*. The real question is how the media should handle it.

Remember that blasphemy, obscenity, and pornography are the unfortunate by-products of freedom of expression. However, freedom of expression is of such overriding importance – the reasons for this will be discussed later in this chapter – that these filthy by-products should be accepted as such. This is not intended to propagate an "anything goes" policy. On the contrary, responsible media should take great care never to offend people unnecessarily and always to keep society's norms and values in mind, even if blasphemy, obscenity, and pornography are not illegal.

The media should regulate themselves in this regard, as they are already doing. For example, a church magazine would surely never contemplate publishing pornographic material. Neither would most self-respecting newspapers in South Africa. Likewise, it would be unthinkable for the national broadcaster to screen hard-core pornography at peak hours when many children are likely to watch.

In summary, then, it should be said that the media should exercise great responsibility, especially when it comes to portraying violence and matters that affect the norms of society. In addition, it is very important that media practitioners should themselves avoid antisocial behaviour such as breaking the law (it puts them in a weak position), and that they should cover the news responsibly so as not to encourage or incite further crime and violence (Day 1991, 204–212).

The need to protect children

The South African youth constitutes an important and growing market for the mass media (newspapers, magazines, television, books, radio, music, the Internet, etc.) in the market economy of South Africa's growing democracy. The Constitution guarantees freedom of expression, and the media are naturally targeting the youth as an important niche market.

On the other hand, South African children are protected in many ways. Chapter 2 (Section 28) of the Constitution codifies the basic rights of children. In addition, there are laws against child pornography and child labour; laws establishing the legal age to marry without parental consent; laws for buying alcoholic beverages and tobacco products, for holding juvenile court proceedings *in camera*, and for not publishing the names of juvenile offenders.

There are also international conventions that protect the rights of children. South Africa is a signatory to the United Nations Declaration of Human Rights as well as the UN Convention on the Rights of the Child. Article 17 of this convention explicitly calls on governments and non-governmental organizations (NGOs) to adopt measures to protect the youth from exposure to negative media content.

Partly because of these commitments, the South African government passed the Films and Publications Act 65 of 1996, regulating all film and publication material produced and distributed or exhibited in the country. This Act was amended by the Films and Publications Amendment Act 34 of 1999. The amended Act provides for the protection of children against exposure to any form of the media containing material that is morally or ethically questionable. In the Amendment of Section 1 of Act 65 of 1996, "child pornography" is defined as including "…any images, real or simulated, however created, depicting a person who is or who is shown as being under the age of 18 years, engaged in sexual conduct or a display of genitals which amounts to sexual exploitation, or participating in, or assisting another person to engage in sexual conduct which amounts to sexual exploitation or degradation of children."

Together with the realization that the mass media are important agents of socialization (Day 1991, 302), the tension between the protection of children and freedom of expression raises several questions (Day 1991, 303): what role should the media play in the lives of the youth of this country? Should the media attempt to inculcate the youth with positive values? What responsibility do the media have when they develop programmes targeted at adults but which are accessible to children? How graphic should material be in confronting children with sensitive and controversial subjects? The challenge "is to construct strategies that will avoid the intellectual and emotional prudishness of a bygone era while maintaining a sense of moral obligation toward children and adolescents as impressionable audiences in the media marketplace" (Day 1991, 303).

In South Africa, the media have taken several precautions, some of which are required by law, to protect children:

- Certain magazines are wrapped in plastic to discourage children from browsing though material that is meant for adults.
- Films are classified in various ways.
- Age restrictions are put on films and videos.
- Pre-programme information or prior warnings are usually given if a programme contains strong language, sex, nudity, or violence. This will be accompanied by verbal warnings.
- Heavy emphasis is nowadays placed on the

responsibility of the viewers, especially the parents, to decide what their children may watch. The SABC, for example, applies the principle of a "watershed" between family and adult viewing. That watershed is 21:00 from Monday to Thursday and 21:30 for the rest of the week. Programmes after this watershed are not censored. M-Net has a system of parental control.

- The more controversial a programme, the later it will be shown.

The Internet

On 20 June 1999 the *Saturday Star* reported the first case of prosecution in South Africa under the Films and Publications Act of a person in possession of child pornography. A Pretoria administrative clerk allegedly possessed about 100 images of child pornography that he had downloaded at work. We can only guess how many paedophiles are using the Internet for their own sick purposes. The problem, of course, is that it seems to be an impossible task to regulate and monitor the Internet sufficiently in order to protect children against the excesses of freedom of speech.

Media freedom

Before another word is said about restricting free expression, it has to be stated emphatically that any type of restriction (however necessary, especially in the case of children) is highly dangerous. Why? Because the arguments in favour of free speech are of vital importance. Anthony Ellis (Kieran *et al.* 1998, 166) cites the main arguments in favour of freedom of speech. He says that *freedom of speech is necessary for the proper working of democracy* for three reasons:

- The government cannot be responsive to all preferences if those preferences cannot be voiced.
- It stimulates the accountability of the government to the people if criticism cannot be stifled.

- The truth is better served, which should make for more soundly based political decision-making.

The argument that *the discovery of truth requires a free marketplace of ideas* gives much wider scope to the search for truth. This idea, formulated and made popular by John Stuart Mill, has been widely misunderstood. Contrary to popular conception, it does not mean that if people are always allowed to speak their minds, then true ideas will necessarily triumph over false ones. The argument does not depend on the assumption that the truth always, or generally, drives out falsehood. It also does not depend on the relativistic view that truth is only that "entity" which is socially accepted as such (Kieran *et al.* 1998, 166).

To be sure, the proponents of freedom of speech need not claim that speech is to be protected always and everywhere. "All that needs to be claimed is that in our circumstances, in the modern, western democracies, allowing the government to hold a monopoly on speech is likely to hinder progress towards the truth. And that is surely true" (Kieran *et al.* 1998, 166). In addition, the argument should not be stated in terms of truth at all. This restricts its force unnecessarily "...since we need not judge the worth of all communications – music and dance, for instance – in terms of truth" (Kieran *et al.* 1988, 166, 167).

Ellis quite correctly points out that these arguments are consequentialist: giving the government a general licence to regulate speech is likely to do more harm than good. There are also non-consequentialist arguments that are based on the conviction that the government must allow freedom of speech in order to respect the moral dignity of its citizens. Mill, for example, held that the freedom to speak is intimately tied to freedom of thought. To prohibit speech is to attack the freedom of thought and thus one's identity.

Closely linked to this is the argument that the denial of freedom of speech is also the denial of the freedom to hear. A democratic government "... must treat its citizens as responsible adults who must be trusted to hear dangerous opinions and who therefore have the right, within very large limits, to decide for themselves what they will hear" (Kieran et al. 1998, 167). Free speech is indeed the freedom upon which all other freedoms depend. This means that *the defence of the freedom of speech is an integral part – even the core – of the media's responsibility towards society.*

Not an absolute right

However, certain questions must be asked: at what cost should free expression be defended? And at the expense of whose pain (Owen 1998, 33)?[9] When may a government override the right to freedom of speech or expression? Although freedom of speech is of the utmost importance to any democracy, it is not an absolute right (that should never be restricted at all). Very few people indeed would, as previously stated, tolerate hardcore pornography in a programme for small children.

Article 10 of the European Convention on Human Rights explains that freedom of expression carries with it duties and responsibilities. Freedom of expression may therefore:

> ...be subject to such formalities, conditions, restrictions or penalties as are prescribed by law and are necessary in a democratic society, in the interests of national security, territorial integrity or public safety, for the prevention of disorder or crime, for the protection of health or morals, for the protection of the reputation or rights of others, for preventing the disclosure of information received in confidence, or for maintaining the authority and impartiality of the judiciary.

Christians calls this the great paradox of democratic theory: "Liberty can never be absolute, censorship can never be absent" (Christians et al. 1995, 313).

Hate speech

Hate speech, Ursula Owen writes, is a troubling matter for people who believe in free speech. "It is abusive, insulting, intimidating and harassing. And it may lead to violence, hatred or discrimination; and it kills" (*Index on Censorship* 1998, 32). This antisocial influence of the media on society with regards to hate speech is unfortunately unavoidable. The genocide in Rwanda in 1994 and the wars in the former Yugoslavia are pertinent examples of how hate speech in the media can turn into deeds that kill (*Index on Censorship* 1998, 31).

The most dangerous threat behind hate speech "is surely that it can go beyond its immediate targets and create a *culture* of hate, a culture which makes it acceptable, respectable even, to hate on a far wider scale" (*Index on Censorship* 1998, 36). As one ominous example of this, Owen points to the events leading up to the assassination of the Israeli prime minister, Yitzhak Rabin. A culture of hate was created through the efforts of right-wingers, who constantly shouted that Rabin was a "traitor" and a "murderer"; through placards which showed Rabin's features overlaid with the thin black circles of a rifle sight; and through elements of the rabbinical leadership, who continually questioned the "Jewishness" of Rabin's land-for-peace policies.

This leads to Owen's important question:

> So, as dedicated opponents of censorship and proponents of free speech, we are forced to ask: is there a moment where the *quantitative* consequences of hate speech change *qualitatively* the arguments about how we must deal with it. And is there no distinction to be made between the words of those whose hate speech is a matter of conviction, however ignorant, deluded or prejudiced, and hate speech as propaganda, the calculated and systematic use of lies to sow fear, hate and violence in a population at large? (*Index on Censorship* 1998, 37)

In the United States, one of the least censored societies in the world, the First Amendment (which guarantees freedom of speech) has hampered attempts to make provisions against hate speech. On the other hand, Article 19 of the International Covenant on Civil and Political Rights – which also states that everyone shall have the right to hold opinions without interference and the right to freedom of expression – also makes provision for restrictions necessary for respect of the rights or reputations of others and for the protection of public order, health, and morals. Article 20 states that any advocacy of national, racial, or religious hatred that constitutes incitement to discrimination, hostility, or violence must be prohibited. The point is this: hate speech is the price society must pay for safeguarding free expression (*Index on Censorship* 1998, 37).

Owen cites a disturbance in Skokie, Illinois, in 1977, as perhaps the most famous defence of the right to express hate. When a US neo-Nazi group tried to march in a community populated by many Holocaust survivors, their right to march publicly was confirmed by the courts, based on the First Amendment. "Such a ruling, they believed, was ultimately to the benefit of racial and other minorities, protecting their right to express their own views freely" (*Index on Censorship* 1998, 33).

Owen offers the following statement as a serious warning:

> Censorship backfires: the biter gets bit. The powerful and painful paradox of laws against hate speech is that again and again they have been turned against the very people we would see as the victims of that same hate speech.
> (*Index on Censorship* 1998, 33, 34)

One example of this is the way South African laws against racial hatred were used systematically under apartheid against the victims of the system. Other examples can be found in Eastern Europe and the former Soviet Union, where "laws against defamation and insult were used to persecute critics of the Communist regimes" (*Index on Censorship* 1998, 34).

Internal control

The enormous social influence of the media on society, and the corresponding responsibility this entails, poses some serious questions: is the freedom of speech an absolute right? What is to be done if the media do not fulfil this role properly? Who decides if it does or does not? What are the penalties – the "or else" part of the "social contract" (Hausman 1992, 47)?[10]

But first this question: "What would *lead* the news media toward greater social responsibility, without the implication of government sanction?" (Hausman 1992, 48). Whether we like it or not, social responsibility firstly means *control*. This can be internal, in the form of a code of ethics, management dicta, or simply a good conscience. It can also be external, like a press council, an ombudsman, or a commission. (Governmental control will be discussed later in this chapter.) These control mechanisms are not meant to curb press freedom, but to serve as a guide to exercising that freedom, provided by the "social contract", in a responsible manner.

Self-regulation

The ideal, then, is that the media "regulate" themselves to such an extent that it would be unnecessary for the government to do it for them. The South African media already do this to a great extent (as discussed earlier in this chapter).

The term "self-regulation" is a dangerous one, however, and it is necessary to understand clearly what is meant by it. There is a clear distinction between self-regulation and self-censorship. Self-regulation simply means doing journalism in a responsible way; self-censorship means toning down the truth or even ignoring stories. Many journalists admit to self-censorship. A US survey conducted in 2000,[11] revealed the following, *inter alia*:

- A total of 41 per cent of journalists either admit to personal self-censorship or to the softening of a story.
- Younger journalists are more likely than older colleagues to admit they have avoided or toned down stories.
- The most common reasons for not pursuing good stories are that they are too complicated or too boring.
- Local journalists face especially difficult challenges.
- Investigative reporters are more likely than either local or national journalists to cite the impact of business pressures on editorial decisions.

Just to be clear: this is *not* what is meant by self-regulation.

It is probably correct to say that few people would dismiss outright the legitimacy of government controls (especially in broadcasting, which is licensed in the public interest), or libel laws (a citizen's tool for redress of grievances), or the protection of minority groups. According to John Merrill, some even argue that social responsibility necessarily means government control (Hausman 1992, 47, 48). The question is where the line should be drawn between state interference and media freedom and self-regulation. For example, should violence in the media be regulated by law? Few journalists would be in favour of that. Christians summarizes their arguments (Christians et al. 1995, 264):

- Artistic freedom and aesthetic integrity demand a laissez-faire approach. Government has no business policing writers and directors.
- Indirect effects are the consequence of living

in a world of mediated messages and cannot be made the basis of criminal prosecutions.
- Violence is a social and historical problem, not the result of violent television or film. To think otherwise is to blame John Wayne for the Vietnam War.
- Much of the concern about media violence is really our fear of changing social institutions. To suppress television and film is to forcibly maintain traditional notions of family, friendship, and marriage in an era when these social arrangements are undergoing radical change.
- Boundaries between news and entertainment programming are falling fast. All of the free marketplace arguments that traditional news has enjoyed must now be applied equally to entertainment programmes. The public has a right to know.

The general "rule" seems to be: the less government interferes, the better. But then the media must act responsibly.

External control (censorship)

In South Africa, there are two main instances where the state overrides the freedom of opinion and expression. The first is Article 16 of the Constitution (Chapter 2, the Bill of Rights), in which the right to free expression is not extended to propaganda for war, incitement of imminent violence, or advocacy of hatred that is based on race, ethnicity, gender, or religion.[12] This goes for films, entertainment, plays, and publications.

These provisions were sharply criticized by the Freedom of Expression Institute (FXI). It was argued that it was the wrong time to place restrictions on racial and other forms of hatred – that should have been done 300 years ago when the seeds of racism were sown by the colonial cultures. "Contemporary South Africa was emerging from racism, not going into it" (*FXI Update* April/May 1996, 1). Furthermore, it was argued that the Constitution is not the right place to put limitations on current problems facing the country.

The second instance of external control is Section 29 of the present Films and Publications Act 65 of 1996, which was passed in April 1997. This Act regulates the creation, production, possession, and distribution of certain publications and films by means of classification, the imposition of age restrictions, and the provision of consumer advice. In particular, care is taken to protect children against sexual exploitation or degradation in publications, films, and on the Internet. It is a punishable offense to exploit children in pornographic publications, films, or on the Internet.

Since the start of television in South Africa, the Directorate of Publications was responsible for classifying films. The board also instructed the SABC on what to cut and at what time the films could be broadcast. This changed in 1995 when the legislation regulating the directorate was scrapped. (It was seen as an apartheid institution and thought to be in conflict with the provisions of the new Constitution.)

The provisions of the Films and Publications Act as they affect broadcasters are:

- A new Films and Publications Board and a Review Board have been established to review and classify films and publications. The Act provides four ratings for films: XX, X18, R18, and 18.
- Broadcasters are not obliged to submit films for approval. They should acquaint themselves with the legal requirements, evaluate the material and decide for themselves what may and what may not be broadcast.
- Broadcasters are not allowed to intentionally broadcast material that is rated XX (this could be classified by either the Board or a court).

They are also prohibited from broadcasting a programme that advocates hatred based on race, religion, ethnicity, or gender.

- Apart from these provisos, the broadcaster is autonomous. Members of the public can, however, lodge complaints with the Broadcasting Complaints Commission of South Africa (BCCSA).

The ratings are formulated as follows and include both films and publications:

- *XX Classification.* Material that falls into this category includes:
  - showing a person under the age of 18 engaging in, or assisting someone else to engage in sexual conduct or a lewd display of nudity;
  - scenes of explicit violent sexual conduct;
  - scenes of bestiality;
  - advocating hatred based on race, ethnicity, gender, or religion and aimed at inciting to cause harm;
  - scenes of explicit sexual conduct that degrades a person and that constitutes incitement to cause harm;
  - scenes of the explicit infliction of extreme violence, or the explicit effects of extreme violence, which constitutes incitement to cause harm.
- *X18 Classification.* This affects material that contains any scene (real or simulated) of explicit sexual conduct which, in the case of sexual intercourse, includes an explicit visual presentation of genitals. Such scenes should be judged within context.
- *R18 Classification.* This affects material that is harmful or disturbing to people under 18, and which requires consumer advice for adults regarding sex, nudity, violence, and language.
- *18 Classification.* Any film that does not fall under the above-mentioned three classifications may be classified in this category.

There are important exemptions to the Act. The XX and X18 classifications do not apply to *bona fide* scientific, documentary, dramatic, or artistic films – but on condition that no exemption applies to scenes of sex with children under 18. The same goes for advertisements that fall under the jurisdiction of the Advertising Standards Authority of South Africa.

Though it may be true that censorship "can never be absent", it is a slippery road. The reasons are obvious: once you set out on the censorship road, where does it end? In addition, "Censorship can kill and maim, for when people draw a cloak of secrecy over their actions, gross abuse may happen with impunity... Censorship backfires: the biter gets bit" (*FXI Update* April/May 1996, 33).

| Obscenity, nudity, indecency

Public morals are difficult to define, and the media have a great deal of freedom to operate in. Where children are not protected, however, the freedom of speech argument weighs less strongly.

The Broadcasting Complaints Commission of South Africa (BCCSA) is inundated with complaints about obscenity, nudity, and indecency. The reasoning behind the BCCSA's adjudication of these matters is noteworthy. Here are some examples. (Clause 7.1 of the BCCSA's code is relevant in each case.)

1 During a *Chuckle and Chat Show* aired on 30 May 1999, an interview was conducted with two women in the nude. The BCCSA said that before the broadcast viewers were repeatedly warned that this interview was not for sensitive viewers. The presenter mentioned on at least two occasions that this was "an adult show, and very much an adult show now". Sensitive viewers could have opted not to watch the programme. Those who did watch it therefore had no reason to complain. In any case, the *Chuckle and Chat Show* is broadcast at 22:30 – long after the "watershed" of 21:00.

   The BCCSA said it served this particular complainant no purpose to debate the meaning of nudity. "The variety and diversity of cultural and religious beliefs in South Africa will always give us a diversity of reactions and understandings towards the meaning of topless and naked." The complaint was therefore dismissed.

2 On the news feature programme *Top Billing*, model Cindy Crawford was asked about her *Playboy* pictures and the reason why she had agreed to have these published. In this case, the complainant argued that the "nude pictures full frontal and the complete nude" that were shown were completely unacceptable. "Our standards are slipping at an alarming rate", she added. The BCCSA adjudged that:

...it is clear to a great extent, the guideline applied (to matters of indecency or obscenity) boiled down to the question whether the nudity was treated in a manner which was blatantly shameless. ...it would appear that nudity in itself is not indecent or obscene, but ... the final issue is whether the nudity has been treated in a manner which could be regarded as indecent or obscene. Both 'indecency' and 'obscenity' would seem to accentuate the blatantly shameless invasion into the privacy of the human body.

The question of whether the material is calculated to excite lust never comes into play because of the subjective nature of lust. In this case the photographs "do not dwell on nudity and the nudity is in no manner exploited". In addition, given the timing of the programme, "it can also not be concluded that there was a large number of children in the viewing audience". Even if some children were in the audience, "the article would not have interested them and, in any case, the nudity was not so pronounced that it would have drawn their attention in a manner which would have harmed or shocked them in their emotional upbringing". Consequently, the complaint was dismissed.

3 On 30 October 1998, Highveld Stereo broadcast a sequence on *Rude Awakening* based on a game show in which a mystery answer would be disclosed to the audience before the guest

arrives. The guest then could ask twenty questions. In this case the mystery object was a black man's penis.

The first question by the guest (a well-known Afrikaans female singer and actress) was whether one could eat the object. The host hesitated, then said "yes". The actress immediately responded: "Is it not a black man's penis?" (translated and crudity omitted).

Citing various court cases all over the world, the BCCSA concluded that terms such as "indecent" and "obscene" are highly subjective and therefore particularly vague. "All the members of the panel concluded that ... they had felt that the broadcast ... had probably gone too far." However, the panel decided that although the majority of radio listeners, if polled, would simply reject the broadcast, the effect of the limited likely audience and the well-known fact that the programme caters for modern-thinking tolerant listeners, led the commission to the conclusion that no constitutionally acceptable reasons could be given for finding that the code had been transgressed. According to the BCCSA,

...we are living in a (sic) open-minded society which is supported by a (sic) open-minded, individual rights respecting, Bill of Rights. Questions which are relevant in this connection are whether the rights of dignity, privacy and the protection afforded to freedom of expression and the arts, given the freedom of choice and the likely audience, have been transgressed in such a fashion that the very foundations on which our democracy rests, have, in this respect, been undermined.

...ultimately one has to live with matters which are utterly offensive to one's sense of propriety, so as to ensure one's own freedom of choice and freedom of expression.

The conclusion was that the material was in poor taste, vulgar and crude – but not legally indecent or obscene. The complaint was dismissed.

4 The BCCSA received a complaint about an interview aired on 29 December 1998 on the John Robbie Show on Radio 702. In the complainant's opinion, an interview done by Aki Annastasiou (standing in for John Robbie) with a "porn actress" was "in extremely bad taste, potentially morally corrupting to young listeners and prurient in the extreme". It was broadcast at 08:19 during the school holidays. The actress was questioned on her professional and personal sex life, including her favourite sexual position. After she had answered the latter question, she was subjected to more detailed questions on the reasons for her preference. "The presenter did not succeed in soliciting any 'interesting' responses from her and attempted to liven the interview up by some heavy-handed ribaldry. The interview ended with the actress playing a tape of the sound effects of her work."

The Commission again acknowledged that the terms "indecent" and "obscene" are difficult to define, saying: "When defining 'indecent' the accent should fall on that which is grossly offensive." The presenter's questions were about sex, it was rude, distasteful, and vulgar, and, according to the BCCSA, he had no respect for either the interviewee or the subject. "Despite these crude attempts at risqué humor the interview never reached a humorous stage. Instead ... the presenter attempted to save it with tasteless comments and offensive questions. The presenter's tasteless treatment of the subject offended against the contemporary taste and recognized standards of decency."

It was quite possible that a large number of children were listening – the subject of the interview "would definitely appeal to young teenagers" – and the possibility of harm to children could not be overlooked. "Consequently the particular broadcast falls outside the protection of the right to free speech. The Commission found the interview including the tape played by the actress ... tasteless, offending and legally indecent. The complaint is accordingly upheld."

5 On 3 February 1999 at 21:30, SABC 3 broadcast a part of the series entitled *Close Relations*. A complaint was received in regard to nudity and sexuality. The question was whether the SABC was justified in simply making use of a classification for a film, without also publishing an age restriction.

Licensed broadcasters are, generally, exempted from the provisions of the Films and Publications Act 65 of 1996. "A special responsibility, accordingly, rests upon broadcasters", the BCCSA said. The commission held that "where an age restriction is regarded as necessary, the necessary publication should also be given to that age restriction". Mere classification would not be sufficient. Such an age restriction (in this case, of 12 or 14) should furthermore be made known "in its publicity and immediately before the screening commenced" – as well as immediately after any advertising break. The complaint was upheld and the SABC was requested to give publicity to the decision on channels 1, 2, and 3 during its evening broadcasts.

Analysis

Due to the highly subjective nature of terms such as "indecency", "obscenity", and "vulgar", they are extremely difficult to define. So is "public morals", for that matter (Clause 7.1.1 of the BCCSA code). It is clear from the BCCSA's adjudication in matters pertaining to this issue that the media certainly have a wide scope to operate in. Freedom of expression is guaranteed in the Constitution, as long as material is not harmful or offensive to public morals, religious convictions, or feelings of a section of the population.

However, where children were not be protected, the freedom of speech argument weighed less than that of possible harm to children. It is therefore of extreme importance that "sensitive" viewers are warned in advance, and that these warnings are repeated whenever possible. The time slot of a broadcast is also of vital importance. For example, if two women are interviewed in the nude and it is done after the watershed of 21:00 and with proper warnings, the media are free to proceed.

Nudity is indeed in itself not indecent or obscene, as the BCCSA quite correctly pointed out in the Crawford case. The pictures were in any case not shown to excite lust. *Rude Awakening* was indeed tasteless, vulgar, and crude, as was Annastasiou's interview with the "porn actress". It is impossible even to give rough guidelines on the matter of taste, for the simple reason that taste is impossible to define; standards differ widely, and people are brought up differently. Someone once said: "I cannot define pornography, but I know it when I see it". The same can be said of taste (or the lack of it).

"Blasphemy"

Normally, taking the Lord's name in vain is not in itself regarded as blasphemous or offensive, but merely annoying. It is a different matter if a programme advocates hatred based on religion (incitement to cause harm).

The BCCSA is equally inundated with complaints about blasphemy. Here are some cases.

1 J. Boshoff complained as follows about a programme screened on e.tv on Sunday 8 August 1999 at 20:30:

> In the latest episode of *Jesse* certain child actors are supposed to put up a 'nativity play' where one child is playing the role of 'the Virgin Mary' and the other that of 'Baby Jesus'. The ensuing conversation between these two children constitutes pure blasphemy and offends my religious belief. I would appreciate your looking into the matter and advising me if we as Christians in this free and democratic country are to put up with this kind of attack on our religion.

Mr Krish Patel, for e.tv, explained that the programme was not produced locally and e.tv had no prior knowledge of the possible offensive material. Such pre-screening would be "tremendously expensive". Had this been a local production, e.tv would have had knowledge of it and would have taken the necessary steps, Patel said.

To this, the BCCSA said it understood e.tv's predicament, but that classification, age restrictions, and timing of programmes are "at the heart of our policy in regard to television". The BCCSA is not permitted to pre-screen or censor any programme – that is the responsibility of the TV station. The BCCSA pointed out two things:

- "Offensive" has a narrow meaning, and profane material which is merely annoying would not pass the test. The material has to be repugnant to the religious convictions or feelings of a section of the community. "The mere taking in vain of the Lord's name, for example, is not regarded as offensive."
- M-Net provides a so-called "green channel", in which foul or profane language is removed in most instances, as well as a parental control mechanism, which makes it possible for parents to block out films carrying a certain age restriction.

The BCCSA emphasized that the word "Jesus" in the nativity play is used in a comical sense. The scene is reminiscent of a scene in the film *The History of the World Part 2* about the Last Supper. A "waiter", taking the Lord's name in vain, says "Jesus" – and "Jesus" answers: "Yes".

> Given the fact that the series *Jesse* is intended for family viewing, as well as the time of the broadcast, we have come to the conclusion that the attempt at a comical use of the word 'Jesus' was offensive in terms of the Code. The fact that the script lets a child say it, makes it even more problematic.
>
> If we are wrong here, we are in any case of the view that some form of warning should have accompanied the film. No such warning either on the screen or by way of a verbal caution before the programme, was given.

The BCCSA added that e.tv should, by 1 November 1999, implement a full system of classification, age guidelines, and timing. The complaint was accordingly upheld by a majority of votes in a panel of three. The panel unanimously held that a classification should have been provided for this programme.

2 On 5 February 1998, just before 07:00, the host of a programme on 5FM Music Radio made the following remark: "...Chips people, Jesus is coming, everybody looks busy..." A. G. Klopper complained that the remark was "in bad taste, extremely offensive and (was) a clear attempt to belittle the Christian faith".

The BCCSA stated that "The SABC conceded that the remark was not in line with SABC policy and that it was not part of a prepared script. The host simply made the remark as a time filler." The BCCSA also remarked that although on its own the remark was probably offensive, it loses this effect when judged as part of a programme filled with numerous items. Moreover, the word "offensive" has a limited meaning "and does not relate to matter which is merely 'displeasing or annoying', but to material that is 'repugnant, mortifying or painful'". Although a large section of the Christian community is particularly sensitive about any joke that has a bearing on Jesus, "not all religious feelings are protected by law". Section 16 of the Constitution limits free speech only where it advocates hatred based on religion and that constitutes incitement to cause harm. The BCCSA therefore concluded "that in spite of the questionable nature of the remark, it is not 'offensive' in law", and dismissed the complaint.

3 A complaint was lodged objecting to the name of God being "bandied about" in the course of a joke on *The Breakfast Show* on 27 November 1998 on East Coast Radio. The complainant, Mrs T. Smythe, found this offensive and said that if similar jokes were made about Mohammed, Lord Krishna, or Buddha, the BCCSA would be swamped with complaints.

The joke recounted how Henry Ford arrived at the Pearly Gates. Because he served humankind through the invention of mass production of the motor car, he is allowed to choose with whom he will spend time in heaven. He chooses God. Ford then tells God that he made various mistakes in the creation of Woman. These mistakes are couched in the sort of language one would use about a motor car. So God goes to his computer and says, "What you say may be true, but many more men drive my invention than yours".

According to the BCSSA,

This 'joke' joins a multitude of other jokes about people arriving in heaven. It is slightly out of the mould in that it is not St Peter who exchanges pleasantries with the new arrival but God himself. ...there is a powerful tension between the image of God as remote and utterly other and his image as one of us, with a human son, a person to whom one can pray for anything from spiritual enlightenment to a win in tomorrow's rugby match. We should not, therefore, be surprised if people make jokes about God and certainly this is not a particularly offensive joke insofar as God's role is concerned. If there were anything to be offended about it is the perpetuation of the all-too-common sexist comparison between women and motor cars."

The complaint was dismissed.

4 The SABC broadcast an interview with a poet on 16 February 1997 at 19:00 on the programme *The Poet Speaks*. The complaints were that the sacred was juxtaposed with the scatological in expressions such as "God's Diarrhoea" (sic), Jesus and masturbation, and Mary and prostitution. The complainant mentioned that the content of that programme was totally unsuitable for young listeners such as her nine-year-old daughter (who had an interest in poetry) and that such material should not be broadcast at 19:00.

Regarding the content of the programme, the BCCSA said that the poems in question were not legally offensive to the religious convictions or feelings of Christians. "This is so since the material does not, on analysis, in any way attempt to attack or violate Christian doctrine." The material amounted to *bona fide* poetry, and the poet used these metaphors to ponder the enigmas of life.

The other issue in this case is the timing of the programme. Because of the intricate nature of the poems, the BCCSA said the programme would have drawn an informed audience. The level of the material was much too high for children under 16 and would therefore not harm or disturb a child.

Analysis

Many religious people would probably not agree with this position, but the fact remains that merely taking the Lord's name in vain is not regarded as being blasphemous, offensive, or repugnant to the religious convictions or feelings of a section of the community. It is deemed to be "merely annoying". In order to limit this kind of speech, the programme must advocate hatred based on religion and therefore constitute incitement to cause harm.

It is definitely not realistic to censor the use of God's name as a matter of policy. M-Net's green channel, as well as its parental control mechanism, therefore go a long way in meeting this problem.

The BCCSA's comment on the Henry Ford joke is quite correct. The joke would be particularly offensive only to the most sensitive religious people. The sexist nature of the joke would probably indeed be more offensive to most people than the religious overtones.

In the case of the poet, the works in question are probably not most people's cup of tea.

| Violence (not nudity)

There is a marked difference between the effect of violence in a fantasy setting, and violence in a "real-life" situation.

The BCCSA received a complaint about nudity in an episode of *Rex: A Cop's Best Friend* ("A Murderous Summer") on SABC on 25 November 1998. Applying Clause 7.1.3 of its code, the BCCSA said it regarded the episode as unsuitable viewing for children — but not necessarily because of the nudity.

The commission had the following to say:

- The episode was aired under the banner of *Tube*, which indicates children's viewing. The nudity (which was not frontal) may have offended some viewers. However, it was rather the subject of murder and the accompanying violence that bothered the BCCSA. In a suspense-filled scene in which a woman was

violently attacked, she was shown as injured and bleeding, and she could have been dying. "This sort of depiction conforms more to adult horror and suspense genres than to children's viewing."

- Later there is a discussion about the killer being a dangerous pervert who smears blood on women's breasts. "I (the adjudicator) think this is somewhat disturbing for most people, but more so for children and even young teenagers watching a realistic drama."

- The SABC's own Guidelines on Programme Content state: "Many children enjoy cartoons in which fantastical violence is continually wreaked on a cat, mouse or rabbit. There is, however, a marked difference between the effect of violence in a fantasy setting, and violence in a 'real life' situation. It is the latter that should be avoided as much as possible.

Where it cannot be avoided, the negative results of that violence should also be given full weight."

- There were no warnings to indicate a content of violence and nudity. There is little that parents who are concerned to provide discerning viewing for their children can do to prevent them from exposure to this programme.
- The BCCSA does not regard the particular episode as containing the most offensive material. But while it may even have some merit, it is unsuitable for children (especially those under 12) and should be rescheduled.

In summary, the lack of warning, the violent content, and the timing of the programme make it unsuitable viewing for children.

Analysis

As stated before, children are overexposed to scenes of violence. What makes this case even worse is that the violence was combined with some nudity or sexuality (blood on women's breasts). The SABC should really have taken more care, as the BCCSA suggests. There is a marked difference between fantastical violence and this horror type of real-life violence. The effect of the latter should not be underestimated, especially as far as children are concerned. So why did the SABC not warn viewers? Parents and children alike are powerless to defend themselves against this sort of material unless they are given proper warning.

Case Study 4 | **Change of attitudes**

The case illustrates how the media can be instrumental in changing a person's attitude (social intervention).

A gripping episode of *Carte Blanche* on 25 July 1999 showed how Danie Theunissen (a conservative father) and his estranged gay son, Le Roux, had met (the previous month) after five years of bitterness and fighting. The programme changed forever his view of life.

Le Roux lived with his father after his parents divorced. However, Danie literally threw his son out on the street. "I told him he must leave the house or I would kill him. I couldn't accept him — he was banned forever", Danie said. "I was full of hate. I didn't recognize him as my son. I cut him out of my will; I didn't want to know him. He was as good as dead to me."

Le Roux was terribly disappointed in his father. At the age of 16, he sued Danie "because he felt it was the only way to get his due". So the

discussion (or rather argument) between father and son took place through their respective lawyers. Le Roux won the case – which made his father (who didn't want to pay for a "queer" to go through life) even more hateful.

During the five years that followed, the two had very little contact. Danie's dreams for his son were long gone; self-criticism took its place, with Danie wondering where he had gone wrong.

Despite five years of pain and aggression, Le Roux took a bold step and called his father. "I am still his son… Emotionally he stripped me, it felt as if I had no future. A son needs his father even if he sees me as a 'moffie'". They talked for over an hour. Danie invited his son to visit him, and an excited Le Roux obliged. It took immense effort for Danie and Le Roux to begin to find common ground. Danie said: "We must start from the beginning, we need to pick up from where we left off. I don't think we'll ever be able to pick everything up 100 per cent but we can try." And Le Roux: "...he's looking further and he sees I am still his son. Hopefully we can find each other and go further and build our relationship."

Then events took a terrible turn. A mere three days after the programme was screened, Le Roux was murdered in his home in Cape Town.

Danie: "When he rode away that first day I had tears in my eyes... I was very excited and I came home and made myself a drink and thought of him visiting in the next few months. Everything was planned – the fishing that we were going to do – but here we sit."

Danie immediately drove from his home in Gansbaai to Cape Town, hoping his son was not dead. There he met Le Roux's partner of the last five years in their home for the first time. "Werner was busy with the detective when I arrived. We both went into the bedroom together and found Le Roux lying next to the bed. We cried together – I hugged him. The tears still come on their own."

"He (Werner) had a real fear of me that evening because he thought I would blame him for Le Roux's murder. In the past I had accused him of taking Le Roux away from me. But in times like that you don't think those thoughts", Danie said.

The programme that Danie did for *Carte Blanche* together with Le Roux had become an integral part of his history with his son: "I was a bit uncertain of Le Roux's side of the story when you were going to come down with the cameras for the first time. I had never heard his side and I was a bit scared he would be destructive and negative about me. Well, in the end he was, but it was his right because I had been wrong. How could I have done what I did to my own flesh and blood? How could I deny him?"

This excursion also changed Danie's perceptions. "I was brought up in a conservative home. We believed queers are queers and men are men. But if you look closely at life, those so-called

bum chums or queers or whatever you call them, they only ask that we accept them – nothing more. It cost me a lot to get that insight. It cost my son's death to understand that even if he's queer he'll always be a person."

Danie has been supported by the gay community during the time of crisis, and by a "coloured" group called "Victim Assist". "They are brown people and I tell you my heart bleeds for them – they feel just as I do. They are a group of parents who's had children murdered. That conservative guy from before who grew up believing that right is right and wrong is wrong, white is white, a Hottentot is a Hottentot and a Kaffir is a Kaffir? He looked deeper. If someone's child is murdered, is he still a Hottentot? Or is he a father? That woman is a mother. They are ordinary people who can share my pain and I can share theirs. It's hard to put into words – but I think I grew up and became an adult", Danie said.

Analysis

This case is included as an example of the type of influence – and therefore creation of responsibilities – that the media can have on society.

The story is gripping: a father who shuns his gay son, a son who blames his father for that, and eventually the bridging of a five-year gap between them. But from the outset it was clear that the possibility existed that *Carte Blanche's* involvement could directly influence and change (for better or for worse) the relationship between father and son. The show's involvement in the life of Danie and Le Roux Theunissen radically changed the former's attitude towards gays (and people of colour), although the intention clearly was not to get involved in the life of the Theunissens. Social intervention indeed took place – not intentionally, but as a nearly unavoidable by-product.

Sliding down the precipice

How socially responsible is it to publish a picture of a traumatic event that not only adds to the trauma – even if the decision to publish is well-intended – but can also have negative implications for the community?

On 24 August 1999 *Sowetan* published a picture on its front page of the bodies of a father and a child. The man had first hanged his 18-month-old child, then himself. Next to the photograph was the story of Mr Bennett Nkosi (25) of Daveyton. Nkosi had been depressed since May of that year, when he started threatening to commit suicide, shocked relatives said. A few hours before the suicide Nkosi had a fight with a relative.

Nkosi's suicide note was quoted, and revealed that he thought he had disappointed his mother by fathering a child. He did not want to burden other people with raising the child (whom he reportedly adored) and therefore decided to kill him too. According to the newspaper, this was the second tragedy within days in Gauteng in which a child was reportedly killed by the father.

Unusually, *Sowetan* published a comment next to the photograph itself, in which the editor explained why the newspaper had decided to publish the photograph. The full text reads:

> Today *Sowetan* publishes a horrendous picture of a father who committed suicide after hanging his 18-month-old baby.
>
> This was a decision not taken lightly. In a society brutalised by violence, the question needs to be asked whether another horrific picture of this nature will not further desensitise us.
>
> We have, after all, in the past published pictures of victims which were just as horrific ... pictures of people who had been 'necklaced' ... pictures of the world at war with itself and pictures of people hacked to pieces in faction fights.
>
> But even so, hardened by our trade, we felt outraged enough to demonstrate the level to which our society has stopped caring for its own. As the Centre for the Study of Violence has commented, we have a violent past. And we are reaping the fruits of not exercising more humane methods of resolving our conflicts.
>
> We also have a history as a caring society. When *Sowetan* started its Nation Building campaign more than a decade ago, it was partly to highlight the demise of the supportive societal structures which could have prevented Nkosi's suicide. Our campaign was to sound the alarm bells that if blacks in particular do not go back to their ubuntu roots, generations that followed would be condemned to hopelessness.
>
> This picture is probably only the tip of the iceberg. We need to act fast if we wish to stop the slide further down the precipice. – Editor

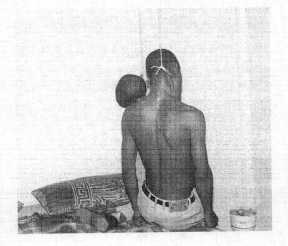

According to its own admission, *Sowetan* was inundated with telephone calls from readers who took strong exception to the picture, and the newspaper received numerous letters to that effect. Here are some of the main arguments advanced against publishing the picture on the front page:

- The picture is immoral because it will encourage people to do the same.

- Children will be terrified because they will think it can happen to them.
- People, especially children, will become desensitized by the picture.
- The story would have been powerful enough without the picture.
- The identity of the baby and the interests of his surviving playmates were not protected.
- The newspaper opted for sensationalism to boost its sales at the expense of black dignity and pride.
- It does not help South Africa's fight against crime.

Edward Bird, Director of the Media Monitoring Project, says that while the picture brought the horror of the event home, it "failed to respect the right to dignity of the victims and their families" (*Sowetan* 1 September 1999). Furthermore, the front-page picture did not prepare sensitive readers for the traumatic nature of the images.

> Images such as these contribute to the dehumanising and desensitising of readers. When pictures of brutalised human beings become the norm, they lose their shock value and fail to engender respect for human life.

However, not all *Sowetan* readers were upset. One reader congratulated the newspaper for a "fantastic story that other papers had not carried". Another said the picture reflected exactly what the story was all about. Yet another called the picture "a wake-up call" to society as it revealed that people were jobless and were suffering.

Analysis

The two points that Bird makes are very valid indeed: the picture failed to respect the dignity of the victims and their families (even though the faces of the deceased could not be seen), and

sensitive readers were not warned in advance. The same goes for most of the points mentioned by readers who were up in arms about the placing of the picture on the front page. Their arguments should be taken seriously, especially that the picture could encourage people to do the same, that children could be terrified because they might think it could happen to them, and the risk of the community becoming desensitized.

Yet *Sowetan* did well to explain the use of the picture. This is commendable. The newspaper felt, perhaps with some justification, there was a serious lack of compassion and support structures in society – which is so unlike the ubuntu tradition. If the community can be made aware of that, tragedies such as this one could be avoided.

However, by the newspaper's own admission this was a "horrendous picture". The truth was already maximized by the report. And serious and unnecessary harm was probably done by the placing of the picture – not only to sensitive readers, but especially to the family. Perhaps the picture could have been used, but smaller and not on the front page. In that way, some harm could have been minimized.

Notes

[1] The article, entitled "The man who counts the killings", is available at www.theatlantic.com/issues/97may/gerbner.htm

[2] Quoted in Stossel 1997, pp. 87, 88. He cites some interesting examples of studies that reveal a link between TV and real-life violence, especially in children.

[3] For a more detailed account and analysis of the Gerbner study, see Lange et al. *Mass media and violence*, pp. 311–339.

[4] At the time Moolman was the director of the Department of Criminology at the University of the North and president of the Criminological Society of South Africa (Crimsa).

[5] Van Vuuren is a psychologist. At the time he was the general manager of the SABC's broadcasting research unit.

[6] Wilson and Herrnstein, *Crime and human nature* (New York: Simon & Schuster, 1985), p. 337.

[7] Referring to the works of Joseph T. Klapper, director for social research at CBS, and the researcher Paul Lazarsfeld, Hausman (1992, p. 44) concludes that people select material from the mass media that accords with their own views, and

largely avoid material with which they disagree.

[8] see Howitt, D. and Cumberbatch, G. *Pornography: Impacts and influences* (London: HMSO, 1990).

[9] Owen is the editor of *Index on Censorship*.

[10] The concept of the "social contract" stems from the philosophy of libertarianism. It refers to the implied (unwritten, of course) "covenant" between the media and society in which the latter "promises" the press the freedom to function and the press "promises" it will serve society's needs for information. However, not everyone thinks the concept of the "social contract" is beneficial to the press. Thomas Hobbes, for example, argued that the social contract leads to the surrender of liberty to the ruler. But that is not necessarily the case. Of course the temptation to abuse that 'contract' will always be there. Undemocratic governments will surely confuse society's needs with that of their own – which can only be to the detriment of a free press.

[11] Andrew Kohut, Director of the Pew Research Center for the People and the Press, in "Self-censorship: counting the ways", cites a major joint survey by the Pew Research Center for the People and the Press and the *Columbia Journalism Review* (*Columbia Journalism Review* May/June 2000, p. 42). The study was carried out over more than a decade. Full results and a complete description of the methodology can be found on www.people-press.org and www.cjr.org.

[12] See Chapter 2

13 | Addendum: codes of ethics

There is a distinction between institutional and professional ethical codes. The first refers to those used by a group of media organizations, the latter to those used by specific media organizations.

Institutional codes

The Press Ombudsman of South Africa

To understand the ethical code of the Press Ombudsman, some background information is required. The South African Media Council was established in 1983 after the media came under political pressure from the government "to get its house in order". The council had its own ethical code, but was dissolved in 1992, mainly because of its political baggage.

The South African Press Council replaced the Media Council in 1992, and also formulated its own ethical code. However, the political baggage of this new council also proved to be too heavy, and the Press Council was dissolved in 1997.

The Press Ombudsman of South Africa then replaced the South African Press Council. The first Ombudsman is Ed Linington, an ex-editor of the South African Press Association (SAPA). His office is in Johannesburg.

The establishment of the Press Ombudsman came about because the founding bodies – the South African National Editors' Forum (SANEF), the Forum of Editors of Community Newspapers (FECN), the South African Union of Journalists (SAUJ), the Media Workers Association of South Africa (MWASA), the Newspaper Association of South Africa (NASA) and Magazine Publishers Association of South Africa (MPA) – were of the conviction that the public could best be served by providing for a readily accessible, impartial, and independent complaints mechanism. They decided to set up such a mechanism in the form of a Press Ombudsman and an Appeal Panel, which would mediate, settle, and, if necessary, adjudicate complaints in accordance with a code and procedure accepted by the founding bodies.

Press Code of Professional Practice

According to the Press Ombudsman's code, the basic principle to be upheld is that the freedom of the press is indivisible from, and subject to the same rights and duties as, those of the individual, and rests on the public's fundamental right to be informed and freely to receive and to disseminate opinions. The primary purpose of gathering and distributing news and opinion is to serve society by informing citizens and enabling them to make informed judgments on the issues of the time. The freedom of the press to bring an independent scrutiny to bear on the forces that shape society is a freedom exercised on behalf of the public. The public interest is the only test that justifies departure from the highest standards of journalism and includes:

- detecting or exposing crime or serious misdemeanour;
- detecting or exposing serious antisocial conduct;
- protecting public health and safety;
- preventing the public from being misled by some statement or action of an individual or organization;
- detecting or exposing hypocrisy, falsehoods, or double standards of behaviour on the part of public figures or institutions and in public institutions.

The code is not intended to be comprehensive or all-embracing. No code can cover every contingency. The press will be judged by the code's spirit – accuracy, balance, fairness, and decency – rather than its narrow letter, in the belief that vigilant self-regulation is the hallmark of a free and independent press.

In considering complaints, the Press Ombuds-man and the Appeal Panel will be guided by the following provisions, which are divided into eight main areas:

1 Reporting of news

1.1 The press shall be obliged to report news truthfully, accurately, and fairly.

1.2 News shall be presented in context and in a balanced manner, without an intentional or negligent departure from the facts, whether by:

1.2.1 distortion, exaggeration, or misrepresentation;

1.2.2 material omissions; or

1.2.3 summarization.

1.3 Only what may reasonably be true, having regard to the sources of the news, may be presented as facts, and such facts shall be published fairly with due regard to context and importance. Where a report is not based on facts or is founded on opinions, allegation, rumour, or supposition, it shall be presented in such manner as to indicate this clearly.

1.4 Where there is reason to doubt the accuracy of a report and it is practicable to verify the accuracy thereof, it shall be verified. Where it has not been practicable to verify the accuracy of a report, this shall be mentioned in such a report.

1.5 A newspaper should usually seek the views of the subject of serious critical reportage in advance of publication; provided that this need not be done where the newspaper has reasonable grounds for believing that by doing so it will be prevented from publishing the report or where evidence might be destroyed or witnesses intimidated.

1.6 A publication should make amends for publishing information or comment that is found to be harmfully inaccurate by printing, promptly and with appropriate prominence, a retraction, correction, or explanation.

1.7 Reports, photographs, or sketches relative to matters involving indecency or obscenity shall be presented with due sensitivity towards the prevailing moral climate.

1.8 The identity of rape victims and other victims of sexual violence shall not be published without the consent of the victim.

1.9 News obtained by dishonest or unfair means, or the publication of which involves a breach of confidence, should not be published unless publication is in the public interest.

1.10 In both news and comment, the press shall exercise exceptional care and consideration in matters involving the private lives and concerns of individuals, bearing in mind that any right to privacy may be overridden by a legitimate public interest.

1.11 A newspaper has wide discretion in matters of taste but this does not justify lapses of taste so repugnant as to bring the freedom of the press into disrepute or be extremely offensive to the public.

2 Discrimination

2.1 The press should avoid discriminatory or denigratory references to people's race, colour, religion, sexual orientation or preference, physical or mental disability or illness, or age.

2.2 The press should not refer to a person's race, colour, religion, sexual orientation, or physical or mental illness in a prejudicial or pejorative context except where it is strictly relevant to the matter reported or adds significantly to readers' understanding of that matter.

2.3 The press has the right, and indeed the duty, to report and comment on all matters of public interest. This right and duty must, however, be balanced against the obligation not to promote racial hatred or discord in such a way as to create the likelihood of imminent violence.

3 Advocacy

A newspaper is justified in strongly advocating its own views on controversial topics provided that it treats its readers fairly by:

3.1 making fact and opinion clearly distinguishable;

3.2 not misrepresenting or suppressing relevant facts;

3.3 not distorting the facts in text or headlines.

4 Comment

4.1 The press shall be entitled to comment upon or criticize any actions or events of public importance provided such comments or criticisms are fairly and honestly made.

4.2 Comment by the press shall be presented in such manner that it appears clearly that it is comment, and shall be made on facts truly stated or fairly indicated and referred to.

4.3 Comment by the press shall be an honest expression of opinion, without malice or dishonest motives, and shall take fair account of all available facts which are material to the matter commented upon.

5 Headlines, posters, pictures, and captions

5.1 Headlines and captions to pictures shall give a reasonable reflection of the contents of the report or picture in question.

5.2 Posters shall not mislead the public and shall give a reasonable reflection of the contents of the reports in question.

5.3 Pictures shall not misrepresent or mislead nor be manipulated to do so.

6 Confidential sources

A newspaper has an obligation to protect confidential sources of information.

7 Payment for articles

No payment shall be made for feature articles to persons engaged in crime or other notorious misbehaviour, or to convicted persons or their associates, including family, friends, neighbours, and colleagues, except where the material concerned ought to be published in the public interest and the payment is necessary for this to be done.

8 Violence

Due care and responsibility shall be exercised by the press with regard to the presentation of brutality, violence, and atrocities.

The South African Union of Journalists

The South African Union of Journalists (SAUJ) is not affiliated to any national trade union and is politically independent. It is however an affiliate of the International Federation of Journalists (IFJ), an international organization representing over 120 journalists' unions in more than 90 countries.

According to the SAUJ Code of Conduct, a journalist:

- has a duty to maintain the highest professional and ethical standards.
- shall at all times defend the principle of freedom of the press and other media in relation to the collection of information and the expression of comment and criticism.

The code also says that every journalist:

- shall strive to eliminate distortion, news suppression, and censorship.
- shall strive to ensure that the information he/she disseminates is fair and accurate, avoid the expression of comment and conjecture as established fact and falsification by distortion, selection, or misrepresentation.
- shall rectify promptly any harmful inaccuracies, ensure that corrections and apologies receive due prominence, and afford the right of reply to persons criticized when the issue is of sufficient importance.
- shall obtain information, photographs, and illustrations only by straightforward means. The use of other means can be justified only by the overriding consideration of the public interest. The journalist is entitled to exercise a personal conscientious objection to the use of such means.
- shall do nothing which entails intrusion into private grief and distress, subject to justification by overriding considerations of public interest.
- shall protect confidential sources of information.
- shall not accept bribes, nor shall he/she allow other inducements to influence the performance of his/her professional duties.
- shall not lend himself/herself to the distortion or suppression of the truth because of advertising or other considerations.
- shall not originate material that encourages discrimination on the grounds of race, colour, creed, gender, or sexual orientation.
- shall not take private advantage of information gained in the course of his/her duties, before the information is public knowledge.
- shall not engage in plagiarism, and shall attribute information used in articles to the original source or individual, organization, media channel, or news agency.

The South African National Editors' Forum (SANEF)

SANEF was conceived at an historic meeting of the Black Editors' Forum, the Conference of Editors, and senior journalism educators and trainers at the Breakwater Lodge in Cape Town from 18 to 20 October 1996. They decided to unite in a new organization called the South African National Editors' Forum, which recognized past injustices in the media and committed itself to a programme of action to overcome them and defend and promote media freedom and independence.

SANEF's objectives are to:

- nurture and deepen media freedom as a democratic value in all our communities and at all levels of society;
- foster solidarity among journalists and to promote co-operation in all matters of common concern among the print and electronic media;
- address and redress inappropriate racial and gender imbalances prevalent in journalism and news organizations in South Africa and to encourage the equitable spread of media ownership;
- promote media diversity in the interests of fostering maximum expression of opinion;
- help aspirant and practising journalists to acquire or develop new skills and professional depth through media education programmes;
- promote rules and regulations guaranteeing professional freedom and independence in broadcast media and all media funded by public authorities;
- encourage government to ensure transparency and openness in administration and to pass laws ensuring maximum freedom of information;
- defend media freedom through all available institutions, including the Constitutional Court.

In terms of an ethical code, SANEF adheres to the Press Ombudsman's Code of Conduct.

The Freedom of Expression Institute (FXI)

According to its constitution, the main objectives of the Freedom of Expression Institute are to fight for and defend freedom of expression, oppose all forms of censorship, and fight for the right of access to information. To these ends, its subsidiary objectives are to:

- oppose any limitations imposed on the freedoms aforementioned, be they at the instance of the state or civil society, that in the opinion of the association constitute censorship;
- create a sense of unity and purpose among those subject to censorship;
- educate the public about the dangers of censorship;
- defend, support, and extend solidarity to the victims of censorship;
- monitor the effect and implementation of censorship in South Africa;
- engage in solidarity with groups opposing censorship locally and internationally;
- work towards the establishment of a Freedom of Information Act;
- promote the right of journalists not to disclose confidential sources of information;
- safeguard the freedom and independence of all media;
- help to ensure a diversity of the media;
- promote the right of all people to communicate;
- engage in campaigns, promotions, projects, and other activities in furtherance of the above aims;
- establish as a separate entity within the association a Media Defence Fund, to raise and disburse funds for legal services as provided for in this constitution.

The Broadcasting Complaints Commission of South Africa (BCCSA)

1 Preamble

The fundamental principle to uphold is that the freedom of the electronic media is indivisible from, and subject to, the same constraints as those of the individual, and rests on the individual's fundamental right to be informed and freely to receive and to disseminate opinions.

2 Reporting of news

2.1 The electronic media shall be obliged to report news truthfully, accurately, and with due impartiality.

2.2 News shall be presented in the correct context and in a balanced manner, without any intentional or negligent departure from the facts, whether by:

2.2.1 distortion, exaggeration, or misrepresentation;

2.2.2 material omission; or

2.2.3 summarization.

2.3 Only what may reasonably be true which has regard to the source of the news, may be presented as facts, and such facts shall be broadcast fairly with due regard to context and importance. Where a report is not based on facts or is founded on opinion, allegation, rumour, or supposition, it shall be presented in such manner as to indicate this clearly.

2.4 Where there is reason to doubt the correctness of a report, and it is practicable to verify the correctness thereof, it shall be verified. Where it has not been practicable to verify the correctness of a report, this shall be mentioned in such report.

2.5 Where it subsequently appears that a broadcast was incorrect in a material aspect, it shall be verified spontaneously and without reservation or delay. The correction shall be presented with a degree of prominence which is adequate and fair so as to attract attention readily.

2.6 Reports, photographs, or video material relating to matters involving indecency or obscenity shall be presented with due sensitivity towards the prevailing moral climate. In particular, the electronic media shall avoid the broadcast of indecent or obscene matter.

2.7 The identity of rape victims or other victims of sexual violence shall not be broadcast without the consent of the victim.

3 Comment

3.1 The electronic media shall be entitled to comment upon or criticize any actions or events of public importance, provided such comments or criticisms are fairly and honestly made.

3.2 Comment shall be presented in such a manner that it appears clearly that it is comment, and shall be made on facts truly stated or fairly indicated and referred to.

3.3 Comment shall be an honest expression of opinion, without malice or dishonest motives, and shall take fair and balanced account of all available facts which are material to the matter commented upon.

4 Elections and referenda

4.1 Where during an election period or referendum period a signatory grants access to its services to a political party, organization, or movement, or a candidate taking part in a national, regional, or by-election, or referendum, or has itself during an election period or referendum period criticized a political party, organization, or movement, or a candidate taking part in such an election or referendum, is under a duty to grant an opposing or criticized (as the case may be) political party, organization, or movement, or a candidate, an equal opportunity to its services to state its policy or respond to the criticism of the signatory or the political party, organization, or movement, or candidate, to whom the signatory has granted access – provided that this clause does not in any way detract from the duties which a signatory has in accordance with the other clauses of this code.

4.2 For purposes of this clause, "election period" and "referendum period" mean a period which commences when the President promulgates an election or by-election for Parliament or referendum in the *Government Gazette* and lapses when polling closes on the (last) election day, or referendum day, as the case may be.

5 Privacy

The electronic media shall exercise exceptional care and consideration in matters involving the private lives and dignity of individuals, bearing in mind that the right to privacy and dignity may be overridden by a legitimate public interest.

6 Payment for information from a criminal

No payment shall be made to persons engaged in crime or other notorious misbehaviour, or to persons who have been engaged in crime or other notorious misbehaviour, unless compelling societal interests indicate the contrary.

7 General

7.1 The electronic media shall:

7.1.1 not present material which is indecent or obscene or harmful or offensive to public morals, which is offensive to religious convictions or feelings of a section of the population, which is likely to harm relations between sections of the population, or is likely to prejudice the safety of the state or the public order;

7.1.2 not, without due care and sensitivity, present material which contains brutality, violence, or atrocities;

7.1.3 exercise due care and responsibility in the presentation of programmes where a large number of children are likely to be part of the audience;

7.2 Controversial issues of public importance:

7.2.1 In presenting a programme in which controversial issues of public importance are discussed, a broadcasting licensee shall make reasonable efforts to present fairly significant points of view either in the same programme or in a subsequent programme forming part of the same series within a reasonable period of time and in substantially the same time slot.

7.2.2 A person whose views have been criticized in a broadcasting programme on a controversial issue of public importance shall be given reasonable opportunity by the broadcasting licensee to reply to such criticism, should that person so request.

Professional codes

Sowetan

Mission Statement

Sowetan is committed to providing excellent service to readers and advertisers through professional journalism, quality printing, efficient distribution, and effective advertising.

Code of Ethics

For our newspaper to thrive and grow, it is crucial that our readers and advertisers have confidence in our newspaper and that they believe what they read in our newspaper.

Accordingly, we the staff of *Sowetan*, bind ourselves to the following code of conduct and agree to abide at all times by its provisions.

Our cardinal goal is to maintain the credibility, independence, and integrity of our newspaper. All our actions must be measured against this cardinal goal.

We acknowledge that as staff members of *Sowetan*, our private and professional behaviour cannot be separated. Therefore, the provisions of this Code apply to us in both our private and professional capacities.

Care should be taken that when staff are hired, there is no nepotism.

We acknowledge that the benefits of our employment at *Sowetan* lie in the remuneration and other employment benefits which are paid to us by the company. We will not accept any other forms of personal enrichment paid to us in money or in kind from any other party, but particularly not from any person or organization which might benefit from enriching us or any member of *Sowetan* staff.

No staff member may use his position at *Sowetan* to enrich him or herself. Staffers are required to refer any free offer of money, goods, entertainment, personal hospitality, or free discounted travel or accommodation to either the Managing Director or Editor for approval.

However, we accept that gifts of an insignificant amount or value are, under certain circumstances, acceptable so long as, by accepting such gifts, we do not endanger our cardinal goal, namely to maintain the credibility, independence and integrity of our newspaper.

Any potential enrichment should be referred to an ad hoc committee comprising of a team of three executive members who will make a decision which will be recorded in writing.

In conclusion, let us remind ourselves that these guidelines exist for the protection of the paper's good name and ours.

Code of Conduct

This code expresses the conviction of all the people employed permanently on the staff of *Sowetan* who bind themselves to its application in both the letter and the spirit.

The people of *Sowetan* subscribe to the Mission Statement of New Africa Publications Limited: to produce *Sowetan* without fear or favour and to protect *Sowetan's* independence by ensuring continuing and improving viability. Our goal is to make *Sowetan* the best newspaper in South Africa.

We recognize the inherent dignity and equality of all our people without exception or qualification of any sort.

We also recognize the inherent right of all our people to preserve and protect their inherent dignity, equality, life, liberty, and personal property.

Accordingly and specifically, we, the people of *Sowetan* – in all departments and sections regardless of company status – agree to respect the personal rights of our colleagues in the following matters:

- sexual preference;
- religious preference;
- cultural preference;
- political preference;
- language preference;
- and the right to hold and express any opinion,

as long as this opinion does not infringe the personal rights of others.

We recognize the rights of our colleagues to associate freely with any lawful organization and to participate in its activities. However, we also recognize the special editorial stance within the columns of the newspaper. When these rights conflict, we believe that *Sowetan's* independence must take precedence over the rights of association of the individual.

We subscribe to the principles of justice, specifically in the application of disciplinary procedures. We agree that all staff will:
- have equal protection of the law;
- have equal protection of the company's disciplinary procedures and Code of Conduct;
- not be presumed guilty before a fair hearing has been held;
- not be subjected to arbitrary interference with their privacy, honour, integrity, or reputation.

We also acknowledge that we have certain obligations:
- to represent *Sowetan* with pride and loyalty;
- to adhere to the prevailing rules of common courtesy;
- to reject any suggestions of bribery or corruption.
- to refuse any offers of gifts, free trips, favours, or special treatment from any source without the specific agreement of either the Managing Director or the Editor.

We support disciplinary steps being taken against any colleague who fails to observe the tenets outlined in this Code of Conduct.

We endorse the letter, spirit, and the application of these documents.

Sunday Times

The preamble of the code of ethics adopted by the *Sunday Times* is the same as that of the Ombudsman and the BCCSA. The newspaper also adheres to the Ombudsman's code.

The following is the proposed new code of ethics for *Sunday Times*, following the South Africa Human Rights Commission's investigation into racism in the South African media.

Code of Conduct (dealing with issues or race, religion, and cultural difference)

Introduction

The guidelines that follow address aspects of how we practise journalism – our treatment of the subjects of news stories, our responsibilities to our society, and our responsibility for the effect of what we publish. It is important that we acknowledge that, while South Africa enjoys a democratic government, its past still lives with us especially as far as race and racism are concerned. We have to acknowledge too, that South Africa is a multiracial and multicultural society and we have to allow ourselves to portray different practices and beliefs in a fair and honest manner in our reporting, gathering, editing, and presentation of information.

Sunday Times staff:
- will act independently when reporting issues of race but will take note of sensitivities regarding race, or other issues, in their work;
- report on these issues where there is a demonstrable public interest; when race is a central issue of the story, racial identifications should be used only when they are important to the readers' understanding of what has happened and why it has happened;
- will not unjustifiably offend others in reporting on sensitive issues relating to race, religion, or cultural difference;

- will not use language or pictures which are offensive, reinforce stereotypes, fuel prejudice or xenophobia;
- will actively seek diversity in sources which represent the whole community;
- will be sensitive to cultural differences and values and will actively seek to ensure that reporting takes these considerations into account;
- in crime reporting, will not make mention of the race or religion of either victim or alleged perpetrator unless that information is meaningful and in the public interest;
- will uphold the newspaper's principles of fairness, especially when dealing with issues of race;
- will, in dealing with the public, be sensitive to cultural differences and not conduct themselves in any way which might unnecessarily offend.

Addendum to reporting checklist: race checklist for reporters and editors

- What is the public interest in this report?
- Has this report been treated differently because of race? If so, why? Is this justified?
- Is the report – even if factually correct – likely to fuel xenophobia or prejudice? If so, is this justified? Is there any way around this?
- Is the report likely to offend people? If so, why? Is this justified?
- What about the language used in the report? Does it unnecessarily reinforce stereotypes? If so, change it!
- What about the voices in the story? Have we actively sought out diverse opinion from ordinary people and experts alike?
- Are there quotes in the story that are racist or possibly offensive? Are these comments balanced by others? Are we justified in using these comments? If so, why?
- Is the report sensitive to possible cultural differences or values? How do we know? Should

anything be changed to be sensitive to these differences? If so, why?
- In crime reporting, have we mentioned race of perpetrators and victims? Why? If so, is it information that is meaningful and in the public interest? Why?
- Has any pressure been brought to bear in reporting this story? Has the issue of race been mentioned? If so, what and why? Do any of these arguments have any bearing on the reporting of the story? Why?
- Have we been fair in the report to all parties?

The Star

Responsibilities

In its reporting and comment, *The Star* should be accurate, fair, honest, and frank.

The Star should aim to give all sides of an issue, by means of balanced presentation without bias, distortion, undue emphasis, or omission.

The Star should be independent of government, commerce, or any other vested interest.

The Star should expose wrongdoing, the misuse of power, and unnecessary secrecy.

The Star should encourage racial co-operation and pursue a policy aimed at enhancing the welfare and progress of all sections of the population.

The Star should endeavor to be positive and constructive but not misleadingly optimistic or bland.

The Star should not pander to personal or sectional interests, but be solely concerned with the public interest.

The public's right to know about matters of importance is paramount. *The Star* should therefore fight vigorously any measure to conceal facts of public interest and any attempt to prevent public access to the news and any effort further to curtail the freedom of speech.

The Star respects the individual's right to privacy, except where it conflicts clearly with the public interest.

Accuracy

- Sources of news should be identified unless there is good reason not to.
- Facts should be checked carefully.
- Reports of a technical nature should always be read back to the source. Other reports should be read back to the source for the checking of facts only, except when time does not permit or there is valid reason to believe that the source will endeavour to frustrate publication on grounds other than factual accuracy.

The Star should not be afraid to admit error, and should publish corrections spontaneously, promptly, and with suitable prominence. Where an apology is appropriate, it should be rendered.

Integrity

The Star should report issues in an impartial and balanced manner. Every effort should be made to reflect all sides of a controversy, if not simultaneously, then in subsequent editions.

The Star should report news without regard to its own interest or viewpoint, and without favour to its advertisers.

No *Star* journalist should identify the source of information provided under a pledge of confidentiality.

News and comments should be kept separate, save in exceptional circumstances. Comment should always be clearly identifiable, as should material from non- *Star* sources.

Advertising or promotional features should be clearly labelled, so as to leave readers in no doubt about the source and nature of the copy.

In its comment, *The Star* should be fair, but outspoken where necessary. It should provide a forum for the exchange of comment, and publish opinions it disagrees with.

The Star should report matters concerning itself or its staff in the same manner as it reports on other individuals or institutes.

Honesty

The Star and its staff should be free of any obligation to news sources and special interests, including political parties. Even the appearance of obligation should be avoided, especially by political and financial journalists.

Neither *The Star* not its staff may accept any gift or service of value, without reference to the editor. No gift, favour, or special treatment may be accepted if it puts a member of staff under any obligation to the donor. Staff should distance themselves from excessive entertainment by seekers of publicity.

No individuals may accept free or reduced-rate travel, without the permission of the editor. Such offers should be made to the newspaper rather than the person. Where a travel or other concession is accepted in order to write a feature, mention of it should be made at the foot of the article.

No individual may accept the loan of a vehicle, except for test-drive purposes.

Star journalists should avoid active involvement in public affairs where a conflict of interest, potential or real, is likely to arise. Any financial, social, political, or personal interest or activity which could give rise to such conflict should be declared to the editor.

Staff may only accept outside commissions, part-time employment, or freelance work for other publications with the knowledge and consent of the editor.

Star journalists should be scrupulous in attending functions to which they have accepted invitations. If any appointment cannot be kept, the host or person concerned should be informed beforehand, or an apology tendered immediately afterwards.

Caxton (*Rustenburg Herald*)

The era of our newspaper only being a third-party witness in the coverage of news is over. Taking this stance brings extended responsibilities as far as ethical reporting and therefore the protection of one of our newspaper's core assets, namely, credibility within the communities we serve.

Credibility is driven by how primary stakeholders view what we do over time, what kind of decisions we make under deadline pressure and the way in which we make them. If media and journalists lack credibility, people vote by keeping their money in their pockets, and circulation figures will show the results of their silent protest.

Professional integrity is the cornerstone of a journalist's credibility.

Our first obligation is to our credibility – that is, to the public at large and not to any other person, business, or special interest. Employees should avoid any activity that would impair their integrity or jeopardize readers' trust in us.

This *Statement of Journalist Ethics* (SJE) has been compiled to give as far as journalistic values are concerned – the driving force behind what goes on in the newsroom every day.

Even the best code of ethics is only able to give broad guidelines on how to manage the many ethical issues arising in newsroom everyday. Therefore sound judgment should be the cornerstone in applying the SJE in our newsrooms.

1 Remember! Making the right call is everyone's job
Three basic rules underlie this statement:
- When in doubt, don't.
- After you didn't, talk to your direct supervisor and editor about it.
- Common sense and good judgment should always prevail.

A community test for credibility
- Our paper's writers have a deep understanding of the community and are a reliable source of information.

- Take responsibility for judgment that might affect people.
- Act as part of the community, not just as a passing visitor.

2 Guidelines for making ethical decisions
The next three principles will guide journalists to ethics at work.
2.1 Seek trust and report as fully as possible.
  - Inform yourself continuously so you can inform, engage, and educate the public in clear and compelling ways on significant issues.
  - Be honest, fair and courageous in gathering, reporting, and interpreting accurate information.
  - Give a voice to the voiceless.
  - Hold the powerful accountable.
2.2 Act independently.
  - Guard vigorously the essential stewardship that a free press plays in an open society.
  - Seek out and disseminate competing perspectives without being unduly influenced by those who would use their power or position counter to the public interest.
  - Remain free of associations and activities that may compromise your integrity or damage your credibility.
2.3 Minimize harm.
  - Be compassionate for those affected by your actions.
  - Treat resources, subjects, and colleagues as human beings deserving of respect, not merely a means to your journalist ends.
  - Recognize that gathering and reporting information may cause harm or discomfort, but balance those negatives by choosing alternatives that maximize your goal of truthtelling.

News is gathered in three ways, and each bring about their own ethical dilemmas. Manners of gathering are:

- obtaining information from witnesses;
- witnessing the event yourself;
- information from other sources (releases, books, etc.).

3 Ethical challenges

At the appointment/news-gathering scene – personal conduct:

- Golden rule: always threat others as you would have them treat you.
- Don't take family members or friends with you to an appointment, except when both the reporter and spouse are invited.
- Announce yourself to parties.
- Be appropriately dressed.
- It is better to stay away from alcohol while covering news. It might be difficult during a social event – here moderation is the guideline.

Deception in news gathering:

- Deceptive practices such as misrepresentation, impersonation, the use of hidden tape recorders or cameras in news-gathering can seriously undermine a newspaper's credibility and trustworthiness.
- These practices fall outside the bounds of generally accepted journalistic behaviour.
- Where it is considered, it should first be discussed with the editor for approval. Approval should only be given after thorough deliberation.
- Disclosure: deceptive practices and the reason they were used must be disclosed in print at the time of publishing a story.

Notes:

- Notes are an important instrument in the hands of newspaper management at the moment legal action is pending. But bad notes can also cause a lot of damage to the newspaper's case in the courtroom.
- There is a good likelihood that you will never need these notes again for editorial purposes. But if your gut feeling says you should keep something – do so!
- Handle electronic notes in the same manner. The guiding term is *judgment*.
- This is a practical issue: if every reporter keeps every note he or she ever makes, we will be buried under our own paper in a matter of weeks.
- A word of caution: if you have notes at the time when a hint of legal action arises, don't destroy them! At this stage, it could be regarded as destruction of evidence, which is a criminal act.
- Bundle your material and hand it to the editor for safekeeping or dispatching to our lawyers.

Electronic recording devices:

- We should not audio- or videotape interviews without the knowledge of those being taped.
- It can be a handy device in difficult, technical, or sensitive interviews, but ask for permission and capture both the request and the consent on tape.
- If it is not granted, turn the recorder off.

Freebies, gifts, travel, and apartments:

- There is simply no such a thing as a free meal. The editorial staff will conduct a workshop on the issue.

Privacy and intrusion:

- We will be called upon to make judgment where private and public lives intersect. This judgment should be based on relevance, but also on compassion.
- Our main objective is to get information, but not at the expense of victims and

families who have suffered enough without our intrusion.

- Decisions on identifying victims – minors, relatives of public people – should be made on case-by-case basis.
- As a general rule, we do not identify victims of sex crimes. We would discuss identifying a victim if the victim wants to be identified.
- Discussions are needed as far as sex crimes involving children molested by relatives or neighbours are concerned.
- Collective judgment is needed as far as the identification of witnesses is involved, mentioning background from the distant past, the influence of headlines and posters, crime scenes, photographs of carnage, etc.
- We generally do not cover suicides unless the identity of the victims or the circumstances of the death has thrust the event into the public sphere.

Sources:
- Our human sources are critical to our ability to publish a factual, complete, and credible newspaper. Treat them with courtesy and respect.
- Establish ground rules with regular sources. Is it a casual conversation between acquaintances or is it a politician/public relation officer talking to a reporter etc? This line is easily crossed – sometimes too casually.
- Take care when interviewing people not usually interviewed by the media. You should not hesitate to embarrass a politician uttering something truly brainless on the record, but the ordinary citizen, especially those who are traumatized, should be granted some leeway and courtesy.

Quotations:
- These are overused in writing. Quotations should be reserved for those pithy state-

ments that real people make, for the precise recording of the twists and turns of politicians and others short of memory.
- Good writers can get the point across more clearly with a well-attributed quote, without the quotation marks.
- Good quotations can make a story, but must be precise and must be quoted in the context of the conversation.
- Remember: a quote is exactly what the speaker said – if not, it should come out of quotation marks and into paraphrase.

Attributions:
- Attribution is very important in reporting because it lets our readers know where our news comes from, that we have done our homework and that we are not inventing what we print.
- It gives our readers the chance to judge for themselves.
- When we attribute to documentation, be as specific as possible and add a date or volume number where possible.
- You should have a confidential relationship with some of your resources to do your work. But if you cannot use the information they have shared with you, you can't print it.
- So refuse to be boxed in by your sources. If someone speaks to you off the record, reserve the right to go back on record and ask questions about off-the-record information.

There are four levels of attribution commonly used:
- On the record: all information can be attributed to the source.
- Not for attribution: you may use the story but the source must be disguised. Example: "Informed sources in the city council said that…"

- Background: a source gives you information, but you are not allowed to attribute it in any way. The council has a plan to keep two heads of departments accountable for overspending. This information will certainly be challenged by editors or sub-editors before publishing.
- Off the record: it is provided to the reported to help her/him understand the story, but may not be used in print in any form.

Confidential sources:

- Should be avoided. They risk credibility, stories lose their vitality, and, even worse, confidential sources make lousy witnesses in libel litigation.
- Confidential sources can only be used if we are convinced that the information is of paramount importance to our readers, we believe the source is reliable and truthful, and we have no other means of getting hold of the information.
- A confidential source should be considered as our absolute last resort. Ask your source to lead you to contracts, memoranda, or minutes or to give you enough names to provide a starting point for further reporting.

Confidential agreements:

- A confidential agreement struck by a reporter is binding on the total newspaper. According to a Supreme Court ruling, the entire company is bound to fulfil a reporter's promise.
- Editors should always be informed who the anonymous source is, but the number of senior personnel informed must be limited to prevent accidental disclosure.
- Confidentiality may be withdrawn at the editor's discretion, if the source has misled the reporter.

Ask the source how we can characterize

him without violating the agreement, e.g. "a person who has been working for company X for two years...".

- The source should know that if the information can be got anywhere else, it will be used without the source's consent.

Offensive language:

- This has no place in a paper intended for circulation to a general audience and should be judged narrowly against what is reasonable taste and community standards, and against the value and relevance of the potentially offensive language.
- The same goes for hate speech/language, particularly terms directed towards minority, ethnic, or religious groups.
- If it is decided that the offensive language has news relevance, work on ways around direct use. Its importance does not make it less offensive.

Race:

- Identify a person or group by race only when such identification is relevant or is an essential element of the story.
- In police stories, race is immaterial and should be left out.
- The exception is when there is substantial reason to believe that the crime is racially motivated.
- If a criminal is at large, race might be an important means of identification. But add all other information as well, such as height, hair colour etc.
- Always handle this issue with care. If in doubt, talk to your editor.

Manipulation of photographic images:

- The objective of photojournalism has always been to cover the news truthfully. The objective is the same as a reporter's. Only the tools differ.

- News photos: every photo on a news page must be real. Don't alter content.
- There is one absolute: if the final product misleads the reader, it is wrong.
- If recorded photos have a tendency to mislead – explain it in the caption.
- Photo illustrations: if you have a reason to alter a photograph to make a valid point, it should be labelled as illustration.

The SABC

Whereas the SABC Board and its appointed management affirm their commitment to the principle of editorial independence; and whereas authority for editorial decisions therefore vests in the editorial staff, we, the editorial staff of the SABC, commit ourselves to the upholding of the following principles:

We shall:

- report, contextualize, and present news honestly by striving to disclose all essential facts and by not suppressing relevant, available facts, or distorting by the wrong or improper emphasis.
- be aware of the danger of discrimination being furthered by the media, and shall do our utmost to avoid promoting such discrimination based on gender, race, language, culture, political persuasion, class, sexual orientation, religious belief, marital status, physical or mental disability.
- evaluate information solely on merit, and shall not allow advertising, commercial, political, or personal considerations to influence our editorial decisions.
- respect the legitimate rights to privacy of individuals and shall do nothing which entails intrusion into private grief and distress unless justified by overriding considerations of public interest.

- take due care and be sensitive in the presentation of brutality, violence, atrocities, and personal grief.
- seek balance through the presentation as far as possible of relevant viewpoints on matters of importance. This requirement may not always be reached within a single programme or news bulletin but should be achieved within a reasonable period.
- prevail on news merit and judgment in reaching editorial decisions. Fairness does not require editorial staff to be unquestioning, or the Corporation to give all sides of an issue the same amount of time.
- be enterprising in perceiving, pursuing, and presenting issues which affect society and the individual, in serving the public's right to know.
- be free from obligation to any interest group and shall be committed to the public's right to know the truth.
- not accept gifts, favours, free travel, special treatment, or privileges which may compromise our integrity and any such offer shall be disclosed.
- identify ourselves and our employers before obtaining any information for broadcast. As a general rule, journalism should be conducted openly. Covert methods must be employed only with due regard to their legality and to considerations such as fairness and invasion of privacy, and whether the information to be obtained is of such significance as to warrant being made public but is unavailable by other means.
- not disclose confidential sources of information.
- do our utmost to correct timeously any information broadcast found to be prejudicially inaccurate.
- foster open dialogue with our viewers and listeners, as we are accountable to the public for our reports.

Bibliography

Altschull, J. Herbert. 1990. *From Milton to McLuhan. The ideas behind American journalism*. New York and London: Longman.

Beauchamp, Tom L., and Pinkard, Terry P. 1983. *Ethics and public policy. An introduction to ethics*. Englewood Cliffs, New Jersey: Prentice Hall.

Belsey, Andrew and Chadwick, Ruth (eds). 1992. *Ethical issues in journalism and the media*. London: Routledge.

Black, Jay, Steele, Bob, and Barney, Ralph. 1995. *Doing ethics in journalism. A handbook with case studies*. Boston: Allyn and Bacon.

Bok, Sissela. 1978. *Lying. Moral choices in public and private lives*. Hassocks, Sussex: The Harvester Press.

—. 1982. *Secrets. On the ethics of concealment and revelation*. New York: Pantheon Books.

British Broadcasting Corporation. 1996. *Producers' guidelines*. London: British Broadcasting Corporation.

Buys, Reinhardt (ed.). 2000. *Cyberlaw @ SA. The law of the Internet in South Africa*. Pretoria: Van Schaik Publishers.

Christians, Clifford G, Fackler, Mark, and Rotzoll, Kim B. 1995. *Media ethics. Cases and moral reasoning*. New York: Longman Publishers USA.

Commission on Freedom of the Press (Hutchins Commission). 1947. *A free and responsible press. A general report on mass communication: newspapers, radio, motion pictures, magazines, and books*. Chicago: University of Chicago Press.

Creedon, P. J. (ed.). 1993. *Women in mass communication*. Newbury Park, California: Sage Publications.

Curran, James, and Park, Myung-Jin (eds). 2000. *Dewesternizing media studies*. London: Routledge.

Day, Louis A. 1991. *Ethics in media communications: cases and controversies*. Belmont, California: Wadsworth Publishing Company.

De Beer, A. S. (ed.). 1998. *Mass media towards the millennium. The South African handbook of mass communication*. Pretoria: J. L. van Schaik Publishers.

De Beer, A. S., Steyn, E., and Claassen, G. N. (eds) 1994. *Ecquid Novi. Journal for Journalism in Southern Africa* 15(1). Potchefstroom: Ecquid Novi Publishers.

Dennis, Everette E., Gillmor, Donald M., and Glasser, Theodore L. 1989. *Media freedom and accountability*. New York: Greenwood Press.

Goodwin, H. Eugene. 1987. *Groping for ethics in journalism*. Ames, Iowa: Iowa State University Press.

Griffiths, A. Phillips. 1993. *Ethics*. Cambridge: Press Syndicate of the University of Cambridge.

Gross, Larry, Katz, John Stuart, and Ruby, Jay. 1988. *Image ethics. The moral rights of subjects in photographs, film, and television*. New York and Oxford: Oxford University Press.

Grossberg, Lawrence, Wartella, Ellen, and Whitney, D. Charles. 1998. *Mediamaking. Mass media in a popular culture*. Thousand Oaks, California: Sage Publications.

Hachten, William A. 1992. *The world news prism. Changing media of international communication*. Third edition. Ames, Iowa: Iowa State University Press.

Hausman, Carl. 1992. *Crisis of conscience. Perspectives on journalism ethics*. New York: HarperCollins Publishers.

Hiebert, Ray Eldon, and Reuss, Carol (eds). 1985. *Impact of mass media. Current issues*. New York and London: Longman.

Hulteng, John L. 1976. *The messenger's motives... Ethical problems of the news media*. Englewood Cliffs, New Jersey: Prentice Hall.

Kieran, Matthew (ed.). 1998. *Media ethics*. London: Routledge.

Korzenny, Felipe, and Toomey, Stella Ting (eds). 1992. *Mass media effects across cultures*. Newbury Park, California: Sage Publications.

Lange, David L., Baker, Robert K., and Ball, Sandra J. 1969. *Mass media and violence. A report to the National Commission on the Causes and Prevention of Violence. vol. XI*. Washington, D.C.: Government Printing Office.

Louw, Louis (ed.). 1965. *Dawie 1946–1964. 'n Bloemlesing uit die geskrifte van Die Burger se politieke kommentator saamgestel deur Louis Louw*. Cape Town: Tafelberg Publishers.

Louw, Raymond, Stewart, Gavin, Gillwald, Alison, Raubenheimer, Louis, Marais, Hein, Ngavirue, Mbatjiua, and Vasconcelos, Leite. 1990. *Open media. Media in a new South Africa.* Cape Town: Idasa.

Martin, L. John, and Chaudhary, Anju Grover. 1983. *Comparative mass media systems.* New York: Longman.

Merrill, John C., and Barney, Ralph D. 1975. *Ethics and the press. Readings in mass media morality.* New York: Hastings House.

Pieters, Michelle. 1999. *Verslaggewing oor tragedies: 'n media-etiese perspektief.* Unpublished Master's thesis, University of Stellenbosch.

Schultz, Julianne. 1998. *Reviving the fourth estate.* Cambridge: Cambridge University Press.

Siebert, Fred S., Peterson, Theodore, and Schramm, Wilbur. 1956. *Four theories of the press. The authoritarian, libertarian, social responsibility and soviet communist concepts of what the press should be and do.* Chicago: University of Illinois Press.

Soul City Institute for Health and Development Communication. 2001. *HIV/AIDS. A resource for journalists.* Johannesburg: Soul City.

Sprigge, T. L. S. 1990. *The rational foundations of ethics.* Padstow, Cornwall: T J Press (Padstow) Ltd.

Swain, Bruce M. 1978. *Reporter's ethics.* Ames, Iowa: Iowa State University Press.

Zastrow, Charles and Kirst-Ashman, Karen. 1987. *Understanding human behavior and the social environment.* Chicago: Nelson-Hall.

Index

5FM Music Radio 229

A
absence of fault 33
absolutism 10
   see also deontology
access to courts 28
access to information 26–27, 29–32
accountability 5, 6, 15
accuracy 39, 67, 247
   case studies 57–66
   importance 49–50
   lack of information 53–54
   plagiarism 54–56
   quotations 53
   text and context 51–53
accusations 159
advertisements 87–88
affiliations 136
Allan, Jani 147
ambush interviews 158
American Society of Newspaper Editors 133–134
analytical skills 6
ANC 198, 200
anonymous sources 118–121
antinomianism 10
applied ethics 22
Argus Company *see* Independent Group
Aristotle 10, 72
Armaments Development and Production Act 57
   (1968) 31
Ashe, Arthur 176
authoritarianism 11–12
   see also developmental concept
   South Africa 18–20
AWB (Afrikaner Weerstandsbeweging) 57–59,
   185–186

B
balance 40, 68, 84–85, 86, 95, 141–143
   see also fairness
Bamber, David 147

Barnard, Ferdi 95
BBC code
   accuracy 49, 51, 52
   conflict of interest 134, 135, 136, 137, 138, 139,
     140
   due impartiality 101–102
   fairness 84, 85–86
   invasion of privacy 154–155, 156–157, 157–158
   reporting of traumatic incidents 175–176
BCCSA code 38, 39, 40, 41, 43, 44, 242–243
Beeld
   Andries Cornelissen 130–132
   AWB and Andriette Stofberg 185–186
   farm attacks 214
   Hansie Cronjé report 107
   Leon van Nierop report 50
   role of media in conflicts 103–104
Bentham, Jeremy 8
Bill of Rights (1996) 26–27
blasphemy 44, 216–218
   case studies 228–230
Boesak, Elna 93–94
Bogoshi case 32–34
Bogoshi, Nthedi Morele 33
Botha, Naas 167–169
Brady, James 51
Brandeis, Louis 152
Braude, Claudia 199
Bredasdorp gangsterism 128–129
bribery *see* gifts
British Broadcasting Corporation *see* BBC
Broadcasting Complaints Commission of South
     Africa *see* BCCSA
Bruce, Peter 145–146
Burger, Staal 162
Business Day
   editorial independence 145
   Hansie Cronjé report 107, 108

C
Cals (Centre for Applied Legal Studies) report
     26–31

Cape Argus
 fake report of Parker's death 78–79
 Hansie Cronjé report 106–108
 Rashaad Staggie case 125
Cape Times
 Breyton Paulse 127
 fake report of Parker's death 78, 79
 Information Scandal 144
 journalists as spies 146–147
 Rashaad Staggie case 125
capitalism 12
Carte Blanche reports
 ambulance delays 79–81
 Danie Theunissen and son 231–232
 elderly abuse 161–162
 hospital theft 81–82
 stress 181–182
case studies
 accuracy 57–66
 confidentiality 125–132
 conflict of interest 141–149
 deception 75–82
 fairness 89–97
 objectivity 105–116
 privacy 161–169
 social responsibility 225–234
 stereotyping 205–211
 trauma 181–191
Castle Lager advertisement 88
Caxton 20, 38
 code 247–252
censorship 219–221, 222–224
charities 138
Chaskalson, Arthur 119
children 230–231
 attitude of media 218–219
choice of words 84
Chuckle and Chat Show 225
Cilliers, Rob 181
City Press 33, 145, 209
codes of ethics 35–37
codes of ethics (South Africa) 37–45
 institutional 237–243
 professional 244–252
Coetzee, Hendrik 147
communications revolution 13–14
Communism 17
confidentiality 41–42, 251
 case studies 125–132
 examples 123–124
 sources 117–121

conflict of interest 42, 133–134
 affiliations 136–137
 case studies 141–149
 freebies 134–135
 friends and relatives 137
 moonlighting 136
 payment for information 137–138
 political involvement 136–137
 promotional activities 138
 vulnerable journalists 138–140
conflicts, role of media 102–105
conglomerates 14, 20
consequences of actions 7, 8–9, 10
consequentialist approach *see* teleology
context 51–52, 84, 86
Control of Access to Public Premises and Vehicles
 Act 53 (1985) 32
Cooke, Janet 70
Cornelissen, Andries 130–132
corrections 52–53
credibility 49, 137, 248
Criminal Procedure Act 28, 29, 119–120
Cronjé, Hansie 106–108, 159
Cronjé, Karin 182–185
Cultural Indicators Project 213–214

D

deception 40, 68–82, 249
 case studies 75–82
defamation 55–56
 defences 32–34
Defence Act 44 (1957) 31
deontology 9–10, 71, 77, 194
De Reuck, Tascoe Luc 50
developmental concept 17
 in South Africa 21, 22
De Wet, Deon 126–127
De Wet, Petronel 126–127
Die Afrikaner, report re dog attacks 208–209
Die Burger 125, 147
 Bredasdorp gangsterism 128–129
 Hansie Cronjé report 107
 Leon van Nierop report 50
 manipulation of photo 75–76
 as mouthpiece of government 19, 20
 Planet Hollywood bombing report 182–185
Dlamini, Victor 181, 182
D'Oliviera, J.A. van S. 62–63
due impartiality 101–102
Du Plessis, Wilhelm 54
Du Preez, Max 59–62, 141–143

E

East Coast Radio 229
editorial independence *see* independence of media
egalitarianism 13–17
    in South Africa 20–21, 22
Eikestad Nuus 127
element selection 85, 113
Emmerson, Benjamin Webber 76–77
empathy 173–174
Equality Act 27–28
ethical guidelines 22, 38–45
ethics, relationship with law 25–26
e.tv
    complaint re blasphemy 228
    Felicia Mabuza-Suttle broadcast 172
    filming of paedophile's home 76–77

F

Fairburn, John 18, 19
fairness 40–41, 68
    case studies 89–97
    definitions 83–84, 85–86
    public relations and advertisements 87–88
    quotes 86
Fairness Doctrine 86–87
farm attacks 208–209, 214
Faultlines: Inquiry into racism in the media 199
Federal Communications Commission (FCC) 86–87
Films and Publications Act 65 (1996) 223–224
financial journalists 139
Financial Mail 145–146
Flame Lily Foundation 59–62
freebies 42, 134–135
freedom of expression 26, 27, 29, 217, 219–221, 227
Freedom of Expression Institute *see* FXI
freedom of press 14–15, 17, 38
    in South Africa 18–19
freelancers 140
friends as sources 137
funerals 178
FXI 38, 41, 44, 141, 177, 222
    code 241
    criticism of SAHRC racism report 199

G

Gerbner, George 213–214
gifts 42, 134–135
golden mean 7, 10–11, 72, 194
Goosen, Liezl–Mari 176
gossip 159
government 12, 16, 21
government controls 219–220, 222
    see also censorship
group rights 16

H

Hadland, Adrian 146–147, 148
handicapped 202
Harber, Anton 162
hate speech 27–28, 44, 220–221
Hefer, Stefanie 75–76
Heintz dilemmas 8–9
Hermanus, John David 114–116
Hermanus Times 164–167
Heyns, Fanie 107, 108
Highveld Stereo
    complaint re Jeremy Mansfield 210
    complaint re nudity 225–226, 227
HIV/AIDS 176–177
HIV/AIDS-A resource for journalists 177
Holmes, Justice 12
Holomisa, Bantu 95–97, 145
Holtzhausen, Wicus 78–79
horizons 100–101
Huisgenoot 167–169
Hutchins Commission 14–16, 20–21
Hutchins, Robert Maynard 14

I

Ilanga 198
impartiality 41, 101–102
in camera hearings 28
indecency 44, 225–227
independence of media 12, 22, 79, 82, 141–143, 144–146
Independent Communications Authority of South Africa (ICASA) 201
Independent Group 20
individual human rights 16
Ingram, Andrew 125
Inquest Act 28
institutional codes
    Broadcasting Complaints Commission of South Africa 242–243
    Freedom of Expression Institute 241
    Press Ombudsman of South Africa 237–240
    South African National Editors' Forum 241
    South African Union of Journalists 240
integrity 49, 247
International Covenant on Civil & Political Rights 221
Internet

child pornography 219
    invasion of privacy 153
    plagiarism 55–56
interpretation 101
invasion of privacy *see* privacy

J
Jason, Fanie 163–164
Jewish Defence League (JDL) 65–66
John Robbie Show 226–227
Johnson, Paul 188
Jooste, Anna 167–169
journalistic privilege 28–29
'just lie' criteria 73
juvenile criminals 159

K
Kansas Code 35
Kant, Immanuel 9, 71
Kfm 126, 127
Koppel, Ted 103
KRON-TV policy 203
Kummer, Tom 72

L
Landman, W.C. 63–64
law
    and media 26–34, 119–120
    relationship to ethics 25–26
Legislation infringing freedom of expression:
    a call for amendment 26
Letsoalo, Paul 54
libertarianism 12–13, 16
in South Africa 18–20, 22
Linington, Ed 115, 116, 165, 235
Lötter, Christo 125
Lubowski, Anton 129–130
Luyt, Louis 206–208
Lyne, Alistair 181, 182

M
Maartens, Deon 57–59
Mabuza-Suttle, Felicia 172
Macozoma, Saki 89–91
Mail & Guardian 197
    criticism after report of arms deal 21
    Marthinus Van Schalkwyk report 114–116
    misappropriations by SABC cameramen during
    Mozambique floods 143
    plant of bugging device 162
Malamud, Bernard 54

Mandela, Nelson 75–76, 200
Mankahlana, Parks 177
Mansfield, Jeremy 210
Maphumulo, Amos 198
marketplace of ideas 12–13, 14, 68, 219
Mazwai, Thami 21
Mbeki, Thabo 200
Mdude, Mzi 143
media
    role in conflicts 102–105
    as watchdog 12
media ethics
    importance 5–7
    meaning 4
media ownership 14, 20
media theories
    applicability 17–18
    authoritarianism 11–12, 18–20
    developmental concept 17, 21
    egalitarianism 13–17, 20–21
    libertarianism 12–13, 18–20
    South Africa 18–22
metaethics 7–11
Meyer, Roelf 95–97, 145
Miller, William E. 35
Mill, John Stuart 8, 219
minorities 202–203, 204, 205–206, 210
Mokgoba, Stanley 112–114
Molefe, Phil 62, 141–143
moonlighting 136
morality 3
moral reasoning 6
Morgan, Piers 139
Mulder, Connie 143–144

N
Nail (New Africa Investments Limited) 20
Nando's advertisement 202
Nasionale Pers *see* Naspers
Naspers 20, 50
National Key Points Act 102 (1980) 31
National Media Ltd 33
National Party 19, 20
national security 30–32
National Supplies Procurement Act 89 (1970) 31
nation-building 17
Ndebele, Njabulo 21
neutrality 102, 104, 105
New Africa Investments Limited (Nail) 20
New York Times 123

Nierop, Leon 50
Nkabinde, Sifiso 91–92
non-consequentialist approach *see* deontology
normative ethics 11, 22
nudity 225–227

O
objectivity 68, 99–100
  case studies 105–116
  due impartiality 101–102
  horizons 100–101
  interpretation 101
  social intervention 102–105
obscenity 44, 216–218, 225–227
Observer 129
ombudsman *see* Press Ombudsman of South
    Africa
Ordinance No. 60 (8 May 1829) 19

P
PAC (Pan Africanist Congress of Azania) 63,
    112–113
Pagad 125–126
parachute journalism 195
Parker, Abdullah 78–79
patriotism 17
Paulse, Breyton 126–127
Pauw, Jacques 95
payment for information 137–138
Pentagon Papers 123–124
Perskor 20
perspective *see* context
photojournalism 251–252
  and deception 69–70, 74, 75–77
  in traumatic events 179–180
Pitchford, Jessica 57–59
plagiarism 54–56
Planet Hollywood bombing 182–185
Plato 72
political involvement 136–137, 139, 143–144,
    145–149, 242–243
pornography 216–218
Poschardt, Ulf 72
Poynter Institute 73, 161
Press Ombudsman of South Africa 201
  code 37, 38, 39, 40, 41, 43, 44, 201, 235–240
principles *see* deontology
Pringle, Thomas 18, 19
privacy 42–43, 151–152, 249–250
  accusations and gossip 159
  ambush interviews 158

case studies 161–169
  definitions 152–153
  invasion 153–154
  juvenile criminals 159
  public interest *vs* privacy 159–160
public and private people 154–157
  sexual matters 158–159
  surreptitious recordings 157–158
  trauma 158
professional codes
  Rustenburg Herald 247–252
  SABC 252
  Sowetan 244–245
  Sunday Times 245–246
  The Star 246–247
Promotion of Access to Information Act 29–31
promotional activities 138
Promotion of Equality and Prevention of Unfair
    Discrimination Act (Equality Act) 27–28
Protection of Information Act 84 (1982) 31–32
public figures 155
public interest 159–160
public officials 154–155
public relations 87–88
public *versus* private property 156–157

Q
Qoboza, Percy 20
quotations 53, 86, 250
Qwelane, Jon 21, 65–66

R
Rabin, Yitzhak 220
racism 43, 195, 197–202
  report re police dog attacks 208–209
  Rustenburg Herald code 251
  Sunday Times code 245–246
Radio 702
  interview with porn actress 226–227
  Jewish Defence League complaint 65–66
  slur against Voortrekker Monument 205–206
Radio Jacaranda 211
Ramaphosa, Cyril 145–146
Rand Daily Mail 144
rape 43, 159
Rapport
  Cliff Saunders as NIA spy 147–148
  report of Pretoria bombing 187–190
Rashomon effect 84, 99
Record of Understanding 29
relatives as sources 137

responsibility
  see also social responsibility
  moral 194–195
  personal 6, 36
Riccard, Carmel 34
right to know 38, 159–160, 163–164
right *versus* wrong 4, 5, 7–8
Ronge, Barry 205–206
Rosenberg, Wilf 206–207
Rude Awakening 225–226, 227
Rustenburg Herald code 39, 40, 41, 42, 43, 44,
  247–252

S
SABC
  children's programme with violence 230–231
  code 39, 40, 41, 42, 43, 44, 252
SABC reports
  Attorneys-General at TRC 62–63
  AWB activities 57–59
  Boesak trial 93–94
  complaints re blasphemy 229–230
  complaints re nudity 225, 227
  discussion on homosexuality 110–111
  Eikenhof murders 63–64
  Ferdi Barnard 95
  "kangaroo court" in Guguletu 108–109
  Louis Luyt 206–208
  Max du Preez re necklacing 59–62
  Max Du Preez's contract 141–143
  Meyer & Holomisa visit to U.P.E. campus 95–97
  misappropriations during Mozambique floods
    143
  PAC conference speech 112–114
  Saki Macozoma 89–91
  Sifiso Nkabinde 91–92
SAHRC 20, 43
  report on racism 197–202
SANEF 21, 26, 38, 44, 146–148, 177, 241
SAUJ code 38, 39, 40, 41, 42, 43, 240
Saunders, Cliff 147–149
Sedres, Roger 182
sexual matters 158–159
Smith, Adam 12
Smith, Hannes 129–130
social intervention 102–105, 231–232
social responsibility 44
  blasphemy, obscenity, pornography 216–218
  case studies 225–234
  external control 222–224
  internal control 221–222

media freedom 219–221
  need to protect children 218–219
  reinforcement of ideas 215–216
  violence in media 213–215, 216
Society of Professional Journalists 134
sources 28–29, 51, 117–118, 121–124
  anonymous 118–121
  Rustenburg Herald code 250, 251
South African Breweries (SAB) advertisement 88
South African Broadcasting Corporation *see* SABC
South African Human Rights Commission
  see SAHRC
South African National Editors' Forum *see* SANEF
South African Union of Journalists *see* SAUJ
Sowetan
  code 38, 42, 44, 102, 244–245
  trauma case study 233–234
Spencer, Charles, Earl 163–164
sports journalists 139
Staggie, Rashaad 125–126
state *see* government
Statement of Journalist Ethics 248
stereotyping 43, 193–194, 204
  case studies 205–211
  handicapped 202
  and media 194–196
  minorities 202–203, 204
  racism 197–202
  women 196–197
Steyn, Pierre 183, 184
Stofberg, Andriette 185–186
stress
  case studies 181–185
  coping mechanisms 179
strict liability rule 32, 33
stutterers, complaint re Jeremy Mansfield 210
suicides 177–178
Sullivan, Peter 135
Sunday Express 144
Sunday Times 145, 197
  code 38, 43, 245–246

T
teleology 7–9, 10, 71–72, 77, 194
Terre'Blanche, Eugene 57–59
text 51–52
The Argus see Cape Argus
The Citizen 54, 143–144
The Poet Speaks 229–230
The Star code 38, 39, 41, 42, 43, 246–247
Theunissen, Danie 231–232

Times Media Ltd 20, 145
Top Billing 225
trauma 43, 158, 171–172
    case studies 181–191, 233–234
    coping mechanisms 179
    photojournalism 179–180
    victims and media 172–178
travel journalists 139
trials 28, 29
truth 22, 39–40
    case studies 75–81
    deception 68–74
    importance 67–68

U
utilitarianism 8–9, 71
Uys, Fanie 185, 186

V
Vaal Weekly 190–191
Van Niekerk, Danie 165–166
Van Schalkwyk, Marthinus 114–116
Van Wyk, Dries 79–81
Van Zyl, Marcelle & Peter 164–167

Van Zyl, Ronél 112–114
victims of trauma 172–178
violence 44, 213–215, 216
    case studies 230–231
Volksblad 50
Vulliamy, Ed 105

W
Warren, Samuel D. 152
Washington Post 70, 118, 123, 124
Webster, David 95
Wiese, Tobie 167, 168
Williams, Moegsien 34
Wolfaardt, Alwyn 185
women 196–197
Woodward, Bob 123
World 20

Y
You 167–169

Z
Zikalala, Snuki 89–91